Date: 2/11/19

782.42164 MIT
Mitchell, Joni,
Joni on Joni : interviews and
encounters with Joni Mitchell

JONI
ON JONI

JONI
ON JONI

INTERVIEWS AND ENCOUNTERS
WITH JONI MITCHELL

EDITED BY SUSAN WHITALL

CHICAGO
REVIEW
PRESS

An A Cappella Book

Published by Chicago Review Press Incorporated
814 North Franklin Street
Chicago, Illinois 60610

A list of credits and copyright notices for the individual pieces in this collection can be found on pages 381–383.
ISBN 978-0-914090-35-9

Library of Congress Cataloging-in-Publication Data

Names: Mitchell, Joni, interviewee. | Whitall, Susan.
Title: Joni on Joni : interviews and encounters with Joni Mitchell / Susan Whitall.
Description: Chicago, Illinois : Chicago Review Press, [2019] | Includes index.
Identifiers: LCCN 2018021888 (print) | LCCN 2018022334 (ebook) | ISBN
    9780914090366 (Pdf) | ISBN 9780914090403 (Mobipocket) | ISBN
    9780914090441 (Epub) | ISBN 9780914090359 (cloth)
Subjects: LCSH: Mitchell, Joni. | Women singers—Canada—Interviews. |
    Singers—Canada—Interviews. | Women composers—Canada—Interviews. |
    Composers—Canada—Interviews.
Classification: LCC ML420.M542 (ebook) | LCC ML420.M542 A5 2019 (print) |
    DDC 782.42164092 [B] —dc23
LC record available at https://lccn.loc.gov/2018021888

Cover and interior design: Jonathan Hahn
Interior layout: Nord Compo

Printed in the United States of America
5 4 3 2 1

For all good dreamers

CONTENTS

Part III • Sweet Bird of Time and Change

Part IV • A Defector from the Petty Wars

INTRODUCTION

"We need goddesses, but I don't want to be one."
—Joni Mitchell to CBC's Jian Ghomeshi

Joni Mitchell is a goddess to her most ardent fans, whether she likes it or not, and to some critics, too—those who have been effusive in their praise for her mid-career albums, anyway—*Blue, Court and Spark,* and *Hejira.*

In the summer of 2017, a group of National Public Radio contributors voted *Blue* number one on its list of "The 150 Greatest Albums Made by Women." It was just the latest in a flood of accolades that have come her way since the turn of the century, partially soothing an ego bruised by her dismissal from a star-making machinery that prefers younger, more pliant women.

Joni earned her status as a pop legend with earthy, poetic images such as "geese in chevron flight" in "Urge for Going," and the effortless way she could define a cultural moment with a lyric: "They paved paradise and put up a parking lot." All this, and those unusual melodic intervals traced by that lissome voice.

In the '60s, Joni's writing saved her from being just another pretty coffeehouse blonde. She scribbled lyrics on any paper she could find, and these scraps bearing painterly words would fall out of her guitar case like confetti, delighting her manager, Elliot Roberts.

She was a pioneer, because it was impossible to identify women who had done what she wanted to do. It was business as usual when the male-dominated music industry tried to box her up in a more acceptable, understandable feminine persona. There were consequences for refusing to live a conventional feminine life. During her Laurel Canyon years, at a time in hip society when the line between friend and lover wasn't always sharply defined, *Rolling Stone* printed a chart with Joni's name in the center of a lipstick print. Lines pointed out from her name to those of Stephen Stills, David Crosby, and James Taylor. It got worse: later in 1971 the magazine proclaimed her "Old Lady of the Year." Almost as bad were the "Women in Rock" features, when she was lumped in with female artists whose careers were almost entirely designed by men.

Born November 7, 1943, in Fort Macleod, Alberta, Joni bounced around several other dusty prairie towns with her parents, Bill and Myrtle Anderson, before they settled in Saskatoon. She was an artistic and musical child. Her first instrument was a hurdy-gurdy—played backwards, of course. She swooned over Rachmaninoff's *Rhapsody on a Theme of Paganini* when she heard it in the 1953 movie *A Story of Three Loves*. Because her mother believed that guitars were the province of hillbillies, Joni bought a ukulele.

She was always singing, and not everybody was happy about it. While in the hospital in 1952, recovering from polio, Joni was ordered by the boy in the next bed to stop singing Christmas carols. She sang louder. Soon after, she joined a church choir where she volunteered to sing the descant, or countermelody—even then, she was drawn to the less obvious, "prettier" melody.

Joni replaced the ukulele with a guitar while attending art college in Calgary, and with a friend, plunked out folk songs in coffeehouses for cigarette money. After moving to Toronto, she discovered that she was pregnant, but when her boyfriend (or, by her account, "friend") Brad MacMath left her on her own and took off for California, she eked out a living working for a department store and playing in the lower rung of Toronto coffeehouses.

It didn't work out well. Pregnant and alone, she was reduced to accepting food from friends and strangers at her rooming house. So in

February 1965, after Joni gave birth to a daughter, Kelly Dale, she surrendered her to foster care—under pressure, she said, from hospital staff who were cruel and scornful of her unwed status. But Joni had realistic fears that she couldn't support the baby.

That spring, Joni met Detroit folksinger Chuck Mitchell at a Toronto club. After a whirlwind courtship, they married in June at his parents' suburban Detroit home, and she moved into his apartment in the inner city. Joni has said many caustic things about the marriage, and about Detroit ("decadent and internally decaying," she said to the London *Evening Standard* in 1970), but the close to three years she spent in the Motor City with Chuck was when she found her voice as a songwriter.

Such early songs as "Both Sides, Now" and "Circle Game" sound as if they were written under endless prairie skies, or in hippie California, but it was in gritty Detroit that Joni scribbled their lyrics in a coffee shop. (A waitress advised her, just before the 1967 riots, that it wasn't safe for her to go there anymore.) Some of those songs, among the most iconic pop/folk anthems of the 1960s, were transcribed by a jazz musician with Motown credentials.

Only Chuck and Joni can say what really went on in their marriage. Joni did credit her first husband with setting up her publishing company, a strong clue that he took her writing seriously and knew she needed to protect it. Chuck also got her into the recording studio. The couple recorded several numbers at the Jam Handy studio on West Grand Boulevard in Detroit, produced by Chuck's father, Scott Mitchell, who worked there.

In some interviews, Joni complained that Chuck, an English literature major, made her feel stupid for not having read the right books. But she also admitted that she probably wouldn't have read Saul Bellow's *Henderson the Rain King*, which led to "Both Sides, Now," if not for her husband's prodding. Chuck also remembers suggesting J. R. R. Tolkien, and the *Lord of the Rings* trilogy was an enduring influence on her.

Living in Detroit as a married woman enabled Joni to have a green card so that she could tour and build her reputation in the United States as a singer/songwriter. Later, it allowed her to settle in California, where she forged a career as one of the defining voices of the West Coast folk rock scene.

There is a binary split in the public consciousness of Joni Mitchell, between her early folk music days and the later jazz years. But her career should really be divided into at least three segments, with her most commercially successful time being the middle years, anchored by *Blue* and *Court and Spark.*

Joni's jazzy experimentation on albums such as *The Hissing of Summer Lawns*, coming right after the irresistible pop genius of *Court and Spark*, alienated many of her fans. And then there were the critics. In *Rolling Stone*, Stephen Holden complained of *Hissing*, "There are no tunes to speak of" and dismissed the "uninspired jazz/rock style" of Tom Scott and the L.A. Express, who backed her up. Mingus's biographer dismissed her *Mingus* album as the kind of "bland fusion music" that Mingus didn't like. (Joni admitted she was glad Mingus was physically unable to sock her over the work but had no creative regrets.)

The collective disappointment over her musical direction led to grievances Joni accumulated over the years—against the music business, disapproving fans, and society in general. But she never turned away from her jazz collaborators. Joni may have been patronized as a girl singer by a huge swath of the rock world, but she felt that jazz players such as Jaco Pastorius, Charles Mingus, and Wayne Shorter "got" her, and in interviews, she basks in the warmth of their mutual esteem. You can hear her dancer's love of rhythm in her earliest recordings, but when she teamed with Pastorius, his singing bass lines brought that out even more.

After Joni did it, it became a well-trod path for rock stars to bring jazz musicians into the studio to infuse their songs with musical depth and gravitas, whether it was a jazz solo leading up to the bridge or a hip, dissonant chord in an unexpected place. But Joni's collaborations with jazz players stood apart from the usual pop-jazz hybrid; she connected with the musicians on a deeper, peer level. Was she right to move away from what brought her platinum sales, from *Blue* and *Court and Spark*? She had no choice, as she told Cameron Crowe. Whether or not her fans were ready to follow, she was dreaming her way to a new sound.

Joni was hesitant and Canadian-polite in her early interviews, but after the "El Lay" coverage, her relationship with the press turned prickly. She could go for months or years refusing to do interviews, especially in the 1970s, icing out *Rolling Stone* for seven years after its 1971 offenses. She complained about the invasion of privacy that doing press interviews entailed and attacked reporters when she felt misquoted or misunderstood. But when she did agree to an interview, interviewee and journalist would end up talking and smoking and talking, for hours on end. Some of those crushes faded. Others endured; after Crowe profiled her for *Rolling Stone* in 1979 (an interview he allowed to be anthologized for the first time in this collection), they forged a friendship that continues to this day.

Joni was as candid in conversation as she was in her lyrics. She revealed her insecurities but also the supreme confidence that led her first husband to dub her "Queen Joan." But early on, before the sun-washed, California mythmaking took hold, she was shy and unassuming, with only occasional flashes of the now-famous ego. She could be a fan girl when talking about artists such as Laura Nyro or Sinéad O'Connor but also sharply critical, dismissing Bob Dylan, and her female acolytes, as "unoriginal."

In later interviews, she is often angry, railing about the "white, straight men" who controlled the press. But consider the backstory. Here is one of the most important songwriters of the twentieth century, but for much of her career Joni is depicted as the "chick singer." She was, and still is, described in stories and books as "beautiful," when that would never be the lead sentence about a man in the same position—think of Jackson Browne, or any of her more photogenic male peers. It seems to startle many writers that an attractive woman could also be an original talent, even, yes—a pop genius.

In 2010, *Rolling Stone* chose its "100 Greatest Artists of All Time." Joni ranked at number sixty-two. There were only eight female acts on the entire list. Of that eight, Madonna—whom Joni has both compared to the Roman emperor Nero and described as a "living Barbie doll"—was perched well above her, at thirty-six.

Joni's talent wasn't always received graciously by her male musical counterparts, either. Although those who put down her work or told her she was a groovy chick who should forget music and be a model usually had no qualms about asking for one of her songs.

As a young woman, and even as a cranky veteran, Joni could be mischievous, but that wry, Canadian humor didn't always register with Americans. "It's been a problem through my life, to get men to do my bidding," she complained to a laughing Tavis Smiley.

In recent years, Joni's health has been a concern. She suffered for years with post-polio syndrome, as well as Morgellons disease, in which the patient feels as if strings or foreign matter is coming in and out of the skin's surface. In late March 2015, she was found unconscious at her home in Los Angeles, having suffered a brain aneurysm. After being released from the hospital, Joni went through a slow recovery, although she eventually regained her speech, and by 2017 she was walking again, with a cane. But during the long months of recovery there were no interviews and no public statements, which makes every past interview she's done all the more precious.

There shouldn't be a concern that Joni's music will fade in relevance anytime soon. The meaning of her songs seems to evolve with time and affects each younger generation differently. "River" was a highlight of her album *Blue* for most fans, exposing her raw emotion over a romantic breakup. But in an intriguing, post-millennial phenomenon, the melancholy song has become part of the holiday music canon. Society may not have realized that it needed such a sad Christmas song, but young people have grown up in a world in which there is one, and we are better for it.

These interviews are culled from all parts of Joni's career, starting when she barely had one. She often did a quick barrage in a month to promote an album she feared would otherwise sink, then she would happily disappear—especially in the 1970s. When Joni did talk, more often than not she would dispatch with the album promotion fairly quickly and go into general conversation, harking back to her childhood, righting the wrongs that had been done her, and telling wonderful stories. The topics would vary, depending upon the charisma of the interviewer and the phase of the moon.

Whether she is bragging and scornful, philosophical and deep—or a beguiling flirt—you'll find all those Jonis and more, within these pages.

My sincere thanks are due to many, including Yuval Taylor and everyone at Chicago Review Press; David Dunton; Pam Shermeyer and Felecia

Henderson at the *Detroit News*; Robert Hull; Steve Shepard; Les Irwin of jonimitchell.com; to Joni for never boring me in many months of research; and to her first husband, Chuck Mitchell, whom I met at a benefit concert in Detroit. Several years ago, Chuck sent me digital copies of the beautiful black-and-white images showing the young Mitchells at the Verona Apartments, photos that had "disappeared" from the *Detroit News* photo archives but are back now, thanks to his kindness.

—Susan Whitall
Detroit, Michigan, 2017

PART I
We Are Stardust

Tucked away in Canada, then Detroit, Joni's creativity takes flight when she starts writing songs such as "Both Sides, Now" and "Circle Game" and recording the albums *Song to a Seagull* and *Clouds*.

TWO SINGLE ACTS SURVIVE A MARRIAGE

A. L. McClain | February 6, 1966 | *Detroit News* **(US)**

In the spring of 1965, Joni met Detroit folk singer Chuck Mitchell at the Penny Farthing coffeehouse in Toronto. On June 19 they were married in the backyard of his parents' house in the Detroit suburb of Rochester, as a string quartet played. The couple moved into Chuck's apartment on the top floor of the Verona, a once grand nineteenth-century apartment building on the edge of Detroit's seedy Cass Corridor. The Verona was the "tenement castle" of Joni's song "I Had a King," and Chuck, of course, the king who "carried me off to his country for marriage too soon" (and changed the locks on her later).

In between gigs at Detroit folk clubs including the Chess Mate and the Raven Gallery, Joni sewed curtains and transformed their lair into a medieval green and gold–hued fantasyland. The couple put up visiting musician friends such as Tom Rush, Gordon Lightfoot, and Eric Andersen in their spacious pad. Hosting Andersen was fortuitous; he showed Joni some open tunings on the guitar, which led her music in a new direction. Joni had already written four or five songs before she met Chuck, but it was at the Verona, where she lived with him from 1965 through 1967, that she wrote some of her best-known early compositions, including "Circle Game" and "Both Sides, Now."

There is even a Motown connection. Chuck said he sought out someone to write lead sheets for Joni's songs, and he found a musician he describes as a lean six footer, "definitely from Motown, African American, fortysomething, a reed man," which fits the description of flutist/saxophonist (and, for a time, Motown bandleader) Thomas "Beans" Bowles. The "reed man" trudged up the many stairs to their bohemian pad, Chuck remembered, but was skeptical of Joni's unusual tunings until he watched her hands on the guitar and found himself caught up in the melodies. —Ed.

In this era of computers serving as matchmakers, it seems unlikely that Chuck and Joni Mitchell would have been paired off as matrimonial partners.

But seven months after their marriage, they seemed to have beaten the machines.

Their wedding required more sacrifice than the average couple's. Each was a folk singer. Chuck had played numerous engagements as a single in the Detroit area; Joni filled dates in her native Canada as a soloist.

They decided to combine single acts into one, and the honeymoon took a slight detour. Chuck explained it, "We are both strong-minded people, and we both had our own ways of doing a number. There were some hectic times until we blended our styles."

Joni's disposition also suffered when he took her home to his apartment in the Wayne State University area. They had to climb five flights of stairs, and he was too exhausted to carry her across the threshold. Joni walked in herself.

"But I carried her the last flight of stairs," laughed Chuck.

Chuck grew up in the Rochester area. Joni was used to Canadian customs. She had wanted to be an artist and had gone to school to study art.

The girl who bears a striking resemblance to Mia Farrow, of TV's "Peyton Place," explained it:

"I got interested in a ukulele, and from there I turned to the guitar and folk singing. Thirty-six hours after I met Chuck, he asked me to marry him. But we waited two months."

Now their marriage and careers are on firmer ground. They recently finished an engagement together at the Chess Mate, and hope to get a tryout at the Playboy Club in Detroit.

Occasionally, they break up the act for separate engagements. This weekend, Joni backed up blues singer Jesse Fuller at the Chess Mate and Chuck sang at the Alcove on Woodward.

On Feb. 15 they join forces again for a week's stand at the Chess Mate, and on Feb. 22 they appear together at the Living End, a nightclub.

Chuck said, "Joni and I have developed our act. We are not just folk singers now. We do comedy, sing some ragtime and do folk-rock. We're ready for the big clubs now."

Joni nodded her approval, as any dutiful wife would do.

URBANITY REVISITED: MODE IS MOD FOR CITY LIVING

Jo Ann Mercer | March 20, 1966 | *Detroit News* (US)

This follow-up *Detroit News* story puts the Mitchells on display as the bright young things of the time, living in an edgy neighborhood in the Cass Corridor and evincing boho chic before it was a thing. It's also instructive to see how women artists were portrayed in 1966—creative, but mostly within the confines of domesticity, expected to be quiet and supportive of the artist husband. Joni spoke to both reporters, and her information is used on background, but there is just one quote used—one! Joni made up for it later.

Joni was, of course, a songwriter who was the equal of any man, but she was also skilled in the traditional home arts such as sewing, and in fact later dismissed feminism in part because she felt the domestic arts were unfairly denigrated.

At twenty-two, her complex nature was already evident. Chuck described their marriage as an "Irish marriage," full of fun but also tumultuous—they would smoke and play gin rummy all night and argue. Joni's decision to give up the daughter she bore out of wedlock in 1965 was a cloud over the marriage. It was also a sorrow that bubbled up frequently in her lyrics, most notably in "Little Green" on *Blue* but also in "Chinese Café/Unchained Melody," with its line "I bore her but I could not raise her."

In some interviews, Joni blamed Chuck for not encouraging her to reclaim her baby. But Chuck points out: "That was pretty much a fait accompli by the time I arrived. When she would ask me what she should do, I said very calculatedly that it was her choice."

As other artists started to have hits with her songs—Judy Collins with "Both Sides, Now," particularly—and the money started rolling in, Joni was primed for flight. The affair documented in her song "Michael from Mountains" prompted one last fight with Chuck.

6

"She tried to brain me with a candlestick," he said. She missed but took off anyway. Note: Chuck Mitchell says the rent on their Verona pad was $75 a month, not $70. A bargain, still. —Ed.

A walk-up apartment in the city is mod—it's camp—but a fifth-floor walk-up is something else. For Chuck and Joni Mitchell, it is many things.

It's a walk in the park . . . a browsing session in a library . . . a midnight view of the city . . . a stroll through an art gallery.

These are just a few of the reasons this young couple, appearing in Detroit-area nightspots as a folk-singing duo, chose an inner city apartment.

For them, the setting is perfect. Located at the corner of Cass and Ferry, close to the campus of Wayne State University, they are near the heart of the city, its people and its culture. And the city is their life.

They thrive on excitement, the fast pace. Young intellectuals, entertainers and artists are their friends.

Although they dream someday of having a second home in the country, modern suburbia does not now fit their needs. Because their rent is low (only $70 a month) they can do many things which would be "impossible" were they living in an expensive suburban project.

With a little ingenuity, design and splashes of paint they have transformed their half of a dark, drab fifth floor into a bright, gay home which reflects their personality, their lives and their era.

But "living at the top" of an old urban building has its disadvantages. For instance, the elevator has not been in operation since 1942.

Sprinting up five flights of stairs can sometimes be quite an ordeal for friends of the couple. One acquaintance, who Chuck says is somewhat overweight, is able to survive the climb. But when he reaches the top, he is barely able to announce his arrival with one short rap on the door before collapsing on a nearby bench.

"But this is a good way for them to get rid of their aggressions," Chuck says of their friends.

The steep climb no longer poses a problem for Chuck and Joni, who feel the daily exercise is good for keeping in shape. But Joni admits that on a trip to the grocery it is wise not to forget anything.

Chuck moved in three years ago, in his bachelor days, but when he and Joni were married eight months ago, things began to take shape and the apartment turned mod. "Now," says Chuck, "it's camp."

Working together in the afternoons and between shows, they started out on what friends considered a "hopeless cause." Chuck is manager, organizer and chief construction expert, while Joni is in charge of ideas, painting and decorating.

When they first began, Chuck considered writing a book on repairing and modernizing an urban apartment. But now it seems that the job itself demands his undivided attention.

Occasionally friends come to their rescue, but mostly they do everything on their own—from manipulating long sections of plywood up the narrow, treacherous stairway to shingling the bathroom wall to cover up the falling plaster.

They haunt estate sales and prowl through antique shops. Often when they leave work at 3 or 4 a.m., they windowshop for bargains in out-of-the-way places. "The next day," Chuck says, "if we feel affluent, we go out poking around and buy some things."

These nocturnal quests have yielded such goodies as a black bear rug (for only $5) which now sprawls in front of a couch they bought for $15. They bartered for the couch and Joni found this much more exciting than just straight buying.

They like to experiment for special effect. Trunks intrigue them. They boast three such accessories. Two were gifts and one they found abandoned in an alley. One claims both gift and heirloom status. It originally belonged to Chuck's grandfather, who used it when he was in college.

Another item which rates high on their "special effect" list is a set of stained glass windows depicting a pastoral scene in brilliant blues, reds and greens. This specialty, a birthday gift for Joni, is destined to become part of their bathroom shower partition.

Joni, who once studied art, has her decorating department well in hand. Because they like country colors, she has carried the antique golds, reds and greens throughout the decor. From the glazed trunk tops to the Oriental paintings, design and planning is evident.

A whisky advertisement, antiqued and framed in red, is one of Joni's favorite objets d'art. "I hung this in protest of the rising tide of conformity," she says with a sparkle of rebellion in her large blue eyes.

Their private "urban renewal" project has meant a lot of hard work, but they've "loved every minute of it." And it hasn't been a haphazard operation. They take one room at a time and work there until they finish.

What do their friends think of this "kookie" dream? Chuck says they reveal their attitude the minute they walk in. Their reactions vary from "It's a gas!" to "You did this . . . and you're only renting!"

But most of their guests marvel at the change. There's something different to investigate on every visit.

As for Chuck and Joni, they are optimistic. Although the building is located in a section that is destined to be torn down for urban renewal, and they don't hold a lease, they believe it will stand for at least 10 more years.

"In the meantime," Chuck says, "maybe we'll get rich and buy the building."

But for the present, they concentrate on their assets and dismiss the elements of insecurity. "This is the chance one has to take in renting in this area," says Chuck.

JONI SAID

On Her Favorite Club, in 1967

"A place called the Sippin' Lizard in Flint, Michigan. . . . It began with this family's sons being interested in folk music and having friends over on the weekends, and soon they had 150 kids in their basement. . . . So they moved the club into a pool hall. And it's marvelous, it really is, the enthusiasm. And the thing that's great about it is the age breakdown, because you get college professors and you get young kids and you get whole families. . . . So I have a following from seven to seventy in Flint."

—to Ed Sciaky, WRTI-FM Philadelphia, March 17, 1967

JONI SAID

On Her Music Lacking Depth

"Well, I started out doing traditional ballads, which were these long English things about Lady So-and-So whose husband killed her while her lover was standing at the foot of the bed, and 'House of the Rising Sun' about a girl that's been led astray, and I think maybe that's why my songs are so happy, because in the beginning they were all so dreary. They're beautiful, but just very miserable songs."

—to *Take 30*, CBC-TV, 1967

JONI SAID

On Openings for Women Artists

"I spent months knocking on record company doors, but suddenly music is accepting so much more. There is now an accepted female point of view. And my problem now is that I have to decide on an image that I have to fill."

—to Peter Goddard, *Globe and Mail* (Toronto), July 27, 1967

AN INTERVIEW WITH JONI MITCHELL

Dave Wilson | February 14–27, 1968 | *Broadside* **(US)**

Dave Wilson interviewed Joni for *Broadside*, the Boston folk publication, in February 1968—one of the busiest years of her early career. Joni had split from Chuck, whom Wilson knew and liked from the Mitchells' previous visits. Her first album, *Song to a Seagull*, would be released in early March, and she played well-received sets in the spring and early summer at the Bitter End in New York and the Troubadour in Los Angeles.

Because engagements at area clubs stretched to a week at least, the Mitchells—and later, Joni—would often stay with Wilson at his small Cambridge apartment rather than at a motel. "It was a very rich time, a magic time. We lived in poverty through it," Wilson said.

He always figured on Joni making it. "She just had it. It was palpable." What was also already evident was that quintessential Joni mixture of bravado and insecurity. There was no reason for doubt, Wilson believed—for him, she was at least as important an artist as Dylan. "She was much better at melodies, her poetry was much better . . . Joni's lyrics have always touched me, right to the heart," he said.

Wilson lost touch with Joni over the years but kept up with her music. Still, he was "stunned" when he heard her sing "Both Sides, Now" at the Winter Olympics in Vancouver, British Columbia, in 2012. Wilson exclaimed at how different she sounded, "how marvelous it was. It brought tears to my eyes, that she's continued to grow. I like her more alto voice. She probably could have done a lot of things in a lower register back in the '60s. The purity of that [earlier] soprano kind of obviated exploring any of her other ranges."

Note: The spelling of Joni's birthplace has been corrected to Fort Macleod, Alberta, not Fort "McCloud."

The Kurt Weill song has been corrected to "Mack the Knife" (not "Mac").

Joni's song "Nathan LaFinire" has been corrected to "Nathan LaFaneer."

The Leonard Cohen song transcribed as "Susan" has been corrected to "Suzanne."

The character in the Bob Dylan song "Hattie Carol" has been corrected to "Hattie Carroll." —Ed.

BROADSIDE: Let's find out where you came from and how you got here. Why don't you give us, in 200 words or less, the entire story of your life.

JONI MITCHELL: Well, I was born in Fort Macleod, Alberta. I moved from there to a small town in Saskatchewan called Maidstone, then on to North Battleford, and on to Saskatoon. I was always pressured by my mother to be involved in music; my father was involved in music with bands when I was small. You know, marching bands and things like that. He played the trumpet and I always was more interested in painting than anything else. And the summer I went to art college, my cronies and I used to go up to the lake every summer and sing around a campfire. We always sang unaccompanied songs. One summer I decided . . . Oh! I remember. I went to a coffeehouse to hear some jazz, because my friends were interested in jazz and I was kind of curious to find out what it was all about. I still was a rock and roller, teeny-bop go-to-dances-on-Saturday-night type. That night there was no jazz, there was this terrible folk singer. I didn't enjoy it at all, but I kept on going down there. And I found out there were some things I liked, and I liked a group that was very Kingston Trio-ish; they were local, and they were very amusing. It was really funny to hear comedy in music. And I wanted the leader of the group to teach me how to play the guitar, and he wouldn't. So I went out and bought myself a ukulele, because my mother thought that guitar . . . she sort of associated guitar music with country and western, which was sort of hillbillyish there. (It's like in the south. If you ask, people are afraid to admit to you that they like country music. It's sort of, not really country people, not earthy people, but some of the people who are really hillbillies think it's unhip. You know, my mother was a real hillbilly, so she thought it was unhip, so she said no guitar, and banned the guitar.) I bought myself a ukulele and I plunked my way through most of the summer. Then I went off to art college and started playing in a club there with Peter Albling, who was the headliner. He and I became the house acts; he's Mycroft of the Times Square Two now. For both of us, it was our first professional gig in Calgary, Alberta. Then, at the end of the year, during that year, Michelle Andrei came through. They went West and I went East, to the Maripose [*Mariposa —Ed.*] Folk Festival, just as someone in the audience that year. I sort of struggled over to Y clubs, and church clubs, and did a part time job in Toronto, too. Until I met my husband, Chuck. Chuck and I moved to Detroit, and we worked as a duo for a while. We stayed mostly in Michigan until Tom Rush came there and Tom sort of encouraged us to get out of Michigan. We came to New York and went to the Gaslight; we didn't do all that well. We drew a few interesting people, but nothing really startling.

So we got out of Michigan and went down to the Carolinas, and found out that South Carolina was too far south. I refused to work there any more. North Carolina was very nice; we met a lot of interesting people—very nice service people—which gave me a whole new point of view on the war. I know a lot of really nice, a lot of really tragic, and a lot of really gung-ho soldiers. A captain who owned my guitar before me wanted to give it to me because he thought I was better than Peter, Paul and Mary. He used to come in every night and get drunk and say, "Oh, you are better than Peter, Paul and Mary." So I bought the guitar from him at a very, very, very good price. Love it dearly.

B: How long have you been working solo?

Joni: I've been working for about a year now. Chuck and I worked a long time as a double bill, where I did individual sets. But I've been working a year totally on my own.

B: When did you start writing your own songs?

Joni: Well, I wrote one song in Calgary. I don't remember what it was about, I wrote it for Peter. I don't remember how it went and I am sure he doesn't either. The next one I wrote was "Day After Day." I wrote it going out to the Mariposa folk festival [*near Toronto —Ed.*]. That was in August, 1964. I wrote my first real song in August, 1964. And my second one, called "What Will He Give Me?" in November of 1964. I didn't write anything until the following April, when I wrote a song called "Here

Today and Gone Tomorrow." And about three or four more; I had one called "The Student Song." I guess I had written about five songs when I met Chuck; that was in May of 1965.

B: Is there any common theme?

Joni: In the early ones, love lost. I met a wandering Australian who really did me in. As a matter of fact, he continued to be the theme for a lot of songs that I wrote. It's really difficult to write love found songs; I only have one and a half. I only have one really true love found song, and that's "The Dawn Treader." They are very difficult; they really take a lot of confidence, not only that you are in love, but that the other person is in love with you. Otherwise you are afraid to say all the things that you want to say, for fear of being made. It's a standard thing. You don't want to look foolish and commit yourself to all these things. So I didn't really, at that time, have very much. The way my head was working, I didn't have very much to write about. I was sort of relatively contented.

I wrote "Circle Game" about a friend of mine named Neil Young, who was lamenting lost youth at 21. He decided all the groovy things to do were behind him now, he was too old to do them; suddenly he was an adult with all the responsibilities. He had been told all his life that all the things he wanted to do, they said, "Wait 'til you're older." Now he was older and he didn't want to do those things any more. So that was the idea for one song.

"The Urge for Going" I wrote after the second Mariposa I ever went to, the first one I ever participated in. That was the first year I was married and that was a very bad year. I suppose Newport had a bad year; one where it was full of drunks and people were there looking for action rather than music. So I was pretty unprepared. I wanted to do all my own material; I didn't have much variety. I wasn't very good, but I had a lot of trouble with the audience booing and hissing and saying "Take your clothes off, sweetheart." Things like that really shook me up because I didn't know how to counter or how to act. I thought I'd bombed; I wanted to quit and I was really desperate. On the way back in the car I wrote a line that said "It's like running for a train that left the station hours ago/I've got the urge for going but there's no place left to go."

What I really meant was that the folk movement had died at that point and that the music I loved had no audience left. And so it was futile and it was silly, and I may as well quit.

So then I forgot about the line and I was cleaning out my guitar case, which is full of scrap songs, lyrics that I've started. Every once in a while I clean it out and read them over, and suddenly I find something. I can't even remember what the original thought was, but there's a line lying there and it will stir up a whole fresh idea, completely new. That's what happening with "Urge for Going." I wrote that in August, and the next thing I knew it was September, and then October. It was really cold, and I was saying, "I hate winter and I really have the urge for going someplace warm," and I remembered that line. So I wrote "Urge for Going" as it now stands, from that.

B: The song became your introduction to a lot of . . . not only people who first heard about Joni Mitchell from "The Urge for Going," but into the music industry as well.

Joni: Well, that was the beginning of it, because that was the one Tom picked up and Dave Van Ronk was the really first one to pick up on that, too. I met Dave and Patrick Sky in Winnipeg in September or October. I had just written it, and it must have been October. They were doing a Canadian television show called "Sing Out" which is like American "Hootenanny." I thought that once again, it was sort of following Mariposa, I was shaky and I thought I was awful and amateurish and I wasn't growing fast enough. And I could feel how good my peers were; I could feel how amateurish I was, and I really needed encouragement. They didn't give me any as far as I could see. Van Ronk was saying things like "Joni, you've really got groovy taste in clothes, why don't you become a fashion model?" And Patrick Sky was saying "It Sucks." Here you are, a hopeless romantic, and doing all sorts of crude Patrick Sky things, that I now think are really dear, because I know him. But Dave did like "Urge for Going" and he asked me for it, I remember. I wondered what ulterior motive he had in mind after saying all those dreadful things to me. "He must just want to laugh at it or something," I was that insecure about my writing. I really thought it was awful. And then when Tommy

[*Rush —Ed.*] took it; he took it with Judy Collins in mind at that time. He took it to her and she apparently didn't like it, it just didn't excite her enough to do. So he didn't know what to do, and he learned it in the meantime. And I got a letter from him one day saying I'm going to do "The Urge for Going" I don't think it's my kind of song, but I'm going to try it anyway. And he had beautiful success with it. So then, Tommy really started it. He opened doors. The Philadelphia circuit, I probably never would have . . . I was running out of clubs to play and there wasn't very much money where I was playing and everything. And the only way I did work was through Tom. He'd go into a club and he'd stand up there and sing my song and build me up and people would get curious, you see. So he really opened up a whole circuit for me. That's where I grew and through experience got some other ideas, lived some other things.

B: "Urge for Going" has been recorded by some other people as well.

Joni: It was a country hit last year. George Hamilton IV recorded it and I think it was in the top 20 Country Songs of the year. Saw that in Cash Box and Billboard, I guess.

B: Has anyone picked up on any of your other songs?

Joni: Buffy [*Sainte-Marie —Ed.*] did "Circle Game" and "Song to a Sea Gull," and Ian and Sylvia did "Circle Game" and Judy [*Collins —Ed.*] did "Michael from Mountains" and "Both Sides Now." She also does "Chelsea Morning" in her live performance. Dave Van Ronk does "Both Sides Now" and "Chelsea Morning." The songs are also being done in England. And there, you see, I don't know exactly what's happening. But I've heard that there have been about eight or nine recordings made, some of them by rock and roll groups. And Julie Felix [*an American folk singer who found more fame in Britain —Ed.*] is doing quite a few of my songs; not very common ones, she's picked peculiar ones that I've forgotten. She's doing them from lead sheets and old tapes. So that's good. That means that some of the old ones will . . . I get very nervous, you see, because I've written about 60 songs now. And of course I'm only going to get twelve of them down on my new album. By the time I do a second album I'll have twelve new songs. So there are going to be about 40 songs that I'll never get down. Because I'm so prolific.

B: What, to you, is the trademark of your growth? What is the change in your writing that indicates to you that you're writing better songs now then you were before?

Joni: Now, better is a point of view. My mother and a lot of my relatives will think I'm more ambiguous. I think I'm a better poet now, and my melodies are much more complex. The music is, and this is a dirty word to use, much more intellectual. It's more complicated; it has more meat to it. So things like "Carnival in Kenora," which is just a pretty little courtship song that people really loved—I'm not writing any more like that. I get halfway through them and I realize they're not saying anything and I throw them aside. I have more philosophy in my songs; it's not really protest, it's more contemporary. If a historian read into it, he would see more of our time in my music now. Before it could have been anything. While I was married to Chuck, what topics did I have to write about? I was limited in writing short stories, character sketches, of people in love for fear that people would say "Listen to that song, there must be something wrong between them." You know what I mean. You have to be very careful not to give the opinion that you're running around. At least I always did and now I have no one to answer to no one to be afraid of offending. My songs are very honest, they are very personal, extremely personal. Sometimes they really hurt to sing. Some nights you really get into them, and they really take a lot out of me, which is something music never did before.

B: You seem to make heavy use of "symbolism" in your music. I've noticed that every once and a while a symbol will recur.

Joni: What?

B: Dreams, for instance.

Joni: Are you talking about early stuff or later stuff?

B: Earlier stuff and wasn't there a bird symbol that recurs?

Joni: Sea gull. My new album will be called "Song to a Seagull" and I've used that as continuity. I found that "Song to a Seagull" is a summary of all the songs I've ever written.

B: Do you work consciously with symbols or do you become aware of them afterwards?

Joni: I think you do afterwards, I think it is subconscious. Just as a songwriter steals from his own melody. Life, if you want to get technical, Kurt Weill's stuff, you can pull "Mack the Knife" out of almost any melody of his. It repeats itself. The same with images. Like, Donovan got hung up and used a really strange thing. It wasn't really a symbol, just a word, he used silver bicycles in two songs. That's a very strange image to use in two songs and I think when you put it in, you're not really aware, maybe he was. There's a friend of mine who uses doves a lot, Mark Spoelstra, he uses doves and gun images a lot, negative gun images. I use dreams a lot, I thought I could say certain things in dream images that I couldn't say in factual things. So now I'm writing more as a narrator, I'm writing more matter of factly. Like I told a very true story from my own life in the form of a fairy tale but instead of telling it completely as a fairy tale, I told it part in modern day and part in fairy tale. It's called "I Had a King in a Tenement Castle."

B: That's what I'd hoped to get to, because "Both Sides Now" is totally lacking in symbolism.

Joni: Right, "Both Sides Now" was the first song of a new bag. And when I go into stories, it's just like . . . I wrote a song called "The Gift of the Magi," which is just O'Henry's [O. Henry —Ed.] short story done in a poem and set to music. And I wrote another called "The Pirate of Penance" they're just my stories, and are not symbolic. My stories are just for story sake, and my songs in the first person are, for the most part, very personal. Like I have a new song called "Nathan LaFaneer." Nathan LaFaneer is a New York cab driver who really exists, who drove me to the airport one day. After I got on the plane, I wrote most of the song. It relates my feelings that day as I left and exactly what he did; just exactly my trip from the door to the airport. The way my album is going to run . . . the song "Song to a Seagull" is divided into two parts. And the first part "I came to the city and I lived like old Crusoe in a cobblestone sea, and the beaches were concrete." And then it goes out of the city and down to the seaside, so I want the album to be divided into two parts, one called "I came to the city" and the other called "Out of the city and down to the seaside." New York has left a big impression on me: good and bad. It's made me very paranoid which is a thing I never was. I've always been sort of naive and completely trusting. No one would ever do me dirt. And I'm beginning to learn that people, even nice people, would do me dirt. Because they have their own selfish things in mind. I'm learning that, and it comes into my songs, it's just like my eyes are opened up. It's not disillusionment, I always cop out in all my songs, no matter how bleak they get, they have something at the end that said, "Well, there's something lost be something gained in living every day." Like even in "Both Sides Now" there is something at the end of each verse that sort of lifts it out of where it's going. So I still have some optimism left.

B: You mentioned Kurt Weill earlier, influence?

Joni: In a couple of my songs, I think it is. It's more a Chuck Mitchell influence. It's sort of like . . . Chuck always talked about wryness, he has a very wry streak. He loves irony and since I've been away from him, that's come to me. It's like everyone that I've met; I've been influenced by all sorts of people who aren't musicians. You spend any time with a person you soak up some of them, but generally it doesn't come out until you've left them. It's like since I've been away from Chuck I have become aware that he's given me a lot. He's given me my music, different things. And a friend of mine, Michael, who is "Michael from Mountains," it's the same thing. Every once in a while I find myself, he's also an artist and lately I found myself doing drawings that were much more him than me. It's been a long time since I've seen him, so his influence is coming out in me now. It's like everyone I meet does that to me, it's just sort of delayed reaction. I don't feel their presence or what they've given me until a long while later. Until all the confusion of leaving them is gone. I'm a late Dylan fan. I was almost anti-Dylan, and I made a lot of enemies, going around saying . . . I thought he was putting me on. I couldn't accept him. It's a trait of mine, I used to be more outspoken, now I'm more concommital [*noncommittal —Ed.*] until I really figure out what they are saying. The thing was I shared no experience with Dylan at that time, so the thing was, I thought that a lot of his stuff . . . the things I thought were ambiguous and were not written honestly I find out now were just things I had no idea of at that time. So as I experience some of his experiences, or bring some of my experiences to his music . . . it's like I always thought Shakespeare was really worthy and weird, right until I went to Stratford [*the Shakespeare Festival in Stratford, Ontario —Ed.*] and saw a man who recited Shakespeare like it was really 20th century. It lost all that super-drama stuff that really turned me off and flowed like 20th century English and I understood it. So it's the same thing with Dylan, now when I listen to him the things that I thought were just words for word's sake, make sense to me. Every single line or almost every line even if it's not the same thing that he's experiencing, at least I'm experiencing something from what I'm hearing. Like, "Yeah, I know what that means to me, maybe it's not what it means to him." So now, this late in the game, I think I'm Dylan influenced. I wrote a song called "Cactus Tree" which is Dylan influenced in its melody, even in its style. I even lengthen my "a's" when I sing it, because it sings better. It's all sort of in monotone. I wrote that after I saw "Don't Look Back," which I think left a big impression on me. My other favorite writer, or one of my others, is a Canadian named Murray McLaughlin, who is an offshoot of Dylan and Donovan; he writes in long verse lines. He is a great character painter, he writes wonderful character sketches of people in song. He's young, only about 19 or 20 now, and he's really together, he's really happy, and he brings a certain amount of cheerful wisdom to his songs. I'm influenced by him, too. I think I'm rather Cohen influenced. I wrote a song called "Marcie" which I don't think would have happened if it hadn't been for "Suzanne," which is another character sketch song. The total character sketch of a person, many people have done it. Dylan wrote "Hattie Carroll" [*"The Lonesome Death of Hattie Carroll" —Ed.*] and all sorts of . . . I'm not a political person, it's only lately that I'm being moved by troubles, but I'm still not very political. "Suzanne," of course, is going to be more the kind of song that is going to influence me, because it's more romantic, a romantic character sketch rather than something done for dramatic purposes.

I'm very Judy Collins influenced because for the first year and a half of my career I memorized her albums. And that's what I sang, my sets were her sets.

B: How about the artistic climate around Canada? Is it any different working here and working there?

Joni: I can't see a difference from country to country. I see a difference from city to city. Toronto: I always get good reviews there, and I guess I'm somewhat of a local hero, because I am Canadian and they really want to identify with Canadians.

B: When is your album going to be released?

Joni: I'm going out in two weeks. There's a lot of problems with studio time out there right now, everybody wants studio time. I've decided that the studio that's best for me is Sunset Sound; it's monopolized. The room I want and the engineer I want—the Buffalo Springfield have it booked up solid until March. So it's whenever they say, "Hey, we don't need it today." It's like, stand by for a flight. I have to do that and try to get it done as quickly as possible.

The reason I waited so long: I could have recorded a year ago, but I waited until I was in a bargaining position. And Judy Collins' album was the thing that really put me in a position where I could get the things I really want. They weren't really outrageous, but I wanted complete and total artistic control over everything concerning the album, which eliminated everybody; it eliminates the liner man and the artist; I did my own album cover. They accepted that, which was good. It's a combination of . . . well, I did the drawing, and then I left spaces.

B: What kind of arrangements are you doing? I know at one point you were considering trying to develop a group [behind] you.

Joni: Well, I think everybody sort of thought that. I've already told you about my feeling of being part of a dead movement. I think a lot of people thought (that) with the growing of rock and roll. For a while, it was unhip to be a folk singer. We very apologetically sort of mumbled,

"Well, I'm a folk singer," and a lot of times I said, "I'm not a folk singer," and I tried to think what I was, a better word so I wouldn't sound so old hat. In the last six months I've just been observing people. I've observed at the Cafe Au Go Go after a long string of rock and roll bands had been there. And I came in after Richie Havens had been playing there for two nights; everybody's faces were relaxed. You used to walk in there and everybody would say, "Hi," and they'd start a sentence, and they'd snap at you, and they snapped and they were busy, and they were rushing around. I think the music was making people snap at you. I noticed I went into a recording session on the album I was working on on the coast, and the engineer who'd been working with nothing but rock and roll bands for two years, he said, "I really want to stay on this session." He's groovy with it because it's clean. And rock and roll, sort of, not all of it, but a lot of it, has gotten so complex that it's back where music was, in a different form, but it's the same thing. It's overcomplicated. Just before the Kingston Trio came out, and they were so fresh because they were so unique. I think we've come around to that again, and I'm now very confident in leaving my acoustical out. We're doing some fun things, I want to do some things that I can't do on a stage, but they'll be ever so subtle; they'll hardly even notice them. I'm doing some vocal over-dubbing. But not a lot. The first thing I found out when I went into the studio, I went crazy and thought of all sorts of harmonies; but between David [Crosby —Ed.] and me, we managed to laugh and sort of realize that we were ruining it. Cut back and take maybe one little three-note passage that really did enhance it, and scrape all that other gunk that we'd put in. I'm working with just vocal dubbing mixed a way back for the most part.

I might play an electric guitar, you can get different effects. I'm going to try and play exactly the same notes and passages that I play on my acoustical with an electric, maybe with a little fuzz on it. But it will be all in control of myself. I won't have an arranger enforcing his own personality on my music, because I'll be, for the most part, alone with David Crosby, who is the most into my music of any outsider I've ever met. He has very good judgment. He also gets very good sound out of me in the studio. He has taught me a lot of things about recording.

Nobody would notice it. I could reproduce what I'm doing on stage. But there is something that goes down in a live performance, there's a certain presence, because you're really there, he's trying to get that on the album—to try to compensate for the fact that I'm not really there. It's really kind of exciting.

JONI SAID

On Leonard Cohen

"My lyrics are influenced by Leonard. We never knew each other in Canada, but after we met at Newport last year we saw a lot of each other. My song 'Marcie' has a lot of him in it, and some of Leonard's religious imagery, which comes from being a Jew in a predominantly Catholic city, seems to have rubbed off on me, too."

—to Karl Dallas, *Melody Maker*, September 28, 1968

JONI SAID

On Being Canadian

"We Canadians are a bit more nosegay, more Old-Fashioned Bouquet than Americans. We're poets because we're such reminiscent kind of people. I love Leonard [Cohen]'s sentiments, so I've been strongly influenced by him. My poetry is urbanized and Americanized, but my music is influenced by the prairies. When I was a kid, my mother used to take me out to the fields to teach me bird calls. There was a lot of space behind individual sounds."

—to Susan Gordon Lydon, *New York Times*, April 20, 1969

—— **JONI SAID** ——

On Rest

"I need a rest. I'm going through a change as an artist . . . I've had two weeks off between three weeks of touring, but when you know you're going back on the road there's so many things to do—every minute becomes vital—and my writing suffers. As a woman I have a responsibility to my home and it takes me a week to get the house reperking."

—to Caroline Boucher, *Disc and Music Echo*, January 10, 1970

—— **JONI SAID** ——

On Paving Paradise

"When I was in Hawaii, I arrived at the hotel at night and went straight to bed. When I woke up the next day, I looked out of the window and it was so beautiful, everything was so green and there were white birds flying around, and then I looked down and there was a great big parking lot. That's what Americans do. They take the most beautiful parts of the continent and build hotels and put up posters and all of that and ruin it completely."

—to Ray Connolly, London *Evening Standard*, January 1970

PART II
Stoking the Star-Making Machinery

Joni finds fame and infamy in the sunny canyons of L.A.; receives plaudits for *Blue* and *Court and Spark*, then critical spankings for *The Hissing of Summer Lawns*. There is weeping in the dormitories of America.

JONI: LET'S MAKE LIFE MORE ROMANTIC

Jacoba Atlas | June 20, 1970 | *Melody Maker* (UK)

Joni had been touring the clubs and coffeehouses on her own throughout the latter part of 1967 and into 1968, her split from Chuck Mitchell becoming more of a breakup than simply geographical distance. A brief romantic liaison with Leonard Cohen ended, although the two would comment on each other—approvingly and not so much—in the future.

After she teamed up with manager Elliot Roberts, they moved to Los Angeles in 1968, at the same time her friend David Geffen made the move. She made *Song to a Seagull* with David Crosby producing. She wasn't happy, years later, with the sound of the album; somewhat tellingly, it was the last time she allowed anyone to have credit as producer over her. In April 1969 she was officially a rising star on the national scene, as she flew to Nashville to appear on *The Johnny Cash Show* on ABC-TV. Bob Dylan was also a guest, and a competitive yet fond friendship was sparked. Her album *Clouds* was released in May and earned Joni her first Grammy Award, for Best Folk Performance. The album was an important step forward from the somewhat twee fairy princess of *Song to a Seagull*.

In June 1970, Jacoba Atlas was making money for graduate school by selling interviews with the cream of L.A.'s music world to outlets including *Circus* and *Melody Maker*. It was a golden moment in music journalism, with almost no wall between artist and journalist. A writer could spend hours, and sometimes days, at the subject's home, with no manager hovering, and no rules. That was the setup when Atlas interviewed Joni at her Laurel Canyon aerie for *Melody Maker*.

The two women spent hours talking at the famous rustic cottage tucked into a Laurel Canyon hilltop—with two cats in the yard and a broken grandfather clock too beautiful to toss out. Atlas remembered that Graham Nash, the adored and adoring boyfriend, was in residence, but that was most likely from one of her earlier visits. By that spring, he and Joni were well along in the painful process of breaking up.

That June, Joni's third album, *Ladies of the Canyon*, and her Grammy for *Clouds* were both just a few months old, so despite the romantic turmoil she was at the first peak of her first wave of California fame.

Ladies of the Canyon included the wistful "Willy," for Nash; some wry commentary on her guilty disconnect from a street musician ("For Free"); a big radio hit ("Big Yellow Taxi"); and one of the defining anthems of the 1970s, written about a festival she never attended, "Woodstock." —Ed.

Joni Mitchell is a poet whose time has come. Because she uses the vehicle of music, her words and thoughts reach out to countless minds. With Joni, there is no restriction of reading or schooling; she sings her poetry and brings it to the people.

In the past year, Joni has emerged as a major force in music. Her songs, once the exclusive property of a few, have become the catchword for many.

No longer is she only known to the few connoisseurs who read album credits; instead her creations are sought after and her work applauded.

Her songs are reflections of a very feminine way of looking at life. All too seldom in music, and indeed in any art form, is the female view of the world set down. Joni does just that.

One critic suggested that women think in a complicated manner and speak in simple terms. This could certainly be said of Joni's material; but her simplicity reveals a sensitivity and awareness that few composers possess today. With phrases like "know that I will know you" and "while she's so busy being free," we are given an entire picture of a woman's mind and heart at work.

Joni has been seeing situations and storing them in her memory and in her music since her birth in Canada some 25 years ago.

She had originally wanted to be an artist, a desire she still retains. Interestingly enough, most of her musical objectives relate directly to a painter's vocabulary: "umbrella's bright on a grey background." Joni describes her home as "a musical one" and her interest in writing "was there since (she) I was nine."

In the mid-sixties Joni came to America and played in clubs, travelling the folk circuit in the East, bravely waiting out her turn to make the mark.

But the single folk singer was on the way out—rock was coming in, and managers figured with a Joan Baez and Judy Collins, who needed a Joni Mitchell.

Fortunately, fellow folk singer Tom Rush, heard Joni's songs and introduced her material to his following and the writer to Judy Collins.

The result was an invitation to sing at the Newport Folk Festival and Miss Collins' recordings of "Both Sides Now" and "Michael From Mountains."

Exalted

Her present manager, Elliot Roberts, brought her to the attention of Reprise records. Her first album was "Song To A Seagull." It sold only moderately; but she became an underground "find." With "Clouds," Joni's second album, it was evident that she had arrived; with "Ladies of the Canyon" her third album, it is evident that she is exalted. With each album there has been more music, more of an effort to bring in other musicians; but despite added instruments and group singing on various stages, Joni remains forcefully a loner.

"I used to be in a duo and that was the last time I played with anyone else except for my friends. I like Graham (Nash) and Judy (Collins), but we sing together for fun.

"I flat-pick my music and I know there are places to be filled in. There could be more texture to it. When I finger pick, I play the melody line and in many cases that's the way it stays. When I've finished a song, I've honed it to a point where it's a completed song to me. And anything that is added . . . might to other people sound better and more complete, but to me it sounds extraneous.

"I'm very serious about my music and so I like that seriousness to remain. When I play with other people, I like that to be for fun. It's on another level . . . a looser level, where a sense of my own imperfections doesn't enter into it, because it's just for my own pleasure. It would be difficult for me now to learn to play with other people, like teaching an old dog new tricks."

Until "Ladies of the Canyon," Joni's melodies have emphasized her past association with folk music: simple and straightforward, they encompassed little of what rock has brought to the music scene.

However, her present association with rock musicians has somewhat liberated Joni from the confines of the folk idiom, and you can hear that change in "Ladies." "I guess there will just come a time when I'm hearing more music than I am able to play and then the change will come about naturally."

Joni does not see adding musicians as back-up men as a step toward co-writing. "I don't think I could do that for the same reasons I can't play professionally with other people. I know what colours I want to use, I'm too opinionated . . . no that's not the word I want. It's just that I feel too strongly about what the finished thing should be, whether it's music or a painting.

"I mean, how many times do you hear about painters working together? The Fool are three painters who paint together, but how many times do you hear of that? I feel very much about my music like I feel about my painting.

"If I were working for a master and he came up to me and said 'Well, if you put a brush stroke of red in that corner, you'll save it' I would have to reject his way of saving it or improving it until I could find a solution of my own which was equally right."

Joni's strong desire to be independent and an entity unto herself can seem at times a contradiction with her own gentleness and music. However, it somehow isn't. Early on Joni was criticised for being too feminine, too romantic ("secrets and sharing sodas that's how our time began").

But just how a woman can be too feminine isn't really clear to Joni who sees the lack of womanliness in her contemporaries as one of the worst aspects of progress.

"I think there's a lack of romance in everything today. I went to see the film version of 'Romeo and Juliet' which is supposed to be the epitome of romance and I thought it was very unromantic. Everything was too perfect.

"I think that women are getting a bum deal. I think we are being misguided. It's just follow the leader. Like for a long time I wouldn't go out without wearing my false eyelashes because I thought that without them I was plain. You know, that's really silly, isn't it? But that is what happened.

Now she rallies her defences
For she fears that one will ask her
For eternity . . .
"Cactus Flower"

"There's the fear of the big hurt, we're taught to be very cool. And be noncommittal. That's the thing about places like Italy. Like they're encouraged to say 'oh I love you my darling' and then if it doesn't work out they all say 'poor little Emilio his heart is breaking' and nobody puts him down.

"You know, they're all very kind, they shelter him because he's mourning openly for the loss of someone. Whereas in America, you stifle that so much . . . well, anything that's repressed and goes underground really gets distorted. You don't know what you want after a while if it's repressed."

Sometimes in the evening
He would read to her
Roll her in his arms.
"Blue Boy"

"Even if I'm writing about myself, I try to stand back and write about myself as if I were writing about another person. From a perspective. I wrote this one song, I can't remember the name of it now, a triangular story where I wrote about myself from the point of view of another woman. It's written about one person and myself, and still another rolled into one. To give the person more dimensions.

"It's really tough because I want to explain to you how I write, but I can't. It's just standing back and getting another perspective on it. I step back and carry on a conversation with myself.

"It's almost schizophrenic. You lay out a case and argue with yourself about it and with no conclusions. But I have to write a long time after something has happened, because when I'm in the middle of something, I'm totally emotional and blind. I can't get a perspective on it."

> *I asked him would he hurry*
> *But he crawled the canyons slowly*
> *Thru the buyers and sellers*
> "Nathan La Freneer"

Like many poets, Joni insists that her lyrics be worked over until every word is absolutely necessary and cannot be altered. She admires both Dylan and Leonard Cohen, although each for their differences.

"Leonard's economical, he never wastes a word. I can go through Leonard's work and it's just like silk. Dylan is coarse and beautiful in a rougher way. I love that in him. I think I'm a belated fan, at least my enthusiasm is growing the longer I live in urban places.

"The last two years have made me a very strong fan; but before I lived in cities I couldn't see what he meant. I'd never known what the street meant. I was sheltered, I hadn't seen the injustices. Now I can understand him."

Her ability to understand and transform has made her almost a legend in the United States. Critics and listeners alike rhapsodise over her songs and her psyche. She is fulfilling something of a "goddess" need in American rock, a woman who is more than a woman; a poet who expresses a full range of emotions without embarrassment.

Her legend is beginning to obscure her work; because she is virtually without competition (Joan Baez and Judy Collins don't have the output; Buffy Saint Marie doesn't have the immediate newness), she is without comparison. Her work for now, goes almost totally without question, without debate.

> *Now I play if you have the money*
> *Or if you're a friend to me*
> "For Free"

Success has worked its hardships on Joni's life as well. With sold-out concerts comes demands on personal time and involvement. After "Ladies of the Canyon" she split to Greece for sun and silence. She said she needed the time to be alone and find her creativity again.

Her house, redwood and hand-honed, high in Laurel Canyon (Los Angeles) stands empty and waiting.

One of her many treasures within the house is a Grandfather clock which refuses to tick . . . it's too old to be repaired . . . it stands idle, useless and beautiful.

That in itself tells us as much about the lady as anything she might write.

> We are stardust
> We are golden
> And we've got to get ourselves
> Back to the garden.
> "Woodstock"

JONI MITCHELL: GLIMPSES OF JONI

Michael Watts | September 19, 1970 | *Melody Maker* **(UK)**

Melody Maker readers were able to enjoy another update on Joni in 1970, this time in September, by way of Michael Watts, who encountered her during a performance in a London television studio. Joni had endured a bumpy appearance at the Isle of Wight in late August. She appeared shaken when a fan rushed onto the stage during her set and demanded that the festival be free. (It turned out to be "Yogi Joe," who, as he rushed at her, also invoked Matala, Crete, where she'd lived for a while after her breakup with Graham Nash. Joni explains the encounter, and the envy of rock star privilege that prompted it, in an interview she did with *Q* years later, included in this volume.) The word "fragile" was still being used to describe her; and photos show her as the dreamy, detached hippie princess, plucking her dulcimer and singing of lost love.

Note: Once again, Joni's hometown has been corrected to Fort Macleod. —Ed.

Scene in a television studio: a girl in a long pink shift, which catches at her ankles when she walks, picks hesitantly at a few bars on the piano, reluctantly gives up, and asks for a glass of something hot, maybe tea.

Her manager, looking like a thinner, less ebullient version of David Crosby, brings her a drink and she tells the audience sitting out there in the darkness of the television theatre that she must have picked up a cold in London, she always gets colds when she is in England; does everybody get colds when they go to America? Gives a nervous little giggle.

She resumes the song, unfolds it carefully like a love letter written on finest paper, pouring out its lines with a peculiar little sob in her voice, as if she cannot bear to let the words slip away. And they are deep, genuine words, about the lover who, "when he's gone, the bed's too big, the pan's too wide," which says it all so simply yet so fully.

Still in the same low key, she moves into the lyrics of 'Woodstock,' and the line about the "bombers in the sky turning into butterflies above the nation," which is tremendous imagery, and then 'Willy'; "he is my child, he is my father, I would be his lady all my life." No other contemporary songwriter could compose lyrics the equal of these in tenderness and innocence, a sweet combination.

She plucks at a couple of tunes on a dulcimer, which she has only been playing since February, and then picks up her guitar to sing 'Big Yellow Taxi,' which gets great applause, of course, as does 'Clouds.' She falters a bit on it, and cannot quite reach the pitch at times, but it is the final number and she has made it through all right.

Short pause while she stands timidly in the centre of the stage, looking vulnerable and dreamy, then fade-out.

Cut to the dressing room, and a typical dressing room scene, with a few friends, one or two press, a lot of record company representatives, and the usual well-known visitor.

In appearance, she seems rather severe in an attractive sort of way with her fine blonde hair scraped back from her tanned face, which has large bones around the cheeks and forehead, and a wide generous mouth. It's a pleasant, open face, that sits on top of a body whose seeming fragility inspires a feeling of instinctive protectiveness.

Joni Mitchell is not her real name. At Fort Macleod in Alberta, Canada, she is known as Roberta Joan Anderson, but in 1965 she got married to one Chuck Mitchell, a marriage dissolved about 12 months later. Her first album, *Song To A Seagull*, reflects the sadness of this marital split, and, indeed, the motions that have inspired many of her songs are always tangible, beating like veins near the surface of her work.

'Willy,' for instance, refers to her association with Graham Nash, now ended, while the impetus for writing 'For Free' came from a clarinettist she saw playing on a London street—"nobody stopped to hear him, though he played so sweet and high," one line goes wistfully.

"There is a certain amount of my life in all my songs," she told me softly.

"They are honest and personal, and based on truth, but I exercise a writer's license to change details. Honesty is important to me. If I have any personal philosophy it is that I like the truth. I like to be straight with people, and them with me. But it is not easy to do this all the time, especially in this business where there is so much falsity."

Her first album was not released until late 1968, but she had been singing for five years then in clubs and bars, while her name was attracting public attention through other artists' interpretations of her songs: Judy Collins' version of 'Both Sides Now' is probably the best example.

More recently too, Crosby, Stills, Nash and Young cut their interpretation of her lovely, floating song, 'Woodstock,' whipping it up in the process into something fierce and pounding, far removed from the original in tone and execution.

"I liked their performance too, in its way," she said. "They were seeing Woodstock from the point of view of the performers, while my version is concerned with the spirit of the festival. I never did actually get to Woodstock itself, you see, because the traffic jams to the site were nine miles long, so I sat in my New York hotel room and saw it on television."

If anyone has helped her, though, in popularizing her work it has been the cowboy rock and roll singer Tom Rush who, she said, had got her to leave Michigan, where she was doing the round of folk clubs, and securing her a gig at the Gaslight in New York.

This was not a total success, but Rush put out a version of her 'Urge For Going,' after it had been turned down by Judy Collins, and this became a favourite on the club circuits, opening doors for her in consequence.

"Yes, he was the first to help. Until he played that and 'Circle Game' nobody really wanted to know; they would time me when I went on as an opening act, so you can see that I have had to work my way up. It has all been very gradual. Tom helped me as well in that period because I was unsure about my writing, and didn't think it was very good. But there have been a lot of people who have been good to me."

Count among these David Crosby, who produced her first album. He has given her lots of hints on recording techniques, she says, and has captured in the studio her stage presence—"he helped to keep the music simple and basic."

"No-one paid much attention to folk music three years ago," she remarked quietly, "and the record companies wanted to change my music, so I had to wait until I was in a position so that I could play as I wanted."

The Judy Collins' album, *Wild Flowers*, which included some Mitchell compositions allowed her to bargain, and the subsequent albums had been made completely under her direction, even down to the sleeves.

All of the album covers she has painted herself, from the rather plain but expressively poignant self-portrait on *Clouds* to the stark simplicity of the sketch on *Ladies Of The Canyon*.

But it is the songs within the covers that are important, and they are tender and sensitive, and as spare in construction as the line drawings on the sleeves.

Her great quality is her spirit of humanity: the compassion for the solitary clarinettist on the street corner, the unalloyed romanticism of 'Willy,' or the comradely feelings for the half million gathered at 'Woodstock.'

At the same time as being deeply emotional, though they manage to avoid the clingings of nostalgia, her work shows no signs of being mushy. Rather, it is built of sturdy bones, and in 'Big Yellow Taxi,' for instance, shows humour, as she herself does ("Clean linen and funk is my idea of a good life," she told me with a laugh).

For those who saw her on the Isle of Wight, or will be able to see the T.V. programme on BBC2, it was a brief glimpse of an American artist who bids fair to have the same impact in the Seventies on the popular musical consciousness that Dylan and Baez had in the Sixties. For those who miss her . . .

You don't know what you've got till it's gone.

JONI TAKES A BREAK

Larry LeBlanc | March 4, 1971 | *Rolling Stone* (US)

Toronto-based writer Larry LeBlanc was just twenty-one when he wrote this interview story for *Rolling Stone*. He had known Joni for some years from the Yorkville coffeehouse scene in Toronto. He interviewed her at the Mariposa Folk Festival in the summer of 1970, clearly a pivotal time in her life and career. Although the story that appeared in *Rolling Stone* the following March included a photo of Joni with Graham Nash, identifying him as "Willy," LeBlanc recalled that she attended the festival with James Taylor.

The songs she would record for *Blue* were obviously on Joni's mind, and she speaks in the interview about issues and worries that turned up in that album, including changes in her life that she was uneasy about—notably, her growing fame.

LeBlanc had been paid for his writing since 1965, when he wrote a column, *Teenbeat*, for 10 cents an inch, reporting on high school dances.

Because LeBlanc arrived late at the Mariposa Folk Festival in 1970, he didn't hear the order for journalists to not even think about approaching Joni for an interview—and so he did.

Joni made it easy by sitting down near him at a Mariposa picnic to say hello and that she hadn't seen him for a while. They talked, Joni played her dulcimer, and LeBlanc shot photos with his Pentax XL. He asked for an interview, and she agreed, but only if it was later, around 7:00 PM. When he arrived backstage, Mariposa staffers tried to stop him, but he persisted. A reluctant Joni came out, as promised, and talked to him for over an hour as they sat in the grass just off the backstage area.

In this story, LeBlanc, as a Canadian, was particularly deft at putting Joni in the context of her Saskatchewan childhood. And he is cheeky enough to repeat a claim that in her Canadian coffeehouse days, "Joni did more for the uke [ukulele] than Tiny Tim."

Some years later, LeBlanc interviewed Joni's mother, Myrtle Anderson, at Joni's childhood home for a book on Canadian songwriters (which was never published). Myrtle showed him Joni's bedroom, a time capsule of her youth, complete with her 1950s record collection stored in a poodle record box and her five-pin bowling trophies. Later, Joni's mother wrote him a fifteen-page letter with background on her daughter's childhood. When he told Joni about it, she quipped, "Heck, it's winter, and the prairies. What else is she going to do?"

Notes: The city near Crete where Joni lived in a cave for a while with that mean daddy Carey is corrected to "Matala."

Also corrected are spellings of the songs "Nathan LaFraneer" and "Marcie." —Ed.

TORONTO—Canadians are stunned by the vague, awesome level that Joni Mitchell has reached. She was the least-known of the Toronto group of folksingers of the Sixties.

Joni returned to Toronto, this summer, to appear at the Annual Mariposa Folk Festival on Toronto Island (15 minutes by ferry from downtown)—her first public performance in more than six months. She has an undisputable genuine affection for the Mariposa event. One reason is it is possible to find a degree of privacy here among old friends. In the afternoon workshop she freely doodled a dulcimer, smiled, and hummed in rhythm with her hands.

She appeared shortly before eight, backstage, dressed in a short robe belted loosely around the middle which hung without tightness to all of her. In the shelter of the trees along the lagoon we talked. The sun was gone, there was a shadow all across the grassy prairie-like opening and a small cloud of insects hovered over.

A few feet away Gordon Lightfoot sat on a park bench and said how great it was to be a spectator for a change. David Rea, who at last is emerging from the relative obscurity of guitarist to Lightfoot, Ian and Sylvia, and Joni, were there, cheerier than ever. Jack Elliott, with significantly smiling eyes, pulled his broad-brimmed cowboy hat over his forehead, put his thumbs in pockets and waited his turn at the bottle being shared by Mississippi Fred McDowell, J. B. Hutto and Lightfoot.

Joni sat watching, curiously and quiet, nodding hello now and then. With her chin resting on her crossed legs, she seemed just a little self-conscious, but most inwardly serene. So perfect with high soft cheek-bones, great bright blue eyes, bittersweet blond hair dribbling down past her shoulders; she has a broad smile worth waiting for and a tremendous vanilla grin which makes her always magical.

Carefully, almost cautiously, she picked the words to describe self-exile from the pop scene.

"In January, I did my last concert. I played in London and I came home. In February I finished up my record. I gave my last concert with the idea I'd take this year off, because I need new material. I need new things to say in order to perform, so there's something in it for me. You just can't sing the same songs.

"I was being isolated, starting to feel like a bird in a gilded cage. I wasn't getting a chance to meet people. A certain amount of success cuts you off in a lot of ways. You can't move freely. I like to live, be on the streets, to be in a crowd and moving freely."

She confirmed that she was still uneasy of the great army of photographers scrambling around her, of the crowds' fawning on her at every turn, wanting something, wanting to touch her. In the center she worked hard to smile constantly, answer the seemingly endless questions, and make that magic.

"It's a weird thing," she said solemnly. "You lose all your peripheral view of things. It has its rewards but I don't know what the balance is—how much good and how much damage there is in my position. From where I stand it sometimes gets absurd, and yet, I must remain smiles, come out of a mood where maybe I don't feel very pleasant and say 'smile.' Inside, I'm thinking: 'You're being phony, you're smiling phony. You're being a star.'

"I was very frightened last year," she said quite directly, wiping some hair out of her eyes. "But if you're watching yourself over your own shoulder all of the time and if you're too critical of what you're doing; you can make yourself so unhappy. As a human you're always messing up, always hurting people's feelings quite innocently. I'll find it difficult, even here. There's a lot of people you want to talk to all at once. I get confused and maybe I'll turn away and leave someone standing and I'll think—'oh dear.'

"I've changed a lot," she said "I'm getting very defensive. I'm afraid. You really have to struggle."

She paused, frowned and laughed. She leaned forward, suddenly, and said: "I feel like I'm going to be an ornery old lady."

Last January she made the surprise announcement of her self-imposed retirement, and canceled two important gigs—in New York's Carnegie Hall and Constitution Hall in Washington. She took a vacation instead.

"I've been to Greece, Spain, France and from Jamaica to Panama, through the canal. Some of my friends were moving their boat from Fort Lauderdale up to San Francisco. I joined them in Jamaica and sailed down through the canal. It was really an experience.

"On the plane to Greece we—I travelled with a friend, a poetess from Ottawa—met a man who was studying in Berkeley. He was a fairly wealthy Greek, very into the family. They're very family-oriented people. He invited us to his home for supper. In that tradition, his sister, cousins and aunts were there. It was very formal. They had a maid who brought the dinner and prepared all the national dishes of Greece kinda in our honor.

"From the peasant on up, when they have guests in the house, they're hospitable and lay on their best feed. Then he took us to a couple of nightclubs with Greek musicians playing. It was a very sophisticated introduction to Athens. Not sophisticated like New York sophistication, but on that level of their culture.

"He would always say, 'We must be spontaneous. The Greek is spontaneous. Let us dance, drink some wine, throw the gardenia to the singer.'"

She giggled, bringing to her freckled and tanned face a smile that almost closed her eyes. She remarked she was delighted with Crete. It was a beautiful country, she said.

"I hiked in boots through the fields. It's very rugged, very simple, so basic. People live from the land much more. The seas are very small, very countryish. Peasants walked donkeys. There were very few cars.

"Even the poorest people seem to eat well: cucumbers and tomatoes, oranges and potatoes and bread. They ate that well. They lived in concrete huts with maybe one or two chairs, a bed where the family slept and a couple of burrows and chickens."

After a brief pause, she added, "To me, it was a lovely life, far better than being middle class in America. I lived for five weeks in a cave there. The only trouble was it was very commercialized. The magazines were writing it up. As a result, you had a lot of prying tourists all of the time. Even that was kinda funny, because most of the people living in the caves were Canadians, Americans, Swiss and French. They'd say, 'Oh, here come the tourists.' It was kinda funny, the Greeks being the tourists."

Then she described the Matala surroundings: "It was a very small bay with cliffs on two sides. And between the two cliffs, on the beach, there were about four or five small buildings. There were also a few fishermen huts.

"The caves were on high sedimentary cliffs, sandstone, a lot of sea-shells in it. The caves were carved out by the Minoans hundreds of years ago. Then they were used later on for leper caves. Then after that the Romans came, and they used them for burial crypts. Then some of them were filled in and sealed up for a long time. People began living there, beatniks, in the Fifties. Kids gradually dug out more rooms. There were some people there who were wearing human teeth necklaces around their necks," she said with a slight frown.

"We all put on a lot of weight. We were eating a lot of apple pies, good bacon. We were eating really well, good wholesome food.

"The village pretty well survived from the tourist trade, which was the kids that lived in the caves. I don't know what their business was before people came. There were a couple of fishing boats that went out, that got enough fish to supply the two restaurants there.

"The bakery lady who had the grocery store there had fresh bread, fresh rice pudding, made nice yogurt every day, did a thriving business; and ended up just before I left, she installed a refrigerator. She had the only cold drinks in town. It was all chrome and glass. It was a symbol of her success.

"Then the cops came and kicked everyone out of the caves, but it was getting a little crazy there. Everybody was getting a little crazy there. Everybody was getting more and more into open nudity. They were really going back to the caveman. They were wearing little loincloths. The Greeks couldn't understand what was happening."

Sadly, she confirmed she didn't find much privacy there.

"I just kinda took it anyway. Well, because the people living in the caves were all Canadians and Americans and young. So it wasn't there. I didn't meet any Greeks.

"When I first got there I found I was carrying around a sketch pad, pens, paper. I was all prepared should inspiration strike in any shape or form—'I'm going to do something with my time'."

She agreed things rarely happen that way.

"Well, I somehow felt like I do sometimes about photographers. When I was in Jamaica with my friends, we went up into the mountains, suddenly we stopped in this village. It was beautiful and primitive. We all got out, jumped around, cameras up to our eyes. I thought from their point of view we must've looked like creatures from outer space, real monsters. I got into 'capturing the moment' as kind of a rape. Even with a pencil or a brush. It was just an attitude I had at that time. I couldn't do anything really until I got away from Crete. When I got to Paris and back into the city, with time to reflect, I began to realize differently."

Like most Canadian artists she was discovered only after other artists began recording her material. A much-needed punch was given to her early reputation (mostly Canadian) when Tom Rush picked up on "Urge For Going" during a gig in Detroit.

Judy Collins noticed a distinct Canadian feel, a more old-fashioned bouquet than American. Canadian composers seem to write closer to nature, away from the competitive rush.

Commented Judy: "There are lots of writers who write good material but there seems to be feeling about Canadian writers that is a very special feeling. I sing Joni's songs because I like them immensely. There doesn't seem to be anyone quite as good. Her lyrics are exquisite and it all fits together."

As the composer of strange autobiographical songs like "Urge For Going," "Michael From Mountains," "Both Sides Now," "The Circle Game" and "Chelsea Morning," she gained the respect, friendship and endorsement of the music world before recording them herself.

New York gave her the inspiration to write the songs on her first album *Songs To A Seagull* [*sic*], produced by David Crosby. The cover had fine pen-and-ink drawings, and Joni's picture was on the back, from a fisheye lens on a New York backstreet.

The songs inside had lots of grace notes, showed trickling-light and beautiful melodies. They dealt with people like Nathan LaFreneer, the crass, hardbitten cabdriver; Marcie, Joni's Canadian girlfriend, who moved to New York the same time as her; and Chuck Mitchell, Joni's old man who carried her off to the country for marriage too soon.

The original cover for *Clouds* showed seasons with a castle and a moat. She had become depressed with it, left it, and only finished it when boyfriend Graham Nash encouraged her.

Song structures were simpler, more reminiscent. Clouds came on in "Both Sides Now" as "rows and flows of angel hair / And ice cream castles in the air / and feather canyons everywhere." "The Fiddle And The Drum" offered subtle comment on war.

Ladies of The Canyon is the most overtly autobiographical of all Joni's albums. "For Free" expresses thoughts on the way her musical life has been rolling:

> Now me I play for fortune
> And those velvet curtain calls
> I've got a black limousine
> And two gentlemen
> Escorting me to the halls
> And I play if you have the money
> Or if you're a friend to me
> But the one-man band
> By the quick lunch stand
> He was playing real good, for free.
> ©1969, Siquomb Music Co.

She wasn't at Woodstock, but her song shows she was alive to what went down there. "Willy," the soft, still, brooding ballad was written about her relationship with Graham Nash. "Big Yellow Taxi" received saturation airplay in Canada, and was covered Stateside by the Neighborhood.

And she finally recorded "The Circle Game," which she'd written years ago in Toronto.

The cover of *Ladies of the Canyon* is the simplest of the three albums. There is a fine, one-line profile of Joni and a homely watercolor of Laurel Canyon. Like the other illustrations, its mood perfectly fits the contents of the album. "The drawings, the music and the words are very much tied together," she agreed, coiling and uncoiling the ends of her belt, occasionally looking at the ground and slowly rolling the pebbly earth.

"It's like taste. It changes and reflects in everything you do creatively. I never get frustrated to where I'll say—'quit writing.' I come to dry periods where either I feel I don't have anything new to say or feel like I'm repeating patterns."

Her expression became serious when she spoke of the kind of material she wants to sing now: "Like now I don't really want to write. The kind of material I want to write—I want it to be brighter, to get people up, to grab people. So I'm stifling any feelings of solitude or certain moods I might ordinarily develop into a song. I steer away from that now because I don't want that kind of material to perform."

Has her writing passed its complicated stage?

"Well," she answered, "I don't notice what I'm doing so much until I've done it and then look back at it. At the time, you're really not aware you're doing it.

"In order to be simplified it has to be honed down more. It takes a lot more polishing for that simplicity than it did for anything complicated. I do a lot of night-writing. I need solitude to write. I used to be able to write under almost any condition but not anymore 'cause I have to go inside myself so far, to search through a theme.

"First of all I'll write something down and then I think: 'Oh, I like how the words sound together but it doesn't say anything.' When I finish a new song I take it and play it for my friends who are fine musicians and writers. I'm very impressed by their reaction to it. If they like it, I'm knocked out. I guess I write for those people. They're really my audience.

"My music now is becoming more rhythmic. It's because I'm in Los Angeles and my friends are mostly rock and roll people . . . and being influenced by that rhythm . . . I've always liked it. When I was in Saskatchewan, I loved to dance."

Joni's father, in the Royal Canadian Air Force, was stationed in Fort Macleod during the war. Joni was born there as Roberta Joan Anderson. The Anderson family moved when her father was transferred to bases in Calgary, and then Yorkton. Following the war, her father worked for a grocery chain in North Battleford. Her mother taught school. Joni was about six, and started school there.

Joni's loving memory of the fresh prairie air and budding things stems from the prairie kingdom that stretched at her feet. The flat prairie of Saskatchewan, a have-not province plagued by droughts and wavering wheat prices, holds things that must be seen and touched: crocuses spreading a mauve mist along railway ties before the last patch of snow was melted; wheatfields merging into a wave-surfaced golden ocean: and telephone wires strung like popcorn.

The family finally settled in Saskatoon—a small, dry, proud town right in the middle of the sea of wheat and atop the potash swells sprawled pleasantly along the high east bank of the South Saskatchewan River. The town is sober to the point of dullness. It was founded 88 years ago by the Ontario Methodist Colonization Society, which dreamed of creating a teetotaler's paradise far from the corrupting influences of civilization.

Joni grew up straight: won trophies for bowling, liked to swim and dance. She took art lessons, and, for drama presentations or dances, Joni always pitched in to provide the decorations. Polio at age ten brought her close to her mother, who taught her at home for a few months before she was well enough to return to school.

At Mariposa, she looked back and gave credit to her 7th grade teacher at Queen Elizabeth public school for getting her interested in writing.

"He encouraged us to write in any form that we liked," she said. "Even at that age I enjoyed poetry, the structure of it, the dance of it, to essays or any other form. His assignments were very free like that. He'd just tell us to write something."

The teacher, Dr. Kratzman, is surprised that Joni dedicated her first album to him. He remembers her as "a blond, bright-eyed kid. Very receptive to ideas. I can see her now, in the back seat of the second row."

"Later on, in the 10th grade," Joni reminisced, "I joined an extra-curricular writer's club. Again I wrote poetry, because there wasn't much poetry assigned in the writing class. I really haven't read too much except for assigned readings in school. Even then, I only read the quota of books on the program. I've been more of a doer, especially painting. Any free time I have, I'd rather make something."

And she loved to dance and listen to music: "I guess I liked the hit parade in those days 'cause I was looking at it from the view: 'Can you dance to it?' There wasn't much to the lyrics, although 'Get out in the kitchen and rattle those pots and pans,' that's great music, great. I love 'Shake Rattle and Roll,' the Coasters, Chuck Berry. I've been with rock and roll from the beginning, and it's just starting to come out now."

In Saskatoon, she didn't show much interest in playing until her last year in high school. She bought herself a ukulele, taught herself the rudiments of guitar playing from a Pete Seeger do-it-yourself manual, and took to hanging out at a coffee house called the Louis Riel.

In the Saskatoon club, Joni met up-and-comers like Joe & Eddie, and Bonnie Dobson, who wrote "Morning Dew." She began playing a baritone uke, taking it everywhere and going plunk-a-plunk every time she learned a new change.

At a weiner roast, a TV announcer from nearby Prince Albert heard her sing and asked her to appear on his program. She only knew four or five songs, but it came off all right.

Then she went to the Art School of Calgary because she wanted to become a professional illustrator. She worked for nothing at The Depression, the local coffeehouse.

"She looked just tremendous," John Uren, the club's owner recalls, "with all that blonde hair. I brought Peter Elbing in from Toronto. And he listened to Joni and said she could sing. She met a lot of people. Will Millar was around. He's one of the Irish Rovers. It was a good scene in those days. And Joni was part of it. She did more for the uke than Tiny Tim."

She migrated East at the end of the first school year to see a Mariposa Festival. Although intending to return to college, she found work in Toronto and stayed with only a hint of what she would find. She worked as a salesgirl to earn the $140 union fee so she could perform. She began writing her own songs (about four a week) and made the rounds of long-shuttered clubs.

She was hired at the Penny Farthing, one of several clubs in Yorkville Village which has been the early training grounds for Jose Feliciano, The Irish Rovers, and Neil Young. While she was playing in the basement section, Chuck Mitchell and Loring James came into town and played upstairs.

Joni was a strange young girl in those days—an all-around golden girl, running around discovering life for the first time. Playing and singing on Yorkville Avenue, she was part of the early scene. Walk down the street, during an evening then, and you'd hear David Clayton-Thomas, Bonnie Dobson, Jack London and the Sparrows (later Steppenwolf), Gordon Lightfoot, the Dirty Shames, the Stormy Clovers, Elyse Weinberg or Adam Mitchell (who joined the Paupers). Buffy Ste. Marie wrote "The Universal Soldier" in Yorkville. Phil Ochs wrote "Changes" there, too.

Her short marriage with Chuck Mitchell was described in "I Had A King": "I had a king in a salt-rusted carriage/Who carried me off to his country for marriage too soon." Their show was pasted together like a collage. Chuck played heavy Brechtian material ("while he sings them of wars and wine"). They did a handful of Gordon Lightfoot songs. But basically, Joni did her own thing and Chuck did his.

With help from friends, the two broke New York, worked the Gaslight Cafe on MacDougal in the Village, and gained some recognition. Next they made the Toronto-Philadelphia-Detroit circuit.

Gradually the breaks started to unfold. Bernie Fiedler at The Riverboat coffeehouse booked her and other clubs followed. Canadian Broadcast Corporation producer Ross McLean got her to compose the title theme of CBC's *The Way It Is*. Television and radio engagements followed.

After Tom Rush and Judy Collins performed her material, her own career moved in full swing. She moved to New York, where she met her managers Elliot Roberts and Joel Dean. They put the finishing polish on her act, got her a Reprise recording contract, and sent her out on tour.

Her personal life became a series of interruptions. But she accepted it with a certain quiet gratitude even when it bore down on her with an overpowering weight.

She retreated to her isolated, wood-hewed home in Laurel Canyon, about three miles north of Hollywood's Sunset Strip and immeasurable social light years away from Canada. Surrounded by stained Tiffany glass windows, oak-beam wooden floors, a Priestly piano, a grandfather clock, and a black cat named Hunter, a nine-year-old tom; she read her rave record reviews and equally enthusiastic stories about her public appearances.

But, she said, just about every songwriter reaches a point where he feels uncomfortable.

"The experiences I was having were so related to my work. It was reflected in the music. I thought I'd like to write on other themes. In order to do this, I had to have other experiences."

JONI MITCHELL: AN INTERVIEW, PART ONE

Penny Valentine | June 3, 1972 | *Sounds* **(UK)**

Penny Valentine, a pioneering woman journalist on the London scene, was already a veteran music writer in 1972, having interviewed the Beatles when she was a teenaged scribe in the early 1960s. When she was assigned to interview Joni in 1972 for *Sounds*, she caught her at an interesting time. Joni had performed two shows in London at the Royal Festival Hall in early May, with Jackson Browne in tow, then traveled to France and Germany for concerts before returning to London in late May for a series of TV appearances and press.

The sit-down with Valentine was the first print interview Joni did after two years of seclusion from public life, recovering from her first flush of fame (and scrutiny) with the success of *Clouds* (1969), *Ladies of the Canyon* (1970), and the album that's now acknowledged as her masterwork, *Blue*, in 1971.

She had endured the "Hollywood's Hot 100" chart *Rolling Stone* published in 1971, which had placed her name in the middle of a chart of her presumed lovers, insinuating a promiscuous love life. It didn't single out any of the men as being lads about town, and it's no wonder she seethed for years at such treatment.

Interestingly, Joni told Valentine that she was still "not ready for 'frau' duties." Although she made no mention of the baby she gave up for adoption in 1965, Valentine managed to convey the singer's conflicted feelings about motherhood and how hard it was for a woman to balance domestic life and a career. Reading carefully, one comes away with more questions than answers.

Later on, Valentine found out that Joni was angry when *Sounds* allowed the story to run in the United States. Joni reportedly felt that the interview contained enough clues hinting at her unwed motherhood that it imperiled her secret.

Note: The spelling of the Hawaiian island, Kauai, and the spelling of Matala, in Crete, were both corrected. —Ed.

THE LADY WHO walks on eggs is sitting in her hotel suite overlooking St. James' Park with her legs tucked up, her chin resting on her knees.

She is wearing a pair of jeans, a tiny printed shirt and a plain sweater over the top. Her feet are bare where she's kicked her clogs off, and her fine, fair hair trails across her shoulders almost hiding the silver hoops she wears in her ears. There is a tidy casualness about her appearance, a cleanliness and unrumpled freshness. And after the perfunctory look at you there's an acceptance that's surprisingly warm when you consider the image that has been built up around her over the years.

It was Richie Havens that called Joni Mitchell 'the lady that walks on eggs' some years back when we were discussing star signs and environmental characteristics. And not knowing her, it seemed from her music she was careful, delicate, going through life frightened of breaking it. It was quite a capsuled insight then—rightly capturing the fragility of a girl whose relentless pursuit of happiness appeared destined to fail. And yet, here and now, Joni Mitchell is a contradiction in terms that shows almost before you speak to her.

That star syndrome, though, produces contradictions in itself. The biggest with Joni is that metamorphosis on stage and off. At the Festival Hall she was like a Hans Christian Andersen snow queen, a throwback to her Scandinavian/Canadian origins, the vocal pitched to hang like icicles on the night air.

This Saturday, in a rainswept London, she is a comfortable encounter, and—for all the outward initial purity—the bright red painted toenails she wiggles while she talks make you smile, simply because they are in themselves a contradiction to the image.

After the Festival Hall she went to Europe for some concerts and then came back to London on Thursday. That night she took herself off to see Kurt Weill's *Threepenny Opera*, found it had moved, tried to see *A Day in the Death of Joe Egg*, found it had started. Undismayed, and she laughs now telling it, she had gone back to the hotel, stuck her hair up in a beret and prowled midnight Piccadilly alone with her notebook of half-finished poems so that she could sketch people in bars. On Friday she had taped an *In Concert* for Stanley Dorfman and afterwards, at dinner, we'd talked about her newly-completed house in Canada, and the plan in her own mind that had never materialized: 'I thought I'd lead a kind of *Heidi*-like existence, you know—with goats and an orchard.'

The interview she has promised on Saturday is her first for two years. She made a lot of decisions, back in 1970, one of which was to give up working and travel around, the other being to stop giving interviews. She'd had a rough time of it mentally and physically, a whole wrong outlook on her life and work. And to her, interviews were beginning to hurt: 'All people seemed interested in was the music and the gossip—I felt then that the music spoke for itself and the gossip was unimportant.'

'I have in my time,' and she grins at the pseudodramatic air in her voice, 'been very misunderstood.' But you can feel that the constant intrusion into her private life got too much to bear.

A lot of new songs have emerged from the two-year hiatus, and in themselves are interesting insights into the change in Joni's outlook: the loving humour of 'You Turn Me On (I'm a Radio),' the pain in 'Cold Blue Steel and Sweet Fire,' the retrospective bitterness in 'Lesson in Survival'. But then there is that feeling—haven't all her songs been directly autobiographical, total personal emotions?

'Well, some of them are, yes, directly personal and others may seem to be because they're conglomerate feelings. Like, remember we were talking before about the song for Beethoven and I was telling you that's written from the point of view of his Muse talking to him. But that comes from an understanding that I thought I perceived. By reading books about Beethoven I got a feeling which I felt was familiar, as I had felt about people that are friends of mine. So that's from my own experience, because it's my feeling for other people.'

And yet one had stuck particularly in my mind—'Cactus Tree'—the song about a girl who everyone loved and yet who was 'too busy being free' to concentrate on returning that feeling properly . . .

'I feel that's the song of *modern* woman. Yes, it has to do with my experience, but I know a lot of girls like that . . . who find that the world is full of lovely men but they're driven by something else other than settling down to *frau*-duties.'

But then, I say, there is this impression she gives out—someone on the move all the time, someone intent on having freedom, even if it's a deceptive kind of freedom.

'Freedom *is* deceptive, though. It's like that line of [Kris] Kristofferson's: "Freedom's just another way of nothing left to lose" [*sic*]. Freedom implies a lot of loneliness, you know, a lot of unfulfilment. It implies always the search for fulfilment, which sometimes is more exciting than the fulfilment itself. I mean, so many times I've talked to friends of mine who are just searching for something and one day they come to you and they've FOUND IT! Then two weeks later you talk to them and they aren't satisfied. They won't allow themselves to think they've found it—because they've come to enjoy the quest so much. They've found it—then what?

'I think that there's a new thing to discover in the development of fulfilment. I don't think it necessarily means trading the search, which is more exciting than the actual fulfilment. I still have this dream that you can come to a place where there's a different kind of medium—a more subtle kind of exploration to do of one thing or one place or one person. Like, drifting through lives quickly and cities quickly, you know, you never really get to understand a person or a place very deeply. Like, you can be in a place until you feel completely familiar with it, or stay with a person until you may feel very bored. You feel you've explored it all. Then, all of a sudden, if you're there long enough, it'll just open up and flash you all over again. But so many people who are searching and travelling come to that point where it's stealing out on them and they just can't handle that and have to move on.'

We talk about the time she spent travelling and how—although songs came out of it and so it was a productive experience—there was an innate disappointment. A sense—and this came out in her spoken intros at the Festival Hall—of disillusionment that what she had believed would be magical somehow never turned out that way. She was affected by that too, she admits, and yet after a thought she smiles at her own naïveté in expecting places to be untouched, in expecting to be totally absorbed into them and accepted.

'You tailor-make your dreams to "it'll be this way" and when it isn't . . . like, if you have a preconceived idea of anything, then inevitably it can't live up to your hopes. Hawaii had so many really beautiful parts to it, and the island of Kauai is agricultural. I guess I had thought of [Hawaii] from all those *Occa Occa* movies I had seen—sacrificing the maidens to the volcano, rivers running with blood and lava, guava trees and,' she laughs, 'Esther Williams, you know, swimming through the lagoon. And you get there and have to sort through the stucco and the pink hotels. Crete was for the most part pretty virgin, and if you walked to the market you'd find farmers with *burros* and oranges on the side; it was wonderful. Matala was full of kids from all over the world who were seeking the same kind of thing I was, but they couldn't get away from, ummm—I mean they may as well have been in an apartment in Berkeley as in a cave there, because the lifestyle continued the same wherever they were. And the odd thing to me was that after my initial plans to be accepted into the home of a Greek family fell apart, we came to this very scene—the very scene we were trying to escape from—and it seemed very attractive to us. There were so many contradictions, so much I noticed about life generally on those trips. Like, the kids couldn't get used to seeing all the slaughtered meat hanging in the shops—they'd only ever seen bits of meat wrapped in cellophane, and to see it there on its frame turned their stomachs. Most people have that reaction—look at last night over dinner when we started to complain because people were talking about eating birds. We got so upset, and yet at the same time we were eating chicken by the mouthful without even thinking. I go on vegetarian things every so often—well, fruitarian really. In California it's easy because it's warm most of the time. I think you need meat in winter. I have this friend who's a vegetarian and helped me build my house in Canada. We lived on fruit all summer, and he was a fanatical vegetarian—sneering at me when I looked at sirloin—but as winter approached he got colder and colder and I said "Look, you've got to eat some meat if we're going to finish this house." I had visions of him collapsing. He actually did break down finally and have a steak, and I felt really terrible corrupting, breaking down a man's principles, like that.'

I wonder if the house in Canada is a permanent move, whether she's had enough of the California scene and is moving back to her roots.

'Not really—moving back is like burning your bridges behind you. For one thing, I don't want to lose my alien registration card, because that enables me to work in the States. So I have a house in California—not the one in Laurel Canyon I used to have—for an address. The house in Canada is just a solitary station. I mean, it's by the sea and it has enough physical beauty and change of mood so that I can spend two or three weeks there alone.

'The land has a rich melancholy about it. Not in the summer, because it's usually very clear, but in the spring and winter it's very brooding and it's conducive to a certain kind of thinking. But I can't spend a lot of time up there. Socially I have old school friends around Vancouver, Victoria and some of the islands, but I need the stimulation of the scene in Los Angeles. So I really find myself down there almost as much now as when I lived there—because then I was on the road most of the time anyway. I'm so transient now that, even though I have the house in Canada, I really don't feel like I have a home—well, it's home when I'm there, you know, but then so is the Holiday Inn in its own weird way.'

We get on to the two-year break and I wonder how she'll take the intrusion into her reasons and her personal kick-back. But she's relaxed and forthright and somehow feel it's a question she feels right in answering now that it's in the past.

'The first year I traveled, the second year I built my house and—in the process of building it and being alone up there when it was completed—I had written a lot of new songs. And it seemed to me that [they weren't] like a completed art until they were tried in front of a live audience. Well, not "tried", but there's a need to share them. I kept calling people in the bar of this lodge and saying, "Listen, want to hear a song?" and they say, "That's really nice—know any Gordon Lightfoot?" No, that's not really true—but I really did want to play in front of people, which was a strange feeling for me to get because two years ago, when I retired I felt I never really wanted to do it again—ever.

'Like, I gained a strange perspective on performing. I had a bad attitude about it, you know. I felt like what I was writing was too personal to be applauded. I even thought that maybe the thing to do was to present the songs some different way—like a play or a classical performance where you play everything and then run off stage and let them do whatever they want, applaud or walk out. I was too close to my own work. Now I've gained a perspective, a distance on most of my songs. So that now I can feel them when I perform them, but I do have a certain detachment from the reality of the story.

'I was too close to my own work. Now I've gained a perspective, a distance on most of my songs. So that now I can feel them when I perform them, but I do have a certain detachment from the reality of the story."

Did it help her in that troubled time to get her feelings out on paper?

'Yes, it does, you know, it translates your mood. You can be in a really melancholic, depressive mood, feeling downright bad, and you want to know why. So you sit down and think "Why?" You ask yourself a lot of questions. I find if I just sit around and meditate and mope about it all, then there's no release at all, I just get deeper and deeper into it. Whereas in the act of creating—when the song is born and you've made something beautiful—it's a release valve. And I always try and look for some optimism, you know, no matter how cynical my mood may be. I always try to find that little crevice of light peeking through. Whatever I've made—whether it's a painting, a song, or even a sweater—it changes my mood. I'm pleased with myself that I've made something.'

JONI MITCHELL: AN INTERVIEW, PART TWO

Penny Valentine | June 10, 1972 | *Sounds* (UK)

In Part Two of her talk with Penny Valentine, Joni confessed that she had seen a psychiatrist—no big surprise, to anyone who's heard her album *Blue*.

She also talked to Valentine about some of the songs she was preparing for what would become her October release, *For the Roses*, that were largely written at her rustic retreat on the Sunshine Coast in British Columbia. —Ed.

Last week Joni Mitchell spoke for the first time in over two years about why she virtually 'retired' from the music scene during a period of searching and self-exploration. How her writing had become a therapy for her to overcome something of a real crisis in her career and in her outlook.

In her London hotel, happily chain-smoking her way through the afternoon, she continues our discussion of her life and attitudes . . .

For Joni, then, the emotional release to her problems came through her artistic involvement, her sense of achievement. But the subject brings up theories on psychiatrists and whether the ordinary person, who perhaps does not have the artistic satisfaction of creating, is ever helped through times of stress by them.

Surprisingly, it turns out, that despite her own forms of release, Joni did once visit a psychiatrist herself just before she made the decision to come off the road.

'A couple of years ago I got very depressed—to the point where I thought it was no longer a problem for burdening my friends with. But I needed to talk to someone who was very indifferent, so I thought I'd pay this guy to listen to me. I had done a lot of thinking beforehand as to what was eating me, so there wasn't a great deal of uncovering to do. I went to see him and said, "Okay blah blah blah" and just started to rap from the time I came through the door—which turned out to be 40 minutes of everything I thought was bothering me. Which included a description of myself as being a person who never spoke, which naturally he found hard to understand! But it was true that in day-to-day life I was practically catatonic. There were moments when I thought I had nothing pertinent to say, but there I was, blabbing my mouth off to him.

'So in the end he looked at me and said "Well do you ever feel suicidal?" and I said "Sometimes I feel very bad, but I have to make another record . . ." telling him I had all these things to live for. So he just handed me his card and said, "Listen—call me again sometime when you feel suicidal." And I went out into the street—I'd come in completely deadpan, my face immobile even when I talked—and I just felt this grin breaking over my face at the irony of it all. At the thought that this man was going to help me at all. I don't see that [psychiatrists] really do much good. The idea that you disclose all these things to a person who remains totally anonymous seems not very helpful.'

But isn't that why people go [to therapy]—that they are anonymous beings?

'Oh sure—that is why people talk to strangers on trains and buses, for a release. But I wanted more than a release. I wanted some wisdom, some kind of counsel and direction. He didn't know. He only knew the way to his office in the morning and the way to the bar afterwards.'

Well, some people use them like a priest—almost as a confessional . . .

'True, but . . . did you read Hermann Hesse's book *Narcissus and Goldmund*? In reading that book—and I have never had any Catholic experience—but at the end when Narcissus the priest gives Goldmund a mantra to repeat over and over again, not reproaching him for his life, but just giving him a focus because he's so spaced out, kind of "You're out of focus—get yourself in focus", I thought that was so brilliant; so many priests and psychiatrists miss the whole point of getting right to the heart of the person. Giving him rehabilitation and setting up a solution. Hesse is certainly my favorite author—although I must admit I hardly ever read. As a result, I find difficulty in expressing myself—suddenly I find how limited my vocabulary is. I never was a reader, I always was a doer. To me, reading was a vicarious experience. But I have a hunger now; there are times when I am among my friends and I feel like an illiterate.

'It's like I came through the school systems completely unscathed in a way, and completely unlearned in another way. Which makes me feel terribly ignorant. I find now that the most common phrase in my vocabulary is,' she lowers her voice sternly, 'I DON'T KNOW, I just don't know.'

Sadly, it's a common link between us—something we have to laugh at but knowing it's only a cover-up, in exactly the same way as an excuse for scholarly learning is that 'living is more important.'

'Oh well, I think that both those sides are true. I think that a lot of people who [are] glued into books can only learn from books. Like, one thing I love is the exploration of learning. I love teaching myself things. In a way, that handicaps me, because when someone tries to instruct me, I can't be instructed. This is particularly painful to me in my music, because someone will say, "Oh, I like the way you play piano, will you play these key changes, C to E?" And I can't do it. The only way I could is if they play the tapes and let me wander around and choose my own chords.

'I was constantly rapped on the knuckles at piano classes because I'd listen to what the teacher played and I'd remember it. So I never learned to sight read properly and she'd bust me on it. I'd fake it—like, I'd read the music and it wouldn't be quite right, there was a certain amount of improvisation in it. And she'd say, "Those notes aren't in there". That kind of killed my interest in piano for a good 15 years or so. From the beginning I really wanted to mess around and create, find the colours the piano had buried in it. You know, I always feel like such an irresponsible creature.'

We move back to the songs. At the Festival Hall she debuted 'Lesson in Survival', which now, having discussed the two years away from the business, seems even more pertinent than it did that evening. She apologized for it on stage, saying she didn't necessarily feel that way now, but obviously it was a very bitter time.

'Yes, that was when I came off the road. I had a friend at that time I was very close to and who was on the verge of tremendous success. I was watching his career and I was thinking that, as his woman at that time, I should be able to support him. And yet it seemed to me that I could see the change in his future would remove things from his life. I felt like having come through, having had a small taste of success, and having seen the consequences of what it gives you and what it takes away in terms of what you *think* it's going to give you—well, I just felt I was in no position to help. I knew what he needed was someone to support him and say it was all wonderful. But everything I saw him going through I thought was ludicrous, because I'd thought it was ludicrous when I'd done it.

'It was a very difficult time, and the song was actually written for that person: "In the office sits a poet and he trembles as he sings/And he asks some guy to circulate his soul . . . okay on your mark red ribbon runner." Like, go after it, but remember the days when you sat and made up tunes for yourself and played in small clubs where there was still some contact and when people came up and said—maybe they did before, but you didn't care, you know? Ummm, well, I've got to clarify that—it is appreciated when someone says it and genuinely means it and you can see it's moved them, maybe changed them a little. Like, I've been really moved by some performances and I've been unable to tell them from my side of it because I know what it's like to receive praise. It's a very difficult thing to give sincerely and communicate that sincerity.'

Having gone through all those feelings, didn't she find it hard to come back to concerts and get involved in it all again—knowing what she knew and how she'd reacted to knowing it?

'Well, that part of the song I apologized for the most was the bitterness, I had felt so pressurized. I don't feel pressurized by it now, mainly because I intend to express myself in more than one medium, so if I go dry in one, I'll move into something else.

'You come to dry periods as an artist, and you get real panicky. I've known people that haven't written for maybe a year, and they're chewing their fingernails right down to the wrist. And I've known people who maybe haven't put out such a good fourth record and they feel they're on some sort of decline. Either they feel it personally or they're led to believe it. Their record company is beginning to withdraw from them, the spark is going out. Or maybe it's the fact that at 17 they were so pretty and all of a sudden in the morning they have bags under their eyes.

'But now I feel personally unaffected by all that, in that I feel my creativity in one form or another is very strong and will continue. I may, of course, just dry up all around some sort of . . . hey, I may become the whole Gobi desert next year! You know, I always say to Elliot (Roberts, her manager), "Oh, I haven't written anything for three weeks," and he's always laughing at me because I'm very prolific. But I'm also very lonely—which is one of the dues you pay. I don't have a large circle of friends. I have a few very close friends, and then there's a whole lot of people I'm sort of indifferent to. And I sometimes think that maybe that's not so good, that maybe I should go out of my way and be nice to everyone, you know?'

But it must be difficult for her—the star system is a trap where it's hard to work out who is a friend for simply what you represent and who for the person you really are.

'I used to see that as a problem, but there was also this thing where I'd be nice to anyone who was nice to me—that I had this obligation to be nice back. But that's a discrimination I've learned. I'm older and wiser now.'

The rain had stopped outside and the last rays of a 7:00 p.m. sun are filtering across the trees in the park. Joni plays a little piano, eats a little butterscotch, and we move on to the new album—her first for Asylum, the label that her co-managers Elliot Roberts and David Geffen started and which she joined as a friend to lend her support to.

'Well, I've started on it. I've been into the studio to cut a publisher's dub, when the songs were very new. I just cut most of them by myself. For 'Cold Blue Steel' I got in James Burton, who's really a great guitarist. Like, that song is a real paranoid city song—stalking the streets looking for a dealer. I originally thought it needed a sliding steel, but we tried that and it didn't work. Finally I ended up with James playing really great wah-wah—a furtive kind of sound. It's a nice track, but in the meantime, the bass line and the drums didn't work solidly, so I have to recut that. I have a take of "Lesson in Survival" which is really magical, the feeling is there, and I don't think I'll do it again—so I have that cut and finished.

'Then I tried to do "You Turn Me On (I'm a Radio)". I've never had a hit record in America, so I got together with some friends and we decided we were going to make this hit—conjure up this bit of magic for AM radio, destined to appeal to DJs. Graham [Nash] and David [Crosby] came and Neil [Young] lent me his band, and he came and played some guitar and somehow it didn't work. There were too many chefs, you know. We had a terrific evening, a lot of fun, and the track is nice, but it's just . . . it's like when you do a movie with a cast of thousands. Somehow I prefer movies with unknowns. So I'm going to start looking for people who are untried, who have a different kind of enthusiasm that comes from wanting to support the artist.

'Like, Miles Davis always has a band that [is] really great, but [the musicians] are cushions for him, you know. That sounds very egotistical, that I should want that, but this time I really want to do something different. Like, the music is already a growth, a progression from *Blue*, the approach is stronger and melodically it's stronger, I think that will be noticeable whether I make a sparse record as I did with *Blue* or not. But I feel I want to go in all directions right now, like a mad thing, right! I'd think, "This is really rock and roll, this song, isn't it?" and I see it with French horns and everything and I really have to hold myself back, or I'll just have a monstrosity on my hands. No, I don't feel trapped in this held-back careful image. I could sing much stronger than I do, you know, especially on the low register. I've got a voice I haven't used yet and haven't developed, which is very deep and strong and could carry over a loud band. And I'm very tempted to go in that direction experimentally.

'But rushing ahead of ideas is bad. An idea must grow at its own pace. If you push it and it's not ready, it'll just fall apart.'

JONI SAID

On Retreating from the Business

"All people seemed interested in was the music and the gossip. I felt that the music spoke for itself and the gossip was unimportant."

—to *Circus*, February 1973

JONI SAID

On Interviews

"I don't like talking about my life. It seems to me that when you may say at one time may be quite different from what you might say two weeks later. I hardly ever do interviews at all. I don't care if I need them for my career or not."

–1974 Asylum Records biography

JONI SAID

On Living up to Her Words

"The thing is, you can express all these high and beautiful thoughts, but your life may not back it up."

—to Marci McDonald, *Toronto Star*, February 9, 1974

JONI SAID

On Outdated Mores

"It was then and still is a constant war to liberate myself from values not applicable to the period in which I live."

—to David DeVoss, *Time*, December 16, 1974

THE EDUCATION OF JONI MITCHELL

Stewart Brand | Summer 1976 | *CoEvolution Quarterly* (US)

The author of this piece, Stewart Brand, coproduced the Trips Festival in San Francisco in 1966, which featured the Grateful Dead and Big Brother and the Holding Company and is credited as one of the seminal events kicking off the counterculture. Brand also founded *The Whole Earth Catalog* in 1968, one of the quintessential publications of the 1960s: a guidebook to using tools, living off the land, and becoming more independent of society.

After the catalog ceased publication, Brand launched the *CoEvolution Quarterly* in 1974, a more intellectual journal specializing in the natural sciences, philosophy, and the arts, with less hippie do-it-yourself material than its predecessor.

As Brand describes in his introduction, his interview with Joni about her education was meant to be part of a public event, a debate on education featuring a panel of pundits including William F. Buckley Jr., Governor Jerry Brown—and Joni.

It seems that Joni accepted but then canceled not long before the event because she wanted to accompany Bob Dylan and the Rolling Thunder Revue on what would be her final concert with them in December 1975—a huge benefit show at Madison Square Garden in New York to benefit imprisoned boxer Rubin "Hurricane" Carter. The tour kept rolling on without Joni in 1976. Typically, she would have much more to say about Carter in later interviews (one of which is included here).

Joni had joined the Rolling Thunder Revue after a very hectic 1974, having released *Court and Spark* to great acclaim, toured extensively, and then released the live set *Miles of Aisles*. After a year of constant activity and scrutiny, she thought it would be relaxing to disappear into the large, frenetic circus of the Revue, playing on a song or two and having fun the rest of the time while others performed.

It proved to be a frantic, unhealthy time in her life, Joni said later on. But having missed Woodstock, she wasn't going to be left out of this party. And she indulged in the shenanigans of the road, doing a lot of cocaine, not taking care of herself, and having what she later termed a "flirtation" with Sam Shepard while on the road. The experience was so intense, Joni had to rest and detox afterward at a beach motel in Florida.

Somehow, in the midst of the frenzy, she found time to talk to Brand about her education, her favorite teacher and books, and her approach to lifelong learning. Despite the cancelation of her appearance at the live debate, Brand loved the interview and ran it in his *CoEvolution Quarterly*. —Ed.

Jerry Brown, Governor of California, got us into this one. Last Fall he wanted to help Immaculate Heart College in Los Angeles through their financial crisis and agreed to participate in a benefit for them. His idea of what might be interesting was a public debate on education. At this point he called me to Sacramento for consultation. I suggested that the debate be threeway, that Bill Graham produce it, and that we have a musician.

"Joni Mitchell," said Governor Brown.

(The debators were to be Brown, William F. Buckley, Jr. and Ivan Illich—Illich wouldn't debate publicly and was replaced by Clark Kerr. At the last minute Joni Mitchell cancelled her appearance so she could be with Bob Dylan and The Rolling Thunder Revue at their Madison Square Garden finale—which explains why Brown said in his Playboy *interview, "Bob Dylan is a man with power." Our debate, called "Education and Wisdom," substituted James Taylor for Joni Mitchell and was rather a flop at the Hollywood Palladium.)*

In the course of preparing a snazzy program brochure for the $50-a-seat debate, I phoned all of the participants for accounts of their educations. This is Joni's, with details added later. I think it's more interesting than anything that was said at the debate. Artists are educated, but never through a curriculum. —SB

Stewart Brand: Where'd you go to grade school?

Joni Mitchell: I went to different schools in Saskatchewan, all along one highway. Then high school in Saskatoon, Saskatchewan.

SB: Was much education happening for you there, or was it just a holding tank?

Joni: I was fortunate in the public school system to have one radical teacher. He was an Australian and a handsome spirited man and a reverer of spirit. The year before he taught me he approached me in the hall where I was hanging my drawings for a parents' day. He criticized my habit of copying pictures. No one else did. They praised me as a prodigy for my technique. "You like to paint?" he asked. I nodded. "If you can paint with a brush you can paint with words." He drew out my poetry. He was a great disciplinarian in his own punk style. We loved him. He was more of a social worker or a renegade priest. I wrote an epic poem in class—I labored to impress him. I got it back circled in red with "cliche, cliche." "White as newly fallen snow"—"cliche"; "high upon a silver shadowed hill"—"cliche." At the bottom he said, "Write about what you know, it's more interesting."

I think at that time there was very good academic opportunity. However, I was only interested in art—painting and music and things which weren't supplied by the school system until a later time. I went back to my high school last summer and found it to be extremely progressive—theatre in the round, advanced study rooms with provision for video tape, individual music practice rooms, a fairly advanced musical school, two classes devoted to fine arts.

When I was there it was an academic school of a very high order. It did attempt to make you do things for yourself, and function in a more adult way, but it was wasted on my particular interests. I must add at this point that this marvelous teacher who extracted the individuality of his pupils created monsters who were almost ungovernable within the rigidity of that system. We nearly drove our next year's teacher nuts!

SB: If they had had the art stuff then that they have now, do you think that would have made a difference?

Joni: I'm not really sure if it would have or not. I mean the pattern that it produced in me was independent thinking, I have no regrets definitely in retrospect. I do know that some of my art education has been something that I've had to undo. It's been a long time coming for me to find myself as a painter because I was educated badly in that area.

SB: Badly means what?

Joni: Badly means being taught to copy things rather than to use my own imagination. And not to copy masterpieces, even, but the covers of magazines and postcards. Bad education in a small town, not progressive enough. They didn't know what to do with a creative child in that environment.

SB: Was the art you were doing mostly painting and that sort of thing or were you doing music by then?

Joni: No, I wasn't into music. It's interesting, I wanted to play the piano but I didn't want to take lessons. I wanted to do what I do now, which is to lay my hand on it and to memorize what comes off of it and to create with it. But my music teacher told me I played by ear which was a sin, you know, and that I would never be able to read these pieces because I memorized things. So again there was a misunderstanding. In my drive to play the piano I didn't fall into the norm for that system, so I dropped that. And I finally dropped my art lessons too through a similar disillusionment. I belonged to an extracurricular writers' club in my school, although I was a bad English student because I was good in composition, but I wasn't good in the dissection of English, you know. So even in a subject which I later enjoyed, I wasn't scholastically good in it because I didn't like to break it down and analyze it in that manner, and I liked to speak in slang.

I failed the twelfth grade, finally. It just caught up to me that I would cram at the end of the year and then I would go into the new year with not enough knowledge to continue to build on that subject. So finally in the 12th grade I ended up repeating a couple of subjects and at the end of that year I went to art college where I became an honor student for the first time in my life. And I found that I was an honor student at art school for the same reason that I was a bad student—an equal and opposite reason—because I had developed a lot of technical ability. I was already aware of tonality and light source, and a lot of things that were taught in the first year. As a result I found that I seemed to be marked for my technical ability so that in free classes where I was really uninspired, my marks remained the same standard. Whereas people who were great in free class, who were original and loose who didn't have the chops in a technical class, would receive a mark that was pretty similar to their technical ability. So I became pretty disillusioned with art college, even though I enjoyed being near the head of my class for the first time in my life.

SB: What was the name of the college?

Joni: Alberta College of Art, situated at a technical institution in Calgary, Alberta.

SB: You were there how long?

Joni: One year. And the first year was like a time to decide whether you wanted to be a commercial artist or fine artist. They were going to decide what your fate would be. So I quit there and went to Toronto to become a musician. In that town there were about 18 clubs supporting singers, so I went up to see if I could get work. This was in '61.

Well, in Toronto there was a very strict union. It cost $160 to get into the union. If you weren't in the union, you couldn't play. So I had to take a job in a clothing store which paid $36-something a week, you know, the minimum wages at that time, out of which a very high rental had to be paid, black dresses for the department I was working in had to be paid, and I could never get ahead to get in the union. And I couldn't write home, because my parents were pissed off at me because I didn't go finish out my art college.

SB: You were what about now–18?

Joni: No, I was 20 at this point. Anyway. I finally found a non-union club in the city that took a chance on me that I worked at for a while. So I made a little money.

SB: Did you ever get in a Canadian union?

Joni: I finally did, yes. I finally got enough money saved up. And then I came to the States and gradually began performing around the country.

SB: Have you done any schooling since then?

Joni: No, but I've learned a tremendous amount from personal encounters. I continue to paint. I continue my work as a fine artist and a commercial artist.

SB: I wonder where that distinction comes anymore.

Joni: Well, I still feel there is a distinction. You've got to remember that at that time, for modern abstractionism there was no real commercial vent. That was what the fine arts were. You didn't see too many Christmas cards, album covers, car ads, or anything like that which incorporated that aspect of painting.

SB: Maybe the distinction is: a commercial artist is any artist whose audience is anybody besides personal friends.

Joni: I think that's about it. The fine artist decides that there are only about 13 people in the world who understand him and resigns himself to it. I don't get much from most contemporary art. I find it too non-communicative.

SB: You're still doing some of that sort?

Joni: I'm still experimenting with very personal painting as well as more commercial illustration of my own album jackets and things. I haven't taken any formal training but I have discovered my own educational system. I know how I learn best and I know how I learn most rapidly and how to feed myself information for my particular kind of growth, so I'm out of this a self-educator, but people do feed into me. I'm aware of sources of growth, people who have laid short cuts on me. I can mark the days of those encounters as points of departure. So I'm continuously in school. I do read some, though I seldom finish a book. I read it till I come to a point of inspiration and then work from that point into my own work.

SB: Do you ever look for more in the same book?

Joni: Some books I do. Rather than overload myself with fact—like in the school system where they gave you so much information that at best all you could do was regurgitate—I've found that at certain points in a book

I would say, "Oh, that's interesting," and I would want to spend some time to develop it or pursue it. I'm interested in the relativity of one thing to another. That's a thing that I do continually, collect information and seek what may seem to be strange correlations. For instance, I know a great studio guitarist, Larry Carlton, whose linear aesthetic tends to arc and splash—Dolphins, I used to call his lines, until I found out he was a weekend flycast fisherman. I find that I interview people all the time. I feel like I'm more in a state of growth and education at this point of my life than when I was in the school system.

SB: Do you think that's true for most of your contemporaries?

Joni: I can't speak for them.

SB: Do you find yourself hanging out with people who are more in the learning mode or ones who tend to know something that you feel like you can learn from them. They're not mutually exclusive, I realize.

Joni: In my early twenties I met two men who were best friends from childhood—one a sculptor—one a poet. My association with them was catalytic in opening my gifts in two areas. The sculptor, Mort Rosenthal, gave me a very simple exercise which freed my drawing—gave it boldness and energy. He gave me my originality. The poet Leonard Cohen was a mirror to my work and with no verbal instructions he showed me how to plumb the depths of my own experience. It's funny the way information falls in for me, you know. There are people at large . . . I wanted so badly to go and visit Picasso, even on the fan level that people come to me, even with the possibility that I would be turned away, I wanted desperately to go and see him. Picasso is one of my teachers although I never met the man, I have applied some of his philosophy of painting to my song writing. I don't seek out those things. I'm very fatalistic about the reception of information.

SB: Are there others like that?

Joni: Yes. But they live in books. The Castaneda books are a magnificent synthesis of Eastern and Western philosophies. Through them I have been able to understand and apply (in some areas) the concept of believing and not believing simultaneously. My Christian heritage tends to polarize concepts; faith and God—doubt and the Devil—it creates dualities which in turn create guilt which impedes freedom. Jean Grenier and Camus also are teachers of freedom. I feel closer to Camus since he is more savage—Grenier being somehow to me wise but passive.

SB: Is there anyone you've looked up personally? I should explain partly why I'm curious about this. I've just spent some time with Marlon Brando, and he is very much an adult educating himself by going around hanging out with people whom he admires. He just shows up at their door.

Joni: That's a wonderful way to do it. Warren Beatty also approaches things that way. He calls people that interest him and flies to meet them. Warren and Marlon have that ability—who's going to turn them away from the door? That's why I was hoping Picasso would like my music, and wouldn't turn me away. I wanted to go and play him a song while he painted or something, because I had so much respect for his prolonged creativity. I've chosen books I guess because I lack the chutzpah to just go up and knock at somebody's door.

SB: When kids come around now to see you, wondering what they should be doing about their own education, do you give them any counsel?

Joni: Well, the last time I had contact with a group of kids they had come over here because they had a class in career choice. They live in the valley, and they were all interested in music, but music again in the school was not considered a career and they were being channeled into what they would describe as straight jobs. So they asked me to tell them how I had come to have an outlet for my music, how I had Achieved Success. Well, in talking to them, most of them felt they had to make it like the Beatles— by the time they were 21. They seemed to have a feeling of urgency, they didn't seem to have the patience to develop and hone their craft over a long period of time. They were rushing, which I felt would interfere with their growth in a way—setting their goals too high and too close at hand.

SB: You can tell them if they're famous by the time they're 21, it will turn their brains to hamburger and they'll be sorry.

Joni: I told them, "You should see the Beatles now, at 30, with all of their glory behind them." I said, "Wouldn't you rather come to fruition later on in life, sort of slow and gradual, so you're still working toward something when you're 30?" I said, "I am 30," and I looked them right in the eye, because 30 you know to a kid is that magic number where you begin to fall apart or something.

SB: Middle-aged.

Join: Right, they can't conceive of it. So anyway, anybody that comes to me, I don't have any stock thing to say, because they all ask different questions. I find one thing: they'll ask a question and they'll get an answer that I feel could be useful to them. I can tell by how they relate to it that it's interesting enough for them to use for themselves. Then instead of taking that one bit of information, they get excited and they get greedy in a way, so that they wind up with more information than they can do anything with.

SB: One handball instructor I know of tells you one thing during the course of an afternoon's workout, and that's all you get.

Joni: That's why I never finish books I think. I get to a point where something hits me so strong that it takes me out of the reading, the non-active activity of intake, and puts me into an output situation, it inspires something, it triggers my work habits, it triggers my . . . at that point I put that book down.

SB: What books have done that for you lately?

Joni: The Boho Dance in Tom Wolfe's book *The Painted Word*. He described the Boho Dance as that period in an artist's existence when he's a Bohemian, when he's established all of his moral justifications for poverty while still striving for success. The second stage is the consummation which he has aimed himself toward, when the public says, "Yes, we like your work, we would like to buy it," and he is celebrated, he finds himself sucked into a social strata which he deplored as a Bohemian. There are different reactions. Picasso went right into it you know and bought himself a Rolls Royce and some little black and white maids, and everybody said, "Look at Picasso, man, he's going to blow it," like he sold out. Jackson Pollock said, "I won't sell out," went to all of these fancy cocktail parties and pissed in the fireplace and did everything just to show he wasn't going to enjoy it. That's the point in that book when I said, "Oh, my God, that is a liberating statement and an understanding to me," and I created a song called "The Boho Dance," taking his title and taking my own experience. I experienced my own understanding of what he was saying so strongly that it almost paralyzed me from reading further. Do you know that feeling? Carlos Castaneda, Rimbaud, Leonard Cohen—they do that for me too.

SB: The only way I can continue is if I can get hold of a pencil and make some mark on the page, turn down the corner, and then I can go on. I've done at least something to acknowledge the hit, and I can come back to it if I need to.

Joni: I am fatalistic about my reading lessons. I was working on a song when I was up in Canada. I had gone up to this lake with John Guerin and we got into a discussion about Genesis and Adam and Eve, and I said let's look up the story. I'd taken two books with me, and there happened to be this Gideon Bible in the cottage, in the dresser drawer. One book I took was a book on the history of modern art from a lot of critics' points of view. They were critical essays on the modern art movement through history, and I was still trying to understand. As I said before, I don't understand this period of modern painting, which is why I was reading Wolfe's book. We were looking for how they had arrived at this, since a lot of it seemed humorous and they wouldn't cop to it being funny. And there was such an elitist attitude.

Well, this other book I had was called *The Disorderly Poet*, which was an explanation of the creative trance, you might call it, taken to different extremes—drug-induced, natural chemical body disorders such as epilepsy, and speaking in tongues. And these three pieces of information were so related. In the art book I came upon a passage about witches and how they had actually been used to further the scientific method, and out of the whole book that's all I recall—that's it in a nutshell, believe me. It was as if the rest of the book wasn't intended for me to discover at that moment. And the information from those three books, in conjunction with one another, was my lesson for the day. And it was completely random, it was, you know, opening the book on page 92 or something. It was almost like the *I Ching*. It was almost like an oracle. But it was the perfect information for that moment. It connected for me in its randomness. So I do feel kind of mystical too about education. I feel that somehow the answers come to you through your inquiry.

JONI SAID

On Musical Pigeonholes

"Eventually, if not in the next album, I'd like to experiment more with rhythm. I might do a completely acoustic album, almost like a folk album, but harmonically it would be different from folk music . . .You know, pigeonholes all seem funny to me. I feel like one of those lifer-educational types that just keep going for letters after their name. I want the full hyphenate-folk-rock-country-jazz-classic . . . so finally, when you get all the hyphens in, maybe they'll drop them all and get down to just some American music."

—to Leonard Feather, *Los Angeles Times*, June 10, 1979

JONI MITCHELL DEFENDS HERSELF

Cameron Crowe | July 26, 1979 | *Rolling Stone* **(US)**

Cameron Crowe describes his 1979 interview with Joni Mitchell as his favorite of the many stories he did for *Rolling Stone*. It was to be Crowe's last cover story for the magazine.

The interview came about because Joni had read Crowe's other stories and felt that he was sympathetic to musicians, resisting the temptation to be cruel to prove he was tough enough for the big league. She had a lot to talk to him about: *For the Roses* came out late in 1972, and then her sunny pop-rock masterpiece, *Court and Spark*, in 1974. The latter went to number two on the *Billboard* charts and achieved platinum status. But when Joni ventured further into jazz with *The Hissing of Summer Lawns,* her brief reign as the queen of pop came to a crashing end. Looking back, it's a bit puzzling. On the surface, *Hissing* still has that jazzy-pop polish, and several songs should have been radio-friendly, certainly "In France They Kiss on Main Street."

It's hard today to comprehend the widespread disdain the album received from critics and fans. Surely she was doing nothing more radical than Steely Dan did a few years later, or Sting, or Paul Simon. But, as Joni said to Crowe, the times eventually caught up with *Hissing*. She also describes how her album *Hejira* came about.

The album she was ostensibly promoting at the time of the interview was *Mingus*, which was made up of music Charles Mingus wrote with her in mind, set to Joni's lyrics. The jazz great died in January, five months before the album came out. But with Crowe, the conversation meandered and touched on everything, such as the nude photo of her on the inside of *For the Roses* that predictably shocked her mother.

Still, Joni resists being put in a box, knowing that once her image was firm in the public's mind as the hippie chic princess of dorm-room fantasies, she would always be that. The counterculture's dismay when she appeared in public in sleek, Yves Saint Laurent pants is recounted with glee. (Much like Warren Beatty sneering at her quilted Chanel bag as "unbecoming an artist.") And she reflects upon her early years, talking about her friendship with Dylan and other peers, and opening up about former boyfriend Graham Nash.

Her musings to Crowe about motherhood, and how she finally felt ready, are poignant. She hadn't yet reunited with her "lost" child Kelly (now Kilauren Gibb), given up for adoption in 1965, and she was not yet ready to admit publicly that she had already experienced motherhood.

From the time she championed him in the 1970s and granted him this interview, Joni has remained close friends with Crowe. One of the rare photos taken of Joni in public after she suffered her brain aneurysm in 2015 was of the two of them at Clive Davis's 2017 pre-Grammy party. —Ed.

Several days before beginning these interviews, I overheard two teenagers looking for a good party album in a record store. "How about this," said one, holding up Joni Mitchell's *Miles of Aisles*. "Naaaaaah," said the other. "It's got good songs on it, but it's kind of like jazz." They bought a Cheap Trick album.

When I told this story to Joni Mitchell later, I could see the disappointment flicker across her face for an instant. Then she laughed and took a long drag from her cigarette. "Here's the thing," she said forcefully. "You have two options. You can stay the same and protect the formula that gave you your initial success. They're going to crucify you for staying the same. If you change, they're going to crucify you for changing. But staying the same is boring. And change is interesting. So of the two options," she concluded cheerfully, "I'd rather be crucified for changing."

Joni Mitchell, 36, has been living in exile from a mainstream audience for the last three years. Her last resoundingly successful album of new material was *Court and Spark*, a landmark in poetic songwriting, performing and in the growth of an artist we had all watched mature. From folk ballads through Woodstock-era anthems to jazz-inflected experimentalism, Joni Mitchell had influenced a generation of musicians.

Then, in 1975, she released *The Hissing of Summer Lawns*, her ambitious follow-up to *Court and Spark*. She introduced jazz overtones, veered away from confessional songwriting and received a nearly unanimous critical drubbing. Mitchell reacted to the criticism by keeping an even lower personal profile. She spent most of her time traveling (the road album, *Hejira*, was released in 1976), associating with progressive jazz artists and asking questions. With *Don Juan's Reckless Daughter*, a double album released in the winter of 1977, she and pop music had nearly parted ways. In a time when the record-buying public was rewarding craftsmen, Mitchell seemed to be steadfastly carrying the torch for art. Her sales suffered, but this direction was leading to a historic juncture in her career.

Word first reached her in early 1978 that Charles Mingus was trying to get in touch with her. The legendary bassist-bandleader had been battling Lou Gehrig's disease out of the public eye. She contacted him and they began a long distance friendship. Mingus had noticed her ambitions and wondered if she would assist him by condensing T. S. Eliot's *Four Quartets*, recite it and play guitar behind it for a composition he had been working on. She read the book and called him back. "I'd rather condense the Bible," she told him, and Mingus said he could dig it. They didn't speak for a time. Then, another phone call.

Mingus had written what would later become his last six melodies ("Joni I–VI," he called them), and he wanted Mitchell to write and sing the lyrics for them. She spent the last year and a half working on the project, her first collaboration, working mostly in her apartment in New York's Regency Hotel.

When Mingus died on January 5th this year, Mitchell continued writing and recording and finally finished in late spring. Including tape recordings of Mingus' voice as segues between tracks, she eventually chose to simply title the album *Mingus*.

About marketing an all-jazz Joni Mitchell album, Elektra/Asylum Chairman of the Board Joe Smith says this: "She has taken a chunk out of her career and accomplished something truly monumental. When we received this album, I got on a conference call and talked with all our promotion men. If any radio station calls itself a trend setter, it must recognize this album and Charles Mingus. I'm also having a contest for my promotion men," he laughed; "first prize is they get to keep their jobs."

Had Smith, in the course of running the company, ever discussed commercial direction with Mitchell?

"You don't tell Joni Mitchell what to do," he said.

It was Joni Mitchell's idea to do this, her first in-depth interview in over ten years. She entered the office of her manager, Elliot Roberts, one afternoon and sat down on a sofa. She wore no makeup, a tan blouse and slacks.

"Let's turn the tape on," she said, addressing my recorder. "I'm ready to go."

An enthusiastic conversationalist, Joni Mitchell speaks quickly and purposefully, structuring her thoughts like a writer's third draft. The sessions continued at various locations over the next three days.

"If I'm censoring for anyone," she warned, "it's for my parents. They are very old-fashioned and moral people. They still don't understand me that well. I keep saying, 'Mama, Amy Vanderbilt killed herself. That should have been a tip-off that we're into a new era. . . .'"

Would you like to shatter any preconceptions?

I do have this reputation for being a *serious* person. I'm a very analytical person, a somewhat introspective person; that's the nature of the work I do. But this is only one side of the coin, you know. I love to dance. I'm a rowdy. I'm a good-timer. Mind you, I haven't seen too many good parties since I left my hometown. People go to parties here mostly to conduct business.

There's a private club in Hollywood that usually is very empty, but on one crowded evening, I stumbled in there to this all-star cast. Linda Ronstadt was running through the parking lot being pursued by photographers, Jerry Brown was upstairs, Bob Dylan was full of his new Christian enthusiasm—"Hey, Jerry, you ever thought of running this state with Christian government?" Lauren Hutton was there, Rod Stewart. . . . There were a lot of people and this little postage stamp of a dance floor, and nobody was dancing on it. These are all people who dance, in one way or another, in their acts.

So the *renowned introvert* comes in, and I just wanted to dance. I didn't want to dance alone, so I asked a couple of people to dance with me and nobody would. They were all incredibly shy. So I went to the bathroom, and a girl came in and hollered to me from the sink over the wall, "Is that you? I'll dance with you." I said, "Great." It was just like the Fifties, when none of the guys would dance. And it was at this moment that the girl confided to me, "You know, they all think of you as this very sad person." That was the first time that it occurred to me that even among my peer group I had developed this reputation. I figured, these guys have been reading my press or something. [*Laughs*] But as far as shattering preconceptions, forget it. I feel that the art is there for people to bring to it whatever they choose.

I wonder if you feel like you've beaten the odds at this point? Even the biggest pop performers usually become the victims of a fickle audience.

It's typical in this society that is so conscious of being number one and winning; the most you can really get out of it is a four-year run, just the same as in the political arena. The first year, there's the courtship prior to the election—prior to, say, the first platinum album. Then suddenly you become the king or queen of rock & roll. You have, possibly, one favorable year of office, and then they start to tear you down. So if your goals end at a platinum album or being king or queen of your idiom, when you inevitably come down from that office, you're going to be heartbroken. Miserable. Nobody likes to have less than what he had before.

My goals have been to constantly remain interested in music. I see myself as a musical student. That's why this project with Charles [Mingus] was such a great opportunity. Here was a chance to learn, from a legitimately great artist, about a brand new idiom that I had only been flirting with before.

How did you decide to make this commitment?

Every year, when I've completed a project, I ask myself, "What am I going to do now?" In the process of asking myself that question, a lot of possibilities come up. I heard on the street that Charles was trying to contact me. He tried through normal channels and never made it. People thought it was too far-out to be true. They had all sorts of reasons for thinking it was an impossible or ridiculous combination. To me, it was fascinating. I was honored. I was curious.

Mingus was a man who generally was difficult to get close to. When did you know that you had really made the connection with him?

Oh, immediately. Immediately I felt this kind of sweet giddiness when I met him. Like I was in for some fun. He teased me a lot. He called me hillbilly; it was charming. We went through some of the old songs. "Goodbye Pork Pie Hat" was the one we decided on immediately. So there was this search for another one, and he played me a lot of material. Charles put on this one record, and just before he played it, he said, "Now this song has *five* melodies going all at once." I said, "Yeah, I bet you want me to write *five* different sets of words for each one of the melodies, right?" And he grinned and said, "*Right.*" He put on the record, and it was the *fastest*, smokingest thing you ever heard, with all these melodies going on together.

Did you find yourself cast in the role of easing Mingus from his fear of dying?

No, that was up to him. You can't do too much to assuage someone of their fears. I wasn't in that personal a role that I was his comforter. It was a professional partnership with a lot of affection. But one day I called him up and I said, "How are you, Charles?" I never really asked him too much about his illness, but that day I did. And he said, "Oh, I'm *dying*. I thought I knew how to do it, but now I'm not sure." At that point I had three songs to finish, and I thought, "Oh boy, I want him to be in the studio when I start to cut them. I want his approval on this. I want him to like my direction."

This was a unique position. I've never worked for somebody else before. Although in the treatment of the music, it was much more *my* version of jazz. As far as the music was finally recorded. He's more traditional in a way—antielectronics and anti-avantgarde. I'm looking to make modern American music. So I just *hoped* that he would like what I was doing. I was taking it someplace where I would be true to myself. It was never meant as a commemorative album while we were making it. I never really believed completely that he was going to die. His spirit was so strong.

Did he hear all the songs before his death?

He heard everything but "God Must Be a Boogie Man," which he would have liked, since it is his point of view about himself. It's based on the first four pages of his book [*Beneath the Underdog*].

How did you go about writing lyrics to "Goodbye Pork Pie Hat"? This is a classic piece of music that has . . .

. . . Been around. That was a very difficult one. I had to find my own phrasing for the notes. The real difficulty for me was that the only thing I can believe is what has happened to me firsthand, what I see and feel with my own eyes. I had a block for three months. It's hard for me to take someone else's story and tell only *his* story in a song.

Charlie assailed me with historical information about Lester Young [in whose memory "Goodbye Pork Pie Hat" was written] and his family background, concerning his early playing days. He used to tap dance in his family band with his father and mother. He was married to a white woman, traveling through the South in a time when that was just taboo. A lot of the great black musicians were forced into cellars or the chitlin circuit. So I had all these details, but I still couldn't, with any conscience, simply write a historical song.

Then something very magical happened. One night Don Alias and I—he plays congas on the album, and he and I have been very close for the period of the last two years—were on the subway, and we got off, I don't know why, two stops early. We came up into this *cloud of steam* coming out of a New York manhole. Two blocks ahead of us, under these orangeish New York lights, we see a crowd gathered. So we head toward the crowd. When we get up on it, it's a group of black men surrounding two small black boys. It's about midnight, and the two boys are dancing this very robotlike mime dance. One of the guys in the crowd slaps his leg and says, "Isn't that something, I thought *tap dancing* was gone forever." Immediately I'm thinking about Lester Young. They were dancing under one of those cloth awnings that goes out to the curb of a bar. I look up—and the name of the bar is the Pork Pie Hat. The music they were dancing to was jazz coming off the jukebox inside. There were big blown-up pictures of Lester Young all around the place. It was wild.

So that became the last verse of the song. In my mind, that filled in a piece of the puzzle. I had the past and the present, and the two boys represented the future, the next generation. To me, the song then had a life of its own.

Looking back, how well did you prepare for your own success?

I never thought that far ahead. I never expected to have this degree of success.

Never? Not even practicing in front of your mirror?

No. It was a hobby that mushroomed. I was grateful to make one record. All I knew was, whatever it was that I felt was the weak link in my previous project gave me my inspiration for the next one. I wrote poetry and I painted all my life. I always wanted to play music and dabbled with it, but I never thought of putting them all together. It never occurred to me. It wasn't until Dylan began to write poetic songs that it occurred to me you could actually *sing* those poems.

Is that when you started to sing?

I guess I really started singing when I had polio. Neil [Young] and I both got polio in the same Canadian epidemic. I was nine, and they put me in a polio ward over Christmas. They said I might not walk again, and that I would not be able to go home for Christmas. I wouldn't go for it. So I started to sing Christmas carols and I used to sing them real loud. When the nurse came into the room I would sing *louder*. The boy in the bed next to me, you know, used to complain. And I discovered I was a ham. That was the first time I started to sing for people.

Do you remember the first record you bought?

The first record I bought was a piece of classical music. I saw a movie called *The Story of Three Loves*, and the theme was [*she hums the entire melody*] by Rachmaninoff, I think. Every time it used to come on the radio it would drive me *crazy*. It was a 78. I mean, I had *Alice in Wonderland* and *Tubby the Tuba*, but the first one that I *loved* and had to buy? "The Story of Three Loves."

How about pop music?

You see, pop music was something else in that time. We're talking about the Fifties now. When I was thirteen, *The Hit Parade* was one hour a day—four o'clock to five o'clock. On the weekends they'd do the Top Twenty. But the rest of the radio was Mantovani, country & western, a lot of radio journalism. Mostly country & western, which I wasn't crazy about. To me it was simplistic. Even as a child I liked more complex melody.

In my teens I loved to dance. That was my thing. I instigated a Wednesday night dance 'cause I could hardly make it to the weekends. For dancing, I loved Chuck Berry. Ray Charles. "What I'd Say." [*sic*] I liked Elvis Presley. I liked the Everly Brothers. But then this thing happened. Rock & roll went through a really *dumb* vanilla period. And during that period, folk music came in to fill the hole. At that point I had friends who'd have parties and sit around and sing Kingston Trio songs. That's when I started to sing again. That's why I bought an instrument. To sing at those parties. It was no more ambitious than that. I was planning all the time to go to art school.

[*Informed of the time, Mitchell realizes with a familiar shudder that she is already an hour late for a hairdresser's appointment. There are several more errands to be run before an evening photo session with Norman Seeff, and Mitchell invites the interview to continue along with her.*

After a short drive down Sunset Boulevard, we arrive at the shop, situated directly across from a gigantic Bee Gees billboard. She is greeted warmly by the attendants, who find her exactly "on schedule," as usual. We resume the interview with Mitchell under the hair dryer, cloaked in a plastic coverall that coincidentally bears a repeating pattern of two be-bopping couples and the phrase, The Jazz Age.]

What kind of student were you?

I was a bad student. I finally flunked out in the twelfth grade. I went back later and picked up the subjects that I lost. I do have my high school diploma—I figured I needed that much, just in case. College was not too interesting to me. The way I saw the educational system from an early age was that it taught you what to think, not how to think. There was no liberty, really, for free thinking. You were being trained to fit into a society where free thinking was a nuisance. I liked some of my teachers very much, but I had no interest in their subjects. So I would appease them—I think they perceived that I was not a dummy, although my report card didn't look like it. I would line the math room with ink drawings and portraits of the mathematicians. I did a tree of life for my biology teacher. I was always staying late at the school, down on my knees painting something.

How do you think other students viewed you?

I'm not sure I have a clear picture of myself. My identity, since it wasn't through the grade system, was that I was a good dancer and an artist. And also, I was very well dressed. I made a lot of my own clothes. I worked in ladies' wear and I modeled. I had access to sample clothes that were too fashionable for our community, and I could buy them cheaply. I would go hang out on the streets dressed to the T, even in hat and gloves. I hung out downtown with the Ukrainians and the Indians; they were more emotionally honest, and they were better dancers.

When I went back to my own neighborhood, I found that I had a provocative image. They thought I was loose because I always liked rowdies. I thought the way the kids danced at my school was kind of, you know, *funny*. I remember a recurring statement on my report card— "Joan does not relate well." I know that I was aloof. Perhaps some people thought that I was a snob.

There came a split when I rejected sororities and that whole thing. I didn't go for that. But there also came a stage when my friends who were juvenile delinquents suddenly became criminals. They could go into very dull jobs or they could go into *crime*. Crime is very romantic in your youth. I suddenly thought, "Here's where the romance ends. I don't see myself in jail. . . ."

So you went to art school, and at the end of your first year you decided to go to Toronto to become a folk singer.

I was only a folk singer for about two years, and that was several years before I ever made a record. By that time, it wasn't really folk music anymore. It was some new American phenomenon. Later, they called it singer/songwriters. Or art songs, which I liked best. Some people get nervous about that word. Art. They think it's a pretentious word from the giddyap. To me, words are only symbols, and the word *art* has never lost its vitality. It still has meaning to me. Love lost its meaning to me. God lost its meaning to me. But art never lost its meaning. I always knew what I meant by art. Now I've got all three of them back [*laughs*].

Did your folk-singing period include the time you spent in Detroit working with Chuck Mitchell?

Yes. We never really were a full-fledged duo. I'm a bad learner, see. I bypass the educational system. I learn by a process more like osmosis. It's by inspiration and desire. So when we would try to work up songs together, we would bang into differences of opinion. Some people say, "Oh, Joan, that's just because you're lazy." But in a way, more than laziness, it's a kind of block that runs all through my rebellious personality. If someone tries to teach me a part that I don't find particularly interesting, it won't stick. I'll end up doing what I wanted to do in the first place, and then they're annoyed.

We had a difference of opinion in material. It was more like two people onstage at the same time, sometimes singing together. We had a difficult time.

When your marriage broke up, you moved to New York City, and artists like Tom Rush began covering your songs. You became totally self-sufficient—booking your own tours and handling all your financial affairs. Was that your nature, or was it a reaction to the end of the marriage?

Both. At that point, I didn't know how far it was going to carry me. I had a little circuit of clubs that I could go in and say, "Okay, your capacity is such and such. I've got you up to full capacity now. Last time I made *this* much; this time, why don't you pay me *this* much more, and you can still make a profit. Let's be fair." People were starting to record my songs; I drew [audiences] even though I didn't have a record out. I really felt self-sufficient. I was working constantly, every night, and I was trying to build up a bank account because I didn't think it was going to last too long. I thought I was going to have to go back into what I knew, which was women's wear. Become a buyer for a department store. But I was going to go on with it as long as I could. Or maybe into commercial art. Whatever.

So you were less sure then that the songs would keep coming?

In some ways I had *more* confidence. I was outspoken. I *enjoyed* performing. I loved the compliments I received when I came offstage. Everything seemed to be proportionate to me. I had $400 in the bank. I thought I was *filthy rich*. I liked the liberty of it all. I liked the idea that I was going to North Carolina, visiting all these mysterious states. I used to tell long, rambling tales onstage. It was very casual.

I remember the first time I played the Newport Folk Festival. It was the first glimmering of what was to come. We went to a party—it was held at a fraternity house, and it was guarded. Only people who were supposed to be there were there. I was with a road manager at that point, a girlfriend who was helping me out. They said, "You can't come in." My girlfriend said, "Do you *know* who this is?" She said my name, and these people standing by the door let out this *gasp*. My eyes bugged out of my head. I had the strangest reaction: I turned on my heel and I ran for ten blocks in the other direction. It pumped me so full of adrenalin, I bolted like a deer. I came back to Janie and said, "I'm *so* embarrassed, man, why did I *do* that? It's a mystery to me." Well, she had lived with . . . [*laughs*] retarded children, right. And a retard is smart in a lot of ways. They're simplified down to a kind of intelligence that a more complex mind is not hip to. Janie said, "I think that's one of the sanest things I have ever seen, you know."

Then it began to get really disproportionate. I couldn't really enjoy it after that. I know it was *good*, but the adoration seemed out of line. The next thing was going through the primary adjustments, where more people are attracted to you because you smell of success. And they're simultaneously saying to you, "Don't change." But as soon as you have so many hangers-on, you have to change, and then you go through the pains of hearing that you "*Changed*, man." It goes to your head. There's a whole lot of levels of adjustment. There are no books written on it;

nobody tells you what to expect. Some people get all puffed up and say, "I deserved it." I thought it was too much to live up to. I thought, "You don't even know who I am. You want to *worship* me?"

That's why I became a confessional poet. I thought, "You better know who you're applauding up here." It was a compulsion to be honest with my audience.

You and Neil Young have always been close. How did you first meet?

I was married to Chuck Mitchell at the time. We came to Winnipeg, playing this Fourth Dimension [folk] circuit. We were there over Christmas. I remember putting up this Christmas tree in our hotel room. Neil, you know, was this rock & roller who was coming around to folk music through Bob Dylan. Of course. Anyway, Neil came out to the club, and we liked him immediately. He was the same way he is now—this offhanded, dry wit. And you know what his ambition was at the time? He wanted a *hearse*, and a chicken farm. And when you think of it, what he's done with his dream is not that far off. He just added a few buffalo. And a fleet of antique cars. He's always been pretty true to his vision.

But none of us had any grandiose ideas about the kind of success that we received. In those days it was *really* a long shot. Especially for a Canadian. I remember my mother talking to a neighbor who asked, "Where is Joan living?" And she said, "In New York; she's a musician." And they went, "Ohhh, you poor woman." It was hard for them to relate.

Later, you know, Neil abandoned his rock & roll band and came out to Toronto. I didn't know him very well at the time we were there. I was just leaving for Detroit. We didn't connect then. It was years later, when I got to California—Elliot [Roberts] and I came out as strangers in a strange land—and we went to a Buffalo Springfield session to see Neil. He was the only other person I knew. That's where I met everybody else. And the scene started to come together.

By this time, David Crosby had "discovered" you singing in a club in Coconut Grove, Florida. What was he like back then?

He was tanned. He was straight. He was clearing out his boat, and it was going to be the beginning of a new life for him. He was paranoid about his hair, I remember. Having long hair in a short hair society. He had a wonderful sense of humor. Crosby has enthusiasm like no one else. He can make you feel like a million bucks. Or he can bring you down with the same force. Crosby, in producing that first album, did me an incredible service, which I will never forget. He used his success and name to make sure my songs weren't tampered with to suit the folk-rock trend.

I had just come back from London. That was during the Twiggy-Viva era, and I remember I wore a lot of makeup. I think I even had on false eyelashes at the time. And Crosby was from his scrub-faced California culture, so one of his first projects in our relationship was to encourage me to let go of all this elaborate war paint [*laughs*]. It was a great liberation, to get up in the morning and wash your face . . . and not have to do anything else.

Is there a moment you can look back on when you realized that you were no longer a child, that you had grown up?

There's a moment I can think of—although I'm still a child. Sometimes I feel seven years old. I'll be standing in the kitchen and all of a sudden my body wants to jump around. For no reason at all. You've seen kids that suddenly just get a burst of energy? That part of my child is still alive. I don't repress those urges, except in certain company.

My artwork, at the time I made the first album, was still very concerned with childhood. It was full of the remnants of fairy tales and fantasia. My songs still make references to fairy tales. They referred to kings and queens. Mind you, that was also part of the times, and I pay colonial allegiance to Queen Lizzy. But suddenly I realized that I was preoccupied with the things of my girlhood and I was twenty-four years old. I remember being at the Philadelphia Folk Festival and having this *sensation*. It was like falling to earth. It was about the time of my second album. It felt almost as if I'd had my head in the clouds long enough. And then there was a plummeting into the earth, tinged with a little bit of apprehension and fear. Shortly after that, everything began to change. There were fewer adjectives to my poetry. Fewer curlicues to my drawing. Everything began to get more bold. And solid in a way.

By the time of my fourth album [*Blue,* 1971], I came to another turning point—the terrible opportunity that people are given in their lives. The day that they discover to the tips of their toes that they're *assholes* [*solemn moment, then a gale of laughter*]. And you have to work on from there. And decide what your values are. Which parts of you are no longer really necessary. They belong to childhood's end. *Blue* really was a turning point in a lot of ways. As *Court and Spark* was a turning point later on. In the state that I was at in my inquiry about life and direction and relationships, I perceived a lot of hate in my heart. You know, "I hate you some, I hate you some, I love you some, I love you when I forget about me" ["All I Want"]. I perceived my inability to love at that point. And it horrified me. It's something still that I . . . I hate to say I'm *working* on, because the idea of work implies effort, and effort implies you'll never get there. But it's something I'm *noticing.*

Having laid so much of your life out for public ears, do you now look back on some things and wince?

The things that I look back on and sort of shrug off, maybe in a weak moment *grimace* over [*smiles*], are the parts when I see myself imitating something else. Affectations as opposed to style. It's very hard to be true to yourself. For instance, I don't care too much for the second album I made [*Clouds*]. I like the first one; the first one's honest. *Blue* is an honest album. *Clouds* has some honest moments on it, but at the time, I was singing a lot with Crosby, Stills, Nash and Young, and *they* had a style, out of necessity, to blend with one another. They had a way of affecting vowel sounds so that when they sang together, they would sing like a unit. I picked up on that and there's a lot of that on the album. I find it now kind of irritating to listen to, in the same way that I find a lot of black affectations irritating. White singers sounding like they come from deep Georgia, you know? It always seems ridiculous to me. It always seemed to me that a *great* singer—now we're talking about excellence, not popularity—but a great singer would sing closer to his or her own speaking voice.

I think Billie Holiday was a very natural singer. In the context of opera, Maria Callas was an excellent singer. I think the lead singer from the Doobie Brothers [Mike McDonald] is a very natural singer.

[*"I think Bob Dylan had the right idea when he wore the same leather jacket for ten years,"* Mitchell says on the way back to her Bel Air home to pick up several changes of clothes. *"Georgia O'Keeffe has got it down to a uniform she wears every day."*

She buzzes open her gate, whips her Mercedes sedan into the garage and disappears into an upstairs bedroom. Her home is spacious, filled with plants and with her own paintings. The Mingus oil works—done at the Regency during her worst periods of writer's block—lie stacked in the hallway just outside the kitchen.

A few minutes later, Mitchell comes bustling into the living room with a small wardrobe, and it's back down Sunset Boulevard to Norman Seeff's studio. It's her fourth session in as many years with the photographer, and they work well together. Both coach each other. Mitchell lectures him on how *"you try celebrities here, you push them to the limit, test them against your zen training."* Seeff shouts at her to be quiet and *"transcend yourself."* Every now and then Seeff puts down the camera and they have a brief cross-fire philosophical discussion. They continue working all night.

The interview continued the next afternoon by Mitchell's pool. We sat in a small nook under the scorching sun, and for several hours, she talked with unflagging energy.]

Ten years ago, you had begun to represent the Woodstock ethic. Someone could say, "There is a Joni Mitchell type," and you would know exactly what he meant. Was that a concern of yours?

Very much so. I remember showing up at a Carole King concert in Central Park in a pair of Yves St. Laurent pants. And a good shirt. They were simple clothes, but they were of a good quality. And I felt . . . really *uncomfortable*. I felt there were certain things that I liked, that were a part of me, that were outside the hippie guard. Things that were a part of me from before this delicious period in the Sixties when we were fresh and were thinking fresh things. . . . It was a good time period. It was a healthy idea that we were working toward, but there came a time when it had become a ritual, a flat-out style.

I began to make this transition, under a lot of peer pressure. I remember seeing, even when I went to *The Last Waltz*, "Miss Mitchell showed up looking like a Beverly Hills housewife." I was outside the uniform of rock & roll and it was annoying to some people. And as a reply to this prejudice, I wrote that song, "The Boho Dance": "Nothing is capsulized in me/In either side of town." As a demand for liberty.

There was a time when you and Laura Nyro were considered to be the two purveyors of female singer/songwriting. Now it's all but taken for granted that Laura Nyro wasn't "tough enough" to survive in the business. Do you think that your own survival has meant a certain toughness?

Gee, I don't know if that's the case. Inspiration can run out, you know. Laura Nyro made a choice that has tempted me on *many* occasions. And that was to lead an ordinary life. She married a carpenter, as I understand, and turned her back on it all. Which is brave and tough in its own way. Many, many times as a writer, I've come to a day where I say, "None of this has any meaning." If you maintain that point of view, if you hold onto it and possess it, that's *it* for you. There's a possibility that you can come firmly to that conclusion, as Rimbaud did, and give it up. I've always managed to move out of those pockets.

At a certain point, I actually tried to move back to Canada, into the bush. My idea was to follow my advice and get back to nature. I built a house that I thought would function with or without electricity. I was going to grow gardens and everything. But I found that I was too spoiled already. I had too much choice. I could take the more difficult, old-fashioned way for a short period of time, but the idea of doing it *forever* would not work. I have reclusive fits, though, all the time. Not that it isn't rewarding, you know. It is. I mean, I do it for myself first, but I don't want to do it for myself only. I feel I can still share my work with people and they appreciate it. I guess it is my calling.

Around 1971, after *Blue*, it was reported that you had retired from the road. You returned a year and a half later with *For the Roses*. Was that material that you had written up in Canada?

Yes. Most of *For the Roses* was written there.

What did your parents think of the inside shot?

I remember my mother putting on glasses to scrutinize it more closely. Then my father said, "Myrtle, people *do* things like this these days." Which was a great attitude. It was the most innocent of nudes, kind of like a Botticelli pose. It was meant to express that line: "I'm looking way out at the ocean, love to see that green water in motion, there's this reef around me" ["Lesson in Survival"]. Joel Bernstein is the only photographer I would feel comfortable enough to take off my clothes for. It was part of our concept for the cover when we were going to call the album *Judgment of the Moon and Stars*. We were originally going to set that photograph in a circle and replace the daylight sky with the starry starry night, so it would be like a Magritte. At that time, no one was paying homage to Magritte. Then Elliot said, "Joan, how would you like to see $5.98 plastered across your ass?" [*Laughs*] So it became the inside.

How aware were you that your songs were being scrutinized for the relationships they could be about? Even *Rolling Stone* drew a diagram of your supposed brokenhearted lovers and also called you Old Lady of the Year.

I never saw it. The people that were involved in it called up to console me. My victims called first [*laughs*]. That took some of the sting out of it. It was ludicrous. I mean, even when they were drawing all these brokenhearted lines out of my life and my ability to love well, I wasn't so unique. There was a lot of affection in those relationships. The fact that I couldn't stay in them for one reason or another was *painful* to me. The men involved are good people. I'm fond of them to this day. We have a mutual affection, even though we've gone on to new relationships. Certainly there are pockets of hurt that come. You come a little battered out of a relationship that doesn't go on forever. I don't live in bitterness.

I'm a confronter by nature. I have a tendency to confront my relationships much more often than people would care. I'm always being told that I talk too much. It's not that I like to, but I habitually confront before I escape. Rather than go out and try to drown my sorrows or something, I'll wallow and muddle through them. My friends thought for a long time that this was done out of some act of masochism. I began to believe it myself. But at this time in my life, I would say that it has paid some dividend. By confronting those things and thinking them through as deeply as my limited intelligence would allow, there's a certain richness that comes in time. Even psychiatrists, mind whores for the most part, don't have a healthy attitude toward depression. They get bored with it. I think their problem is they need to be *deeply* depressed.

My relationship with Graham [Nash] is a great, enduring one. We lived together for some time—we were married, you might say. The time Graham and I were together was a highly productive period for me as an artist. I painted a great deal, and the bulk of my best drawings were done in '69 and '70 when we were together. To contend with this hypercreative woman, Graham tried his hand at several things. Painting. Stained glass. And finally he came to the camera. I feel he's not just a good photographer, he's a great one. His work is so lyrical. Some of his pictures *are* worth a thousand words. Even after we broke up, Graham made a gift of a very fine camera and a book of Cartier-Bresson photographs. I became an avid photographer myself. He gave the gift back to me. Even though the romance ended, the creative aspect of our relationship has continued to branch out.

This is the thing that *Rolling Stone*, when it made a diagram of broken hearts, was being very simplistic about. It was an easy target to slam me for my romantic alliances. That's human nature. That hurt, but not nearly so much as when they began to tear apart *The Hissing of Summer Lawns*. Ignorantly. I couldn't get together, in any way; it being human nature to take the attacks that were given certain projects. I got very frustrated at the turning point, when the press began to turn against me.

When did you first meet Bob Dylan?

The first official meeting was the *Johnny Cash Show* in 1969. We played that together. Afterward Johnny had a party at his house. So we met briefly there.

Over the years there were a series of brief encounters. Tests. Little art games. I always had an affection for him. At one point we were at a concert—whose concert was that? [*Shrugs*] How soon we forget. Anyway, we're backstage at this concert. Bobby and [Dylan's friend] Louie

Kemp were holding up the wall. I went over there and opened up the conversation with painting. I knew he was discovering painting. At that point I had an idea for a canvas that I wanted to do. I'd just come from New Mexico, and the color of the land there was still very much with me. I'd seen color combinations that had never occurred to me before. Lavender and wheat, like old-fashioned licorice, you know, when you bite into it and there's this peculiar, rich green and brown color? The soil was like that, and the foliage coming out of it was *vivid* in the context of this color of earth. Anyway, I was describing something like that, really getting carried away with all of the colors. And Bobby says to me [*an inspired imitation*]: "When you paint, do you use *white*?" And I said, "Of course." He said, "'Cause if you don't use white, your paint gets muddy." I thought, "Aha, the boy's been taking art lessons."

The next time we had a brief conversation was when Paul McCartney had a party on the *Queen Mary*, and everybody left the table and Bobby and I were sitting there. After a long silence he said, "If you were gonna paint this room, what would you paint?" I said, "Well, let me think. I'd paint the mirrored ball spinning, I'd paint the women in the washroom, the band . . ." Later all the stuff came back to me as part of a dream that became the song "Paprika Plains." I said, "What would *you* paint?" He said, "I'd paint this coffee cup." Later, he wrote "One More Cup of Coffee."

Is it true that you once played Dylan a just-finished tape of *Court and Spark* and he fell asleep?

This is true.

What does this do to your confidence when Bob Dylan falls asleep in the middle of your album?

Let me see, there was Louie Kemp and a girlfriend of his and David Geffen [then president of Elektra/Asylum Records] and Dylan. There was all this fussing over Bobby's project, 'cause he was new to the label, and *Court and Spark*, which was a big breakthrough for me, was being entirely and almost rudely dismissed. Geffen's excuse was, since I was living in a room in his house at the time, that he had heard it through all of its stages, and it was no longer any surprise to him. Dylan played his album [*Planet Waves*], and everybody went, "Oh, *wow*." I played mine, and everybody talked and Bobby fell asleep. [*Laughs*] I said, "Wait a minute, you guys, this is some different kind of music for me, check it out." I knew it was good. I think Bobby was just being cute [*laughs*].

Prior to *Court and Spark*, your albums were mostly kept to sparse interpretations. Had you always heard arrangements like that in your head?

Not really. I had attempted to play my music with rock & roll players, but they couldn't grasp the subtlety of the form. I've never studied music, so I'd always be talking in abstractions. And they'd laugh, "Aww, isn't that cute? She's trying to tell us how to play." Never negatively, but *appeasingly*, you know. And finally it was Russ Kunkel who said, "Joni, you better get yourself a jazz drummer."

One night I went down to the Baked Potato [an L.A. jazz club] to hear the L.A. Express play. I knew Tom Scott; I'd done some work on *For the Roses* with him. When I heard the band, I was very enthusiastic, and I asked them to play on my next session.

When they got in the studio, it was the same problem. They didn't really know how heavy to play, and I was used to being the whole orchestra. Many nights I would be very discouraged. But one night we suddenly overcame the obstacles. The next thing we knew, we were all aware we were making something quite unique.

A commonly asked question among your long-term fans right now is, what happened to the melodies?

The album with Charles is incredibly melodic. What it is, is *more* melody. Granted, "Coyote" is not a melodic tune. It's rhythmic, it's almost chant-like. A lot of it is spoken: "No regrets, Coyote." But I've always been a lover of melody. I don't think that I've ever lost that. It's just that at a certain point, my poetry began to spill out of the form and into something more relative to a jazz sense of melody, which was restating the melody in variation. If you have four verses, maybe it'll be slightly different every time it comes around. But that's just different. It doesn't always have to be melodic. So what, you know? You take a painter, and maybe he's been painting multicolored canvases. All of a sudden he decides to paint two-tone compositions. I figure anything Picasso could do [*laughs*] . . .

Don't you believe in compromise?

I don't believe so much in compromise as I don't believe in art that has become so elitist that only fourteen people in the world can appreciate it. For instance on this project, there was a possibility that people would have this prejudice—"Oh, it sounds like cocktail lounge music." Or, "That sounds like Johnny Carson show music." I wanted somehow or other to make something that transcended that prejudice. I feel that I solved that problem. It remains to be seen, but I feel that the music, while being very modern, still contains an almost folk-music simplicity. I don't think that it's intimidating. Some people get intimidated by jazz. It's like higher mathematics to them.

Was *The Hissing of Summer Lawns* more of an L.A. album for you than *Court and Spark*?

Yes, because *Court and Spark* still contains a lot of songs written up in Canada. The song "Court and Spark" itself was written up on my land there. It deals with a story based on Vancouver and the Sunshine Coast.

The Hissing of Summer Lawns is a suburban album. About the time that album came around I thought, "I'm not going to be your sin eater any longer." So I began to write social description as opposed to personal confession. I met with a tremendous amount of resentment. People thought suddenly that I was secure in my success, that I was being a snot and was attacking *them*. The basic theme of the album, which everybody thought was so abstract, was just any summer day in any neighborhood when people turn their sprinklers on all up and down the block. It's just that *hiss* of suburbia.

People thought it was very narcissistic of me to be swimming around in a pool, which I thought was an odd observation. It was an act of *activity*. As opposed to sexual posturing, which runs through the business—nobody ever pointed a finger at narcissism *there*. I had stopped being confessional. I think they were ready to nail me anyway. They would have said, "More morose, scathing introspection." They were ready to get me; that's the way I figure it. It was my second year in office. The cartoonists had their fun. There weren't enough good jokes left, so it was time to throw me out of office and get a new president. It's politics.

It sounds like it surprised you when it actually happened.

It really surprised me. In retrospect, it doesn't surprise me at all. I listened to that album recently, 'cause I was going to rework "Edith and the Kingpin." I was surprised. I feel that the times have caught up with it. At that time, I was beginning to introduce—for lack of a better word—jazz overtones. Nobody was really doing that. In the two years that followed, it became more acceptable, and when Steely Dan finally made *Aja*, with some of the same sidemen, it was applauded as a great, if somewhat eccentric, work. I fail even to see the eccentricity of it, myself. Perhaps there was a weary tone in my voice that irritated people, but there was so much of it that was accessible.

I remember having a conversation with you about a year ago. Months had gone by and you were still smarting over the criticism you'd received for your last album, *Don Juan's Reckless Daughter*. What exactly was your frustration?

If I experience any frustration, it's the frustration of being misunderstood. But that's what stardom is—a glamorous misunderstanding. All the way along, I *know* that some of these projects are eccentric. I *know* that there are parts that are experimental, and some of them are half-baked. I certainly have been pushing the limits and—even for myself—not all of my experiments are completely successful. But they lay the groundwork for further developments. Sooner or later, some of those experiments will come to fruition. So I have to lay out a certain amount of my growing pains in public. I like the idea that annually there is a place where I can distribute the art that I have collected for the year. That's the only thing that I feel I want to protect, really. And that means having a certain amount of commercial success.

It's a credit to the people that have supported me in spite of the bad publicity of the last four years—the out-and-out panning of a lot of fine and unusual projects—that at least they felt this work had some moments of accessible beauty. If a reviewer sits down and he plays [one of these albums] two or three times, it's just going to sound freaky to him. There are moods I'm in when I can't *stand* to listen to some of my own music. I don't expect it to always be appropriate. But come the right moment, where we're on the same wavelength, it might slip in on you.

I feel frustrated sometimes. I feel bitterness, but I'm not embittered. Feelings pass. A lot of the humor in the music is missed. They insist on painting me as this tragic . . . well, not even a tragic, because in this town people don't understand tragedy. All they understand is drama. You have to be *moral* to understand tragedy [*laughs*].

Elliot Roberts, your manager, realized not too long ago that he had canceled more shows than you'd actually played. Was there an instance when you walked offstage after two songs?

There was one time that I was onstage for one song. And I left. I felt very bad for the audience. It was impossible for me to continue. There's that old show-business axiom that the show must go on. But if I listed for you the strikes that were against me that night, I think that you could dig it. It's not easy to leave an audience sitting there. I was still in bad health from going out on Rolling Thunder, which was *mad*. Heavy drama, no sleep—a circus. I'd requested before the show went on to get out of it. But it was too late. I had bronchitis. A bone in my spine was out of place and was pinching like crazy. So I was in physical pain. I was in emotional pain. I was going with someone in the band and we were in the process of splitting up. We were in a Quonset hut and the sound was just ricocheting. And I just made the decision.

That can get to be costly.

The money is not the motivation anyway. I use one of two analogies all the time with Elliot. One that I was his racehorse. Or if I really wanted out of something I would say to him, "Be a good pimp, Elliot, don't put me out [*laughs*]."

I stopped touring for a while for a couple of reasons. One of them was that I felt it threatened my writing, that it limited my experience to that of a traveling rock & roll singer. I didn't want only to be a scribe to that particular facet of life, a minority experience. There were so many people documenting that already. That's rock & roll calling itself rock & roll simply by talking about rock & roll.

You may tour this summer with a band including Pat Metheny and Jaco Pastorius, presumably to play material from the Mingus album. What kind of set would you do?

With these players, we're talking about young musicians who have no real musical or categorical preferences. We all love rock & roll. We all love folk music. And we all love jazz. If anything, we want to be considered a musical event. We're going to do some traditional African ceremonial drum pieces. I would like to get loose enough to dance. Jaco, you know, is a bass player, but he's also a fantastic keyboard player. In this band, we're going to try to switch instruments. It should be very creative.

What were the origins of *Hejira*? That album seems to have a sound all its own. . . .

Well, after the end of my last tour, it was a case of waiting again. I had an idea; I knew I wanted to travel. I was sitting out at the beach at Neil's [Young] place and I was thinking, "I want to travel, I don't know where and I don't know who with." Two friends of mine came to the door and said, "We're driving across country." I said, "I've been waiting for you; I'm *gone*." So we drove across country; then we parted ways. It was my car, so I drove back alone. The *Hejira* album was written mostly while I was traveling in the car. That's why there were no piano songs, if you remember.

Hejira was an obscure word, but it said *exactly* what I wanted. Running away, honorably. It dealt with the leaving of a relationship, but without the sense of failure that accompanied the breakup of my previous relationships. I felt that it was not necessarily anybody's fault. It was a new attitude.

You were nowhere to be found in the Dylan film from *Rolling Thunder—Renaldo and Clara*.

Yes. I asked not to be in it.

Why?

I joined *Rolling Thunder* as a spectator. I would have been content to follow it for three cities just as an observer, but since I was there I was asked to participate. Then, for mystical reasons of my own, I made a pact with myself that I would stay on the thing until it was over. It was a trial of sorts for me. I went out in a foot soldier position. I made up songs onstage. I sang in French, *badly*. I did a lot of things to prevent myself from getting in the way. What was in it for me hadn't anything to do with applause or the performing aspect. It was simply to be allowed to remain an observer and a witness to an incredible spectacle. As a result, the parts of the film that I was in . . . for all I know, it was powerful and interesting footage. But I preferred to be invisible [*Laughs nervously*]. I've got my own reasons why.

Do you make it a point to check out some of the newer female song-writers—like the Wilson sisters from Heart or Rickie Lee Jones?

I'll tell you, the last three years I have been very narrow. In a way, I turned my back on pop music and rock & roll. I was concentrating mostly on jazz, modern classical music, Stravinsky, polyphonic music. During that time I developed a lack of appreciation for pop music.

Out of cynicism?

No no. It was part of an artistic process. It seemed to me, in the context of what I was exploring, there was no reason in the world you should be comparing Stravinsky to Heart. But if you're given Heart or Stravinsky, I was more interested in Stravinsky. Or *In a Silent Way*.

Now, I don't even listen to the jazz station in my car. The jazz station is full of mediocrity, too. I listen to AM, and I like what I hear. There's only a certain amount of fine work in *any* idiom. The rest of it is just copyists. Regurgitation. Obvious rip-offs. Mingus has a song, "If Charlie Parker Was a Gunslinger, There'd be a Whole Lot of Dead Copycats." Sometimes I find myself sharing this point of view. He figured you don't settle for anything else but uniqueness. The name of the game to him—and to me—is to become a full individual. I remember a time when I was very flattered if somebody told me that I was as good as Peter, Paul and Mary. Or that I sounded like Judy Collins. Then one day I discovered I didn't want to be a second-rate *anything*. I have to remember to be compassionate. Otherwise it really *pisses* me off to hear somebody getting a whole lot of public roar and, "Oh, this is the newest and the greatest," when it's really the newest and greatest *copy*. There are bands coming now that are really good. They're interesting; they've got some vitality and some fire, but—say they're Englishmen who sound like Bob Dylan. I listen to it and it's pleasant on the radio, but as an artist I say to myself, "If you're that good, how come you can't be yourself?"

Has anyone played you Elvis Costello? Any New Wave music?

I don't know enough to talk about it. It's ignorance speaking a bit, but one of the things I like that's coming out in rock & roll now is the Archie and Betty and Veronica aspect of the characters. I like the way [Rick Nielsen] wears a high school sweater and bow tie and beanie. [Bun E. Carlos] will have an accountant's short-sleeved shirt and short haircut and wire-rimmed glasses. I love the look of Cheap Trick.

I understand the punk movement. It reminds me of a very exciting time in my own life. It's nothing new—I was a punk in the Fifties. Devo, I think, is great. I love them. They are like Dadaists to me. Everything that they express is a complete reaction against everything that we stood for. But they do it so well, theatrically speaking. And with a great sense of humor. I love it. Now, as far as putting on a Devo album? It wouldn't be something I would do. It's the visuals that make them fresh and fascinating to me.

Do you think you've achieved greatness?

[*Long pause*] Greatness is a point of view. There is great rock & roll. But great rock & roll within the context of music, historically, is slight. I think that I am growing as a painter. I'm growing as a musician. I'm growing as a communicator, a poet, all the time. But growth implies that if you look back, there was improvement. I don't see necessarily that this album is any, to use your word, *greater* than the *Blue* album. This has a lot more *sophistication*, but it's a very difficult to define what greatness is. Honesty? Genius? The *Blue* album, there's hardly a dishonest note in the vocals. At that period of my life, I had no personal defenses. I felt like a cellophane wrapper on a pack of cigarettes. I felt like I had absolutely no secrets from the world, and I couldn't pretend in my life to be strong. Or to be happy. But the advantage of it in the music was that there were no defenses there either.

The vocals are real on this *Mingus* album. The interplay between the musicians is spontaneous and real. I can put my dukes up now if I have to in life, but out of appreciation for honesty. I won't settle for anything less in the studio. So much of music is politics. It's going for the big vote. It amounts to a lot of baby kissing.

Do you listen to Fleetwood Mac?

I enjoy them. To make a whole album like that, I think, would leave me wanting something more. For my own self. Not to put them down in any way. I'm still obsessed with pushing the perimeters of what entails a pop song. I can't really let go of that impulse yet. I don't know where I'm going. I never really do. My songs could come out any shape at this point. I *am* thinking now of keeping it simpler. Quite naturally, my experimentation has led me to a conclusion, and I feel myself returning more to basics and to my roots in folk music. But I don't even know what that simplicity might turn out like.

Do you still feel a comradeship with the Eagles, Jackson Browne and Linda Ronstadt?

The Eagles have really stretched out thematically. Jackson writes fine songs. Linda is very special. I'm a great appreciator of all those people. But at a certain point, I don't know if it was to protect me from getting a swelled head or what, I was denied any kind of positive feedback from a lot of sources. Like I go to a party and everybody shows up. I figure everybody must have a tape of their album on 'em. I figure, "Let's sit down and play these things." *Right*? A lot of times it would end up where I would be the only one who would end up being that pushy.

I always had this childhood idea that artists in a scene, you know, compared and discussed and disagreed with each other. But it was all done openly, perhaps in a shadowy cafe over wine. But because of this pressure for commercial success, maybe in a way we're deprived of this interchange.

[Mitchell adjourns the day's session with a quick and soundless dive into her pool.

As I walk into her kitchen the next day to finish the interviews, she is on the phone with a friend who is inquiring about the possibility of visiting Georgia O'Keeffe, the reclusive, great American artist, at her home in New Mexico. Mitchell herself became friendly with O'Keeffe only after several tenuous meetings; once she turned around and returned to Los Angeles before even knocking on O'Keeffe's door and introducing herself. Now in her nineties, O'Keeffe has few visitors, and Mitchell was careful about providing instructions to the house.

Later I would learn the caller was Warren Beatty, who, in researching his next film, about the revolutionary John Reed, wanted to speak with people who were alive in his day.

"I don't know," Mitchell allows with great affection. "Georgia might say, 'Ah yes, it was a very . . . yellow time period.'"]

Have you moved to New York City?

I consider myself spread across this continent in a very disorganized manner. I have three residences. One is wild and natural. One is New York, which needs no description. California, to me, represents old friends, and health. I love to swim. If there's anything that I love about this place here it's the luxury of being able to swim, which is like *flying* to me. I could get in the pool, float around for about two hours and never touch the sides. That's better than any psychiatrist to me. I'm working out my body, working out my lungs—the poor things are blackened with cigarette smoke—and looking at nature. I don't have that in New York.

New York gives me an opportunity to flex a muscle that I don't really get to use; for instance, out there there is directness. I find that it makes me stronger. You don't have so many anonymous encounters out here. In New York, constantly, the street is challenging you to relate to it.

What do you think of the theory that great art comes from hunger and pain? You seem now to be living a very comfortable life.

Pain has very little to do with environment. You can be sitting at the most beautiful place in the world, which doesn't necessarily have to be private property, and not be able to *see* it for pain. So, no. Misery knows no rent bracket [*laughs*]. At this time in my life, I've confronted a lot of my devils. A lot of them were pretty silly, but they were incredibly real at the time.

I don't feel guilty for my success or my lifestyle. I feel that sometimes having a lot of acquisitions leads to a responsibility that is more time-consuming than the art. That's probably one of the reasons why people feel the artist should remain in poverty. My most important possession is my pool—it's one luxury I don't really question.

Do you have many close women friends?

I have a few good women friends. I like them and I trust them. But generally speaking, I'm a little afraid of women. I don't know, it's a funny time for women. We demand a certain sensitivity. We've made our outward attacks at machoism, right, in favor of the new sensitive male. But we're just at the fledgling state of our liberty where we can't handle it. I think we ask men to be sensitive and equal, but deep down think it's unnatural. And we really want them to be stronger than us. So you get into this paradoxical thing.

I believe in equality. I believe that I am male and I am female. Not that I'm saying I'm bisexual—I believe in heterosexuality. I think ultimately it's the most difficult and nourishing of them all. But I do understand homosexuality in these times. It seems to be a peculiar, in many cases, necessary, alternative to this *mess* that's happening between the men and the women. I know a lot of women now who have come through the whole gamut and they're at the position where they almost don't want to *deal* with it anymore. They want to be celibate. Men are not at this place at all. The new woman is embracing this as a possibility. If there wasn't always this intense sexual competition between women, it *might* provide a climate for them to develop a camaraderie. In my observation, what passes for feminine camaraderie is conspiracy. I would *love* to make new women friends, but I hardly have time to do justice to the ones I have.

Did it change your concept of dying to spend the last year and a half with Charles Mingus?

Not completely. See, in my lifetime, I've had so many brushes with death myself, not that I'm saying that I'm not afraid to die—of course I still am. *Afraid* of it. 'Cause it's so *final*, you know. As far as a ceremony, of how I would like it to be treated, I'm not really sure. I mean it's an inevitable thing. I feel I'll live a long time. I'm confident that I'll live to be in my eighties. So I have a more immediate problem than confronting death.

Filling those years?

Aging gracefully. Which is easier in some societies than in this one. Especially in this very glamour-conscious town where women become neurotic at a certain age and go for surgery and any number of things to disguise that fact.

I had an interesting experience concerning aging in Hollywood. A friend of mine and I went to this Beverly Hills restaurant. It happened to be Fernando Lamas' birthday. So, sitting at the table next to us was this long supper of the old Hollywood. They were drinking toasts to Marilyn Monroe and there were lots of stories flying around about celebrities and people who they had known. There was a tremendous amount of glamour represented. *Well-tended* glamour. The fourth face-lift. Maintaining the youthful silhouette. I looked around and thought, "Is this the way that we must go in this town?" Is our hippie philosophy going to surrender to *this*?

I think if you're healthy, aging can be quite a beautiful process, and I think we've created an artificial problem for ourselves. Generally speaking, men are very generous. But I think that's the main problem, you know, at thirty-six, I'm examining.

You hold Georgia O'Keeffe as an ideal. Yet there she is in her nineties, living in the middle of the desert with only her art. She has no children. It seems like it could be a very lonely life. . . .

That's the part about it. I don't know, really, what your choices are. Obviously, that's a constant battle with me. Is my maternity to amount to a lot of black plastic? Am I going to annually bear this litter of songs and send them out into the marketplace and have them crucified for this reason or that. . . .

Or praised.

Or praised. Let me not get lopsided about that. I certainly get my fair share of appreciation. You know, in a few years, I'll be past a safe child-bearing age. I don't see many women raising children successfully alone, and as yet I haven't been able to bond with a man who I could see myself with in constant company for the twenty years that're necessary to do a good job of that. I would take that job seriously. I wouldn't just frivolously get pregnant and bring a child into this world, especially a world that has such a difficult future as the one we're facing. Also, the children of celebrities have been notoriously troubled. But when it comes to the business of raising children, I *finally* feel emotionally stable enough to deal with it. It's taken me this long, but it may be something that's denied me. It may be one of my little regrets in my old age. I still leave the future open, and given the right relationship, even if I thought the relationship had a potential longevity of, say, *six* years, I might do it.

David Crosby once said this about you, with all affection: "Joni Mitchell is about as modest as Mussolini." [*She smiles, shakes head.*] And while it's been my observation that you have a much better sense of humor than Mussolini, it's also true that you have no apologies to offer for anything in your career.

I like to work myself up to a state of enthusiasm about anything I do, otherwise, what's the point? I see a lot of people and say, "Hey, you got an album coming out, what's it like?" They say, "Oh, it's *okay*." I say, "Gee, you're putting out an album and you think it's *okay*? Where is your enthusiasm, man?" They don't like to hear that. I'm not talking about arrogance, but I believe in real enthusiasm. That's probably where Crosby's quote comes from.

There is also a deeper point to be made. In looking back over all that we've talked about, it seems that everything about you is geared to your creative muse, and it is to that muse that you have remained true. At any expense.

I'll tell you, any acts of frustration or concern or anxiety in my life are all peripheral to a very solid core. A very strong, continuing course I've been following. All this other stuff is just the flak that you get for engaging in the analytical process in the first place. Even Freud knew that; to me it was the hippest thing he ever said: "Dissection of personality is no way to self-knowledge." All you get out of that is literature, not necessarily peace of mind. It's a satisfying, but dangerous, way to learn about yourself.

Ever find yourself the only one speaking out on certain subjects?

All the time. On many nights I go home and say, "Mitch, you know, you're gonna have to start going only to comedies now. And only reading Kurt Vonnegut. Put those Nietzsche books away."

Last question. What would you have listed, as Woody Allen did at the end of _Manhattan,_ as your reasons why life is worth living?

It would be very similar to his. I would name different musicians, but it might finally be a beautiful face that would make me put the microphone down. I would just be thinking fondly of someone who I love, you know. And just dreaming of . . . Basically if you want to say it in one word? Happiness?

It's a funny thing about happiness. You can strive and strive and _strive_ to be happy, but happiness will sneak up on you in the most peculiar ways. I feel happy suddenly. I don't know why. Some days, the way the light strikes things. Or for some beautifully immature reason like finding myself running to the kitchen to make myself some _toast._ Happiness comes to me even on a bad day. In very, very strange ways. I'm very happy in my life right now.

PART III
Sweet Bird of Time and Change

Joni works more and more with jazz musicians, enraging and delighting Charles Mingus while recording *Mingus* and finding musical soulmates in Jaco Pastorius, Wayne Shorter, and Herbie Hancock.

JONI MITCHELL IS A NERVY BROAD

Vic Garbarini | January 1983 | *Musician* (US)

Joni Mitchell loved a good conversation, and she met her match in Vic Garbarini. Then editor of *Musician* magazine, Garbarini interviewed her at length in late 1982 about her new album, *Wild Things Run Fast*, and the story turned out to his satisfaction, and that of readers. But despite their bonding during the interview, Garbarini picked up later that Joni wasn't happy with the finished piece.

He ran into her several years later, backstage at the Amnesty International benefit at Giants Stadium in New Jersey, in 1986. Joni, her bassist husband Larry Klein, and drummer Manu Katche were doing a last-minute set, filling in for Pete Townshend.

Garbarini asked her what she didn't like about his *Musician* piece. He thought maybe it was because he'd written in the story that Henry Lewy was her producer, when he was always identified as her engineer. "She said, 'Oh, that wasn't a big deal,'" Garbarini recalled, although she had long been sensitive about Lewy's status, which many believe fell somewhere between engineer and producer. Having had too many men tell her what to do in the studio over the years had hardened her resolve.

No, what she was upset about, it turned out, was that they had a great conversation, but Garbarini was hardly in the finished story. "She said I had her stuff in all right, but I'd cut out a lot of what I had said. I said, 'Well Joni, it was a choice between me *blah blah blahing*, or putting in what you said. I had to condense my points to fit in your answers. I had five thousand words, do you want two thousand to be me? But thank you for saying that." At that point Larry Klein, Joni's husband, leaned over to say that he'd told her that was probably the case.

Later, Joni asked Garbarini to escort her onstage because she felt a little overwhelmed and nervous. He did, taking her arm in his and leading her to the microphone. Then the writer retreated, to stand behind the amplifiers and watch her performance. "She played her first song and it was amazing—but the audience was rowdy. Some of the idiots in the front were even throwing things, balled up pieces of paper at her. She said later, 'I wasn't that bad was I?' It was the best show I've ever seen her do!"

Notes: The following names were corrected: Don Alias, Jackson Pollock, as well as the song title "Marcie."

In the original *Musician* story, Garbarini has Joni referring to Henry Lewy as her producer instead of engineer. The writer said he must have misheard her on the interview tape—and it has been corrected here.

Joni's claim that *Rolling Stone* pronounced *The Hissing of Summer Lawns* the worst album of the year wasn't correct, as she herself has acknowledged in later years—although the magazine's review, by Stephen Holden, was largely negative. –Ed.

Joni Mitchell is a nervy broad. That's what Charles Mingus said, and he should know. Dressing up like a black dude on her own album cover, out of tune orchestras on "Paprika Plains," Burundi drummers and synthesizers, Wayne Shorter soloing over a 12-string guitar. . . . Check it out. 'Course, Charles had been dealing with nervy broads all his life, but this one was different. This one took risks not just to impress folks or for cheap thrills, but because her restless muse demanded it of her. What's more, she was usually able to pull off these stunts. And when her leaps of faith sometimes ended in belly flops, she invariably picked herself up and jumped right back in. Charles liked that. Liked it so much, in fact, that—knowing he was dying— he asked her to write lyrics for and record his last series of compositions. Some folks thought it was a pretty risky proposition for one of America's greatest black composers to leave his final legacy in the hands of a young white woman from Saskatchewan. Maybe it was, but that didn't seem to bother Charles. Artists, it seems, have a predilection for that kind of thing.

When *Court And Spark* was released eight years ago it was universally hailed as a near-miraculous synthesis of folk, pop rock and jazz (well, the L.A. lounge lizard variety, in any case). A careerist would have dug in and consolidated at that point, happy to mine a formula that had both critics and fans jumping for as long as the vein held out. But Joni Mitchell felt compelled to heed a different drummer—quite literally. Her next few albums followed a trajectory that took her farther and farther from the pop mainstream. Melody gave way to modality, conventional song structures were shattered, and the standard four-beats-to-the-bar pop format was lost in a stampede of African and Caribbean polyrhythms. Each new album attempted to stretch more boundaries, explore new compositional elements and rearrange old ones. *Hejira* eschewed the security of pop melodicism, opting instead for free-form verse shoved up against the beat. She kicked the remaining props out from under the rhythm section on *Don Juan's Reckless Daughter*, and finally broke free into traditional and hybrid jazz arrangements on *Mingus*.

Mitchell garnered little credit for introducing these fresh elements and innovations into popular music. In fact, she was often roundly castigated for even trying. That's what you get for debuting the Burundi beat back when Bow Wow Wow's Annabella was toddling off to kindergarten and David Byrne was signing up for art school. Or for attempting to work through musical, conceptual or spiritual puzzles under public scrutiny. Her latest release, *Wild Things Run Fast*, heralds Mitchell's reentry into the pop mainstream. You could call it the Concorde version of *Court And Spark*: supersonic production values, razor-edged guitars, streamlined hooks and melodies—all the nuances of vocal phrasing and rhythmic sophistication she picked up on her jazz pilgrimage applied to good ol' rock 'n' roll. In short, rock strategy enhanced by jazz tactics. *Wild Things* also signals a shift back to the first-person confessional style of her earlier work. And, as usual, the main action takes place in the arena of male/female relationships. Mitchell's ongoing fascination with documenting the cat and dog fights of modern lovers can be a bit much at times, but she effectively utilizes her own well-publicized romances over the years with musicians from David Crosby to Don Alias as a laboratory in which she can investigate and explore her chief fixation: paradox and duality. *Shadows And Light*; love and hate; fire and ice; Don Juan's Eagle of Wisdom and Snake of Desire . . . unresolved contradictions honeycomb her work and conversation. Like a Zen Master in front of a *koan*, Mitchell confronts paradox from every angle. Like the Indian cultures she feels a kinship with, she works more by intuition than through calculated design. For Mitchell, ordinary life is a semioticist's paradise, a place where coincidence and synchronicity can be the catalysts that reveal glimpses of a deeper pattern, a unity that underlies and ultimately resolves what appear on the surface to be irreconcilable opposites. In Mitchell's tales of incredible coincidences on steamy streets or chance encounters with affable drunks in hotel lobbies, vital pieces of the puzzle drop into place, and the whole is glimpsed.

Okay, I know what you're thinking: later for the artsy stuff . . . what's she *really* like? A fair question, and one that occupied my thoughts as I tossed down another Martinelli's Sparkling Cider, waiting for the good lady to arrive at her manager's Sunset Strip office. Obviously she was no longer the skittish, intense folk princess I'd first encountered at the Philadelphia Folk Festival fifteen years ago. Nor did I expect the glamorous Queen of Cool who, with a little help from a stellar crew of sidemen like Pat Metheny and Jaco Pastorius, had wowed the crowd at Forest Hills in 1979.

"Hi, got your letter!" says Mitchell cheerily as she sweeps through the door and plops into a director's chair. She's dressed in a smart grey skirt, white blouse and blue and white striped knee socks. The operative buzz words for the '82 model Mitchellmobile are elegant, open, secure and curious. And by elegant, I don't mean the ersatz Cosmo artiness of her album cover photos, but a natural, relaxed, *earned* sense of character and confidence, forged and tempered by struggle and suffering. After some small talk I ask why, two years after I sent it, she decided to answer my written request for an interview. "Oh, I liked your natural loose approach and the questions you raised about the creative process and inner growth. Sounded like we might have a decent conversation. I also like what you *didn't* want to ask me about." Such as? "My romances!"

As you'd soon discover, Joni speaks like she paints and composes. She's an ace storyteller, right out of the Homeric tradition, not so much describing or analyzing a situation as conjuring up visionary landscapes of cinematic power that take the listener vicariously through the event, like stepping into one of Don Juan's shamanistic visions. You emerge from the other side with the feeling that you've lived the event yourself and learned whatever lessons it inherently had to offer. Very exhilarating and a little spooky. But then, artists have a predilection for that kind of thing.

MUSICIAN: *After eight years of experimentation with jazz and poly-rhythmic music, you've come back to rock 'n' roll. What caused you to take the leap in the first place, and why come back now?*

MITCHELL: Well, after *Court And Spark* I got fed up with four beats to the bar, and by the time I hit the *Mingus* project I was having the rhythm section play totally up in the air. Nobody was anchoring the music. I wanted everything floating around.

MUSICIAN: *Just a need to break up patterns and let go?*

MITCHELL: Yeah, I was trying to become the Jackson Pollock of music (laughs). I just wanted all the notes, everybody's part, to tangle. I wanted all the desks pushed out of rows, I wanted the military abolished, anything linear had to go. Then at a certain point I began to crave that order again. So doing this album was a natural reentry into it.

MUSICIAN: *How would you say your approach to rock has changed as a result of your jazz and experimental work?*

MITCHELL: For one thing my phrasing against the beat changed radically. A rock singer usually sings tight up with the rhythm section. The rhythm section on the new album is still expressive even while they're anchoring, so if they come in on the downbeat I don't have to sing (heavily on the beat) "DOWN TO DAH RIV-AH BAY-BY." I can come in on the end if I want to, or cluster up anywhere—jazz phrasing—and still keep the rock groove going.

MUSICIAN: *Yeah, comparing this album to* Court And Spark, *it's apparent that you've learned how to bend and stretch the music to complement the lyrics and the emotional tone of each song. That first line of* "Underneath the Streetlights" *isn't about being in love, it* is *that exhilaration . . .*

MITCHELL: Yeah, you know how to get into that song? Just run down the street, throw out your arms, and shout *"Yes, I do, I love you!"* That should do it. I've been trying to do that with the music and lyrics for years, but I don't think it worked as well in the past because I wasn't *as* anchored to the rhythm. I was pushing it, kind of creating a certain friction against the rhythm. "Coyote," for instance, is a lot of stacking up. When I first started doing that years ago, there was a lot of criticism along the lines of "Hey, there's no melody, and it sounds like she's talking." In other words, the limitation of meter became oppressive, and wouldn't contain the poetry anymore, 'cause it wanted to go in a more blank-verse direction. I think now it's compromised, but not in a bad way and that's why this album is more accessible than some of the other projects. It's still anchored to the beat, which is, for lack of a better word, the heartbeat of the people.

MUSICIAN: *Speaking of heartbeat, a number of the songs on the new album shift rhythms between chorus and verse. Did you have any models or precedents in mind when you were working with your rhythm section?*

MITCHELL: The Police. I love that band, and they were definitely a factor. My appreciation of their rhythmic hybrids and the positioning and sound of their drums was one of the main things calling out to me to make this a more rhythmic album. I was in the Caribbean last summer and they used to play "De Do Do Do" at the disco. I *love* to dance, and anytime I heard it, boy, I didn't care if there was no one on the floor, I was going to dance to that thing because of those changes in rhythm. You get into one pattern for a while and then WHAM, you turn around and put a whole other pattern into it. My *feet* got me into that record.

MUSICIAN: *Yeah, considering how conservative radio is nowadays I think the Police have done a real service in bringing reggae and Third World rhythms into the pop mainstream.*

MITCHELL: And hybriding them, not just aping them or trying to sound authentically Caribbean, but coming up with a fresh approach. We did that with "Solid Love" on the new album. It's reggae in principle, and there are gaps between the bass lines, the repetitive figures with space between them. It begins to roll like a reggae, but it's a hybrid and turns into something original again.

MUSICIAN: *It's a lot more nourishing than the musical junk food churned out by radio stations run by computers—or worse.*

MITCHELL: Yeah, radio's like the Catholic Church: you can only paint the saints, that's all we want to see. No more fishes, no more symbolism.

MUSICIAN: *Instead of inspiring or challenging you, they're going for the lowest common denominator, refeeding you yesterday's breakfast. Most of FM radio now sounds like Journey.*

MITCHELL: But Journey does do some good things on a sounds level. As a matter of fact, I learned some things about eq and sonic frequencies from their records that I applied in making my own album. You might think they're antiseptic or too this or that, but when they come on the radio, they have a sound that's outstanding. I began to notice a glitter or clarity to the sound of certain bands that I may not take inspiration from on a compositional, and certainly not on a lyrical, level. I spent a long time mixing this album. Our bass player Larry Klein, who's my boyfriend, is also a sound man. He's twenty-five and he's come up in an era that's more sound conscious than the previous wave. He stretched my ear in certain areas, like drum sounds, which we'd never fussed much with before.

MUSICIAN: *Who took responsibility for the overall production?*

MITCHELL: At the end there was myself, Larry Klein and Larry Hirsh. We were a perfectly balanced team in that I handled the treble aspects and placement of the vocal and horn sounds—"This should go over here because it'll pop if we put it over there." They handled the rhythm section sounds and certain things I couldn't hear. But I *could* hear that the snare had a certain quality, and its placement was related to what we'd liked on the Police albums. And I could hear that supersonic sheen on the Journey album. There's a place on our record where it sparkles so much that if you listen to it too long it'll make you nervous. After about an hour of mixing with certain eq on it, we were ready to snap at each other.

MUSICIAN: *Was there ever a point when you were out on a limb with some of your jazzier material when you asked yourself, "What the hell am I doing* here?"

MITCHELL: Oh, yeah, on the *Mingus* project. I remember sitting down with Charles at first and requesting some input as to the themes. "What does this melody you wrote for me mean to *you*," I asked. He looked at me wryly, like Rumpelstiltskin, and said, "These are the things I'm gonna miss." So I had to get inside his soul from all the way across the nation and write down what I thought he was gonna *miss*. That was the first song done, and he loved it. Next was "Pork Pie Hat," and he played me every version that had been recorded, over and over again, and I chose the one I liked best to work from. The first step was to memorize that piece of music vocally, which was very complicated. It had one passage of triple-tonguing (waggles tongue) BLBLBLBLBLBLBLBL. And I said, "You want me to write words to *that*?" And he smiled and said, "YEAAAAAHHHHHHH!" (laughs)

He gave me this melody, and I didn't know what kind of a theme to lay on it. He kept saying, "This guy was the sweeeetest guy," and he kept saying that over and over about Lester Young, who was gone, and it was given to me to write by a man who was about to go. And somehow or other, I felt that in the lyric—the lyric should contain both of them. So, the first verse was easy. But how to get out of this was a mystery, and the last verse wouldn't come. So one night, we're going uptown, my boyfriend and I, and we decided to get off the subway a block early. And we came out near a manhole with steam rising all around us, and about two blocks ahead of us was a group of black guys—pimps, by the look of their hats—circled around, kind of leaning over into a circle. It was this little bar with a canopy that went out to the curb. In the center of them are two boys, maybe nine years old or younger, doing this robot-like dance, a modern dance, and one guy in the ring slaps his knees and says, "Ahaaah, that looks like the end of tap dancing, for sure!" So we look up ahead, and in red script on the next bar down, in bright neon, it says "Charlie's." All of a sudden I get this vision, I look at that red script, I look at these two kids, and I think, "The generations. . . ." Here's two more kids coming up in the street—talented, drawing probably one of their first crowds, and it's . . . to me, it's like Charlie and Lester. That's enough magic for me, but the capper was when we looked up on the marquee that it was all taking place under. In big capital letters, it said "PORK PIE HAT BAR." All I had to do was rhyme it, and you had the last verse.

MUSICIAN: *I remember at your Forest Hills concert during the* Mingus *tour overhearing a couple of sixteen-year-old girls breathlessly discussing "this new album called* Mingus, *and he was this great jazz person, and Joni worked with him." A critic friend with me got rather cynical about that, but I was quite touched to hear these kids talking about Mingus like he was Tom Petty or Bruce Springsteen.*

MITCHELL: The lovely thing is that while people of my own age jumped ship when I hit a certain pocket, these young kids, who maybe were presented with one of these records for their twelfth birthday, had come easily and open-mindedly all the way up through this whole progression without batting an eyelash. I find that personally very satisfying, no matter how silly it sounds to some New York intellectual. Even with the verbal simplification they gave, you can't beat the young enthusiasm and open-mindedness of something like that.

MUSICIAN: *Along the same lines, is it possible for an artist to make a statement that is rejected by his or her audience, and yet in fact be more in touch with what the audience itself is going through than they are?*

MITCHELL: Well, let's make an assumption here that an artist has a fine nervous system, okay? Now there are also a lot of people with fine nervous systems, more sensitive spinal columns or whatever, who are not artists, who have no outlet of expression. I think the nuancy observations an artist makes are going to get picked up first by these sensitive people. Eventually they'll be picked up by people intellectually and then passed down through the culture . . .

MUSICIAN: *Trickle-down art. Supply side inspiration. I love it. . . .*

MITCHELL: . . . (laughs) There's a sensitivity lag. Some statements that are made by artists in their desire to look at the world in a fresh way have traditionally come up against a shocking reception. When Stravinsky first played, people jumped up out of their seats and booed and hissed. People were infuriated by even less dramatic changes, like Dylan going electric. . . .

MUSICIAN: *. . . or Joni Mitchell going into jazz.*

MITCHELL: Sure. Rock 'n' roll was rock 'n' roll and jazz was jazz. and leaving one camp was a minor act of treason. It breaks down into all kinds of camps: your traditional jazz people who prefer bebop played acoustically and have a prejudice against all electronics. Charles was one of those who didn't like electronic music.

MUSICIAN: *What was his rationale?*

MITCHELL: He felt that on any acoustic axe the central quality of the line was more apparent between an artist and his instrument than in electronics. I disagreed with him. That was one of the battles we had in that I felt there was a new world of music opening up, regarding sounds, and that you had to play with electronic instruments and kind of warp them to get the individual tonality out of them.

MUSICIAN: *And yet people on that creative edge transcend stylistic and generic differences; they recognize a fellow spirit. After all, Charles reached out for you, didn't he?*

MITCHELL: Yeah. He liked . . . *some* things about me.

MUSICIAN: *Such as?*

MITCHELL: He thought I had a lot of nerve (laughs). He was critical of some things I was doing as well, but he was critical of his own work, too.

MUSICIAN: *What made him think you were nervy?*

MITCHELL: Two things: he thought I had a lot of nerve to be dressed up like a black dude on the cover of *Don Juan's Reckless Daughter*. He couldn't get over that. He was sort of thrilled by it. The other thing was the piece "Paprika Plains," which made him mad at one level, and kind of interested him on another. What happened was I hadn't played piano for a few years, and in January, just before making that album, I called up [*Henry Lewy, her engineer —Ed.*] and said "Henry, we've got to go in the studio right now because for some inexplicable reason I'm playing piano better than I have any right to be. I can't hit a wrong note." What I'd done was give myself a freeing lesson and said to myself, "Everything resolves to C; no matter where you go you can't hit a wrong note, just go home to C." We went in the studio and cut this thing four times. It was a trancelike situation. The four improvisations we recorded all clocked in at between twenty-nine and thirty-one minutes, so my attention span each time was almost exactly the same. From those four performances I edited together a piece that was to become the bridge for "Paprika Plains" and months later I wrote a song in which I inserted this segment. In the meantime the piano had been retuned a number of times. Then I gave the piano piece with lyrics to an arranger who added strings. The strings begin in the January section of the piano piece, but when they hit the October part, the piano tuning has changed, so the strings have no chance to retune as they cross over. That really infuriated Charles. "The orchestra's out of tune . . . they're in tune, they're out of tune!" Well, that drove him crazy (laughs). So he thought I was a nervy broad.

MUSICIAN: *Speaking of nerve, do you usually trust your creative impulses, even if you can't explain them to others? Or to yourself, for that matter?*

MITCHELL: Oh, yeah, I work from intuition, so I'm always flying blind and looking to be thrilled. Waiting for the magic to happen. I think it's easier to recognize the truly spectacular from an intuitive position than from your intellect, which is linear, dealing only with knowledge of the past projected into the future.

MUSICIAN: *With all the attention we pay to the intellect in this society. . . .*

MITCHELL: . . . A vastly overrated instrument, the intellect. . . . I get bugged when people call me an intellectual (laughs).

MUSICIAN: . . . *We know relatively little about developing those intuitive faculties, or learning how to deal with the stress of handling those energies when the magic does strike.*

MITCHELL: Sure. The Western world doesn't know anything about the need to prepare yourself for dealing with creativity or the time you have to put in in apprenticeship. Back on the coffee house circuit I loved being a musician, I was a real ham for it. But the moment I hit the big stage, and heard people suck in their breath at the mention of my name, it hit me . . . and there were years and years of maladjustment to contend with. My own apprenticeship, finding my balance, took eight years. The battles I have with it now are minor compared with those.

MUSICIAN: *Was there a clash between your ego and your creative nature over who was going to take credit for those goodies?*

MITCHELL: Are you kidding?! I used to go in the dressing room after a show and just. . . *cry*. People were just discovering you, so you received this radiant enthusiasm and you'd think, "What are they applauding for, that was *horrible* what I just did out there." There was emotional deception, there was technical failure. I couldn't get into this song and they didn't know the difference. There's a danger of becoming contemptuous of your audience at that point.

MUSICIAN: *If they couldn't seem to differentiate between good and bad performances, what do you feel they were responding to?*

MITCHELL: There's a story about a clown that kind of sums it all up for me. I think it's Henry Miller, but I'm not sure. Now pay attention. Anyway, he's the greatest clown in the world, and one night when he's at the climax of his act he forgets his part, he just has this blank spell. It seems interminably long, the audience are on the edge of their seats, and just at the tension point where they're gonna boo him, all of a sudden he regains it. The audience goes crazy! He's never seen such applause. Next night he comes to the same place and seems to be forgetting what to do. He draws it out, draws it out, the audience leans forward, and just then he remembers the part and the audience again goes nuts. So he keeps this up for a while, and one day he wakes up and finds it repulsive that they don't know that he's faking, that he's manipulating them like that. He can't bear himself for doing it, so he quits. Finally, he winds up as an elephant boy in another circus, and one night the head clown takes sick. So our hero volunteers to step in, and he does the guy's part, and from the audience comes the biggest roar he's ever heard. The sick clown in the back room hears this and realizes that this replacement who's never done his routine before is getting more applause that he ever did. It breaks his heart, and he dies. The burden of hearing about this is too much for our hero, so he quits the circus and wanders around as a bum, sleeping in parks. One day he senses that it's his day to die. Coming down the walk is a cop, slapping a billy club on his leg. So he goes into his original routine and he gets up to that point and seems to forget the part, and he pulls the tension out and then regains it. The cop goes into absolute hysterics, just laughs and laughs. And the clown has this great contented feeling, and with that feeling he dies. So there you have the old yin and yang of it (laughs). . . . Kinda subtle.

MUSICIAN: *Did you come to a moment when you realized you had to withdraw, to let go of it all to keep your sanity?*

MITCHELL: In the early 70's I just quit. I built a retreat up in the Canadian bush and swore I was never coming back. I built a house and wrote *For the Roses* during that time, so my little retreat was not complete (laughs). But I became a hermit. I felt extremely maladjusted about . . .the contrasts that were heaped on me. It was just too much input.

MUSICIAN: *So you couldn't trust either the positive or the negative feedback you were getting?*

MITCHELL: Yeah, it was as if (sings like Dylan) "People just got UGLIER and I had no sense of TIME!" (laughs)

MUSICIAN: *Could you find a place in yourself where you could sort things out?*

MITCHELL: One day about a year after I started my retreat in Canada I went out swimming. I jumped off a rock into this dark emerald green water with yellow kelp in it and purple starfish at the bottom. It was very beautiful, and as I broke up to the surface of the water, which was black and reflective, I started laughing. Joy had just suddenly come over me, you know? And I remember that as a turning point. First feeling like a loony because I was out there laughing all by myself in this beautiful environment (laughs). And then, right on top of it, was the realization that whatever my social burdens were, my inner happiness was still intact.

MUSICIAN: *John Lennon spoke of going through the same process in his last interview. He'd gotten in his own way and finally Yoko sent him alone to Hong Kong where it all came back to him while sitting in a bathtub. When he finally let go, he found he had it all again. He found that creative center again.*

MITCHELL: See, during my problems the creative spot never left me. I'm just hyper-creative. I'll create no matter what situation I'm in. If I have no tools, I'll dance. That doesn't go. My problem is my tremendous personal and social self-consciousness, which over the years has lessened and lessened and is now quite nicely balanced, I think. There's a gently undulating pattern between low and high self-esteem, which I think creates the proper tension.

MUSICIAN: *Very early on you documented your personal struggles and conflicts in your music. But around the time of* The Hissing Of Summer Lawns *you shifted your perspective from a sort of confessional stance to that of an outside observer, commenting on what you saw happening around you. Why the shift?*

MITCHELL: Well, first of all, the pop star is very self-promotional. You know, "I'm DA GREATEST LOVER, BAYBEEEEE!" The nature of the beast is to present yourself in the early years as some kind of teen idol. Initially I wrote those extremely personal songs like "Marcie" as a response to the big roars from the audience. I would stand up there receiving all this massed adulation and affection and think, "What are you all doing, you don't even know me." Affection like that usually doesn't come without some kind of intimacy, like in a one on one relationship. So I thought, you better know who you're grinning at up here, and I began to unveil more and more of my inner conflicts and feelings. Then, after about four years . . . I guess it's just the nature of the press, having built you up, they feel it's time to tear you down. So I began to receive a lot of unfavorable attention. At the same time it became harder and harder to sing these intimate songs at rock festivals. The bigger the audience I drew, the more honest I wanted to be (laughs).

MUSICIAN: *Could you sense when real contact and communication was taking place onstage, when something was connecting? And was there anything you could do to help bring on or deepen that contact?*

MITCHELL: Oddly enough, there were a lot of times onstage when my errors were icebreakers. For instance, I'd flat-out forget a piece onstage, or I couldn't get into a song, so I'd start another one. That would be a turning point many a night. I would be oblivious to all this, but (manager) Elliot (Roberts) would tell me later that it had humanized the show. He said it actually made people feel more comfortable and heightened their enjoyment. That was a long time ago, mind you. You couldn't do that playing with a band, because you'd wind up with five embarrassed people.

MUSICIAN: *In a sense, those errors broke a pattern and created an opening for something special to enter. Do you find that because your songs are tied to a narrative format whose structure doesn't alter much that it's harder for that magic to happen—harder than for, say, Mingus or Hendrix, who had large pockets of improvisational material with a lot of openings for something to enter.*

MITCHELL: Well, rather than talking generally, let me give you an example. On *Don Juan's Reckless Daughter* [*in fact,* Mingus —*Ed.*] there's a song called "The Wolf That Lives In Lindsey." It was a live duet between Don Alias and myself; it's a strange piece of music, in that it's an example of a song that *has* a structure that I had completely ignored. I dropped beats, I added beats, there's bars of 3/4 that are in there, and there's all kinds of abbreviated signatures. Don was thrown into a highly alert position as a drummer, to be able to follow this thing, which was not maintaining a groove, just bursts of rhythmic passages. It was very spontaneous. And, when the thing was over, we figured that magic had, in fact, occurred. As raw as it was, and as technically peculiar as it was, you couldn't beat it for spirit. And I turned to Henry and said, "You know what we need on this now? We need wolves and water gongs." And, that was on a Wednesday night. So he was going to make it a project over the weekend to look through the A&M library of sound effects, and we were going to get some wolves.

So, anyway, that weekend I had company coming from Texas, and I had company coming from Canada at the same time. And simultaneously I was supposed to be at the Bread & Roses Festival. When my guests arrived, coming already from long distances, I had to tell them, "We're moving now!" And we all went to this festival in San Francisco. Things kinda got screwed up, and there were some vibes around the whole situation which I won't go into, that made me very introspective. And I noticed at dinner that night, that my introspection was also making the table introspective. So, I thought, "I don't want to be here in this mood with these people, I'm influencing their mood," and so I excused myself.

I had told a friend of mine, Tim Hardin, that I was gonna meet him back at the hotel. So I get to the hotel desk, and I say to a very uptight desk clerk, you know, "Would you please give me Mr. Hardin's room?" And he replied, "Can't you see I'm busy?" He was *really* uptight. The lobby of the hotel was gigantic, and suddenly, across the hall there came a drunk, singing "Why Do Fools Fall In Love?," stumbling across the lobby, snapping his fingers, right? I had nothing but time on my hands, so I perked up, because suddenly there was externally something interesting (laughs), and I was drawn across the hall, and I linked up with him, and we came back across the hall, singing "Why Do Fools Fall In Love?" We ended up standing by the desk, with this uptight guy in the background, and the next thing I knew, we had drawn in two more singers who turned out to be the Persuasions. Well, when we stopped singing, everybody was in great spirits, we all laughed, you know, we patted each other on the back, and we shook hands. "So now," I say to the guy, "Would you give me Mr. Hardin's room," and somebody in the crowd yells, "Oh, Hardin's in the bar." So I go into the bar, there's a kind of loungey jazz band playing, and Hardin is *pissed* out of his mind, and he comes dancing towards me through this crowded room here, singing to the band, "Hello, Joni," and doing improvisational lyrics. So I start dancing towards him, singing "Hello, Timmy! So good to see you!" The bartender says, "What would you like?" And I sing to him, "One white wine," and the bartender raises his hand in the air, and sings back, "One white wine." And the next thing, the whole room was engaged in this spontaneous Broadway show. Anyway, the story hasn't come to an end yet. Now, we're all in very high spirits. We discover that there's a party on the third floor. We go up to this room, and all the way up the hallway—you know, Timmy and I are hamming it up, just being goofy. We get into the room, and suddenly, the same guy that was drunk in the lobby singing "Why Do Fools Fall In Love?" comes up to me and says, "I have a tape of some wolves." And I say to him, not even realizing how profound it is, "Oh, I'm looking for a tape of some wolves. I'll write down my address and you send it to me." He said, "No, I mean, I've got it *on* me." So I said, "Okay," and he produced this box of tapes, all homemade with labels on them, and we thumbed through it. It was all African animal sound effects. Well, the very last entry was wolves. So he loaned me his tape recorder, I put the tape on, and it was a cycle of a wolf—it starts off with the lead wolf, and then you hear yipping of pups and female voices, you know? And then he goes, "Aaaooo-aaooh-ahh." Like, the same yelp, but one note up higher in the scale. And then the yipping of the pups, and the females. And the thing was looped about four times. Well, the first time I did "The Wolf That Lives In Lindsay," I just hit the button right at the beginning, picked up the guitar, and uncannily, *it was the perfect key.* The way the loop was designed, if you started it at the top of the tape and went all the way to the end, it fit the structure perfectly. So anyway, the next night when I went to the concert, my friend Joel Bernstein hooked the tape up and for an encore, I came out and we did this song and we blasted the wolves, mixed them in with the song, and the audience—when I was finished singing, some clapped, but most of them howled me back on for another encore. So you see, there's still ways to get spontaneity into a show.

MUSICIAN: *I guess so. If you had to point to a particular album that realized as much as possible what you were aiming for at a particular time and place, where you thought, "Yeah, that's as honest and clear as it's come through," what would it be?*

MITCHELL: The purest one of all, of course, is *Blue.* At the time I was absolutely transparent, like cellophane. If you looked at me, I would weep. We had to lock the doors to make that album. Nobody was allowed in. Socially, I was an absolute wreck. Imagine yourself stripped of all defenses . . . going to a party! (laughs) Not only did I have no defenses, but other people's defenses were alternately transparent, which made me very sad . . . or people really tend to aggress on you when you're weak. You know what it was exactly like? It was like being in an aquarium with big fish coming at you and they weren't saying anything, and sometimes the sound would shut off. It was just like that scene in *All That Jazz* when suddenly the heartbeat becomes dominant.

MUSICIAN: *But there was a positive aspect to it . . . ?*

MITCHELL: Oh, that would be a beautiful space if it wasn't so scary. If you could just magically wipe out the fear. There's nothing there but . . . but what is there. Having no defense, you have no ability to . . . you have no pretense, which you need.

MUSICIAN: *You need it as a buffer. Like deflector shields.*

MITCHELL: Well, that's what happened. There was no social personality, but still a strong inner life.

MUSICIAN: *That can be an awfully painful state . . .*

MITCHELL: But it produced that beautiful album. There is not a false note on that album. I love that record more than any of them, really . . . and I'll never be that pure again (laughs).

MUSICIAN: *Don't worry, someday you'll be a virgin again.*

MITCHELL: Sure! (Cracking up)

MUSICIAN: *No, I'm half serious. It reminds me of something Robert Fripp once wrote for us, about how you can't regain your innocence, but you can learn to* act *with innocence and reenter that world, and to touch that place without having to shatter the personality.*

MITCHELL: Yeah, I'm spiritually very promiscuous. I've been Shoko Buku'd, I have a TM [*transcendental meditation —Ed.*] mantra. I've been to the mountain, done my hermitage, my self-confrontation pockets. I've hung with Zen Buddhist priests, and all of them have opened some little pocket. I've had my fair share of pushes in the right direction. I *desire* it, though, and that's the key. I'm sort of headed in that direction but I backslide.

MUSICIAN: *Can you see your inner growth reflected in the evolution of your music?*

MITCHELL: Basically I'm a sensual primary, a compulsive creative person. So, yeah, I can see my growth in my harmonic sense, for instance, although I still like dissonance in music, which is not enlightened chord structure. But that dissonance is very full of human travail. I still like conflict in poetry, I'm still in the flames. I guess I'm just a . . . a . . .

MUSICIAN: *. . . a teenager in love? (Joni laughs) Speaking of which, is there a certain sensibility connected with growing up in western Canada that you share with Neil Young?*

MITCHELL: I feel very kindred to Neil, yeah. We're caught between two cultures—we're neither-nor. We still salute the Queen up there, though Canada's becoming more independent lately. We grew up in the pre-TV era, and at that time radio was happening. There was more of an English influence them, a lot of BBC humor. We went to J. Arthur Rank movies on the corner, *Dr. Seeley*, that whole series. So we had an infusion of British comedy, which is a different sensibility than American humor.

MUSICIAN: *Do you feel that Americans sometimes miss the humor in your work?*

MITCHELL: Yeah, people sometimes aren't sure that they can laugh at my stuff. "Coyote," has a lot of that dry humor that can get by people, not jokes per se, but . . . Okay, now if I had a voice like Donald Fagen there'd be no problem. He's got that irony, that black, dry kind of humor that I call a Canadian sensibility. His voice can convey that even though he's not Canadian. Mine had this high (in a high register) earnest kind of melancholic quality that doesn't project a lot of humor unless I break into a Bugs Bunny voice on certain lines and really nail 'em. Like, (a la Bugs) "Now it's gettin' on time to close." Or if I dramatize a character within the context of a song, people will laugh . . . I don't know what I'm talking about! Do you know what I'm talking about?

MUSICIAN: *Sure, you've just exposed your essential wabbit nature to the American people. And we understand.*

MITCHELL: (laughs) But getting back to Neil. He and I have uncanny similarities of background. We both come off the Canadian prairies; we were both struck down by polio in the same epidemic; both in the back, in the precious spine, and in the right leg. That's a great will-forger, you know. There's a big struggle involved with walking around after that. When you're struck down early in your childhood with crippling diseases and have some of the background problems he did, you've got a lot of peer group disadvantage from an early age. Maybe that gives him a tailwind.

MUSICIAN: *If there's one recurring theme that runs through your work, it's your obsession with duality and dichotomy. Shadows and light, fire* *and ice, the Eagle and the snake, love that's hopeless and inspired. Those oppositions form the core of almost every song . . .*

MITCHELL: Well, if you take your intellect as far as it will go, you run smack-dab into paradox.

MUSICIAN: *And then what do you do?*

MITCHELL: Then you forget about it! (laughs)

MUSICIAN: *Okay, maybe you don't try to think your way through them, 'cause that's not possible. But you're constantly placing yourself in front of them. It's especially apparent in your songs about struggling with male-female polarizations in relationships.*

MITCHELL: In spite of all my yelling at my lovers in public (laughs), I've received a lot of affection in my time. People have been as good to me as they could, but . . . yeah, I guess it is all about compatible madnesses. There are pockets where people flat-out don't understand each other, they come to impasses. And they stubbornly hold to one side or another, conflicting points of view. So, yeah, those paradoxes are dramatized in love relationships. All along I guess I've been trying to figure out (sings) "What is this thing called love . . . this crazy thing called love?"

MUSICIAN: *The new album seems to be an attempt to come to grips with just that question. It impressed me as being a cycle about love that starts with the youthful sentimentality of "Chinese Cafe," then advances into emotional adolescence with "Man To Man" and "Ladies Man," where you're the naive victim. Then there's "Solid Love," which is a step up, a genuine contact with someone, not just the old I-need-you-to-complement-my-neurosis situation. "Underneath The Streetlights" is another gutsy affirmation, a commitment and recognition of a real soul to soul contact. Finally, there's "Love," the piece you borrowed from Corinthians, and the last song on the album. It's like a glimpse of the goal, the higher, egoless, transcendent level of love, beyond conflicts and paradoxes: the summation of everything you've been striving for all these years.*

MITCHELL: Yeah! It is! I never really saw that when I was putting the album together, but in hearing you say it, I can see what you see, and it has validity to me. That thing from Corinthians *is* on another level. I'm not talking about hippie sloganeering there, I'm talking about the real shit. There's a qualitative feeling to that kind of love that's beyond the bounds of sexual attachment. I didn't write that, though. I stole it from the Bible (laughs). I appreciated it, then I presented it.

MUSICIAN: *But as with the "Pork Pie Hat" story and the wolves song, you recognized the deeper pattern that your artistic sensibilities were creating with the album. Something in you knew that had to be the last song on the album, the summation.*

MITCHELL: Right, and that was magical, that recognition. Magic doesn't have anything to do with intellect, which is linear. Intuition appears to be more chaotic, even stupid sometimes. . . .

MUSICIAN: *But it can pass through dichotomies and reach something higher.*

MITCHELL: Right, intuition cuts through all that. Intellect comes in paragraphs, ya-da-ya-da-ya-da, and intuition comes ZAP!, like a bolt of lightning. It comes as a pill, and then has to be translated from an impulse into language by the intellect.

MUSICIAN: *When you reach the end of your rope in front of some paradox, you suddenly see the deeper pattern, and know where the pieces fit.*

MITCHELL: That's it. The magical moment comes at the point of despair, where you say, "I can't do this!" At the peak of my frustration, I meet a guy singing in the hotel lobby, or see those tap dancing kids in front of that bar. When all intellectual options have been exhausted and there's no way out, suddenly something cracks open and takes you through to the other side. Finding that song and knowing to put it at the end of the album was the same as stumbling on that drunk guy with the wolves tape. It was the missing piece. The last verse. As you said, most of the other songs were about conflict or paradox, but that song was the resolution. The missing piece. That last verse.

MUSICIAN: *You put in one extra verse that wasn't in Corinthians about having "fragments of faith, hope and love in me." Why did you add that?*

MITCHELL: It's very delicate, messing with the Book. I wanted to add emphasis to what was already vaguely stated in the verse about "As a child I saw face to face, now I know only in part."

MUSICIAN: *I asked because there's a passage in some book by Ouspensky about how the higher impulses of faith, hope and love should be united in the heart of man, but have atrophied and scattered into fragments throughout our being.*

MITCHELL: Oh. I'd never heard that.

MUSICIAN: *Could be another example of synchronicity, flashing of a universal pattern. Jung pointed out that the same dream archetypes symbolize identical concepts in otherwise dissimilar cultures.*

MITCHELL: Jung borrowed an Indian fetish that I quite like and modified it a bit without giving any credit (laughs). He ripped 'em off, just like I ripped off the Bible . . .

MUSICIAN: *Or maybe he was just recognizing the same archetype they were, like you and Ouspensky with the fragmented virtues.*

MITCHELL: Could be. In any case, in my search for a centering device, a unifying fetish, I came upon this North-South-East-West grid in Indian tradition, though I don't remember which tribe. Wisdom was north, heart was south, clarity was east and introspection was west. It was a chief's wheel, designed to develop the ability to speak a whole truth in a person who was to be a central figure in speaking to other people. The concept was that you were born with a predilection towards one of the four, and the opposing arm would be your weak point. If you had wisdom, your weak point would be your heart. If you had clarity, which is overview—the flying eagle, right?—your weak point would be introspection. And your life's work and goal would be the ability to speak from all points and eventually unify them in a central truth. To be able to speak to all people, regardless of their predilections.

MUSICIAN: *Finding that unifying point beyond duality.*

MITCHELL: That's exactly what they all have in common, that intersecting point, the Tao.

MUSICIAN: *Speaking of fetishes, where'd you get those blue and white socks?*

MITCHELL: "T'was brillig, and the slithy toves . . ." Remember that? These are *Alice in Wonderland* socks. And she also had voluptuous Midwestern thighs, too. Kansas calves (laughs).

MUSICIAN: *I'm not gonna comment on that. With all the interest in African music over the last few years, including the use of the Burundi beat by bands like Bow Wow Wow and Adam & the Ants, I'm surprised you've never been given credit for introducing those elements back* on The Hissing Of Summer Lawns.

MITCHELL: The Burundi thing on "The Jungle Line"? They killed me for that. The worst album of the year. That project received an onslaught of negativity.

MUSICIAN: *What prompted you to put those drums under the lyrics?*

MITCHELL: Because I loved that Burundi warriors passage. It had a Bo Diddley lick in it which I took out and made into a loop and then ran this black cultural poem under it. I thought I was black for about three years. I felt like there was a black poet trapped inside me, and that song was about Harlem—the primitive juxtaposed against the Frankenstein of modern industrialization; the wheels turning and the gears grinding and the beboppers with the junky spit running down their trumpets. All of that together with that Burundi tribal thing was perfect. But people just thought it was weird.

MUSICIAN: *Those cultures have some of the directness you talk about in "Love." Did you have any contact with Indians in Canada as a child? And did it make any impact on you?*

MITCHELL: The first dream I remember having was about Indians. The Indians in that part of Canada were mahogany-faced and very serious, at least within the context of our culture. They were woodlands Indians, so they were covered in smoked leathers with elaborate floral beading and satin skirts and long braids. On our sports days they would put up aspen lean-tos and skin tepees, and they'd have their own dances at night. I remember sneaking over and listening to their chants at the fringes of town.

MUSICIAN: *Were you discouraged from having any contact with them?*

MITCHELL: We were told they were dirty and that they stank. I happened to love the smell of that smoked leather and found their creativity fascinating. But they also terrified me because we heard that, like gypsies, they would kidnap us and kill us. But about that dream: I was three years old, I think I was having my appendix out. I wanted one of those little kid's pedal cars, and, oh, I had just seen *Snow White and the Seven Dwarfs*, and heard the stories of Little Black Sambo, with the little leopard that runs around the tree until it turns into butter. And the combination of these desires and inputs, plus my impressions of the Indians around our hometown combined when they gave me the anesthetic and told me to count backwards. So in this dream, round and round the tree went the seven dwarfs in primary-colored shirts with the numbers ten through one on them, 'cause I was counting backwards. They went round and round that tree in pedal cars like Little Black Sambo, chanting, (in a low Indian voice) "HEY, HEY, HEY, HEY, HEY!" (laughs) They made a strong impression on me then, and in later years with dreams like the one that became "Paprika Plains." They come back all the time in my dreams.

MUSICIAN: *You have a very vivid visual and conceptual sense. Can you sometimes capture something through your painting that you can't do with music, or vice versa?*

MITCHELL: Oh, yeah. If I experience something, it will make a better painting than it will a song. For instance, about a month ago I finished driving across the prairie, where I had grown up. When I got back, I started painting enormous collage-like landscapes of the memory of that vastness. Then I thought, "Ah, this could be an album cover. I better write a song called 'Prairie Roads'!"

MUSICIAN: *What would be your first step in translating that portrait into music?*

MITCHELL: I'd meditate on it. Perhaps I can tell something about what my visit to my uncle was like, and can thread in enough material to make a poem out of it, and find a striding, long-legged melody to illustrate that. But the initial impulse was to paint it. Of all the arts, painting shuts off the inner dialogue best for me, and it's currently the most seductive to me for that reason. I get down to the hum of Oms and mantras in my head more quickly through the meditation of painting than I do in other mediums.

MUSICIAN: *Are there any other musicians or artists you've always wanted to collaborate with?*

MITCHELL: Well, once I went to see Miles Davis to present him with a project, a duet for the two of us.

MUSICIAN: *Did he like the idea?*

MITCHELL: I don't know. He just fell down with a death grip on my ankle and passed out (laughs).

MUSICIAN: *Last question. What would you have done if you weren't an artist?*

MITCHELL: I would have killed myself years ago.

MUSICIAN: *Killed yourself?*

MITCHELL: I wouldn't have any outlet for this energy. I don't know. Maybe I would have been an athlete. Well, no, I couldn't because I had polio and my spine's all out. If I hadn't had polio . . . I'm built like an athlete.

MUSICIAN: *I see you've got athlete's feet, too.*

MITCHELL: Yes, I have athlete's feet, and they're long fellows.

MUSICIAN: *Well, that's the key, the unifying fetish that explains everything about you.*

MITCHELL: Yeah, I'm a poet but I don't know it . . .

MUSICIAN: . . . *but your feet show it* . . .

BOTH: . . . they're Longfellows (laughing).

JONI SAID

On Relationships

"Leonard Cohen said years ago that marriage is the new church. I ditto that. Relationship is everything. Obviously both people have to have patience. Everybody is a pain in the ass sometimes. But you can't run out the first time a person is burdensome."

—to Bill Flanagan, *Musician*, December 1985

JONI SAID

On "The Jazz Side of Life"

"[Rickie Lee Jones] said that she could sing jazz and I couldn't because I didn't walk on the jazz side of life. And I thought, 'What does that mean? Do you have to shoot up to like this music?' What is 'the jazz side of life'? Who's to say? She doesn't even know me."

—to Bill Flanagan, *Musician*, December 1985

JONI MITCHELL

Alanna Nash | March 1986 | *Stereo Review* (US)

In 1986 Joni was betwixt and between in both her life and career. She was in the middle of a nine-year marriage to bassist Larry Klein, in middle age (forty-two), and creatively, caught between balancing her need to stretch out musically and the constant pressure to sell albums and remain relevant in the pop world. Her output in the 1980s was not well received, and yet, she persisted.

In early 1986 she spoke to journalist Alanna Nash about *Dog Eat Dog*, the intensely political album she'd released in the fall of 1985. She had hoped that the album was her ticket back to the center of things, but in this piece we begin to hear her increasingly angry remarks about the business and her frustrations with her record company—comments which, at the time, surprised Nash.

Dog Eat Dog turned out to be one of her least appreciated albums, something that Joni herself seemed to agree with, in recent years. She told *Billboard* in 2014 that a trendy sound had been imposed upon her by husband Klein, along with Thomas Dolby and Mike Shipley, and thus the music sounded dated. For her 2014 Rhino box set *Love Has Many Faces, A Quartet, A Ballet, Waiting to Be Danced* she said she was able to take some of those dated sounds off in the remastering process.

Although Joni told the writer that she was happy to be "mated," she couldn't know that a period of difficulty was just ahead of her. *Dog Eat Dog* would continue her slide downward in sales, and she would suffer a miscarriage and split up with Klein.

But her reunion with biological daughter, Kilauren Gibb, would also come in the next decade. And musically, she would please fans and critics alike with 1988's *Chalk Mark in a Rain Storm* and especially 1994's *Turbulent Indigo*. —Ed.

Roberta Joan Anderson was an athletic nine-year-old when the polio epidemic hit western Canada in 1952. By the time she got out of the hospital, her spine "looked like a freeway after an earthquake," and the muscles in her back and right leg were so withered that the doctors said she'd never walk again. The nine-year-old, however, had other plans.

"The fact of the matter is that I was, I am, crippled by it, but I just pretended like it wasn't there," says Anderson, who grew up to become Joni Mitchell, one of pop music's most significant singer-songwriters. "I got through my youth and my teens without any real problem—never missed a dance. I'm sure you can't say that *all* handicaps can be overcome by spirit," she adds, chain-smoking her third Camel of the interview, "but I really believe that a lot of them can."

Mitchell's indomitable "spirit" was called on to perform another near miracle last year, when, after a decade of low-to-moderate sales and quirky, avant-garde experimentalism, the singer decided to resurrect her career with an all-out, Big Business push, *à la* Tina Turner. Predictably, most of the record industry had about the same prognosis for her success as the long-ago doctors had for her dancing.

But Mitchell ignored industry doubts, the same way she'd discounted the effects of polio, and went on to produce "Dog Eat Dog," a beautifully crafted and intelligent appraisal of American culture in decline. Released toward the end of last year, the album had critics somewhat divided. Some put it on their "year's best" lists, while others, expecting perhaps her acoustic or jazz-pop formats of old, quarreled with its modern, synth-rock, audio-effect framework. Most reviewers, however, see it as a relentlessly inventive collage of sound, rhythm, and lyrics and an album that ranks with "Blue" and "Court and Spark" as a milestone in Mitchell's eighteen years of recording.

As a result, Mitchell, at forty-two, is doing something she's always refused to do, and that is to go out and personally hawk an album. In the flesh, she is something of a surprise. Her blond hair is no longer folkie-long and straight but medium-short and curly. Wearing a black beret, a black jumpsuit with purple stripes, and short, black, lace-up boots, she is both beatnik and brainy, charming and offbeat, with a strong Canadian accent. She is also quicksilvery—open, giddy, polite, even vulnerable one moment, and very, *very* cool the next as she stands with her arms folded, smoke-smoke-smoking that Camel and watching the video for *Good Friends*, her first single off "Dog Eat Dog."

The funny thing, she says, sipping black coffee at the Warner Bros. Records office in New York, is that after all these years of invisibility she finds she loves talking to people, even the press—doing as many as ten interviews in a row on one banner day. "I'm in promo mode," she explains with a wide smile. "I want people to know the record is there."

With her first album, in 1968, twenty-five-year-old Joni Mitchell appeared to be a bell-bottomed folkie with a poetic eye and a sure knack for storytelling. Her songs grew musically more ambitious with each album, and her singing likewise grew confident and daring. By the time of "Blue" (released on the Reprise label in 1971), her fourth album, Mitchell had developed into a startlingly mature writer, fusing intensely intimate lyrics with emotional melodies in the contemporary folk tradition.

It was her fifth [*in fact, sixth —Ed.*] album, "Court and Spark" (1974), however, that really showed what she could do. No longer content to stay within the narrow confines of acoustic folk music, Mitchell ferreted out a complementary clutch of jazz-pop musicians (led by Tom Scott) who understood the unorthodox chords she employed in her open tunings on the guitar. Full of emotional rushes, romantic surges, and tight but well-paced music, "Court and Spark" (on Asylum) was a thrilling synthesis of rock, pop, and jazz, an album that assured Mitchell's position in the annals of popular music.

From her most widely hailed effort, however, Mitchell spiraled down with "The Hissing of Summer Lawns" (1975), in retrospect a brilliant album but ahead of its time. Universally drubbed for its use of polyrhythms, Burundi drums, modality, and unconventional song structure, the album began a commercial decline from which Mitchell is only now recovering.

"Hissing" was followed by "Hejira" (1976), a jazz-laced album of romantic introspection; "Don Juan's Reckless Daughter" (1977), a wandering collection of formless jazz; and "Mingus" (1979), a tribute to jazz great Charlie Mingus, which brought her scorn and ridicule from both jazz and pop circles.

Three years ago, Mitchell tried again, with "Wild Things Run Fast." The album won back some of the old fans with a pop, rock, and jazz orientation that was reminiscent of her early Seventies work. But if anyone thought she was about to repeat herself, they did not know Joni Mitchell very well. Her next album would take a 180-degree turn, from musings on love and romance to Mitchell's most overtly political statement yet.

"Dog Eat Dog" is an angry album, one that fairly *seethes* with outrage as Mitchell surveys the general state of things and finds rampant moral decay: government intervention in private lives, Yuppie materialism, Moral Majority censorship, Star Wars sensibility, and the frightening symbiosis of politics and religion. These subjects may seem light years away from Mitchell's best-loved work—confessional, highly personal songs of romance, self-obsession, and delusion—but in truth all of the new songs do have autobiographical roots.

The tone of the album comes from two experiences. The first involves an "unfair" California state tax levied in 1982 against Mitchell and nine other musicians who had artistic-control clauses in their recording contracts. The levy demanded 15 percent of Mitchell's income between 1972 and 1976 in back taxes. "Now I know firsthand what it is to be dealt an injustice by the government," says Mitchell, who has retained her Canadian citizenship. "I got my advance [on a new five-year Geffen recording contract], and the state of California said, 'Thank you very much. That's *exactly* what you owe us.' I'm telling you, it was like finding out that Daddy goes to hookers."

At about the same time, Mitchell married bassist Larry Klein (she was divorced from Detroit folk singer Chuck Mitchell in the late Sixties) and settled in for a "normal American year, spending a lot of time at home, watching a lot of television." In fact, Mitchell says, she would have called the album "Songs of a Couch Potato" except for the seriousness of her message. Believing now that "the government is crooked," she was horrified at what she saw on her screen: an undeniable swing from the liberal, progressive Sixties and Seventies to a decade of right-wing conservatism and repression, best exemplified by the televised sermons of Jerry Falwell and Jimmy Swaggert [*sic*]. "The government," she concluded, "is now in league with the fundamentalists."

When it came time to record, however, Mitchell worried that the times were too superficial for such an album. "In a way," she said, "I don't blame people. It's a period of escape, like the early Fifties were, although for a different reason. Even the cause-mindedness, to me, has a more frivolous nature now than it did in the Sixties. I mean, with the causes this time you've got albums for them flashing on the *screen*," she says, laughing. "So on one level, it's just a great party time. Like my manager said, 'I don't know about these songs, Joan. Don't you have anything about sex and parties?'"

Mitchell left her long-time manager, Elliot Roberts, toward the end of the project and signed with Peter Asher because Roberts was "too busy" with his enormous stable of clients. But she also admits that Roberts, concerned with her loss of power in the industry, pressured her to bring in a co-producer—something she had not had to do since her debut album.

In the end, British electronics wizard Thomas Dolby came in as a "color assistant," sharing producer's credit with Mitchell, Klein, and engineer Mike Shipley on all but three songs. The recording sessions, for the album lasted from February to September.

"This was one of the most difficult albums I ever had to make," she says, knitting her eyebrows. "I had never done any kind of work with a committee where, instead of just going with my natural enthusiasm for something, there were four strong opinions to consider—and a lot of opposition. But frequently, because of the delay and irritation, just like sand in an oyster, a pearl was born."

Some of the shiny, austere sounds on the album—the percussive whir of a cigarette machine on *Smokin' (Empty, Try Another)* or the street ambience of a burglar alarm on *The Three Great Stimulants*—have been criticized as "aural flash." But there is an appropriate uneasiness to this music, the effects lending the lyrics a power they would not have on their own. Better still, the electronics never diminish Mitchell or her material.

So far, with "Dog Eat Dog" selling well and bringing her back to center stage, the rest of Mitchell's life is on track too. "Marriage frees me up in a lot of ways. I feel mated," she says, pointing out that "Dog Eat Dog," for all its foreboding, is bookended by songs about friendship and love, a continuing source of optimism for her. "Relationship," she deems, "is everything."

Just the same, she says she still finds it difficult to express happiness in her music. "I'm a melancholy Nordic, you know. Midnight Sun in all the genes. Writing is very confronting work. A strong emotion—either a misunderstanding or a need to comprehend something within yourself—drives you to sit up all night to plumb the depth of your being. It's only rewarding when the muse coughs up something that has the right sound, as well as confirmation and content. When that happens, or when you get lucky in the studio, man, there's not another job in the world you would want.

"Sometimes I start to feel that the gods are smiling," she says, sounding a lot like Roberta Joan Anderson from Saskatchewan. "To a certain degree I have to feel that there are forces at work beyond me."

JONI SAID

On Rock 'n' Roll

"Rock and roll is about youth and sex. Can it mature? That remains to be seen . . . But I had one grey-haired record company executive tell me, 'I don't like anything unless it makes me feel young and happy.' It becomes a question of whether adult themes can get the vote. You can be doing great work, but unless people buy it, you're condemned to obscurity, and it's only a matter of time before that's it for you."

—to Gary Graff, *Detroit Free Press*, March 27, 1988

AN INTERVIEW WITH JONI MITCHELL

Sylvie Simmons | 1988 | *Musik Express* (Germany)

After the dizzying musical detour of *Dog Eat Dog*, with its banks of synthesizers and lack of Joni Mitchell guitar, she returned to a more familiar sound with her next album, *Chalk Mark in a Rain Storm*, released in March 1988. As part of the promotional flurry for the album, Sylvie Simmons interviewed Joni at a hotel in West London in May of that year. She remembers it as a typical "conveyor belt" press day of the time, with the artist ensconced in a hotel room, enduring interviews by a long line of journalists who would each get forty-five minutes to chat about *Chalk Mark* before being whooshed off by the record company publicist.

Simmons was the last interviewer of the day, and when the record company staffer gave her a five-minute warning hand signal to wind down the interview, Joni intervened. "She put up that big hand of hers like a stop sign, and kept on talking," Simmons said. "We got at least one, maybe two more visits from the record company person, who told her that she had this or that going on, and they had to go."

To her surprise, Joni didn't just prolong the interview, but also suggested that Simmons accompany her to Italy, the next stop on her promotional tour. Simmons remembers a look of abject panic on the record company publicist's face. "I don't remember if they made the sign of a finger horizontally slashed across the neck, but they made it clear to me that this was not going to happen, and don't even think about it." In those days before cell phones, Simmons had no way of contacting Joni after the interview, so that was that.

Perhaps emboldened by talking to a woman, Joni brought up the fact that she felt her all-male band tended to be too critical of her in the studio, and even ganged up on her at times, making it necessary for her to put her foot down and forbid it. She talked about a project Prince proposed that they work on and her eyebrow-raising decision to make herself up as a black male for the cover of *Don Juan's Reckless Daughter* in 1977. We'll let the reader parse Joni's own words on that startling choice.

Sadly for posterity, when Simmons wrote her 2011 Leonard Cohen biography, *I'm Your Man*, she wasn't able to secure an interview with Joni. It would have been instructive, since Joni's views on Cohen have been all over the map over the years. Not long after she ended their brief romantic relationship in the late 1960s, Joni said, "I'm just a groupie for Leonard and Picasso." Being not quite as constant as the northern star, she later dismissed him as a "boudoir poet." Many believe that her beautiful song "A Case of You" was about him.

Portions of this interview appeared in the German publication *Musik Express* in 1988, but the following is Simmons's original transcript, which includes extra material that was never published.

Note: *The Hissing of Summer Lawns* wasn't chosen as the worst of 1975 by *Rolling Stone*, as Joni herself now concedes, but she undoubtedly complained of that to Simmons, who mentions it here. —Ed.

Masculine hands, imposing hat, eyes the colour of package-holiday-brochure sky. Joni Mitchell laughs a lot and smokes even more. She's 45 years old, a dancer in appearance, an artist-painter by inclination, and a singer by accident.

It's been 20 years since her first album, *Song to a Seagull*, set her in many people's minds as the epitome of the pure, pained, virginal singer-songwriter, the centre of the California scene when California was the centre of the universe. Since then her work has developed along a painter's lines: layered, experimental, highly-designed yet emotional, with slashes of dissonance dabbed onto fat, contented chords, or patterns of hope weaved through tragic minor-keys. She has also left a legacy of beautiful, very personal poetry.

However, since *Rolling Stone* magazine named *The Hissing of Summer Lawns* the Worst Album of 1975, much of her work has been misunderstood and maligned by the critics. It is as if the image of Joni Mitchell was expected to remain as pure and pained as it was in the "hippy" days, and never allowed to change. Now, with the release of her latest album, *Chalk Mark in a Rain Storm*, the critics seem to have rallied around to her side again, declaring it to be her most powerful work in years.

It features two cover songs, and a list of guest musicians that includes Tom Petty, Peter Gabriel, Willie Nelson, Don Henley and Ben Orr of the Cars. She says she craved "more living, breathing people" after her last, "synthesiserland" album. It was co-produced by Joni with Larry Klein, her bass player, and her husband for the past six years. They live in Malibu, California, by the sea, and by her own admission she has "settled down." Other than the smoking, the Joni Mitchell who spends the next two hours in a huge, plush London hotel room talking to me seems calm, relaxed and happy with life. The only thing she'd change about herself, she says, is "maybe dye my hair red . . . !"

You say you've "settled down" these days; that implies domesticity and contentment. What do you say to those who believe that you have to have turmoil and pain in order to be able to write poetry and create a piece of art worth having?

Pain doesn't devoid the settled. All I mean by "settled" is that I'm happily married and my husband is not the creator of my difficulties necessarily. He is—the home is—the cocoon. But there's plenty of suffering in the world. It's just *one* problem out of the way; I'm no longer looking for my mate. But there are other problems. People up and sue you or something, she laughs. (She's referring to a lawsuit taken out against her by a former housemaid who claims Joni attacked her).

I picked up a girl once, hitchhiking, going up to my house in Canada, and she recognised me and liked my poetry and said that she had been a poet once. I said, "What do you mean, *had been* a poet once?" "Well," she said, "I used to stutter". I thought that was interesting—when her stuttering cleared up, she stopped writing.

I think if you're having a really wonderful time, you're less likely to stop and withdraw from society and scribble things down. So, pain does help create a withdrawal. I also think that what everyone on this planet has in common is loneliness and suffering, it doesn't escape any of us, and depression is an important part of life. It (*she hesitates*) it forces you to lie down and think about things and hopefully come up with some way back to normalcy. That period is for a poet a very fertile period. I would agree with that: depression provides a climate for deeper thought.

If you were one of those blessedly lucky, "What, me worry?" types, I imagine that you might have a happy existence, but you wouldn't be an artist or a deep thinker. Not that deep thinking is any great shakes (*she laughs*), but it's something to do!

Do you think you avoided marriage and settling down for so long because you worried that it might have affected your life as a poet and artist?

I think I took the idea of marriage fairly serious, and the idea of spending the rest of my life with somebody—that somebody had to be a pretty good fit. See, this is where you choose your family; the other family you're born into you have no choice, but now you have to find your friend and your lover . . . I think what I was looking for changed as I got older. I was more sensible as I went along. I was more capable of choosing a mate correctly as my self-knowledge increased.

You know, I might have gone for pretty packaging earlier in life, or something less substantial. But I really lucked out. We travel well together, play well together, work well together—you know, you don't want unhealthy competition. It just took me a long time to find the right person.

You and your husband have worked together producing the last two albums. Was that a good test?

The last one was difficult. For me it was painful, because I was never in a group, and my processes are peculiar: a lot of it is intuitive and it requires that there be a climate in which there is no fear of failure. So if you have the boys standing around saying, "Oh, no" at the beginning of an idea, "that's not going to work"—which they did—I kind of felt ganged up on.

So when I began this project I started the first three tracks with a big NO BOYS ALLOWED sign on the door. And even Peter Gabriel, whose studio it was and who came to visit from time to time, would make comments like, "Why did you do this or that?"—it's a natural thing, I do it when my husband's in the studio producing someone, it is hard to keep your mouth shut. But this was the way it had to be.

So he had to learn certain things about my way of working. First of all, *spirit*: I'm very sensitive about keeping spirits high in the studio. I find a lot of producers don't really care about spirit, they're more task-masters; I've seen them slog a band into the ground. But that way you don't create a climate in which a lucky accident can occur, and that I'm very fussy about. So, working together on this project, Klein acknowledged that this was a big part of my creative process, so we worked fantastically. Because, (*she laughs*) he's a real smooth cookie!

Is each album that you make part of an ongoing continuum, or do you begin each album as if you were starting afresh from square one?

There is a continuity in that each one gives you the opportunity to correct what you might think were the weaknesses of the one before. For instance, on this album I knew what I would do different from the last one was, I wanted more live playing and less mechanical assemblage, whereas on the last one I wanted to go almost completely into synthesiser. And having done that, it gets a bit like a Detroit product-assembly line, and you crave to see living, breathing people playing off of each other through the glass. Now in regard to the next project I'm going to do, I crave further simplicity—which I've not had for years, because I always craved greater and greater complexity for a while. But I might not, because I'm now kind of used to the synthesisers and they're a great orchestral compositional tool, so it will probably be a mixture of both.

So in that way there's a continuum. As far as the poetry goes, well that is pretty much just what the year coughs up as a vision; it's what you think about in the writing period between albums. And if there's a continuity, it's just the continuity there is in life.

I was wondering if you made albums according to some internal timeclock when a burst of creativity periodically surges to the surface and can't be ignored, or whether you make them according to external pressures, like record contracts.

There's no pressure from the record company. When I signed this contract, I was really reluctant to make any more records. And because of that David Geffen—who's an old friend of mine (the man about whom "Free Man In Paris" was written) [*And Joni's former agent, and record company boss —Ed.*]—said, "I don't care if you don't make a record for five years, it doesn't matter." So there's no, "Isn't it about time you made another album?" Plus with all the technology, there are multiple hundreds more decisions to be made in regard to making a record than there were when I first began in the business; all I had to do then was just get the best performance of my songs with just voice and guitar, so it was fairly simple. A record took two weeks, maybe, at the most; this last one took two and a half years.

Is the desire still there as strong as it was to make them?

As strong as ever. I'm as keen as I was when I was a "green" kid. I think it's because of the varied nature of music itself—there are so many wonderful kinds of music to assimilate. I could make a jazz album now, a rock album. I've never really done any *funk*, for instance. But Prince has kind of approached me with a project that we will probably do sometime—to take my chords, my harmonies—which is not of an idiom, it's not really a jazz harmony or folk harmony or even classical harmony; because of the open tunings of my guitar, my chords are unusual and individual—and he mentioned that that harmony with his funk rhythm would be an interesting hybrid. And I am interested.

Do you intend to collaborate with anybody again on the level you collaborated with Charlie Mingus?

I don't know. See, that was a specific incident. Charles was dying and he had a project in mind. He called me up, basically, after having gone through a lot of black poets, to set words to his melodies. And, having found them either too sentimental or—they didn't satisfy him. So he sent for me, oddly enough. Part of the reason was because I dressed as a black man on that cover (*Don Juan's Reckless Daughter* in 1977). That album was a very misunderstood project in many ways—it introduced some very African sounds which are now quite popular in pop music but then it was very strange, and for a white woman to be playing around with African drums and things confused white pop critics. But the black music papers, seeing a "black man" on the cover, reviewed it as if it was a black album, once they got into it. And Charles seemed to get a kick out of it! Because the disguise was almost complete. It does look like a black man. *I* was amazed when I put on the costume and saw the transformation myself. For several days it was like *Black Like Me* (a novel and movie about a white person who took medicine which caused a change in his skin pigmentation, and suddenly found himself on the receiving end of racial harassment). I was able to feel what it was like, I received prejudice in restaurants. It was a very strange and interesting experience.

Because of that I was sucked into the black culture, and I was required to write from a black point of view: the point of view of a black man dying. I wanted to please a dying man by putting the lyrics that he wanted to his music. I tried a lot of different personnel to capture the music, and ended up going with what I felt was the best jazz band going in the world at that time: Herbie Hancock, Wayne Shorter, Jaco Pastorius. What we came up with I believe is splendid—and noticably undervalued and misunderstood. It was very adventuresome and a *complete* collaboration.

I didn't want a track, for instance, where my voice could be removed and another singer could be put on; I wanted them all listening intensely to each other, like a group dialogue, and my voice was imitated in the horn and so on, all welded together so that you couldn't remove anything—like a piece of fabric, you pull a thread out and the whole thing comes unwoven. Plus, I had all this wonderful candid tape that Sue Mingus provided me—candid moments, at birthday parties, with Charles speaking, and amongst it I found him talking about his own death, so I included that. When a person dies, how frequently do you find a documentary of him discussing what he wants for a funeral? I think some people thought it was in bad taste (*she looks downcast*). It was a very misunderstood project.

Was part of it the same syndrome Dylan found when he went electric: people have an idea of how you should be and get angry when you do something different?

Yes, you do get typecast. But you need new tributaries. Things turn into curios. I don't want to become a jukebox, or something cute and quaint. I want to keep my music alive, and the way I do that is by searching for things that thrill me. I grow through admiration more than anything. Anything I hear that makes me go "Wow, fantastic!" creates a new tributary coming into the source of my music. If years go by and I don't hear anything that thrills me, then I'm a dead musician and a curio for sure!

Still, a lot of people have retained an image of you as the Fragile Lady of the Canyon, the pure, the melancholic, virginal singer-songwriter of the folk days. You must be aware of that?

Well (*she laughs*), you can imagine the laughter of my cronies in Saskatchewan, Canada, who knew me as a real *enjoyer*. You know, I loved to dance, it was a girls-just-want-to-have-fun period, lively, party, dance. And when my music came out, you would think having spent a decade in that fun-loving period that my music would come out that way. But instead it tapped into things internal, and came out in the form of mild and vague longings for a better world.

Because in the '60s—people romanticise them now, but they were very difficult times. America was swaying from the loss of Kennedy—Daddy was dead—the war was on TV and the world looked fearful. I went from being a good-time extrovert to being an introvert during those times. They hit me hard. My twenties were in the Sixties and my twenties were difficult. I feel now more like myself. Like I can still be pensive and write from the inner landscape. I still spend some time there, but I don't *live* there anymore.

But I *was* fairly innocent, late into my twenties. I have always brought out the protective somehow or other in people. My father's like that. I don't know about now because I'm such a worldly creature now (*she laughs*), but people were always reluctant to swear around me or do drugs in front of me. I was quite sheltered, ultra-feminine then. Now that I've come through life and through this business—and it's a man's business—I've become more balanced. I remember when I stood on the brink of entering it, people advised me against it because it's a hard business for women and they thought I'd never make it through. And it *was* difficult, too.

And yet you've come out of the other end far more intact than most of the male musicians of that period, so many of whom are washed up musically, or dead.

The difficult thing is making change. To keep your river alive, you must take in new tributaries. Jimi Hendrix for instance, who was a great talent, one of the greatest talents of my peer group, confided in me that he didn't want to play the phallic, on-fire Jimi any more. It had become distasteful to him. He wanted to drop it and get into more legitimate big band arrangements. But every time he tried to eliminate it, the audience would rise against him. So he ended up doing it in a half-assed way, and during that transitional period, he died.

I think every time you change, you lose a little bit of your following; people don't like change, change is hard. But I have an appetite for change. Every time you go through change, you go through a little death, and it seems to be easier for some than others to go through and survive these little deaths. But it's the only way you keep going.

Do you enjoy the elements of success these days that make you a star, a role model to some people?

I didn't enjoy them until recently. I now realise that it's not going to go away, so I may as well enjoy it!

Who were your own role models?

Miles Davis is a great hero of mine, because of his ability to follow his muse purely; Picasso also for the same reason. Roy Rogers in my childhood. Yes (*she laughs*), we were all Roy Rogers fanatics in my neighbourhood!

You mentioned no women—not surprising when you were one of the first women in pop music to come along and make her name independently of any man. You had no Svengali behind you, no Phil Spector or Motown or whatever.

See, I'm an artist first, I've always been a painter, which is different from a girl who comes into the business to be a singer. She's at the mercy then of men to make her image for her, provide her with material. Maybe that's the difference. See, I just got into this business to make a little money on my way to painting. It was accidental. I was a waitress in a coffee-house in my hometown and I'd been playing around with a ukulele for fun, and somebody didn't show up one night and they said, "Come on Joan, somebody's got to go on", and it was terrifying to me.

It sounds like one of those movies—the big moment when the waitress realises she can sing!

Well, I knew that I could sing, but I didn't think much of it. There were a lot of people who could sing. The town I lived in as a child had classical music pretensions; almost everyone studied classical piano, some instrument or voice, so I had playmate friends who were real singers. So I didn't think much of it. We all would stand around the piano and sing Walt Disney songs, "Some Day My Prince Will Come," or something, and I sang in the church choir. But I didn't have my identity wrapped up in being a singer. I was always the artist—my self-image was of a painter rather than a musician. I have a funny perspective. David Geffen said to me early on, "You're the only star I've ever met, Joan, who wants to be ordinary!" (*She laughs*) And in a way that's true.

The other thing was in high school, I was always kind of a star, know what I mean? And an outsider, too. I always drew the best so that gave me a mystique; it was a talent that wasn't rampant where I came from. And also I had a lot of childhood illnesses (including polio). I would have preferred to be more academic and athletic, but things conspired. And so through my illnesses I developed an inner life, and through moving a lot, I developed an independence. I was aloof, and kept the suffering that accompanies that to a minimum, to hold my head up while being the new kid on the block—which is a good training for wandering the world and everything. It takes a long time to understand why things unfolded the way they did. That's why I'm comfortable now; 20 years into the business and I've decided I like my job (*she laughs*). But there were terrible periods of maladjustment to it.

Back to the current album [Chalk Mark in a Rain Storm —Ed.]; *do you have any particular favourite track?*

I like "The Beat of Black Wings". It's not necessarily my favourite but for instance on "My Secret Place", while I like it very much there are things I would do differently, and on "The Beat of Black Wings" there's nothing I crave to change. I like "Corrina, Corrina"—I think it is kind of miraculous the way it turned out, with its flurry of horns at the end;

all of that happened spontaneously. But "Beat of Black Wings," is the only one I wouldn't change.

You've mentioned that several times—does dissatisfaction constantly niggle at you?

Dissatisfaction is very healthy, because that's where you get your next direction. It's like *divine* dissatisfaction in a way. Because nothing's perfect, there's no such thing as a perfect work of art. If you were a painter you could do a series—you may have 10, 12, 20—every time you try it there's an object that comes out of it as the residue of that experimentation. Whereas on tape you end up with one finished product; things come off and are thrown away and you start over.

Picasso painted like that—he would paint and paint and paint, over and over on the same canvas, more like music, where each image is buried under the last. I could keep going on certain little bits and pieces—what if this was a different colour? or, what if the line was a slightly different shape? It's nothing to worry about, but the dissatisfaction gives you your next period.

You have an interesting and mixed list of guest musicians on this album.

Don Henley I've worked with before, he's a friend and I've called on him from time to time to work backgrounds. The only two people I sent for that I hadn't met were Billy Idol and Tom Petty. I called Billy specifically to bring to life a character in one of the songs. See, people tend to confuse art with the artist, and because I have a reputation for being an autobiographical poet, sometimes the strangest assumptions are made—like, I've seen in print that *I* am the "Free Man in Paris", and I think, "Where is those people's common sense?" They seem to miss the quotation marks. So I thought, this time I'll spell it out for them, I'm going to cast the album and play the narrator. Billy seemed a natural to play the character of Rowdy Yates in the song; just that funny, rowdy spirit of his. The character played by Tom Petty was a difficult one; because it was such a small part it was almost with apology that I offered it to anybody. But in my mind's eye, Petty and Billy facing off seemed to be excellent (*she laughs*).

Ben Orr—my husband [*Larry Klein —Ed.*] was producing him. Peter Gabriel had asked my husband to play on his *So* album because he was in the neighbourhood, and we used his studio. I've always had a lot of people on my records, singing background or playing. Usually they were either friends of mine or recording across the hall. So it's really nothing new, except I've never done it to such an extent as I have on this album, this *casting*.

Will you tour with this album?

I'm not sure, because the drummer I want to use—Manu Katché—is going out with Peter (Gabriel) in the fall; I just found out. Another Amnesty International tour. Peter invited me to go along on that; it's going to a lot of interesting places all over the world; places none of us have ever played before—quite an exciting adventure. So if Manu's going off on that tour, that pretty much throws the monkey-wrench into my own independent tour. So if I do tour, I imagine I'll have to go on that tour (*she laughs*), because it's got the personnel I want.

Outside of music and painting, are there any other big interests in your life?

It all turns back into that anyway; pretty much. Sporting events: I used to go to the Rangers games in New York. I like hockey—I come from the Prairies—hockey-land! Otherwise—what else is there, besides the arts? (*she laughs*) I like talking to people, I like wandering through streets of cities with my eyes and ears open, soaking everything up. But everything will turn back into art anyway. I'm kind of compulsive that way.

JONI MITCHELL: DON JUAN'S RECKLESS DAUGHTER

Phil Sutcliffe | May 1988 | *Q* (UK)

Phil Sutcliffe met with Joni in Los Angeles in the spring of 1988 to interview her for Britain's *Q*, ostensibly on the subject of *Chalk Mark in a Rain Storm*. They convened at her then-manager Peter Asher's office, which Sutcliffe describes as "middling posh," featuring an artsy, sensual photo of Joni and husband Larry Klein displayed on a coffee table. For the interview, Sutcliffe and his rock star subject sat across a table from each other, his cassette player hissing away as Joni answered everything he asked, gracefully.

Her favorite word seemed to be "appropriate," and Sutcliffe remembered that she used it with precision, in her Canadian accent, "as if the concept figured large in her view of the world." She took her time, choosing her words carefully and often beautifully, with no canned answers, it seemed.

Joni brought up some tricky subjects with Sutcliffe, including her awkward encounter with the ailing bluesman Furry Lewis in a dingy Memphis room—captured in her song "Furry Sings the Blues"—and that problematic blackface she adopted for the cover of *Don Juan's Reckless Daughter*, for which she was cheerfully unrepentant. She talked in detail about the misfire of *Dog Eat Dog,* and how record company "politics" helped create a situation in which Thomas Dolby and others gave the album more of a synthetic feel than she liked (Dolby insisted that she signed off on the collaboration).

Sutcliffe had an hour and a half interview scheduled, but Joni started to enjoy herself and was surprised when her interviewer drew the encounter to a close after ninety minutes of chat—but he had a plane to catch, back home to London. The journalist later heard that Joni said it was the first time an interviewer ended the session before she did.

Note: Two common errors have been corrected—Elliot Roberts's first name and the spelling of Fort Macleod, Joni's birthplace—as well as Lionel Richie's name. —Ed.

She's danced to the beat of her own drum all the way from Laurel Canyon to uptown Los Angeles. Joni Mitchell talks about her life, her loves and her courageous musical ventures in a rare interview with Phil Sutcliffe.

On the office wall, in elegantly lit monochrome and framed, Joni Mitchell's husband Larry Klein bends down fondly to bury his face in the hair at the nape of her neck and wraps his arms around her. Nestling against him, she in turn affectionately hugs a bright-eyed cat. A picture of love and fulfilment—at last, you might fairly say.

There is recent evidence too of her public life: copies of Chalk Mark In A Rain Storm, her fifteenth album in 25 years, the last 16 of which have seen her veering away from her early folk roots into a sequence of experiments and unpredictable collaborations which are evolving still with Crosby, Stills & Nash, jazz virtuosos black and white—Charlie Mingus and Jaco Pastorius—and soul singers black and white—Lionel Richie and Michael McDonald. She's even been working with Prince, a devotee of her 1975 LP The Hissing Of Summer Lawns, though nothing has emerged yet.

Now, though, after working for a couple of years in nine British and American studios, she has completed her most elaborate cooperative venture.

The Chalk Mark cast includes Peter Gabriel, ex-Eagle Don Henley, old outlaw Willie Nelson, Hopi Indian Iron Eyes Cody, Wendy Melvoin and Lisa Coleman from Prince's Revolution, Tom Petty and, perhaps least likely of all, Billy Idol ("I saw him at the Grammies, thought he was fantastic, rang him and told him I wanted him to sing with me"). And the result is a wonderfully original album, her most compelling compositions for years moulded, as ever, by her remarkable ear for arrangements.

The picture of wedded bliss hangs on the wall of her manager Peter Asher's office in Los Angeles, between Sunset and Santa Monica Boulevards. There have been rumours that Joni is "under the weather" but she arrives, half an hour late after a 15 minute drive from her home in Bel Air, apparently in the pink, at ease and expansive whichever way the interview turns. We perch on either side of a glass and chrome desk like job applicant and employer. Someone looks in to toss her a pack of Camels.

Joni Mitchell laughs a lot, from the lower end of her range. When she tells a funny story she makes big, comic gestures with her arms. She's 44 now, but there's still something enduringly innocent about her. Her mild accent turns "out" into "oat" and "docile" into "dossl". Talking, as in writing, she takes care with words and relishes what she calls "a well-contoured phrase". Though names and numbers escape her, she has almost total recall of what she saw and what she felt at any particular moment. She can even remember what she was *wearing* at every crisis point in her life.

Roberta Joan Anderson, who has lived her public years in the urban sprawl of Los Angeles, grew up in the rural sprawl of the Canadian prairies. The only child of Bill, a flight lieutenant in the Canadian Air Force, then grocery store manager and part-time trumpeter in a marching band, and Myrtle, a teacher, she had an itinerant childhood following her father's postings and employment across the vast flatness of Alberta and Saskatchewan: Fort Macleod, where she was born in 1943, Calgary, Maidstone—pop. 400, "a two-church town" where the highspot of her day was to watch the only train going through and wave to the driver —North Battleford, and, from the sixth grade on (11), Saskatoon.

Life post-war had a peculiar flavour throughout the victorious nations, even in the rich wheat prairies the tight belt of rationing nipped every waist. "It was a strange, surrealistic time," she says. "Stocks on the shelves were dwindling down to nothing. You were lucky to get soap, and when you did get it, you washed your dishes and your hair and your clothes with it whether it was detergent or shampoo."

Although she was always artistically inclined she was never any good at school. The only period when she made real progress was when she had polio (Neil Young caught it in the same Canadian epidemic) and her mother—"an old-fashioned woman, presser of flowers, scrapbook keeper," says Joni—who had stopped work by then, taught her at home for an entire year while she recovered. "She had this blackboard and when I didn't understand something she would say, For Pete's sake Joan, do I have to draw you a diagram? And that was exactly it—I needed pictorial references."

At first they wondered whether she would walk again. Then she wanted to do nothing but dance. Ballet, she dreamed. Rock 'n' roll, she loved it, jiving with the door handle to the two weekly hit parade shows on the radio. It led her into bad company, bussing downtown in her smart frock, proper hat and gloves to the juke box hangouts, forbidden public dances, brothels even. "If you've seen pictures of me when I was 25 when I started recording, you'll know I looked 12 then," she says, "so you can imagine what I looked like when I really was 12. Awfully wholesome to be in those places. The kids used to say to me, You look too innocent. Smoke!"

Into her teens, she drew a Christmas card for a senior boy at school and in return he gave her The Hottest New Sound In Jazz LP by Lambert, Hendricks & Ross. Strangely enough, this motormouth, avant-grade flare-up took her by storm—"I don't think there's another album I know every song on, including my own." But The Kingston Trio were in the pop charts with Tom Dooley so she bought a ukulele, her mother having decreed that the guitar was "hillbillyish".

While studying at the Alberta College Of Art, Calgary, at 19 she played her first pro dates at The Depression coffee house with a friend called Peter Albling (a comedian in L.A. now) and wrote her first song. The second, Day After Day, came to her on the train to the '64 Mariposa Folk Festival, near Toronto, and inspired her decision to shovel the last clod on the grave of her formal education, quit her course and leave home.

With her few thin songs, "love-lost pieces for a wandering Australian who really did me in", she plunged into the musicianly hurly-burly of Yorktown, Toronto, an area rather like Greenwich Village, where the tough competition on the local circuit was from the folk-rock protest sector: David Clayton-Thomas (later of Blood Sweat & Tears), Jack London & The Sparrows (later Steppenwolf), Gordon Lightfoot, Buffy Sainte-Marie and Phil Ochs. She faced the drunks yelling "Get 'em off, sweetheart!" and the mockery of musos like Dave Van Ronk who listened to her play and then said, "Joni, you've really got groovy taste in clothes. Why don't you become a fashion model?"

She almost did. Initially she worked in women's wear shops to pay for her musicians' union card. And the coffeehouse grind went on for four years. She got married to another folk singer, Chuck Mitchell, in '65, and moved in with him in Detroit. They toured the northeast US circuit as a duo, then split up after a little over 12 months [*They split up over 1967–68 —Ed.*]. But she kept right on, solo, handling her own bookings, enjoying what she calls the "scuffling".

"OK, I've got you up to full capacity now," she'd say. "Last time I made *this* much; this time why don't you pay me *this* much more and you can still make a profit. Let's be *fair*." One regular gig was the army base at Fort Bragg, North Carolina, where, among other broadening experiences, she acquired the guitar she was to use onstage until it was stolen from an airport baggage carousel at Maui, Hawaii, in the late '70s. She bought it from a captain who would get drunk and tell her she was "better than Peter, Paul & Mary".

By then Joni was set up in New York with a small apartment north of the Village. She got into what she calls her "Magic Princess trip", covering the bedroom walls with tinfoil and wrapping crepe paper round the door. Life was good: independent, writing up to four new songs a week, as much as $400 in the bank. This was her Chelsea Morning—she celebrated it with the joyful song eventually recorded for Clouds, her second album.

Then she started to get noticed. Suddenly renowned folkies like Tom Rush and Buffy Sainte-Marie, who both recorded The Circle Game, wanted her songs. Most significantly, in '67 on Wildflowers, Judy Collins covered Michael From Mountains and Both Sides Now, the latter an American Top 10 single some months later (and a lesser UK hit in 1970). Still, in autumn that year Joni was on $15 a night, opening for Richie Havens at the Cafe Au Go Go in the Village when Buffy took one of her agency team, Elliot Roberts, to see her. He has described her as "a jumble of creative clutter with a guitar case full of napkins, road maps and scraps of paper—all covered with lyrics." Immediately, he left his job to manage her.

Roberts negotiated a deal with Reprise and brought Joni to L.A. She didn't like it at first because the pavements were dead, it was a city that lived in cars. But by '69 she and Graham Nash, the former Hollie latterly partnered with David Crosby and Stephen Stills under the Roberts umbrella, were living together in Laurel Canyon—the hill suburb of Los Angeles that had become so fashionable among rock stars. Indeed Stills, Crosby and Cass Elliott (of the Mamas And Papas) comprised their immediate circle of friends and neighbours.

A strange phenomenon ensued around the time of her first album, Song For A Seagull. She and Nash took to conducting press interviews at home and, given the run of the place, journalists from Time or Rolling Stone would stroll about, in effect, conducting inventories. Fascinating. The contents of the fairly bijou two-bedroom residence—previous owners Houdini and Tom Mix—included one grand piano, one grandfather clock (gift from Leonard Cohen), one turkey made of pinecones, one "Souvenir of Saskatoon" ornamental plate, one Art Nouveau lamp in the shape of a frog on a lily pad, one hand-carved hat rack, one sewing machine, musical instruments and brown velvet rocking chairs (various) and one giant antique wooden pig. All reported glowingly on the friendly atmosphere.

With Nash, Joni put herself on the line. Combine this sort of media exposure with her music and the rock public felt an unusual intimacy with her which both demanded and fed the supply of stories about her love life: Leonard Cohen, James Taylor, Neil Young, Stills—there'd been liaisons with all of them but what was the latest? Millions followed the rumours on a need-to-know basis.

At first she held nothing back. She was on the road for 40 weeks in '69. She opened for CSN on a US tour and played major festivals at Miami, Atlantic City, Newport, Big Sur, New York and Monterey (she missed Woodstock, but played the Isle of Wight the following year). Her second album, Clouds, went gold in America and won a Grammy, while her success as a songwriter reached a new peak in '70 with Woodstock, her imaginative response to not actually being there, a massive hit in Britain and America for both CSNY and Matthews' Southern Comfort.

But for all that she became a celebrity it was simply voice, melody and lyrics that established her as an artist of substance. On her great sequence of albums through to the live retrospective Miles Of Aisles in 1974, she had the stillness and purity of Baez or Collins, her immediate forerunners, but she wasn't so cool—there was romance and vulnerability about her. And no barriers. Women were Joni, men were her boyfriends (in fact, she often portrayed herself as the wayward boy's mother too), and her improbably sinuous melodies, playful swoops and sustains made your hair stand on end.

Her lyrics were a joy: built with immense discipline as in Both Sides Now, a song all about "balance" and its limitations; dazzlingly inventive as in Big Yellow Taxi (the firecracker fun and spot-on satire carried by alliteration in "They paved paradise and put up a parking lot" still gives me a big grin). But for the less sentimental, her poetic often lurched towards the poetical and her flights of imagery went airy-fairy. Song To A Seagull stands accused of anticipating Jonathan Livingston of that ilk: the bird as vaguely mystical symbol of our higher aspirations to something or other and harbinger of this and that. The busker in For Free with whom she critically, but romantically, compares her strictly-cash-on-the-barrelhead self would, given a voice, carp at her only for giving herself a hard time while she could have been dropping a dollar in his hat.

Like any writer, she couldn't always evade the current clichés. She did try though, and with remarkable conscientiousness. Already, in January 1970, she was worried that stardom had cost her the observer status in life which she valued so much. Her range of experience, her air supply, was being circumscribed by the common round of rock.

So she stopped. She stepped right away from the music business and went travelling: Greece, Spain, France, Jamaica, Panama. On Crete she spent five weeks roughing it with the hippies in the caves of Matala, until the police came and turfed them out.

She returned with a new policy for personal defence which was to sustain her for some time. Her next album, Blue, 1971, was the ultimate in her "confessional poetry," wide open and apparently vulnerable—and yet not so because, other than in her music, she had determined to keep herself hidden. She refused interviews and gave fewer concerts, and even then pulled out of so many that at one point Roberts did some rueful arithmetic and said she had notched up more cancellations than gigs played. Onstage she would even threaten that if she saw one photographer's flash she would be off.

Towards the mid-'70s a durable solution, artistic rather than career-tactical, began to shape itself quite naturally for her. The first signs of it came when she asked a jazz band, Tom Scott And The LA Express, to play in the studio for Court And Spark (her only US million-seller) and then as her backing band on the Miles Of Aisles world tour. Also she fell in love with the drummer, John Guerin, who moved in to share the 16-room Spanish-style Bel-Air house she lives in to this day. An American magazine interview at the time related scenes of tranquil domesticity: goldfish pond, swimming pool, Chinese paper dragons by the door and Joni and John playing backgammon on a table in the sun.

Q: A media picture of you has emerged from about '69. You were living with Graham Nash and apparently keeping virtual open house to the press.

You have to put it in the context of those times. Back then, we, the musical . . . heroes, for lack of a better word, didn't feel very separated from our audiences. We were all hippies. It's not like now where the musical stars have become like the movie stars of the era before us—transformed by luminous images. We felt we were all in this together. I know I didn't feel separate from the press—which was a mistake. Oh yeah, you must maintain some privacy. I mean, I like my place to be cosy. I like cats. They give the home a heartbeat—in lieu of children. I don't have children. I see home as a sanctuary with a tea kettle rocking and good conversation.

Q: What did you feel at the time then about that public scrutiny via the media?

Oh, I couldn't stand it. All that exploitation and posturing, the gasping at the mention of your name, the pursuit by photographers and phenomenon-seekers . . . you get that shot of adrenalin and it's fight or flight. I chose flight many a time.

Q: Hard to do on stage, you're not supposed to . . .

The *first time* I stood my ground was in front of half a million people at the Isle of Wight. What happened was this. It was a hostile audience to begin with. A handful of French rabble-rousers had stirred the people up to feel that we, the performers, had sold out because we arrived in fancy cars—Neil and I had rented an old red Rolls, the driver had to sit outside, a real horseless carriage. Backstage there was all this international capital—bowls of money, open coffers.

Some acts cancelled so there was a dead space of about an hour. No one would go on. But in a spirit of co-operation, knowing it was death, I said, OK, I'll go out there.

In the second number a guy in about the fifth row, flipped out on acid, comes squirting up and lets out a banshee yell, guttural, demented, devils at his heels. It's as if a whale came out of the water, the waves, the energy from him spreads to the back so fast. Now the whole thing is *undulating*. I go and sit at the piano and this guy I knew from the caves at Matala, Yogi Joe, he taught me my first yoga lesson, he leaps up onstage. He gives me the Victory sign, he sits at my feet and starts to play the congas with terrible time. He looks up at me and says, Spirit of Matala, Joni! I bend down off-mike and say, This is *entirely* inappropriate, Joe. It was Woodstock of all the songs to be singing, because this was so different—it was a war zone out there.

At the end of Woodstock Yogi Joe springs up, grabs the microphone and yells, "It's desolation row and we're all doomed!" or something to this effect. A couple of guards grab him. The crowd then stand up and scream, "They've got one of ours!" And they're moving forward.

Now what would you do? I've run for much less than that. But I thought, I can't. I have to stand up. The place I drew my strength from was very bizarre. I had been to a Hopi snake dance ceremony—it's a very high ceremony to bring rain to their runty corn crops. They dance with live snakes and there was one that stood up on the end of its tail and launched itself like a javelin right into the audience. The people scattered but the musicians, the antelope-priest drummers, never missed a beat. Their earnestness, their sincerity, their need to bring rain, was unaffected. They kept the groove.

So, with my chin quivering, fighting back tears and the impulse to run, I said, "I was at a Hopi snake dance a couple of weeks ago and there were tourists who acted like Indians and Indians who acted like tourists—you're just a bunch of tourists. Some of us have our lives involved in this music. Show some respect." And the beast lay down. The beast lay down.

Q: Did you and your friends live communally?

No, not really. There was a community of musicians but we didn't all live under the same roof and alternate duties or anything.

Q: You wouldn't have wanted that?

I'm too much of a loner. I was too much on the fringes of everything.

Q: But all your personal relationships centred around the "community of musicians"?

They usually began as friendships, burst into flame (*laughs*), and continued after the fact as friendships.

Q: Did the whole hippy cultural and social period feel natural to you?

No, never, because it was a *style*, you know. Lay off the scissors and you were a hippy.

Q: In your group of friends there was a lot of closeness, but was there also competition, rivalry?

Uh-huh. It doesn't suit my body, though. I short-circuit. It feels tense and, uh, vulgar. I was sort of passive in my twenties, very manipulable. I was opinionated, mind you, but . . . I had a desire to be agreeable and co-operative and you can take that desire and move a person around.

Q: Did you get moved to where you didn't want to be?

In some cases. Woodstock, for instance. We were all standing in the airport, CSN and myself, and it was agreed by the managers, David Geffen and Elliot Roberts, that I should not go because it would be difficult to get me out of there and back to New York for a television show that Monday night. If it happened now I think I would have given them a good argument because it kind of broke my heart. But I was the girl in the family. 'Daddy' said I couldn't go.

Q: Where did drugs figure for you?

I was late to try everything. I was so overprotected within this stable. When Crosby, Stills, Nash & Young did their first album all I knew was suddenly all their personalities were changing. Graham was getting thin: he wouldn't eat and he stayed up all night. I didn't know any of them was doing drugs. They would hide them and whisper when I was around.

Q: But you eventually tried them?

Oh yeah, I tried everything. Well, I never tried heroin because I thought, "What's the point? The worst that could happen would be you'd like it." But altered consciousness is completely tempting to a writer. I did some writing, I think, on cocaine—Song For Sharon (*Hejira*)—but it kills your heart, takes all your energy, puts it up in your brain and gives you the arrogance that, you know, ruined Jaco Pastorius. (*After destitute years of drink and drug problems the former Weather Report and Mitchell band bassist died last September after being beaten up outside a Florida club.*) I watched it ruin a lot of people.

Q: Were you aware of being "the spokeswoman for a generation"?

You mean via the song Woodstock? If I was a spokesperson nobody heard me, so big deal.

―――――――――

In 1975 Joni Mitchell took a typically peripheral part in the great rock 'n' roll gang show, The Rolling Thunder Review, which featured Dylan, Baez, McGuinn and friends. But she was preparing to make her own splash with an album which can now be seen as the axis of her career. The Hissing Of Summer Lawns came out in the autumn and its smoky, languorous, jazz tension provoked her first critical pasting, in America at least. She had been revered, "the Goddess of song" no less. Now she stank the place out. The crime seems to have been, as with Dylan a decade earlier, that she had deserted folk and, thus, all the associated purities she had represented.

Some small consolation was that it did strike a chord in Britain. In case anyone was going to miss the point of it all she drew a diagram. Her cover painting showed Amazon tribesmen bearing a giant snake, approaching the outskirts of a cityscape incorporating LA and New York—with the Mitchell homestead bottom left.

She had taken a theme outside love lost and found and worked it to the limits of her imagination and intellect to build a whole album. Offsetting black and white, the jungle and the city, she had a muscular metaphor for the big idea that was eating her—how the orderly and the wild fight it out beneath the skin of everyone. Burundi drums thundering through The Jungle Line or sprinklers hissing like snakes . . . She had her subject, the animal/human/animal. She had her musical field to explore, at last discovering how she might connect with the black and white blending she had loved so much on her old Lambert, Hendricks & Ross LP. (She covered their Twisted on Court And Spark and Centrepiece on The Hissing Of Summer Lawns.) It wasn't that she took a vow against "personal" songs from then on, but they were no longer a trap to her.

Her next, Hejira, was written almost entirely on the road, in the Kerouac sense. She was cooling her heels on the beach at Neil Young's house one day when some friends came by and said they fancied driving across the country. They climbed into her car and did it. Among other things, Hejira actually bade farewell to another lover—presumably Guerin, whom she left that year—but Furry Sings The Blues, a reflection on her encounter with ancient bluesman Furry Lewis, was the piece which attracted controversial attention.

Then, astonishingly, she turned up in blackface on the cover of her next, Don Juan's Reckless Daughter, a yet more ambitiously jazzy double set, with the late bass virtuoso Jaco Pastorius a forceful presence. While it took her further away from a mainstream audience, Charlie Mingus, a jazz immortal composer, acoustic bass player and band leader, listened and liked it. He contacted her through the grapevine with a proposal that they work together on T.S.Eliot's Four Quartets. If she could trim the texts down a bit ready for singing, he would write a score for full orchestra. Joni read the thing and, regretfully, cried off. But Mingus was persistent. In April '78, already crippled by a rare, paralysing disease, he produced what proved to be his last six compositions and told her their provisional title was Joni I-VI.

It was a great gamble. She had never collaborated with anyone to this degree before, and Mingus's music was very difficult, but how could she resist? She spent time with him in Mexico while he consulted a faith healer. The dying of a great man hung over her work, challenging her ingenuity and her artistic integrity. She gave up on a couple of the pieces. She tried his signature tune, Goodbye Porkpie Hat, instead and it took three months to get a lyric. Finally she found she had recorded up to four separate cuts of every track and, although she knew Mingus hated amplified instruments, she chose the electric versions because she felt they were best.

In her touching sleevenote she sees herself "dog paddling around in the currents of black classical music". Referring to the two tunes she had to leave out altogether Joni said they were "too idiomatic" for her. Ironically, this was exactly how the entire album would sound to her fans.

No such nice considerations, though, for Joe Smith, chairman of Elektra/Asylum. On surveying the plush gatefold sleeve and listening to the music therein he made a conference phone call to his promotion men nationwide. "I'm having a contest for them on sales of Mingus," he explained afterwards. "First prize is they get to keep their jobs!"

Q: Your most controversial work in the second half of the '70s came from your unusual approaches to black music from The Jungle Line and on to Mingus. In between there was Furry Sings The Blues. How did the song come about?

I had been out on Rolling Thunder and for my own amusement on that tour I had taken to ripping off cops. I would use my wits and try and get a piece of cop paraphernalia off 'em—I got hats and jackets and tie-clips and badges. One time I chased a cop and he wouldn't give me anything so I said, "What if I get a gang and we pin you against a wall and you tell your superior you were outnumbered?" He was real deadpan. This smile came over just one corner of his mouth and he said "Go get your gang." It was really a charming game. I would introduce myself as Mademoiselle Oink, the liaison officer between rock 'n' roll and the cops.

So when we got to Memphis on my own tour I hit on this cop and he agreed we would trade a badge for a record. Then he said we should go and see old Beale Street, which used to be the heart of blues music in the town. Well, it was an amazing vision, like a Western ghost town three blocks long. Shards of wreckage all around, cranes with wrecking balls still standing there. Two pawn shops were functioning and there was a modern movie theatre with a double bill of black machine-gun movies—next to a status of W.C.Handy, a trumpet player of the jazz era. We came down the street and, if I'm not embellishing, a tumbleweed drifted across in front of the car—it seems to me it did.

Standing in front of one of the pawn shops was a guy in a purplish-blue shirt, bright blue blazer with brass buttons on it, bald, smokin' a stogie. He looks at me and says, You Joni Mitchell? I think, Culturally this is impossible. This guy should not know my name. However, I had heard that Furry Lewis lived in Memphis so I mentioned it to the pawn-broker. He says, Oh sure, he's a friend of mine. Meet me here tonight and we'll go over and see him. Bring of bottle of Jack Daniel's and a carton of Pall Mall cigarettes.

Furry was in his eighties or nineties and senile at this point. Lived in a little shanty in the ghetto there. It was quite a nice visit until I said to him—meaning to be close to him, meaning "We have this in common"— "I play in open tunings too." Now I dunno, people must have ridiculed him about it or something, because he leaned upon the bed and said (*hoarse old voice*) Ah kin play in Spanish tonnin'. Real defensive. Some-how or other I insulted him. From then on it was downhill. He just said, I don't like her, as I wrote in the song.

Q: What do you feel about this whole episode?

I'm too sensitive. I'm likely to feel shitty over things that would just roll off another back. I would like to be appropriate. I would like to be fine-tuned to the point where my instincts are working well, where everything is in alignment. But to say, I play in open tunings too—this is not an insulting remark (*laughs*)! You can't control these things.

Q: And how do you see the experience with Charlie Mingus now?

The musicianship on that album is at a very high level and I'm proud of it. But it's obscure. It hammered the nail into my coffin which said: Joni is dead on pop radio, she's a jazzer. I would do it again in a minute though, that project. To have the experience of collaborating with such an unusual character and a fine jazz musician. Definitely.

Q: Was Mingus's being black a big part of it for you?

No, *my* blackness was a part of it actually because I appeared on the cover of Don Juan's Reckless Daughter as a black man. Charles thought I had a lot of audacity to do that and that was one of the reasons he sent for me.

Q: His response seems unusual. The old "nigger minstrel" blacking-up business is normally taken as racist. Why did you do that?

There's a whole history that led up to that action. The first seed was on Rolling Thunder. Bobby and Joan Baez were in whiteface and they were going to rescue Hurricane Carter. I had talked to Hurricane on the phone several times and I was *alone* in perceiving that he was a violent person and an opportunist. I thought, Oh my God, we're a bunch of white patsy liberals. This is a bad person. He's fakin' it.

So when we got to that last show, which was at Madison Square Garden, Joan Baez asked me to introduce Muhammad Ali. I was in a particularly cynical mood—it had been a difficult excursion. I said, Fine, what I'll say is—and I never would've—I'll say, We're here tonight on behalf of one jive-ass nigger who could have been champion of the world and I'd like to introduce you to another one who is. She stared at me, and immediately removed me from this introductory role. I thought then, I should go on in blackface tonight. Anyway, Hurricane was released and the next day he brutally beat up this woman . . .

So there came Halloween, and I was walking down Hollywood Boulevard. There were a lot of people out on the street wearing wigs and paint and masks, and I was thinking, What can I do for a costume? Then a black guy walked by me with a New York diddybop kind of step, and he said in the most wonderful way, (*croons*) Lookin' good, sister, lookin' gooood. His spirit was infectious and I thought, I'll go as him. I bought the make-up, the wig, the sideburns, I went into a sleazy menswear store and bought a sleazy hat and a sleazy suit and that night I went to a Halloween party and nobody knew it was me, nobody.

The art she professed herself most worried about at the start of the '80s was "growing old gracefully." Further, with mock melodrama, she enquired of a journalist, "Is my maternity to amount to a lot of black plastic?" She had drifted a long way from centre-stage. Like Miles Of Aisles, the Shadows And Light live double, her last recording with Pastorius, seemed to have drawn a line. Then she went to ground for a while.

Wild Things Run Fast, in '82, featured Guerin on drums—she's terrific at staying friends with former lovers—and her new husband Larry Klein on bass. It took a potshot at a single hit with a spunky remake of Leiber and Stoller's (You're So Square) Baby I Don't Care. In Lionel Richie it introduced the first of what, on her last three albums, has become a parade of unlikely guest duettists. It was very good—she really has never made a clinker—and sold moderately.

The same applied to her next, Dog Eat Dog, three years later. While shifting further towards the adult rock consensus it was literate as ever, sharply satirical about fang-and-claw consumerism and the seedy side of pop's efforts for Ethiopia. Joni found new Madonna and Stevie Nicks areas in her voice and, while English new-tech wizard Thomas Dolby's production work didn't make much impression, two straight ahead songs with music by Klein—Fiction and Tax Free—hinted that she might be examining the possibilities of stadium rock.

In the middle of recording, she broke with Elliot Roberts after 17 years. For a few weeks she tried to look after herself as she had done back in the coffee house days but, when she realised it meant the phone never stopped ringing, she turned to her old friend Peter Asher, actress Jane's brother and very late of '60s chart duo Peter & Gordon, not to mention long-time manager of James Taylor and Linda Ronstadt.

No magic wand to hand, though. "I loved Dog Eat Dog," he says. "Other people didn't. Of course, Joni was disappointed when it didn't do well. The thing is every artist has a reluctance to accept that basically, not enough people liked the record. Then anyone who's around gets blamed, which is usually the record company.

"But Joni doesn't have any of this even vaguely on her mind, not for an instant. In the studio her objectives are solely artistic. And I don't say that is a virtue. She doesn't even *think* of pleasing the public. In that sense she's lucky she's as popular as she is. At least, around the world, she still does half a million every time. No danger of Geffen losing money on her—and even if an album didn't get its costs back, another label would sign her right away because of her reputation and creativity."

It turns out that Chalk Mark In A Rain Storm, her latest, is a wonderful album. Apart from the intriguing and varied list of duettists detailed earlier, songs show off her full scope quite beautifully (there's even a nostalgic variant on folk standard Corrina Corrina). The depth of reflection she is putting into her work now emerges in two songs which reach back over 20 years to events touched on elsewhere in this interview. Those Hopi antelope-priest drummers who inspired her at the Isle of Wight are on her mind again in Lakota, a protest against government attempts to take the tribe's land for uranium mining. And Fort Bragg, the army camp where that besotted captain sold her a favourite guitar is recalled in Beat Of Black Wings—it was there, she explains, that she met the song's central character, the Viet Vet, Killer Kyle.

"He was there. Fort Bragg was an interesting place. It gave me a balanced view because everyone I knew was, you know, dodging the Vietnam draft like crazy, pleading insanity and homosexuality, anything. The boys down there were Southern for the most part: they all believed in America, mom, apple pie and the War. They were not at all Bohemian.

"There were some soldiers there who hadn't been to the War yet, and then you had the damaged coming back—Killer Kyle was such a person. He was in the Airborne Division, a paratrooper medic. Terrible experiences, hell on earth, you know? I came off stage one night—I can remember what I was wearing, the whole incident was so vivid: an old '40s purple silk velvet evening gown and my hair plaited up on my head with some roses in it. I looked like an old Sarah Bernhardt poster.

"I went into the dressing room and Killer was there, red-in-the-face angry, his fists clenched, in his neck the veins were standing out—it was kind of frightening. He said to me in a thick Southern accent (*which she doesn't mimic*), You've got a lotta nerve, sister, standing up there and singing about love because there ain't no love and I'm gonna tell you where love went. He ended up crying and shaking. The song doesn't exactly depict what he told me, though. What he told me doesn't make a song,"

Q: Did you start the '80s thinking "I have a problem here"?

I started the '80s by going to a party—at Stephen Bishop's—with the theme "Be nice to the '80s and the '80s will be nice to you". Everyone realised at the brink of it that it was going to be a hideous era. I had this car, my beloved '69 Bluebird [*"Bluebird" was her 1969 Mercedes-Benz —Ed.*] and I was on my way, driving past Tower Records on Sunset, it was that royal blue time of night, just before it goes black. I stopped and ran into the store because I just had to listen to a Jimmy Cliff record, The Bongo Man Has Come. But when I came out there was the empty slot where my car had been. Never saw it again. I loved that Bluebird.

Anyway that's how the '80s were ushered in for me and it was all downhill from there. The government ripped me off—I was one of just 12 people in the entire country who were forced to pay a new tax on a record at the point you hand it over to the record company. Twelve people! What kind of justice is there in this thing? I'm still fighting it. Then my housekeeper decided to sue me for $5 million.

Q: What did you do to her?

I kicked her in her shin because she was ripping me off. She was a Guatemalan and I'd paid for her to go home twice and the second time she didn't even go, she went to Europe, so she'd been lying. Finally I kicked her in the shins. But I can't do that as a public person. She went to the criminal court and they threw it out because it's just laughable. But she's still after me though she's on her fifth lawyer. Then I had trouble with the record company which we don't wanna get into, OK, because I'm still there.

Q: They wanted you to sell more records I expect.

No, no. Anyway, it's like the Anti-Christ is running things in this era.

Q: Why did you split with Elliot Roberts?

He needs a manager (*laughter*). We're still good friends. I don't really want to get into that.

Q: Why did you decide to get married at last?

Because Larry's such a wonderful person and I just love him.

Q: And you've become marriable?

Exactly. I've settled down.

Q: Have you ever been out with a non-musician?

Since my youth . . . not really. I'm drawn to talent. I've been out with a painter. Always in the arts though.

Q: How do you spend your time now, outside of music?

I'm so artsy, you know. When I'm not doing music I'm painting, I'm writing poetry. We enjoy home life. It's fairly simple really, we enjoy movies, I love card games, video games, backgammon . . . I don't go to the supermarket because I hired a cook, but up till then I did. I don't lead a tremendously sheltered life. We frequent a little restaurant in our neighbourhood almost every day. Most of our best friends are not in the Hollywood firmament.

Q: Does it matter to you that this album is a hit?

I could use a hit, yeah. On the last two records the production, the layering of keyboards, was an expensive process and I gotta sell more records to recoup, just to break even.

JONI SAID

On Locker Room Talk

"I like men's humor. I like to be around men in a way that I don't disturb their maleness, so they can be themselves. I don't like to put any coyness into the situation that might make them want to be more like men to a woman. I like locker room talk."

—to Rory O'Connor, *Vogue*, August 1988

JONI MITCHELL

Jeff Plummer and Marty Getz | 1989 | *Quintessential Covina*
Cable Access Interview (US)

It's something that might have happened in SCTV's fictional Melonville: small town open access cable TV show lands an interview with Joni Mitchell to discuss her latest videos—but it really happened. As any Joni observer comes to know, as much as she liked to refuse interviews, she also loved to baffle or defy her managers and give interviews on a whim.

Marty Getz was producer of *Quintessential Covina*—a name that could have come out of the mind of SCTV's Johnny LaRue. The show aired at 10:00 PM Saturday nights in Covina, California, a town of forty-seven thousand some twenty-two miles east of Los Angeles. The show included a segment on current music, so Getz had gotten on a list to receive record company videos.

One day in 1989, the mail brought him three new Joni Mitchell videos, released to support the previous year's album, *Chalk Mark in a Rain Storm*: "Lakota," "Beat of Black Wings," and "Dancing Clown." Included with the videos was a press release asking for his opinion of the videos.

Getz called the number on the release and said he would prefer to talk to Joni directly about it. Some time passed, and he figured nothing would happen—until one day, it did. A call came through from Peter Asher's office. Joni Mitchell would talk to them, on camera. At best, the show would be seen by a few hundred viewers. No matter.

Jeff Plummer was tasked with interviewing the star for the show while Getz produced and Steve Rhoades operated the camera. "She was wonderful in the interview. Not in a hurry and very cool," Getz recalled. He not only saved her bottle of sparkling water, he had it encased in glass.

In the interview Joni is asked what makes her happy, and she gives an agreeably zen answer. She describes her creative process for making videos, talks about film and concert footage, and also complains that at his advanced age Jack Nicholson could still act, but she was expected to look like a "sexpot" in videos. Wasn't there a way for a woman to age gracefully in music, she wondered? Good question.

Note: The "Gloria" Joni refers to is Gloria Boyce, who worked for Peter Asher Management. —Ed.

Jeff Plummer: OK, I'd like to thank you for coming today and welcome to the interview.

Joni Mitchell: Oh, sure.

Plummer: First of all, the main reason we're here is to kind of find out about your new videos that you have out, including "Lakota" and "Beat of Black Wings," also with "Dancing Clown." You felt compelled to make these videos and, if you did, were the ideas you had at the time at the same time the songs were written or did they come later?

Mitchell: They came after the completion of the record in various ways. We should maybe break it down into individual songs—

Plummer: Right.

Mitchell: —and I'll tell you how they came around.

Plummer: OK, first one being "Lakota" since it's the first one we had on the tape. Can you tell me where that came from and how it came to be?

Mitchell: That one came in a kind of a mystical way. We—at the release of "Chalkmark," Gloria and I traveled around the world running off at the mouth in self-promotional mode. In Japan I also had an art show, and I sold a little more than half of the show so I had a little bit of money. So I put that money into an art kitty, with the intention of using it for video since we get—the videos are billed back to the artist anyway.

Now, in regard to my music, it had always been a difficult decision for the record company to make, it seemed, as to what the single should be. And the video always accompanies the single and sometimes the visions, the most visual songs for me were not the ones that would be chosen. So ideas that might come to you would then have no outlet.

Anyway, completing this journey around the world in self-promotional mode, I came back to Los Angeles. And the entry into the country was difficult. We had a mean, kind of redneck customs official, and it was the only country in the world where you suddenly had to have coins to get your shopping cart. We had hit the commercial world.

I guess you'd have to say there's a postpartum kind of depression that accompanies something like that. It was a lot of energy output and very positive experience but coming back to America, I was sort of flattened and overwhelmed because I was requested—people wanted me to do this, do that, do this, do that. What do I want to do, I said. So I lay around the house for a couple of days. On about the third day, on a Tuesday, I got an idea. And my idea was this, I said to my husband, "I've got it! We're supposed to go to the Lakota reservation. We'll take all our Super 8 cameras." We had four Super 8 cameras and a bunch of film. "We'll go onto the reservation, we'll wave a white flag, you know, so they allow us entrance, because I'm a blonde, and as a custom I don't think they take to blondes too much. And we'll say 'We know you love the Black Hills; we want to make a video. Take this camera, here's how it works, go shoot everything that you love, your children, your friends, the landscape, whatever. When you run out of film, come back and we'll load you up again.'"

So this was the dream, the fantasy, on a Tuesday. The following Monday I was talking on the phone to Gloria Boyce, and while we were talking she said, "Oh, Joni, a call is coming in from the chief of the Lakota Sioux." So I said, "Oh! I've been thinking about them. Call me back and tell me what he wants." So what he wanted was for the first time in I don't know how long, the Lakotas, who were scattered over several reservations, seven reservations or eight reservations, had decided to unite and march in protest in regard to the Black Hills and to speak and hold public meeting. It was a baby step for them in organization. I was invited to march with them as a dignitary.

Plummer: That's great.

Mitchell: So we went and when we got there I didn't even have to say here's the camera and here's the film. The children that you see in the film kept running up and taking the camera and running off. And the reason that it's all in slow-mo is because when children between the ages of four and fourteen shoot, they think they're spraying flies and there's a lot of fast movement. Great inside subject matter, but technically you had to milk it to get the stability of the shot so that's why that style evolved.

Plummer: Yeah, it has a great effect—

Mitchell: —dreamlike—

Plummer: It's very interesting to find out actually what was behind that because it seems as if—did it seem something that they didn't understand as far as all these people coming in and wanting to film their way of life?

Mitchell: Well, it didn't come like that, see, because it was never spoken that that's what we were there for. We were there because I had written a song, "I Am Lakota," in the first person and I think they were curious. I was invited to speak among one of the dignitaries there. As one of them. It was really quite an honor.

Plummer: That's great.

Mitchell: And I had some confrontation over some of the lyrics. On the second day we were there, I wanted to film people as we got more comfortable with one another, saying some of the lines. And they all had mimeographed lyrics—the chief had mimeographed my lyrics and passed them out.

So I went around and nobody would touch certain lines. You know, "the poor drunk bastard falls." And I did have some explaining. Some people were very confrontational with me, but it was written with a lot of empathy, and basically it was a magnet to a great adventure. It was quite touching. And at the end when the woman passes the peace pipe to me, I was filming that segment. So I mistimed in a way with her, because she passed the pipe to me and I didn't know whether—I was confused, should I put down my camera and accept it? And you'll see an expression on her face she did it of her own volition but when I hesitated, she looked over to a higher-up, one of the chiefs to see if it was all right to be doing this with me, I think. There's a moment where her expression changes.

Plummer: Hesitation or . . . That's interesting.

Mitchell: It's really a great experience.

Plummer: As far as "Beat of Black Wings," now this is a song that you've carried around with you for quite a while as far as that you haven't put down on recording or video; what brought that to fruition?

Mitchell: Oh, well, that was written for the last album. The vision—that was a collaboration, that piece. The Bauhaus style dancing was contributed by the director. The black soldier was—well, actually, he's multiracial. He looks sort of Sandinista. I mean he/she/it [laughs]. That was my idea. And it's an iffy thing because I had to play gender cross, racial cross, and age cross because he's a young soldier. I think the director would have selected a different piece of footage. The parts that I selected were almost maybe too feminine. You know, we did a lot of takes and some of them were much "butcher" and some of them, I think—what we should do is have another edit. He should edit it also. Because in the middle of it, I felt that it was getting away from my vision and I—it wasn't a hostile takeover, but I took back the reels and edited myself, and it's a compromise of styles because they had begun editing in the long dissolves and things whereas I like—"Lakota" and "Dancing Clown" is my editing. More hard cut, and shorter pieces. That's more the way I would have done it had it been all mine.

So it's almost there, I think, as a piece of art.

Plummer: So the Bauhaus style of dancing in that wasn't your ideal or idea, excuse me. That wasn't something that you had conceived for the video or was it—

Mitchell: No. With video directors they get visual ideas. And then people come to them and sometimes they'll laminate an idea onto a song, whether it has anything to do with the song or not. So Jim Shea had this idea with the sketches from some Bauhaus dance routine that he'd seen. And I thought it was an odd juxtaposition. Originally, you know, I saw this guy drunk in a bar, this soldier, he's mad—he's mad at his girlfriend, he's mad at the powers that be. And I couldn't understand what he'd be doing in a bar with these kind of dancers.

So the idea then metamorphosed. I said what if he's lying in an alley outside of a theater and they're rehearing. That makes sense. So we found the alley and luck was with us again in that the Black Panther insignia was spray painted all over this alley, and the Black Panther insignia is a guy with a beret and a mustache and looks just like my character; you ever seen it?

Plummer: Uh-huh.

Mitchell: So this was sprayed all around in that area. The night we shot—speaking of spraying, they sprayed for—what is that stuff, Gloria?

Gloria Boyce: Malathion.

Plummer: For medflies [*The Mediterranean fruit fly, which was devastating California crops in 1989. —Ed.*]

Mitchell: Medflies. Yeah, so we took a heavy lungful of medfly poison that night. There really isn't much more to say with it. I feel that piece is almost there. I'd like to see Jim's edit now. I think he's going to do another one. I've had my go at it. I can take one more. Editing is an addiction, you know.

Plummer: So as far as "Dancing Clown," is that something you want to talk about as far as including it in the package?

Mitchell: Yeah.

Plummer: How do you feel about that video? It's a different departure, it's light and it's very entertaining.

Mitchell: That's all my idea. And I believe in amateur photographers. The Super 8 was shot by a friend of mine, for many years my art director for my album covers. He'd never filmed before that I know of. But he turned out—he's stocky and he has a beautiful weight and classical moves with the camera and I think his footage was quite successful.

The thing that I didn't want was the imposition of direction. I wanted to be alone in my kitchen listening to this piece of music with nobody telling you how to act alone in your kitchen. Just if I could get friends to shoot it—my mother gave me the idea. When the album came out, she said, "I just love that song "Dancing Clown." She said, "I put my headphones on and I dance around the kitchen." So I thought that's a great idea, you know.

Plummer: That's an entertaining song. And you work on that song with Billy Idol and Tom Petty are in the background at the end.

Mitchell: Right. Originally I wanted to shoot Tom and Billy in their kitchens dancing around mindlessly. But things conspired and it never came off. So my cat El Café—

Plummer: Filled the bill.

Mitchell: Filled the bill.

Plummer: I wanted to get on to talk about producing albums. The majority of your albums are self-produced until the latter—other than your first album—your latter albums you've worked with your husband, Larry Klein, and I believe on one you had Thomas Dolby help you in producing.

Mitchell: And Mike Shipley. Well, now he—that all comes down to internal politics. Thomas was hired—we were moving into synthesizers. Studios are very expensive. If you don't know what you're doing on them yet you're slow setting up yourselves. And with the clock ticking it's a very bad situation economically.

Plummer: A technical advisor in effect?

Mitchell: So Thomas was hired to set us up colors quickly. Then management got involved and he ended up with a production credit, but in fact, he was a player and a colorist. Mike Shipley, who's a wonderful engineer, also gets production credit. I'm not sure where production and great engineering begin and end.

My husband also gets production credit. He helped in the tweaking of sounds, and he has two songs on that album which he pretty much did produce himself. He developed his tracks up to a certain point and then the choral work, half of it is his production and half of it is mine. So those are two collaborations. But aside from those two songs, I don't— I've never liked the word "producer." It's like an interior decorator. It is in the final wash my music. Every note that's selected, no matter who plays it, is arranged by me, moved around and it's very like painting but sometimes other people are holding the brush but you can take those strokes that they made and move them. So . . .

Plummer: So I was just basically wondering if there was any conflict with working with other people producing, but since it's essentially your product, there really isn't.

Mitchell: I'm unproduce-able. I've had my reign too long.

Plummer: Well, I think you have good control over your product and I think it shows.

Mitchell: Thank you.

Plummer: Here's a kind of an off-the-wall question: Do you ever feel a void in creativity, is there ever a time you feel a void and if so, how do you deal with it?

Mitchell: No, I never feel a void. But I work in many fields of expression so when one tires out, which is inevitable, it's like crop rotation, you move to another. So if I'm bored with my music, if I feel that what's coming out is repetitive or I've done it before, I'll go back to painting, give that a rest. And the resting of the soil in the different areas keeps them all fertile.

Plummer: OK. As far as the way the public views you and the way you see yourself, is that pretty much close, the same, or does it differ quite a bit?

Mitchell: Hmmm. "The public" is a lot of people. It breaks down into individuals. One person would hear a song of mine and think it was too sad. Someone else would hear the same song and think it was uplifting. I've tried to avoid image traps, to be myself as much as possible in the course of my career, even if it meant belly-up and revealing some rather unpopular things about my own psyche to keep my humanness, therefore to keep my ability to walk around so I would never get too star trapped. You know, people are pretty good with me because of that. I think they let me be a human being.

Plummer: You have a pretty close following as far as your true fans, I mean they're pretty supportive in whatever avenue you take.

Mitchell: I've got my "loyal-ies," I think. You know, my generation, like all generations, stops listening to music and waxes sentimental at a certain point, "Oh, they don't make it like they used to in the old days!"

So those people, I have fans like that, who have my records say up to *Court and Spark*, and it ends there. Those are the people that say, "Oh, you define a certain era." I say, "Oh, really?" What a limiting idea. So there are some people that say I belong to the '60s when in fact I came in late in the '60s and worked through the '70s.

I still feel like I don't belong to any era. I'm not nostalgic for the '60s. I don't think my life lies behind me. I still see territory.

Plummer: How do you decide, when you get an idea or feeling, between putting it into a song or picking up a paintbrush and putting it on canvas?

Mitchell: Between painting and songwriting, the images fall almost automatically into their categories. One of the decisions is should it be a song or a short story. Sometimes it's hard to get all the information into a song. Like I've got a new one now called "Cherokee Louise" which really is a short story and manages somehow compactly to go into four verses. Sometimes you almost think you need a little more space, that the song form is too short.

But paintings, the ideas that I have for the work that I'm about to do that I haven't done, the main thrust of my work at this point is absorbing surfaces and reflecting surfaces so I—for instance, if you use gold line, in certain lights that line becomes dark and in certain lights it disappears. So I've taken to collecting terrible bad paintings by people with some virtuosity but no imagination so you get a stiff painting that's well rendered but has nothing happening for it, no soul. And then scribbling on it in gold pen. Well, from one angle you don't even see your line. From another angle you've scribbled all over it. So I'm playing around with surfaces like that.

That really doesn't have much to do with songs. Most of the graphic ideas for the art are quite separate. They may have—there's one big canvas I did that was called "Dog Eat Dog," which was the title of an album. And although it depicted a lot of—like the dogs had all kinds of expressions. The world was a dangerous and angry place for me at that particular time, and this was an outlet for it in that, and the music also expressed that theme.

Painting, you express it more broadly, more childlike. Here's the basic thing: like all that a painter—a painter at best because of their juvenile qualities. The reason painters live, I think, to be quite old is because they're children, maybe more than any of the arts, that never grew up, never put their crayons away. And the painting at best is supposed to rejuvenate a person. It's the work of a juvenile, perennial juvenile, intended to rejuvenate. You should get a wonderful "*Oooh!*" It should make you want to get out your crayons, a good painting, more than anything else.

A good poem, the role of the poet is to be an aspirant, at best. You know, they should take their insights and their human experiences and create something, especially in America which blessedly is not a number-one power. Now we can develop some character, some midrange. But because we've been "the Winner" for so long, everything's black and white. You're either a winner or loser. Now we should be able to be a little bit more humane.

But during that winner climate, people didn't talk about their difficulties. You were a social pariah if you had too many problems, people would isolate you, they'd leave you alone. So the poet during that time period, the "Me" '70s and the greedy '80s—well, less than the greedy '80s because people didn't—it was just a mad race for money. I don't think the poet was needed. He may have been but people didn't know he was.

Let's see, painting . . . music is a soothing, tactile expression. Music is really a mystery—how do those notes . . . you hear those sounds and they make you feel things. They do it quicker and more mysteriously than their abstract line equivalent. You may see an abstract painting with certain colors and everything, and get a feeling, but I doubt you'd get as intense a feeling as you would if you heard a certain chord progression which is line and color juxtaposition. Music is abstract; abstract painting is abstract. As a communicating tool, music is instant. It's really great, what it does.

Plummer: About your art, you said you had an exhibit in Japan? Can you tell me a little bit about that?

Mitchell: Yeah, there's a woman named Michiko Suzuki who for years, when she came to interview me for Japanese newspapers, saw that I was always in the process of painting. And after many years she decided that it was time that I would have a show there. We talked year after year after year about it, and I always declined in that they wanted me to perform in the gallery and I didn't want to get one thing mixed up with the other. Finally the climate was right, and there was a boy at the Parco Gallery in Tokyo who five years earlier, when he was writing out his application form, he was asked what his goal was in the gallery in a long-term plan. He said one of his ambitions was to bring the paintings of Joni Mitchell to Japan because he'd seen some of them on album covers.

So in collaboration with Michiko, they came and selected certain pieces and took them to Tokyo and we had the show.

Plummer: Was it well-received, the show?

Mitchell: I think so. We sure enjoyed it. It was fun. It was beautifully lit. The guy who lit it, lit it beautifully, and we sold enough to put together this video kitty to have a little money in there to stretch out and be able to do the videos, because owing to the number of years that I've been around and the type of videos that are being made, you know, the bathing suit girls. I'm not going to be jumping around in a—it's just not dignified at my age.

But I still wanted—I felt surely there are other expressions. If Jack Nicholson is still acting, why can't I be in videos? Why do I have to be a sexpot? There must be some graceful way. If there isn't, then I'm not in the game anymore and I should just quit and become a painter, period. So I didn't really find much company support. David [Geffen] said, "Well, Joan, the kind of videos you do . . ." And that I guess gave me a bit of a drive because I thought, wait a minute, I'd like to see these images. I'm sick of these images that I see.

Plummer: Do you plan to pursue that in long form or down the road more videos?

Mitchell: Well, I've done two illustrated concert films. That's where I started in editing. Just to spice them up.

Plummer: Did you work on editing, say, on "Shadows and Light"?

Mitchell: Oh, yeah, I edited that and what was the other one, "Refuge of the Roads." I did all the editing. "Shadows and Light" was my first one, "Refuge" was the second, and "Lakota" was the third.

Plummer: I think "Shadows and Light" has, at the beginning it starts out with an homage to—it has James Dean at the beginning.

Mitchell: That's right.

Plummer: And you utilized that almost like in a living room of a household or it was on a—could you tell me a little bit about it?

Mitchell: Well, that movie came out when I was twelve. And we all drank milk. I hated milk, but we all drank milk out of quart bottles because James Dean did. And we wore red cotton jackets with our collars turned up, and I mean, he was our hero—*Rebel Without a Cause*, that was right when the women's lib thing was happening. I don't know if you remember the movie but the women of that generation were restless, and while they were still aproned and still domestic, there were things that were bubbling. And the man/woman thing was unsettling. That was kind of the undercurrent of *Rebel Without a Cause,* was his mother was bitter and the father had the apron on, he wanted to be a man, what was happening. This was just at a sociological turning point just before the Pill became available and women were temporarily emancipated until disease struck, and we went back into Victorian.

What really happened with that film was it was a five-camera shoot. So with five cameras, when one magazine comes down, the other guy figures he's got it covered. Well, right before we started shooting, the number one cameraman sprained his ankle. Fifteen minutes into the show, between the heat and the pain, he passed out—then there were four. One of the other guys was Joel Bernstein, who's a great still photographer, who had never moved one of those big, bulky TV cameras, so his stuff was jerky. So then there were three. And two of those were roving handheld on stage, so sometimes when they'd come down, there'd be nothing, there would be no coverage. So we said, "What are we going to do?"

Concert footage at that time was already looking pretty bland, and this was before videos. People were trying to figure out how to make rock and roll look good on television. Because it was never like being there. You put the concert on the little screen and it wasn't quite the same thing.

So we went and did a low-budget thing which was at that time called "shopping the halls"; like the "Coyote" footage for instance, I directed a scene which was pretty literal, with people suffering in hotel rooms, and we rented a floor at this Sunset round tower at Sunset and the San Diego freeway, and we set up the whole scenario. And that's when I realized that if you take an image in a song and you depict it literally, the two [*claps*] kill each other off.

So that was discarded, and I started shopping around for outtakes from different places of coyote footage. When we found this thing with the coyote and the mouse, it was just—everything was there. "He drags her out on the dance floor" and the coyote whops the snow bank and the mouse bounces and they go off like the mouse is a hockey puck. It was just great stuff.

Plummer: It's a great image. I really enjoyed that. A couple of questions about critics. I don't know if they're your favorite people or least-favorite people but how do you handle negative criticism, and does it really get to you or do you just kind of shrug it off?

Mitchell: Well, I think criticism has always bothered just about any serious artist in that the caliber of criticism—well, George Bernard Shaw, I think, had the best line. He said, let's see if I quote this right, "The duty of the critic is to . . ." Let's see, "illuminate"? No. "The duty of the critic is to educate the ignorant, not to emulate them." Right? So most of the time, most criticism is really stupid. I'll give you an example—and the first review that comes out on a project because critics are so lazy, sets the tone for all to follow. Because the second guy gets what's available, what's already been written, and he bases that, that becomes the foundation of everything. On *Dog Eat Dog,* the first review came out in *Time* magazine; they pitted me against James Taylor, because they love to pit someone—not having Carly anymore, they decided to pit the two of us. And I came out the short stick, and what I believe the word they used was, they called it an "adolescent work" in *Time*. And so that came up again and again internationally, all around the world. And yet the music and the ideas that it contained two years later were going to become their headline stories. So in fact, was it adolescent?

You know, you say, "Come on! How can you dismiss this?" That was released into a very "Rah Rah, Reagan" pro period. Any criticism against America, and that album contained some social criticism, was considered negative. "Hey, you know, we're the greatest!" People were having this one last illusion.

Now, when *Chalk Mark* came out, the first review appeared in *Billboard*, and it was a rave. The guy loved it, he got it. I said to Gloria, "Send him some flowers!" because you watch, all of them are going to follow suit and so they did. And so they're lazy and why do we have them?

Plummer: We should be our own judges.

Mitchell: We should be our own judges.

Plummer: I think that point has been made and made, and I don't think people—you know, there's always going to be critics, which sometimes is unfortunate, that people should be able to judge their own opinion, but I think that's something that we're just going to have to live with.

Mitchell: My husband gave me a book that's called *The Critics*. It's a history of criticism, and it's reviews of Stravinsky, masterpieces, you know—all the negative reviews, things that history has proven to be great. It's a pretty funny book to look at. That puts it in perspective.

Plummer: Do you have any plans in the future as far as touring, playing live?

Mitchell: We get offers, to go to Russia, to go here, and of course the omnipresent benefit. I mean, you could do a hundred benefits in a day really. Touring is a strenuous thing, it really is moving the troops. To be able to afford it. It usually ends up costing you money. Prince, I think, it costs him money to put on those shows. Now at this point, even to carry background singers, you want to do it right. And the people that I want to play with are great and therefore they're expensive, and it really is almost cost prohibitive. If I had a hit album that really took off, which guarantees a certain populace, I could tour. Or if I took a trio I could tour. But we were out for nine months in '83 and everyone—if you're going to give up nine months of your life and put yourself through that rigor, changing your water, it's unhealthy—it's really like going to war in a certain way. You should be able to come home with something in your pocket. And I didn't, on that tour. Everybody made more money than I did. Now, money's not your sole motivation, but I think you should be paid for touring.

So in the event—if this next record is a smash, then I'll go out. [*Laughs*].

Plummer: Sounds good. I think we're all waiting, anticipating. You've worked with so many artists, so many great musicians. Is there anybody that you'd really like to work with that you haven't yet?

Mitchell: Yeah. Miles Davis.

Plummer: Miles Davis?

Mitchell: Definitely.

Plummer: Why do you choose him over . . . ?

Mitchell: I just love him, he's—he's one of my great heroes. I learned a lot about singing from him. I learned a lot about pitch, as opposed to perfect pitch. I learned about bending pitch for emotional things. There's a song of Miles's, for instance, called "It Never Entered My Mind," and at the end of it he draws a long, flat note. He lays on it, it is flat all the way—and he holds it flat all the way through the piece of music to the end and it's just brilliant. Because it—you know, music is designed—the technically correct aspects of it, and then there's what it does to your emotional center. That flat note just kills me. Every time I hear it I just go, "Oh! it's so sad!" You know, if he'd played it right on pitch it would have been pretty but he flattened it out and you know it just tears your heart apart. It's so perfect, it's just touching.

Plummer: He's a hero of yours?

Mitchell: Oh, yeah. Definitely.

Plummer: Out of your body of work, what stands out as one of your favorites, album wise or?

Mitchell: I like different ones for different reasons. *Blue* is very emotionally pure. It has its own uniqueness. It's simple and pure. It's like Japanese watercolors or something, haikus. It's very intimate.

Court and Spark was my first record with a band, using other players, so—and I think that one, symphonically speaking, band to band, the movement, especially of the first side, and I built connecting pieces to make it even do this more—the flow of the first album, it goes by like that [*snaps*] because the way—it's not just five songs in a row. They move, bridge each other beautifully. I like that for that reason.

Don Juan's Reckless Daughter was an experimental project. It's spotty and it's double and nobody can ever wade through and digest a double album, it seems. But there are experiments on that. I like the song "Cotton Avenue," I like the spirit of it. We still play that in concert. That has peaks on it.

I like—"Hissing" again was—I let my players go a little freer than I did on *Court and Spark*, because it was the first time I used a band, I practically sang and told them everything to play. I was much more in control of every note . . . On "Hissing," I cut them some slack. As a result, I think a lot of people didn't like it because cut some slack, they reverted to being jazz musicians. My music isn't jazz, the harmony is different from jazz, but a jazz musician cut loose against it will play jazz harmony with it. And that intimidates some people.

But I like the Burundi drummers on that; I think that was a good experiment.

Plummer: So you experiment with all your projects, then. You try different things. You're ever-changing.

Mitchell: Yeah. To keep it fresh sounding. And say, "Oh! I've never heard anything like that before." But sometimes you stick your neck out a bit when you're trying to go for it. That's another reason why Miles is a hero of mine. He and Picasso are restless spirits, always looking to discover. There aren't a lot of those in any field. Jimi Hendrix would have been another, I think, if he'd stuck it out, although he needed more audience support. You have to be able to take the rejection of your audience to go that route, and that's why I don't think a lot of people do it. You know, they may come back to you. You have to dare to be yourself and that's not—yeah, there are some dues with it.

Plummer: I was going to ask you, what makes Joni Mitchell happy and what makes you sad?

Mitchell: Oh yeah, well, that's easy. Let's start with sad; it's more universal. Happy is like the pursuit of—it's more the ideal. I'm sad about the rainforests coming down, I have been for many years. I'm sad about human nature in general, you know, we're so puny really. Our greatest accomplishments backfire ten years later, it seems. You know, every miracle—like DDT was a miracle, the car was a miracle, plastics were a miracle. Although any hippie, you know, hippies were real anti-plastic and now you can see with good reasons why. Plastics ate the sky. Plastics are made from the blood of the mother, from the Earth, and when it's burnt, it goes up and eats the father, which is the sky.

You know, this is the best and the worst of times right now. The best in that the world is beginning to realize how small it is. It's an opportunity to lay down arms with our old enemy, the bear. At the same time, the idea that we will be extincted, not by the big one [*The nuclear bomb —Ed.*] but by a fast food chain, you know, 'cause they're like cutting down all these forests for cattle ranching for hamburger chains. You know, that's some human irony, isn't it? These things make me sad. The '80s in general made me sad, the greed, the negativity, the ostrich-ness, inability of the world to be self-examining and critical, the misunderstanding of the role of depression in a human life, the beauty of depression. You know, that period of retreat, of cocooning where you think through your priorities and your value rather than being seen as a social disease, as a loser.

The things that make me happy are pretty simple. Basically, it's zen mind. If I lose self-consciousness—we go around all the time self-conscious, we're all self-conscious—the moments in the day when I lose self-consciousness are the moments when I'm happy. When you're purely a witness, and "I" is anesthesized, there's no concept of "I." It's just, "Oh! Look at that ruby-throated bird sucking on a petal—you know what I mean? Like stop and smell the roses. It sounds corny but it's always been the greatest high, I think. Even in a smoggy day, you see a bird or sunset. The smog here makes beautiful sunsets.

Plummer: Do you find yourself having time to do that? Just actually stop and forget about things, forget about recording, business, that type of thing and actually just enjoy yourself or enjoy something?

Mitchell: You find yourself accidentally enjoying yourself. You know, if you're rushing around, rushing, rushing, rushing, which we do all day long, you don't see much. But if during your rushing you sort of rush less neurotically, at a stop sign on your way rushing from Point A to Point B, something could come in. You have an exchange, instead of flipping the bird at somebody in the car next to you, you have some kind of pleasant exchange, that'll carry you for a couple hours.

So basically, human kindness is the thing that impresses me the most these days. You see so very little of it, it's always a welcome surprise. It was out of vogue in the '80s. I don't mean smile button mentality either. Little things. My cat! My cat cracks me up. I love that cat! Furry Snake, we call her. Famous cat, yeah. She'll take over from Morris.

[*Joni goes over some of her paintings in a brochure, describing them to Plummer and the crew. .—Ed.*]

Mitchell: This thing, this was the weirdest painting. This thing painted me—we were making the *Dog Eat Dog* album and this was to be the cover. But the company said it was too artsy. "Hey, we know you're artsy, put your kisser on the cover." So anyway, I would come home after a twelve-hour day in the studio, and it was sitting in the living room. And if I looked at it—I had to go up the stairs to bed, after twelve hours' work on the music sometimes you'd be kind of flattened—if I glanced at it at the foot of the stairs, the thing would make me work. And I'd work. It's hallucinatory, a lot of seeing the dogs in the paint. Because it begins with an abstract process, comes from fatigue, you begin to see things. So I began to see a lot of vicious dogs from fatigue. [*laughs*]

There was one up here, it looked so much like Richard Nixon for a while, this guy. And there's a self-portrait in it, there's a cheekbone, teeth, nostrils. There's God Dog over here, he's got sailboats for teeth. He looks pretty bored. Then there's Jesus Dog here too, the crucified one, right in here. He's the long-suffering one. And then you have all the races pushing against each other in here, pink man, yellow man, green man, black man, white man, all nose to nose.

Plummer: Is that—where is that at the end, the portrait? Do you have it? Is it in a gallery?

Mitchell: This one is in Japan. This one sold and so it remains over there. And this is kind of a noble dog, a statesman kind of dog, isn't he this one? He's very noble. Like a wolf. I love wolves. Did you ever meet any wolves?

Plummer: Yes, all the time.

Mitchell: They are a wonderful creature, aren't they?

Plummer: My parents live in the mountains, and they get all kinds of creatures.

Mitchell: OK, this is a portrait of Charles Mingus. I painted this one too in a fever overnight. When I met him, he was in a wheelchair, and his hands, which were big to begin with, were swollen. They looked like he was wearing baseball mitts.

Plummer: That was a unique project for you too.

Mitchell: Wasn't it? Yeah, really something.

Plummer: Is that something that you really treasure or is that—

Mitchell: Yeah. That was fantastic, really.

Plummer: He sought you out, actually, didn't he?

Mitchell: Yeah, it was like Rumpelstiltskin. He had a project in mind, which was a peculiar kind of thing. And this was to be his last project. He, when he discovered he was dying, he called a friend of his who was not a religious person by any stretch of the imagination. And he said . . . "I'm dying, I want you to come over here and talk to me about God." And [his friend] said, "Oh, you're talking to the wrong person."

So he went out and he bought him T. S. Eliot's [*Four*] *Quartets* and he tried reading it. Charles's wife was quite literary. She belonged to—she had a New York magazine of some kind. Anyway, she read it to him and translated for him. So he gets this idea that he wants to do a piece of music with an Englishman, with an Oxford English accent reading from the [*Four*] *Quartets*, pausing, and then me paraphrasing it, spoken, against this cacophony of a full orchestra, and he wanted me to play lead acoustic guitar across it.

So I went out and I got the [*Four*] *Quartets* and I read it and I said, "Charles, I can't condense this stuff. I'd rather paraphrase the Bible than this. I think I can see where his inspired lines are, and where his filler is. I think I can see what I could take out. But somehow or other, the filler is the necessary chain. I can't do it!"

So he wrote six songs, which he called "Joni I, II, III, IV, V, VI," and when I went out to visit him, there was one melody that jumped out at me which became a song called "Chair in the Sky." That was the first one I liked, and I said, "What kind of a theme do you hear? What subject matter do you hear for this?" And he looked at me really wryly with this real wry expression—well, I'll show you the expression, it's in here. It's small though, we'll see if you can capture this. [*Joni shows a picture from the gallery show brochure*] Yeah, and he said, "Well, that's about the things I'm gonna miss, motherfuck." You can edit that part out. [*Laughs*] So that song's pretty much about—he's talking about. "When I come back I'll be bigger, I'll be better than every, I'll be rich as Standard Oil." It was like Rumplestiltskin: "Guess my name! What am I gonna miss?"

When all medical help failed Charles he went to Mexico, and he was seeing a witch doctor in Mexico City named Pachita. He was like one of these "psychic operators" who reaches in with his bare hands, a lot of blood flying by candlelight, all that Catholic—

Plummer: I remember reading about that; there was one down there, surgeon with a rusty knife kind of guy, who was just [doing it] with his hands . . .

Mitchell: Yeah, well this is the kind of scene it was. And he'd taken a place in Cuernavaca, that was when I first went down to Cuernavaca.

[*Joni flips through more brochure pages.*] This is Georgia O'Keeffe and Juan Hamilton. And an old Bowery bum panhandler. This is an L.A. nightscape, it's full of friends of mine: Jaco Pastorius, vegetable woman. I guess vegetable woman is sort of a self-portrait there, turning into foliage and war paint.

Getz (off camera): Do you work in any other mediums? . . . Silk screening, or . . .?

Mitchell: For graphics? No, I don't do much—I draw, and they would translate really well into etching kind of things. But mostly I been messing around with paint. This is called *Still Life with Commotion*; it's a portrait of my husband in Dalhousie Castle in Scotland. See all of that line on there? That's silver pens; a lot of reflective surface on here. It changes in the light. . . . That one's not finished really. This one is called *Marriage of Church and State.* I crucified two canvases together for Easter. All the little dots up in the upper here are the presidents up to Nixon; you can't really but there's the assassinated presidents and Nixon is kind of the black cloud in the middle of the stars there.

These are some of the early abstractions that I got into. I was not a fan of abstract art until I began to pursue it. Now I adore it. This was painted for my wedding. All across the surface—you can't really see it—it says "I do, I do, I do, I do, I do, I do" and I do! [*Laughs*] I still do! This is called *Birth of the Earth*, the Earth is seen as after birthing, Big Bang. That was [*another painting*] one of the early prototypes for the album cover, painting on the photo. [This] is kind of our courtship painting, Klein and I. I painted that of us while we separated, from a [photo from a] photo-buying machine . . . you have to squeeze your heads together. That was the *Wild Things* [*Run Fast*] cover. That one I'm going to scribble on, roll all over like *Still Life with Commotion*. It's not finished, really. I have to have another go at it. They're never finished.

JONI SAID

On Women Singer/Songwriters

"Tracy Chapman wrote a coupla good songs, but generally speaking she's not that musically gifted. And Suzanne Vega, well . . . And now there are dozens of them. But I don't hear much there, frankly. When it comes to knowing where to put the chords, how to tell a story and how to build to a chorus, most of them can't touch me."

—to Robert Sandall, *Sunday Times* (London), September 9, 1990

JONI SAID

On Femininity

"[Dylan] was talking about how he didn't like seeing women onstage, how he hates to see them up there whoring themselves. So he was asked, 'Well, what about Joni Mitchell?' And he says something like 'She's not really a woman. Joni's kind of like a man.' [*Laughs*] The thing is, I came into the business quite feminine. But nobody has had so many battles to wage as me. I had to stand up for my own artistic rights. And it's probably good for my art ultimately."

—to David Wild, *Rolling Stone*, May 30, 1991

JONI SAID

On the Cocaine Era and "Heart"

"Billie Holiday and Edith Piaf were my heroes. I'm a more theatrical singer. Billie had a tone unlike anyone else. It was like . . . no matter how rough it got, it was there, baby. That era, no matter how screwed up people got, they still had good heart. I think the cocaine era, with the coming of that drug, it became more cerebral. The heart went cold, or something."

—to Elvis Mitchell, *Last Call*, CBS-TV, October 24, 1994

JONI SAID

On Freedom

"It's easier to do a portrait of myself and my own foibles, which also helps to prevent too much worship. I'm not comfortable with being too pedestaled, I like my freedom in the street, I like to walk around unchaperoned in the street, so to speak, and feel that I can handle it."

—to *This Morning*, CBS-TV, January 3, 1996

60 MINUTES WITH JONI MITCHELL

Vic Garbarini | September 1996 | *Guitar World* (US)

Vic Garbarini was friendly with Joni Mitchell through much of the 1980s and into the '90s. At that time, he was writing a column for *Guitar World*, "60 Minutes." The column consisted of an interview with a musician about his or her twelve favorite songs. But not every musician could manage eloquent answers. "It was one of the most difficult things I ever did," Garbarini said. "Some musicians can't articulate anything about music they like beyond the word 'awesome.'" But Joni, he thought would be an excellent prospect, as someone who had very specific memories of her favorite songs and a lot to say.

   She didn't even need a lot of words. As with her lyrics, Joni could often say more in a sentence or phrase than others could say after an hour of conversation. —Ed.

The great goddess of open tunings fashions her ultimate travel tape

There probably isn't a serious guitarist-songwriter who hasn't worn out a copy of *Blue* (Reprise, 1970), *Court and Spark* (Asylum, 1974), or the musically and lyrically exotic *Hejira* (Asylum, 1976). Like her fellow Canadian Neil Young, Joni Mitchell has been making groundbreaking music for over three decades. She's also been cited as a role model for every emerging female guitarist and songwriter, having boldly shattered every cheesy gender stereotype with her real-life, introspective songwriting and innovative playing. Plus, she knows more alternate tunings than Jimmy Page and Stone Gossard combined.

   Mitchell took a mostly chronological approach to answering the 60 Minutes question, "You're about to go to Neptune, and you're only allowed one-hour's worth of music on board. What would you put on that tape?"

As Mitchell puts it, "Every once in a while during your life you'll hear something that stops you in your tracks, something that makes the hair on your arms stand up, and there's no explanation for it. You're just ready for it at that moment. The first piece of music that did that to me—I was about eight, I guess—was the title song to a movie I saw called *The Story of Three Loves*, starring Kirk Douglas. Actually, it was a classical piece called . . .

"RHAPSODY ON A THEME OF PAGANINI —VARIATION NO. 18"
Sergei Rachmaninov
Classics At The Movies (RCA, 1934)

"To this day, I can say it's the most beautiful melody I've ever heard. It was the first thing that told me I had to make music. I have this mystical connection with it, because I have a CD that says either his writer's block finally broke, or he performed it for the first time on November 7, 1943. That's the day and year I was born."

"JOHNNY B. GOODE"
Chuck Berry
The Chess Box (Chess/MCA, 1988)

"Why? DA DA DA/DE DE DE DE DE DE/DA DA DA/DE DE DE. That's why."

"WILL YOU STILL LOVE ME TOMORROW"
The Shirelles
Dedicated To You (Capricorn CK, 1960)

"God, the number of quarters I shoved into jukeboxes for that song. I'd sit in the A&M lunchroom and smoke and drink Coca-Cola and just *dream* into that song."

"ANSWER ME MY LOVE"
Nat King Cole
The Best of Nat "King" Cole (Capitol, 1968)

"I love anything that has wide intervals in the vocals like that, where he steps up to a fourth or a fifth. Most melodies are all thirds—singers usually don't get that brave."

"NEFERTITI"
Miles Davis
Nefertiti (Columbia, 1967)

"Also anything from *In A Silent Way* and *Kind of Blue*. I'm still learning from that music. Oddly enough, it's probably still the major influence on my long-term musical plan. If you go back and listen to *Nefertiti*, with Wayne Shorter and Miles playing, they start out in unison. But as the track goes on they pull away from each other—like silk screening. They're still playing the same melody, but they're slightly out of phase with each other. As a painter and musician, I liked that on an audio-visual level. In silk screening, you lay your blue on and then your red, you off-center it a bit, and you get the same kind of slightly out-of-sync feel."

"POSITIVELY FOURTH STREET"
Bob Dylan
Bob Dylan's Greatest Hits (Columbia, 1967)

"It gave you the freedom to write on any topic with a base of any emotion. I thought, 'If he could write a song from self-righteous anger like that, you could write from *anywhere*.' Bob covers so much pictorial territory. Incredible imagery."

"THE STAR SPANGLED BANNER"
Jimi Hendrix
Jimi Hendrix: Woodstock (MCA, 1994)

"'The Star *Mangled* Banner,' yeah. Just for the pure violence of it. The chaos. As far as cacophony goes, that's my favorite bit."

"NORWEGIAN WOOD"
The Beatles
Rubber Soul (Capitol, 1965)

"That was the Beatles album I played and played. I used to sing that song in my coffeehouse days in Detroit. This is before I started writing myself, and it appealed to me as a scenario. It has this whimsical, kind of charming quality. I'd sing it to put some levity in my set. I got a kick out of throwing it in there amongst these tragic English folk ballads. Besides, I have Norwegian blood."

"MEXICO"
James Taylor
Gorilla (Warner Bros., 1975)

"I like so many of James's songs, it's really hard to choose one. I especially like the melody and spirit of this song, it's another one that stops me in my tracks. He's opted, as Dylan has, for the road. You have to make a decision in that respect. If you're going to be a road rat, you can't be a writer. There's just no life to write about. And I think in some ways he regrets his decision. He's not a natural writer in the sense that he's driven to write. Peter Gabriel is the same way. You have to lock them up and make them do it."

"DE DO DO DO DE DA DA DA"
The Police
Zenyatta Mondatta (A&M, 1980)

"I've danced in the Caribbean for weeks to that song. I'm an old rock and roll dancer, you know. The stops, the pauses in that one are really fun. I appreciated the rhythmic hybrids, the gaps between the bass lines, the repetitive figures with space between them. James Taylor and I had dinner with Sting once at our mutual manager's place. He was quite effusive about us being his heroes. So I always think of him as our son."

"PUNK JAZZ"
Weather Report
Mr. Gone (Columbia, 1971)

"Weather Report was the most aggressive 'synthetic' band prior to the punk movement. Zawinul had a keyboard sound that was much more interesting than anything at the time. Jaco [Pastorius] was doing things with the low end I'd been dreaming about, and Wayne Shorter was musically a metaphorical thinker, like me. Probably because we're both painters."

"DEACON BLUES"
Steely Dan
Aja (MCA, 1977)

"The arrangement. The melody. The wit."

"SUZANNE"
Leonard Cohen
Songs of Leonard Cohen (Columbia, 1968)

"That's another one with a mystical connection. I was sitting in a boat in Miami Bay with the biggest liar in town, a guy who was pretending to be Tim Buckley. Looked just like him, but I knew he was a fake. I closed my eyes and recited the Jesus verse [*sings*], 'And Jesus was a sailor when he walked upon the water.' When I opened my eyes the sunset actually turned *green*. I later learned that it's a local phenomenon associated with the Seminole Indians. So that sunset, to me, seemed to be triggered by the watery verse in 'Suzanne.' Sitting in a boat with the biggest liar in Miami."

"DOLL PARTS"
Hole
Live Through This (DGC, 1994)

"Sometimes I could listen day in and day out and hardly hear an honest line. There's being really low, and then there's pretending to be low because it's trendy to be miserable. There's so much falseness in that stuff. There's a line in a Courtney song that stopped me: 'I fake it so real, I am beyond fake.' That, at least, has an element of truth and revelation in it."

JONI SAID

On John Lennon

"When I was recording *Court and Spark* at A&M Studios, John Lennon was recording across the hall. He came in one night. I played him a few tracks. Being a working-class lad, he said all he liked was simple rock 'n' roll, and anything too orchestrated was too sophisticated . . . he said [the intricate arrangements] were a 'product of over education' and 'Why do you let other people have your hits? You want a hit, don't you? Put a fiddle on it!' I don't remember what I said back to him. I wanted to sputter out that I flunked 12th grade twice."

—to Melinda Newman, *Billboard*, August 24, 1996

ALTERNATE TUNINGS

John Ephland | December 1996 | *Down Beat* (US)

In 1996 it was announced Joni would be inducted into the Rock and Roll Hall of Fame class of 1997. It was also the year Joni released two compilations, *Hits* and *Misses*, which pleased her loyal fans but didn't make much of an impression on the charts: *Hits* peaked at number 161 on *Billboard*'s chart, while *Misses* failed to chart altogether. Her reception from the jazz world was a little friendlier.

On the surface, it would seem that there couldn't be two women with less in common than Joni Mitchell and Cassandra Wilson. The former was a Nordic/Irish mix from the Canadian prairie, the latter an African American from Jackson, Mississippi. But that surface view would be deceiving. While singer Cassandra Wilson is now known for her soulful jazz recordings, she launched her professional career playing Joni Mitchell songs in Jackson coffeehouses. The two women share many jazz heroes as well as a freewheeling approach to musical boundaries.

It was an inspired decision for *Down Beat* to pair them for a dual interview, conducted by editor John Ephland in late 1996. Naturally, there is much talk of Miles, and Monk, and the difficulty of getting a pianist who will lay back and play economically, allowing room for a singer.

Notes: Joni tells Ephland that her next album was to be a tentative February 1997 release on which she would be accompanied only by Brian Blade on drums. As it turns out, her next album, which included Blade as well as a number of her favored sidemen, was 1998's *Taming the Tiger*.

Eric Andersen's name and the title of Victor Feldman's book were corrected from the original. —Ed.

Their paths had never crossed. One is from the cold and blustery fields of Alberta, Canada, the other straight out of Jackson, Miss. Joni Mitchell and Cassandra Wilson have more in common now that they've spent a long evening together, but their kinship, a musical bond thick as blood, has deep roots.

Mitchell's latest work involves drums-only accompaniment. With her arsenal of created guitar tunings, she and Brian Blade (that's right, Joshua Redman's drummer) have formed a music both spare and florid, improvisational even as it surrounds that inimitable voice. (Untitled at presstime, the album is scheduled for a February release date.) Mitchell—whose last feature in these pages was a 1979 cover story on the occasion of her recorded collaboration with the late Charles Mingus—has been on a roll of late: among other awards, two Grammys for last year's *Turbulent Indigo*; Billboard's Century Award, a new honor the newsweekly bestows on musicians from all genres who've made a highly significant impact on the arts in this century, also in '95; and induction in the Rock and Roll Hall of Fame this year. This fall sees the release of *Hits* and *Misses*, two career-spanning anthologies of her work with every label she's ever recorded for. Having just turned 53, clearly, she has much to celebrate.

While Mitchell may have worked with Mingus, Pat Metheny, Jaco Pastorius, Michael Brecker and—with the exception of one—*all* of Miles Davis' former mid-'60s sidemen, Wilson's jazz pedigree is better known to Down Beat readers. Witness her recent wins, starting with last year's Readers Poll and continuing with both the Readers and Critics polls for top female jazz singer this year (see Aug. '96, and page 40 this issue). Apart from her success with *Blue Light 'Til Dawn* and *New Moon Daughter*, the 40-something singer's recent work includes guest spots on Javon Jackson's *A Look Within*, David Sanchez's *Street Scenes*, guitarist Pat Martino's next record, a duet with Dianne Reeves on the Bob Belden-produced *Strawberry Fields*, music for the soundtrack to the current film *Rosewood*, and recording and touring with Wynton Marsalis this winter as part of his ambitious *Blood On The Fields* project.

The musicians met in Los Angeles for dinner earlier this year at Adriano's, a fashionable Bel Air restaurant. The conversation/interview, which spilled over to Wilson's hotel, dealt with the mechanics of music, definitions and the relevance of jazz, "that widened harmony," and Miles Davis. Both women were earnest, robust and, at times, a tad wild, Mitchell taking the reins often in a conversation that jumped off the path more than a few times.

JOHN EPHLAND: *Both of you seem pretty restless when it comes to making music. What makes your music sound different?*

JONI MITCHELL: What opened the door for me was that my left hand couldn't get at the chords that I heard in my head. So I tuned the guitar to the chords that I heard in my head. [Folk musician] Eric Andersen showed me open G and D modal tuning. After that, I never played in standard tuning.

CASSANDRA WILSON: That's what I started out doing: playing guitar and singing Joni Mitchell songs. But it was something I had stored away.

JM: What years?

CW: It was '74, '75, '76.

JM: And coffeehouses were still around?

CW: In Jackson, Mississippi, no less. Check that out. I figured out the tuning on [Mitchell's] "For The Roses," and that was it. I was gone. I was taken by the tunings. There was Miles, I remember, when I was four or five; then when I got to be 15, there was Joni. The tunings were the thing. That's what opened up everything for me.

JM: It's that widened harmony that they create.

CW: There's a resonance.

JM: And even just simple bar chords. You can make instant music with them all, with those really wide chords. First of all, you can't get them on a guitar without the tuning. It's physically impossible. You widen the orchestral breadth of the instrument considerably. You've dipped it down into the upper-bass range, for one thing. You've got a lot more bottom on the music than the normal guitar. And there are inversions that it couldn't have been possible to finger.

CW: Unless you have really beautiful, strong, wide hands, you can't get the same kind of resonance inside of a Spanish tuning.

JM: Because the strings are so tight.

CW: Once you find the place for it, the guitar speaks. The only problem is my bass player complains. Because when we do the open tunings, we're off into his space. We overlap.

JM: Now, when I add bass, the bass player wants to go polka-dotting along on the bottom. Especially in pop music. He wants to come in and stay in. I think, "Bump, bump, bump," kind of four-on-the-floor almost, only a little more creative, but not much. So he's putting dark polka-dots across the whole thing. So I'm saying to bass players, "Do you have to stay in all the time? Couldn't you go up in the mid-range and play a counter-melody?" . . . There's a lot of quotes from Stravinsky in my music, if you listen. From *Rite of Spring*. It's a little jazzy, but it's not jazz. It's jazzy in that the harmony is wider, but jazz has its own harmonic laws.

JE: *You're breaking up stuff and you're making your own music.*

JM: According to the guy who wrote a book on jazz, [multi-instrumentalist] Victor Feldman, he defined it and locked it into harmonic laws. Victor Feldman apparently wrote a technical teaching book or some kind of book on jazz harmony [*Musicians Guide To Chord Progressions*]. We were playing on a date. What was it? "Moon At The Window." Victor was playing vibes. Well, on this one, he got really uptight. I thought the words were bothering him because he's a family man and it was about people with the incapacity to love, and he had a very loving family. I thought the words must be bothering him. I said, "Are the words bothering you?" He said, "I hate the harmony and the harmonic movement." I had to stop and send him home. I said, "You can't play on something that you hate!" I played the piece for Sarah Vaughan. She had a comment on it: "That's a strange form," she said to me. I said, "It's not really a strange form, it's an old standard form. It has a verse at the beginning that never comes back, then it's got A-B-C three-part melody like most standards do. There's one chord that changes the interval as it goes into the C section that's a bit shocking. I don't know what it is, whether it's a fourth or—I don't know technically what it is. It comes in a little bit odd, but it's a good odd. It's no odder than any change in life. It's kind of like a "but." The thing is drifting off . . . "but." That's how I think that chord works. It sets up an alternative view point.

JE: *So you were breaking the rules?*

JM: I don't think there are any rules left to break. But she thought so. Wayne Shorter came in, and he's the broadest musician that I've ever worked with. He knows the numerical language, the alphabetical language, and the flyshit, yet he chooses to play through metaphor, as I do. He's the only metaphor guy I know.

CW: Couldn't you find a classical musician that understands?

JM: I'm sure there would be somebody if you knew where to look; but a lot of times, classical musicians can't interpolate. They've always had the guidelines someone else wrote. It kind of kills their ability to improvise, in a lot of cases. Not all. But I think you have to grow up doing both.

JE: *When you say "improvise," what does that mean?*

JM: Making it up [*laughs*], as opposed to reading it.

JE: *What do you think, Cassandra?*

CW: What's the Jazz Age? What is improvisation? What is jazz?

JM: It's a fine line.

JE: *We seem to live in a time where there's a hardening of terms.*

CW: I didn't think about jazz when I started listening to Joni. I think everything we've produced in America is jazz.

JE: *Everything we do is jazz?*

CW: Yeah. Because we've learned how to improvise.

JE: *That's interesting, Cassandra. Have you been thinking about this long, that everything we do in America is jazz? I mean, it swings, too. Right? Excuse me for bringing up Wynton [Marsalis], but . . .*

CW: While I eat?!

"The view may not be the greatest, but it's theirs" read the caption in the March 20, 1966, *Detroit News Pictorial Magazine*. Joni and Chuck Mitchell were photographed at their boho chic top floor apartment in the nineteenth-century Verona building. *Photo by Edwin C. Lombardo/Detroit News*

"Taping a folk song, the young performers can practice without disturbing anyone," noted the *Detroit News*. Chuck remembers that Joni brought the reel-to-reel tape recorder with her from Toronto, after their 1965 wedding in suburban Rochester, Michigan. *Photo by Edwin C. Lombardo/Detroit News*

Joni and Chuck Mitchell were friends with Marji Kunz, fashion writer for the *Detroit Free Press*, and were pressed into service to pose as a bridal couple for the paper's February 1967 bridal fashion supplement. *Via newspapers.com, reprinted by permission of the Detroit Free Press*

Joni was photographed by Canadian music writer Larry LeBlanc at the Mariposa Folk Festival outside Toronto in 1969. She had been out of the spotlight for a while, but she knew LeBlanc from her Yorkville coffeehouse days and sat for an interview and photographs. *Photo by Larry LeBlanc*

Joni, who was involved with James Taylor for a time, was introduced as a "special friend" when he brought her out to duet on his song "You Can Close Your Eyes," at Queens College, New York, December 19, 1970. *Photo by Sherry Rayn Barnett Photography*

Joni refused some obvious interviews and agreed to some unusual ones, such as a 1988 request from *Quintessential Covina*, a local cable access TV show in California. Here she talks to the crew in her manager's office. *Photo by Marty Getz*

Joni appeared at the New Orleans Jazz Heritage Festival on May 6, 1995, playing a set that ignored her early pop hits and focused on her more recent work, including "Amelia," "Happiness Is the Best Facelift," and "Hejira." *Photo by Robert Jr. Whitall*

It was singer-songwriter (and friend) Eric Andersen who showed Joni how to play guitar using open tunings during one of his visits to Detroit, a momentous creative tool for her in the coming years. Here Joni and Eric enjoy a reunion outside the Bottom Line in New York City, in 1995. *Photo by Ebet Roberts*

JE: *I find what both of you sing draws me in. You each ask the listener to get closer as opposed to what belters do with their singing.*

JM: Belters tend to be showy, not intimate. We can probably both belt, if you like that kind of theater. I'm not sure that I do. It's like grandstanding to me. I said to Mingus, "Who's your favorite singer?" expecting Bessie [Smith] or Billie Holiday. He said Judy Garland—a grander, showier kind of singing. It's an interesting question. We both could sing that way, I'm sure.

CW: How do you get a voice like that? And how are you able to maintain a voice like that? How can you sing night after night after night at full broth and not rip your throat out? I'm not into that. I'm a Miles Davis child.

JM: Miles is my favorite singer, and probably yours, too [*laughs*]. So tasteful.

CW: The first Miles I heard was *Sketches* [*Of Spain*]. That was just so damn expansive. I'm a Miles fan. I love all of his work. There's specific periods that I bond to. It's nostalgia, though. But I listen to it all. I love it all.

JM: Miles was a fine, fine sonic innovator. And some of the music of the bands he inspired, and kicked into gear, that's some of the finest music I've ever heard. . . . The later stuff, I think he had less inspiration. It took him longer to play. It seems like he stood around more. He was so pure. He really waited until he heard something the he felt.

CW: So much of it has to do with the emotions.

JM: I'm at that place now, in a way. I'm almost too picky to go on. I'm still making the music, and I've got some new ideas. But you get narrower, in a way. It takes more and more to get you off. Mingus, at the end, couldn't stand anything except a couple of Charlie Parker records. He couldn't stand his own music. He'd go, "He's falsifying his emotion. That ain't shit." He heard all the effort people put forth and very little purity and sincerity. I get that way sometimes. My jive detector gets too sensitive and music just sounds awful to me. All of it. . . . In a certain way, we do most of our enthusiastic listening in our youth. It's the backdrop for our courtships, and you stow it and you're sentimental. The songs with the Pioneers, Roy Rogers' backup band, I'm just thrilled listening to those old songs. That's the music of my preteens. It's much better music than I realized as a child. Sentimental, kind of cornball, classic cowboy stuff. I never was much of a country & western fan, but I love listening to that. It swings. It's got that element of jazz in it.

JE: *And their hearts are in it so much.*

JM: And every track is excellent.

CW: Like *Turbulent Indigo*. I heard it the other night. The song is, "You've made everything I fear and everything I . . ." There's this passage or this space where there are two bars and it's a repeating thing. For me, it's the epitome of the economy of motion. Two changes that just tear everything up. Tears everybody up. And it's only the space of two bars. It's in the middle of it and comes out of nowhere. It's like harmonically, how does this fit in here? Where does it come from?

JM: Weird things. It comes out of the tunings.

CW: I know. That's *you*. And I'm always prepared for it. But this one, I wasn't prepared for it because it's so spare. It's only *two bars*.

JM: Or Miles plays this flat note on the end of "It Never Entered My Mind." This is a really early recording. He draws this note flat, and he holds it flat all the way out. If he played it in pitch, it wouldn't do this to you, what it does. It's the saddest note.

CW: It's not a flatted fifth, is it? [*laughs*]

JM: No! It's a flatted *flat*! Know what I mean? It is FLAT! It's like, out of tune. But if he played it in tune, it wouldn't have the impact. It's the saddest note in the world. It's like he just lost it on this note. Sometimes I go through these periods where I get temporary perfect pitch and everything is driving me nuts! I go and put that thing on.

CW: That's why you had to find those guitars. Because of the tunings. I deal with maybe two or three tunings. I can't imagine what you have to deal with because I know you must have hundreds of them.

JM: I have 60. But that's too many.

Now we're in the lounge of the Hotel Nikko. The bar band starts their set playing Thelonious Monk's "'Round Midnight."

JM: [*To Cassandra*] What do you think about Monk? You're also a piano player. Does he have an influence on you?

CW: Definitely. Monk is the main influence. I took classical piano lessons for seven years, so that was my first introduction to music formally. But Monk, *Monk's Dream*—that album was one of the first albums, along with *Sketches Of Spain*, that I heard as a kid. When I stared playing piano, those were the first piano sounds I heard. Later came the classical things: Tchaikovsky, Chopin, Ravel, that whole piano tradition out of Europe. The first sounds I heard from the piano were this weird kind of [makes '*tink tink tink tink*' sounds]. That's the way I play piano now. Economy playing.

JM: I just discovered Monk two nights ago. I knew that name. I heard all kinds of stories, like, "Monk could paint! He painted a bowl of flowers and an ax!" But I never really knew what he was about. Monk hasn't worked his influence on me, but he's going to. The first thing that caught my eye was that he played flat-fingered like Laura Nyro, instead of with an arch, which is hard, I think, for going fast. Then, of course, the obvious, which everybody notes, is how he's always working from the top down and cross-handing. But the thing that really amazed me is the economy, the minimalism of it. How beautiful it was! I'm a chord-puller. I like hybrid colors, like triads or full-fisted chords.

JE: *I can tell by the way you play your guitar that you do that.*

JM: But this guy is linear and very percussive. On the left hand, he may be pulling totally tonal chords, or sometimes just rocking from the black to the white to the black to the white keys. Very, very minimal, but god! When it fibers in with the other players, a lot of times, if the piano player has a lot of chops—this has been my experience in hiring piano players for my band—they get really pianissimo on you and they start scribbling over all these intricate things and they take up a lot of space and they over-embellish.

CW: That's why I don't have a piano player.

JM: It's hard to find a minimalist.

CW: They figure: "OK—88 keys? I've got to play every one of them. 12 notes? I've got to play every note." And it's the instrument itself, you can't really blame them. Unless you really have the serious discipline and you can focus on bringing the piano into a small space, condensing it, it's hard to do that. I think it's hard for a lot of pianists. Now the old cats, who used to comp with the singers, understood how to do that. A lot of space.

JM: Leaving the vocalist room to breathe.

CW: And for the imagination.

JM: Miles, too. He was Mr. Economy. If you don't feel anything, don't play it.

JE: *The two of you are band players as well as vocalists. But you also imply—Cassandra, you do it more than Joni—the use of space. You both imply a lot, and I sense you don't feel like you have to say everything and put everything out there. You leave stuff out so people can fill it in for themselves.*

JM: Speaking more for Cassandra, because of my wordiness, I am first responsible to my words. So when I play with a band, I have to be the leader. Well, the words have to be the leader. And if there's any room for anyone to get in, well, good luck! We did a jam one time, and it was ridiculous. It was Herbie Hancock's pilot for a series [Coast to Coast, in 1987 —Ed.]. Two drummers: Vinnie Colaiuta and I forget the other one [*Steve Thornton —Ed.*]; two horn players, Wayne Shorter and David Sanborn; Bobby McFerrin and myself. And we're doing "Hejira" and "Furry Sings The Blues." Now, those are two very moody songs. You got all these guys waiting to get in the gaps. Two horn players and a scat singer, so to speak—that is to say, a wordless singer—waiting for a hole to open up for them to get an "ooh aah" out. There's hardly any. A lot of people who heard it thought it was successful. I wish sometimes I could write a song with less story. Let me try it: "The wind, the wind, oh the lovely wind. La la." [*laughs*] You can take a lot of space between those and then give them eight bars to blow around!

CW: There's something about your phrasing that implies space. It's the most unique phrasing. When I first heard the way that you would say all the things you would say, and when I started writing songs, I would try to do that. I would try to write poetry and sing it and I would just sort of—I couldn't get it all in! That's a special art. Not everybody has that.

JE: *This is one of the reasons we got you two together—we kind of saw Cassandra coming from more of a jazz-oriented background and going toward pop music, however savage a description that is.*

CW: Dangerous. Dangerous.

JM: Cassandra, forgive me, but from the little I know, that doesn't sound quite accurate. She's got a classical piano background, she's listening to jazz as a young person, but she's also a singer of folk music. Right?

CW: What do you call all that?

JM: That's just good American fun! [*laughs*] I don't think we're coming from anything that radically different. I'm coming first from classical music, a couple years of piano where they crack you at the knuckles. I could memorize faster than I could read. I was not going to be literate, apparently. Well, as it turned out, I didn't need to. There were rare occasions that I did, but I just needed an interpreter. You hire a guy to write the lead sheets out. Then you're home free. It's an important thing. I mean, I wish I had it.

CW: Well, it's important to have the tools to communicate. Especially in the jazz world. If you don't have those tools, there's no respect there, on a certain level. I treasure both of them now. I'm glad to have it all, but I think there's a certain kind of opening you get when you approach your instrument intuitively. The trade-off is, because you don't know the rules, you can open doors, open windows. That's what the tunings were for me. It was like a way out. When I first tapped back into it, it was like, *whew*!

JM: It's a tool for discovery. That's the great thing about it. It's like a no-man's land. It's uncharted territory.

JE: *You could say you both haven't gone from point A to point B. Instead, you've always been where you are all along.*

CW: We are all complete. I like that.

JONI SAID

On Some Famous Female Fans

"Monday night I played Fez, in New York, Chrissie [Hynde] came down, and I forget what she was drinking, but it seemed like she consumed quite a lot of it, and all through the show she was like, 'Rock it, Joni!' . . . There was a bit of fur flying between her and Carly Simon. As I understand it, Carly told her to shut up, and she wrapped her hands around Carly's throat."

—to Morrissey and David Wild, *Rolling Stone*, 1997

JONI SAID

On "Hip"

"Instead of enthusiasm for something original, you hear, 'Well, what are we going to do with that?' The system trains people to be purchasers manipulated by hip, in and out, hot and not hot. But hip is hindsight, so I stood my ground and plowed on. If you avoid doing what's cool, you won't have bell-bottom pants on your songs down the road."

—to Carrie Bell, *Billboard*, August 22, 1998

THE UNFILTERED JONI MITCHELL

Dave DiMartino | August 1998 | *Mojo* (UK)

Dave DiMartino interviewed Joni in Los Angeles, where he was based, for *Mojo*, at a time when she had gotten past some of her worst times, creatively and personally—the 1980s—and was starting to pile up professional honors.

Was the music business starting to realize what it had, before it was gone? But no worries, she wasn't mellowing in any way. She castigated the Rock and Roll Hall of Fame for waiting three years after she was eligible before inducting her in 1997—and it's true, the hall hadn't been as slow with the music world's male icons.

DiMartino gleaned some intriguing facts: that Bob Dylan wanted to learn some of her open guitar tunings (she discouraged him), that she admired the paintings of Don Van Vliet (Captain Beefheart), and that she was delighted Janet Jackson was a fan.

Dave also got the backstory about why ex-boyfriend Graham Nash, who had accepted her Rock and Roll Hall of Fame statuette in her place, presented it to her later wrapped in a black plastic trash bag. The writer even revealed to the singer a long-ago, accidental hair-pulling incident in which she was a victim. Happily, she had forgotten about it.

Joni was no longer guarding the secret of her unwed motherhood. She had been reunited with her daughter, Kilauren Gibb, a thirty-two-year-old former model, a year earlier, in 1997. Stories about Joni and Kilauren were popping up in the tabloids, and people were recognizing her in airports—more than usual, she thought. Joni had plenty to say about their reunion. She talked about her song "Stay in Touch," and her relationship with Kilauren, which hadn't yet begun to fray, torn asunder by issues of abandonment and control. Mothers and daughters were on her mind; she also talked about how her own mother, Myrtle—often disapproving of Joni's boyfriends and lifestyle—had been perturbed by her song "Facelift."

Note: Joni said in a later radio interview that she didn't say "manure in a pasture" in this *Mojo* interview, but "Man o'War in a pasture," referring to the famed racehorse who, like her, had been put out to retire and graze. (See page 245.) It has been corrected here to reflect her original intent. —Ed.

It's a Saturday night in Burbank, California, and perhaps 200 invited guests are sitting in a circular arrangement of plush chairs, overstuffed sofas, even cross-legged on the floor. Wines and bottled water abound. At the centre of this velvet doughnut is a small, round stage, upon which stand Joni Mitchell and three, sometimes four, other musicians. Video cameras record every detail of this, the second of two private concerts, for a television special to be aired later in the year. Rosanna Arquette introduces Mitchell on both nights.

Joni's paintings are everywhere, hanging on the curtained perimeter of the circle and exhibited proudly on the curved pathway which led the small audience to their seats. Her friends are everywhere, too. There among her dazzling band—including drummer Brian Blade, pedal-steel guitarist Greg Leisz, and trumpeter Mark Isham—stands bassist Larry Klein, Mitchell's former husband of 10 years, whom she'll briefly and conspicuously kiss midway through her performance. And there in the audience is the familiar, greying figure of Graham Nash, her celebrated beau from earlier days. And tonight, the composer of Our House has work to do.

Sure enough, Nash heads to the stage with a peculiar object in his hand, wrapped in what appears to be a disposable plastic bag. It is, says he, the trophy owed to Joni for her induction into the Rock and Roll Hall of Fame last year. The one she never got because she never showed up to claim it. "You had your reasons," Nash says, diplomatically, "but I'm sure they're all fine." Looking at Nash—bemusedly or begrudgingly, it's hard to tell—she grasps the object in its sloppy wrapper and deadpans: "It's perfect in a garbage bag."

One has to love Joni Mitchell, and these days one does. Since 1994's *Turbulent Indigo* netted the singer two Grammy Awards—including Album Of The Year—Mitchell has been on the receiving end of a non-stop series of honours, awards, and the sort of accolades usually given posthumously to bluesmen most decent humans have never heard of. Among them: the Billboard Century Award, the National Academy of Songwriters Lifetime Achievement Award, the Canadian Governor General's Performing Arts Award, even Sweden's Polar Music Prize.

Such awards usually indicate a career nearing the end of its creative lifespan, but in Mitchell's case that's simply laughable. She's been *out there* in 1998—touring with Bob Dylan and Van Morrison on a seven-date concert series verging on the historic, taking part in a memorable Los Angeles Walden Woods benefit (alongside an all-female cast including Sheryl Crow, Stevie Nicks, Björk, Shawn Colvin, Paula Cole and Trisha Yearwood), and completing *Taming The Tiger*, her 17th album. To be released 31 full years after she signed to Reprise Records in 1967, it is as fresh and vital as anything she has ever recorded, and will not come packaged in a plastic garbage bag.

Sitting outside a restaurant she frequents in Brentwood—an area now famous for its association with disgraced celebrity athlete O.J. Simpson—Mitchell is chatty, warm, an excellent smoker and, frankly, among the most magnetic personalities I've ever encountered. She zigs and zags from subject to subject; she is highly opinionated and visibly proud of it. She talks about nearly everything, including her reunion last year with daughter Kilauren—after giving her up for adoption 35 years ago—and her own mother, now 86, and the subject of *Taming the Tiger*'s song Facelift.

So outspoken is Joni Mitchell that she and her publicist are discussing the downside of complete frankness. In these days of Lilith Fairs and tired topics like "women in rock", the press—god bless 'em—continue to run familiar female names by Joni seeking assessment and, ideally, condemnation from the queen herself. Sheryl Crow? Alanis Morissette? Jewel? Even Rickie Lee Jones? Mitchell notes a previous reporter she'd encountered "laid on me questions like, 'What do you think of so and so?' and I deflected and deflected and deflected and finally said something. And I thought, If they cut *that* off and *that* off—and you know they will—he got the dirt. He *got* it." She pauses. "I'm getting a rep for that."

So much for the mudwrestling questions.

It seems like you've been surfacing more lately. A conscious move on your part?

No. I guess things started to take off in the last five years mainly because of the Billboard award. After that, it was a series of sort of copycat crimes, where people remembered me and I was the recipient of a lot of awards in a row. And then I won a Grammy—well, two Grammys, one for the artwork, which also pleased me very much.

I'm really a painter at heart and I can say this now since, you know, Kilauren has come along. Music was a hobby for me at art school, and art was serious. Art was always what I was going to do; I was going to be an artist. But the time that I went to art school was very disappointing—although I romanticised the time that Van Gogh went to art school. I thought that to go to the French Academy at that particular time—even though as a female I would have been considered an associate no matter how good I was—was the best education you could get. And yet in Van Gogh's letters to Bernard, he's begging him to get out of there, saying, "They're providing you with subject matter—if they have their way, they'll make a mistress of your art, and you won't know your true love should you come upon it." He was begging him to get out and just paint from his heart at that time. That was an eye-opener to me—when I read that, I thought, I'm going to give *myself* the art education: I'm going to paint the way I want to, never mind the art world. So I went back to painting landscapes and my friends and cats and not making a mistress of it—stopping trying to be innovative and *moderne*, and painting the kind of paintings that I can't afford to buy that I want to have in my house, you know?

The paintings on display on Saturday night were gorgeous.

People like that kind of painting. The art world will apologise for it if they write about it, you know what I mean? The art world is a funny world—I'm glad I never had to be a part of the gallery scene or anything.

Do you know Don Van Vliet, Captain Beefheart?

Yeah, he's a good painter.

He retired from making music in the early '80s, ostensibly to paint. I spoke with the man who handles his work professionally, and he

mentioned that it was tough for any musician to be taken seriously in the art world unless he devoted his time solely to art. He said it would take a minimum of 10 years for him to be away from the music business to be taken seriously at all.

Absolutely. You're regarded as a dilettante. That's because—here's my opinion on that—America is far away from a renaissance spirit. I've seen shows passing through Rome, the poet as painter, Ferlinghetti's drawings on display. That's a renaissance culture: they understand it, condone it. Why shouldn't a poet be able to render? Not all of them can, but supposing they can? Don't rule it out.

You made that point very well on Saturday night when you mentioned what Georgia O'Keeffe said.

(*Quoting*) "Oh, I would've liked to be a musician, too, but you can't do both." It's a lot of work, you have to give up a certain amount of social-ising—but the way I learn anyway, everything that I admire sparks me: best teach it to me as admiration.

Funny, as a painter I have so many heroes. But as a musician I like one or two in each camp and then I don't like the rest. Like, I don't care for John Coltrane—many people think he's the greatest. Coltrane seems like he's on Valium to me. Charlie Parker, I see his greatness; then Wayne Shorter is a genius—he's a tributary of 'Trane, but he's got so much more breadth and mysticism and wit and passion and everything. So to me, Coltrane is kind of a stepping-off point to Wayne.

I have strong and strange opinions on things which are kinda controversial. As a painter I admire much. And it's been hard—like music, it's been hard to synthesize the many styles that I like. In art school I was criticised for painting in two or three schools at the same time. Music hybrids better than perhaps painting does immediately. I ended up kind of without a country—you know, musically speaking?

Do you derive the same degree of artistic satisfaction from painting as you do from music?

Yeah, as a painter there are so many painters that I bow to. I didn't like poetry, so the poetry that I made is the kind that I like better. So I don't like a lot of poets, and that seems to annoy people, that I'm dismissive of a lot of what they think are great poets. I'm with Nietzsche on the poets. He went into a long harangue: "The poet is the vainest of the vain, even before the ugliest of water buffalo does he fan his tail. I've looked among him for an honest man and all I've dredged up are old gods' heads. He muddies his waters that he might appear deep." That's one of my favourites. I can see the filler in [poetry]—I can see, a lot of times, the effort. It wasn't honest enough for me a lot of times. It was tipping its hat always to the Greeks and classicism in a certain stylistic way. I like Yeats, I love Yeats—the Yeats poem that I set to music [on Slouching Towards Bethlehem], though, I corrected . . . there were parts of it that I added; they let me do it, which was amazing. Because I think they sued Van Morrison for setting something. They just said, "You have to put 'adapted by'." And I think I did it pretty seamlessly because I understand his style—the third stanza is mine, and it's very much in the style of the first one, more so than his second stanza.

For that matter, on-stage you mentioned Bob Dylan's covering your own Big Yellow Taxi.

It's been so long since I heard it, but I don't think he ever mentions the taxi, he just goes straight to the tractor. It was on *Self Portrait*, I believe.

Actually the *Dylan* album, I think. But I wondered if you were as sensitive as the Yeats estate might be when someone was altering your own work.

Oh, no, no. And I love Bobby. I think Bobby thinks of himself as not friendly. I think he just thinks of himself that way. But I'm very fond of him, and over the years we've had a lot of encounters, and most of the discussion has been about painting, actually. No, he can do whatever he wants as far as I'm concerned (*laughs*). He's one of those people like Miles, you know? Even if he wasn't up to it that night—or I saw a performance where he just kinda cruised—whatever it was, I would always be curious about the next. Because he's kind of untouchable in a lot of ways.

And I love his writing—you know, not all of it. And I was a detractor in the beginning. In the beginning I thought he was a Woody Guthrie copycat. I never liked copycats, and I just found out why from these horoscope books that just came out. I'm born the Day of the Discoverer in the Week of Depth. I really love innovators. I love the first guy to put the flag at the North Pole; the guy that went there second doesn't interest me a lot of times. Although some could say that Wayne Shorter is the guy who got there second, but he took it somewhere. So Dylan went to Woody, and you have to build off of something. Not everybody comes out of the blue as a genuine muse—a real cosmic muse. It used to be that's what music was—but now it's formulated. And, especially, it's become a producers' art, who's an interior decorator basically.

Does Dylan know that you were initially a detractor?

Oh, I don't know if he knows that or not, but you know, the thing that turned me around was Positively 4th Street. It stopped me in my tracks, and I went, Oh my God—that's just great. We can write about anything now.

Because up 'til then, I was writing songs. And I wrote poetry in the closet because I didn't like it. I wrote it, I just rhymed, haha. Rhyming Joan, I guess. But I didn't care to show it to anybody, or I did it in school on assignment because I had to. And I was praised for it, but I just figured I got away with it. And songs I loved, stories I loved—I always loved stories from the moment I could understand English. Poetry was kind of like shelling sunflower seeds with your fingers—it just was too much work for too little return, a lot of times. I like things more plainspeak.

And the poems that I did like in school were very visual—and less diaphanous and cryptic. I think people like to say they understand it, but there's nothing really to understand. You can comb it and comb it for understanding, and it may produce a lot of thoughts, but it doesn't get to the heart of the matter clearly enough for me. Most poetry.

In high school, my teacher loved T.S. Eliot and we studied The Love Song Of J. Alfred Prufrock—which essentially needed a translation key to even begin to be deciphered by 14-year-olds. I'm not sure it should've been foisted on people who weren't willing and ready to explore it.

Not only that—but speaking as a poet, I write a song, say, Stay In Touch on this album, and I know what I wrote it about. When my daughter and her boyfriend came, Teddy heard it and said, "Kilauren, that song's about you." Well it was—it's about the beginning unsteadiness in a very passionate new relationship. Any time I have a passionate new relationship, that song will come to life in a new way. If it's overly explained, you rob the people whose lives it brushes up against of their own interpretation and their own experience.

I know how a song falls differently against your life many times. To keep it alive it has to—you're bringing new experience to it all the time, and it's not the experience you wrote it with, so it's open to interpretations. It's a kind of dead poet's society thing—tear those pages from your books. The songs shift around—either it means something to you or it doesn't. And that's one reason why I resent the "who is it about?" fixing it in time, "it's about that over there . . ." No it isn't, it's a mirror—and it reflects you if you take the time to look as you pass it by.

I'm sure you've had people picking apart your songs on the autobiographical level, saying this line is about that person . . .

And they assume that—the new press. The new press is so irresponsible they print their assumptions without using the word. I don't think they know the word 'assume' exists. They print it as a bald-ass fact, "When she wrote this, she meant this," like bad poetry teachers.

I'm still living here, and it's getting me in a lot of trouble, too. Especially if they name a person. Not To Blame caused a lot of friction. Some people said it's about O.J., and some people said it's about Jackson Browne, right? Well, it's about men who batter women—and it has some details that are specific and some that apply to a lot of different situations. It's about the kind of guy who goes around battering women—and if the shoe fits, wear it, you know (*laughs*)?

But there's still a lot personally revealed, I think. On the new album, there are lyrics referring to radio stations playing "genuine junk food for juveniles", and you're singing about "a runaway from the record biz". How do you view yourself as a record maker in the business of making records today?

The business—even the executives are kind of at the mercy of the Wall Street graph. The graph must go up. So it creates a kind of conservative poker playing. And they won't bet on any long shots. And among the long shots there are a lot of generalities. People over 30, especially people over 50. VH1, MTV—all of the outlets for music have been barred to me for many years, 20 years, for one reason or another. For mysterious reasons. In the beginning, when I first started, for the first five years I had no drums on my record, so I didn't go to AM radio. So even in the time when I was a *young* artist. You only get about five or six years before they're sick of you in the business generally, and they let you ride—they don't put any money or effort or interest into you, really. They just let you sit there like Man o'War in the pasture, as a procurer of young artists at the label. But they don't help you get your product to market.

Has that in any way affected your art, your music?

No, it hasn't at all. I was accused of pandering on *Dog Eat Dog*—and my manager told Thomas Dolby, who'd been hired as a colourist, to give me colours and get away. And he was comfortable with that, or so he said—but behind my back, my manager thought that if Thomas was producing it would create some more excitement. And so they negotiated that, and it caused a lot of trouble. And people said that I was selling out or pandering on that record. I wasn't.

What people don't know is I was a dancer—I like some disco. I don't belong to any camp. I like a little of this and a little of this and a little of that—and at any moment, I could be inspired to go in any one of those directions.

No, I've always kept my painting pure and I've always kept my music pure, that's one thing. No matter how disturbed I've been. My predicament wasn't one in which effort worked any way. I was just s*hut out*, period, after the *Mingus* album.

But, as you said, things have changed significantly since the Billboard award. Take the Swedish Polar Music Prize—how exactly did that come along for you?

They're trying to have a kind of Pulitzer Prize for music over there. It's fairly new. McCartney had been a recipient and Quincy Jones, and they have a pop and classical category.

Sounds like a wonderful idea.

Yeah, it was fun. I enjoyed the King, I really enjoyed his company, he was a character—kind of a hippie playboy guy.

Had you met any kings before?

No. He let me smoke, so that was good. I had to ask his permission, though. He smoked with me. He'd say he had to keep pace with me. So sometimes he'd say yes and sometimes he'd say no. Can I smoke now? "No." Well when can I smoke next? "I'll tell you." And he had a silver cigarette case, and he'd say. "OK, we will smoke now (*laughs heartily*)."

How did you enjoy the Walden Woods benefit?

Oh, I loved it. I thought it was a beautiful night. People were talking about it for days afterwards. Weeks, of course, doesn't happen in this town. Maybe even weeks—weeks later *I* was still talking about it.

I've played with a big orchestra before, but never so comfortably. Maybe because I'm more comfortable—maybe because always I had to sing and play and play *with* them with very little rehearsal. This time I just had to stand up and sing, so I was liberated from having to plunk. And I loved the arrangement—I sang Stormy Weather with 60 pieces. The most beautiful arrangement we could find of it. Frank Sinatra had recorded it several times, but this one—I forget the arranger's name, but we just copped it—you couldn't beat it, it was so gorgeous. And to feel all those strings come rising up around you, you know?

When I got to the hall that day, it was the first day that we went to our dressing room, and we'd been rehearsing with a bit of the orchestra, the central kind of little jazz group that was the centrepiece of the orchestra. It was the first time I'd gone to my dressing room, and there was a guy taking me up the stairs to my dressing room, and I was kind of huffing at the second landing and I said, Why would you put the oldest one on the third floor and the young ones all down on the stage? It should be the other way around. So I put all my stuff down and came back down to rehearsal, and I played with this big orchestra—I went back up to my dressing room, we started to do make-up, and when I looked at my face

I was glowing—and I realised I came up those three flights of stairs two at a time after playing with that orchestra. That's how incredible it was. So I have to do that again.

Tonight I'm going to record with Herbie Hancock, he's doing an album of Gershwin tunes. Stevie Wonder's going to be there too. I've got a choice of three songs. I think with Frank Sinatra's death and all, there's a resurgence of interest in that era. Of eras of music, I would say I'm a swing era baby. I love the swing beat. Even though my music doesn't reflect all the kinds of music that I love, it eventually will.

After watching you do Marvin Gaye's Trouble Man on Saturday night, it struck me as odd that you've never recorded a complete album of cover songs.

I've never been *able* to. By contract. It was disallowed.

Would you like to do one?

I'm *going* to do one. I'd love to.

What you brought to that song was fabulous.

Oh, I love that song. I've played that song over and over—I'd only do the ones that I play over and over and over. I own them in a certain way because of my love of them. I love that song. I sang that at the Stormy Weather concert also.

That was quite a group—how did you all relate to each other?

We didn't really—aside from the duet that I did, there wasn't that much co-mingling. People came—they kind of kept us apartheid in case the fur would fly, I don't know. I saw Stevie [Nicks] because she was before me, and Björk and I worked together. I love Björk. No, I think we were all a little out of our idiom—it was hard work, everybody was a little nervous, it was just beautiful. We're going to do it again in San Francisco in September, taping it there.

At the show with Dylan and Van, you all played so very well that I wondered if you felt you all rose to the occasion due to the company? I've seen Van play many, many times, yet when he played Moondance, it was as if I'd never heard it before.

I think we all *did* kick each other up. Bobby—I don't want to be indiscreet to Bobby, but it's beautiful what he said. I don't want to be a tattletale here.

We can go off the record, if you'd like . . .

Well it's for his sake—and it's kind of a brag on my part. I treasure it, but it's not something I really can say publicly, I don't think—just as a person . . . [off the record stuff follows] . . . So anyway he greeted me after the show in Vancouver, he went on last that night, and it was a difficult show for me because I'm not used to playing big sports arenas, and there was a lot of milling, a lot of going for beer, and a lot of talking really loud through all of the shows. It seemed to be that that crowd had come for the beer and the event itself—not to listen, just to be at it, you know? And I thought that was a shame. And you have three people that are really listened-to artists, it's OK if there's no lyrical text or something, but I assumed that this was gonna be a writers' tour, so I picked a set for Bobby. And I think he did for me, too—because he put in one of the best line-ups of songs that I've seen him do for a long time. All of that you can quote me on.

But when he came off-stage, he was there to greet me, and it takes a moment to kind of recover—and I wasn't sure if it was a good experience. I thought we played well in spite of it, but that we weren't properly listened to. It was the first one, you know. Then I realised it was just the nature of the crowd. But Bobby was standing and he was very excited, and he said, (*affecting Dylan's voice*) "Oh those chords, those chords— you've got to show me some of those chords. I love those chords that you play. We're gonna sound like an old hillbilly band when we go on." I don't know whether that's indiscreet or not—what do you think?—I'm so sensitive to it. I said, Bobby you don't want to learn these chords. First of all you have to learn tunings, and tunings are a pain in the butt. And you won't have nearly the fun that you're having now with your music.

When I saw him it was almost as if he was taking songs that he hadn't written and making them his own, in a strange way.

Um-hum, um-hum—that's what I'm doing. Bobby and I played in Tokyo a few years back, three or four I guess, and he called me up just before we went over and he said, "I forgot how to *sing*—but I remember now,

I remember now. The trouble is they want me to do all those Bob Dylan songs—and they're so heavy." And that's exactly what I feel about my material. It's like Meryl Streep at a certain point decided to do comedy. I've done drama, he's done drama; we've done it very well. But we both have a sense of humour. His perhaps is more apparent in his writing than mine is. It's in there, here and there, there's a little bit of comic relief—you know, "Drink up now, it's getting on time to close." But people don't even seem to notice, they're so stunned by the drama of it all, you know?

And I started doing these cover songs with my hands free, like I say—the liberty in it is just exciting, you know? I'd like to make a whole show out of Gershwin. The songs that I write, you see, they're not really so much for singing—they're more dramatic. Like Bob's work, the prettiness of the singer, in the later work especially, is not the point—the point is to bring the words to life like a Shakespearean soliloquy. If you have to talk 'em, whatever it takes, you know? Whereas these old songs don't have a lot of words and there's plenty of time to ride the note and float, and they're real singerly material, and I don't write stuff like that.

It seems to me that maybe around *Hejira* time—not so much that you shifted styles per se, but . . .

The poet took over the singer.

There were melodies that anyone could cover in some of your earlier songs, and it would make perfect sense—they were gorgeous songs that existed unto themselves. And by no means are the newer songs inferior on any level . . .

The writing is superior, really—but, like rap, it's at the cost of melody to a certain degree. Although . . . it's more like jazz melody, it's conversational improvisation. If it didn't have words on it, it's conversational improvisation around a known melody. Except I don't really state the melody.

I had a difficult time trying to describe that when reviewing your show; I compared the speak-singing style to later Lou Reed . . .

It's the same thing that Bob does. The poet takes over. Maybe I guess Lou Reed, although I'm not as familiar with his material as Bob's. The point in the performance is to make the words come alive. Like Ella

Fitzgerald is a beautiful singer, she has perfect pitch and perfect time, but she doesn't illuminate the words—she just sings through it. "S'wonderful, s'marvellous"—that's the way it's written, she sings through it. Whereas Billie Holiday makes you hear the content and the intent of every word that she sings—even at the expense of her pitch or tone. So of the two, Billie is the one that touches me the deepest, although I admire perfect pitch and perfect time.

And you could have that at the expense of the read, but I don't think anybody could have perfect pitch, perfect time and colour the words, right? I'd sacrifice the perfect time and the perfect pitch to colour the words, but that's because I like the text. Dylan does that. He never reads the same thing the same two days in a row—and as a result, you can almost see his state of mind in the reading. And I respect that, I think that's emotional honesty, and when you have this complex creature, the singer-songwriter . . .

Everybody's a singer-songwriter now, but not everybody should be, not everybody can do all of these things, and yet everybody does. And that's why I think music has gone downhill. It used to take three—a great lyricist and a great musician and then a great singer. Like with Frank, and that's why that stuff is so enduring—because you had three gifted people doing it. Now you've got people, they're not really a great singer or a great writer or a great musician doing it, so the standards have dropped severely. And ironically, at the same time that the standards dropped, the machines have increased. These people have 20 times the distribution, so the bad stuff is really *everywhere*.

The album that has one or two good songs, the rest being filler . . .

It's hard to write 10 good songs. I know the fellow that runs my Website said, "You used to put records out one a year." And I did for a long time—and I think that the standard of writing on them is pretty even. People listen to it and for one year they've got three favourites, and then they put it on five years later and some of the ones they didn't even notice suddenly mean something, because they're all about different themes. So either you've experienced that—and if you have, then you're closer to the songs, so you know.

But music now is so disposable. Like this new album—I'm very proud of it, I think the standard is high, I'm very proud of the composition, the tools were available. I play nearly everything, and I guided everything into place on *Court And Spark*—even though I didn't play it, I *sang* it, and then they played it from that and it was pretty much as writ. *Hissing Of Summer Lawns* was a little looser—I let people stretch out, and as result of that it had a jazzier flavour, because they used their own harmonies instead of mine. People weren't really ready for jazz in pop music at that time—jazz-tingeing.

With those older things—lines like "bombers into butterflies"—do you feel like that was a different Joni?

Yeah, there are some things that I'm prejudiced against in my early work. I think they're the work of an ingénue, that I'm miscast in them now, I don't do them for that reason. However I saw this female impersonator, John Kelly, and he did a lot of my early work beautifully—from a spirit point of view, beautifully—and he's in his mid-thirties I think. And in drag, to boot, and singing in a full tenor voice, some of them, not even imitating me, just singing them with all his heart. He sang Night In The City, which I think of as a childlike ditty, and like I was a ghost at my own funeral I saw the audience respond and I heard the song, it gave me some perspective on it that I never had. Not that in a limited show that I feel the need to include it. I'm out for a long time. What I felt when I put this show together, the necessity was to run by these songs that had become considered obscure and difficult. Any chance I get to air them and run them by people so they can make some new memories against these songs . . . they're too good to kill is the way I figure it. So I chose to use this run as an opportunity to revitalise them.

You, Dylan and Van Morrison seem nearly alone among your contemporaries in that your newest work is treated by critics with as much respect and enthusiasm as your earlier material. You don't really seem to be as much tied into a time as others.

Well, they try to tie you to a time whether you're tied to a time or not. Like I've seen recently, "that folk singer from the '60s." I haven't been a folk singer since 1964—and I didn't make my first record since 1967. When I started making my own music, that's not folk music—it has its roots in, and it's classical. The first music that I made that was my own, when I stopped singing folk songs, was rooted in Chuck Berry. Big Yellow Taxi is rooted in Chuck Berry. In my pre-teen years, my best friends were classical musicians. And my parents, we only had five records in the house.

What were they?

Clair De Lune. My father had a Harry James record and a Leroy Anderson record, he was a trumpet player. And my mother had Clair De Lune, Brahms' Lullaby, a lot of classicism, beautiful melodies. And I had personally, until I became a dancer and won records . . . because people didn't buy records like they do now. I've got a godson who lives in a trailer park who's got 50 CDs. These things are expensive. People charge now; they didn't when I was coming up. If you didn't have the cash for it you didn't get it. And I used to go down and take the records out of the brown paper and go in the listening booth and listen to Rachmaninov's [*sic*] Rhapsody On A Theme By Paganini. It was like 75 cents but we couldn't afford it. I'd go downtown and put it on and listen to it and swoon, a couple of plays, and put it back in the paper, and put it back on the shelf. Like Russia or something, it seems like now.

I was wondering when I saw you get that Rock and Roll Hall of Fame Award from Graham on Saturday night—was that staged, or was that really the first time you received it?

No, he'd brought it the night before, and accidentally a friend of mine, Chris, one of the boys who sang with me, broke it, and the top piece came off of it, but he was scared to tell me—he was horrified, he went home and he couldn't sleep. But he did bring it in the garbage bag like that. So I laughed.

Graham has a very good attitude about the Rock and Roll Hall of Fame. My father would have the same attitude. Unfortunately I do not have a good attitude about the Rock and Roll Hall of Fame, and you can say this. It was a dubious honour—in that they held me out conspicuously for three years. To go, Oh, thank you, thank you—I mean, having conspicuously ostracised me for a few projects, how can I be gracious, really?

And the other complaint that I had is that it was gonna cost about 20 grand to take my family—that they charge, and they get a free concert out of you. It's exploitative, I'm sorry. Brian calls it the Hall of Shame, and in a certain way I think it is. It's mercenary, and they're putting everybody in—so the honour is dubious on that level. It's not really rarefied. The best records don't make that record of the year, the best records do not win the Grammys. The best do not win, so all this is is perpetuating the falseness of the victors, you know? It's not correcting history as it should be. There's a lot that's in there that's great, but . . .

When you get these accolades do you feel, good, you deserve it? Embarrassed? Too little too late? Or who cares—it's meaningless because the best things are never recognized?

Every one was different. Most of them fell short of honouring me. If I'm truly honoured, I should be humbled, and most of them made me arrogant, because they didn't seem to know why they were putting me across, only that they should. And yeah, that kind of ticked me off. And then there were tailgaters too—people rubbing up and taking credit for things more than they're deserving of, and that's always annoying too. And again my depth gets in the way. Because I know Graham just has a straight-ahead healthy attitude that it's an honour to be in there. And you know, coming from Manchester or whatever—I come from Saskatoon. It's more of a boondocky place than Manchester, really, although it is the centre of the North American continent, pretty much. It can have that claim to fame, I guess . . .

Yeah, I'm a deep thinker, so I thought a lot, What is honour? I think about things like that. The Governor General award—the Governor General truly honoured me, and I blushed like a schoolgirl when he gave me that award. And it was very sweet, and it was kind of private, I don't need to repeat what he said. But I enjoyed that, but the applause was way too long and he kept saying, "Get back up and take it."

I don't really like a lot of applause. I'm not a natural performer, you know. I'm kind of ambiverted, in that I have hambone—I have enough ham to get up there, and enough introvert to be the writer. But of the two, I have no need to perform like a lot of performing animals do. Some people are just performing animals and need that, and don't feel comfortable anyplace else. But I feel very comfortable—well, Geffen said it years ago, he said, you're the only star I ever met that wanted to be ordinary.

I was always a star. I'm not one of those kids that had a bad high school life. I was always invited to the pretty kids—the doors were opened to the things that most people come to this business wanting. But I always chose my friends—my mother said, "You have the weirdest friends," but I chose them with my heart.

I enjoy the car jockeys down here, you know—one guy brings the cars in like a matador—I enjoy village life, let's say that. This is my small town here; I know the shopkeepers and I tease them. I like that, I'm a small town person.

Celebrity takes all of that away from you in a certain way. There's a tremendous pocket of adjustment where you either take drugs or kill yourself or something. You say you're not gonna change, but everything around you changes, and you eventually have to change. Everybody goes through that awful period. I'm kind of used to it, I'm comfortable with my celebrity, but I don't think anything much of it. But I'm like a mother about my art. I know what's good about it, what's exceptional about it, what's unique about it; I don't like it being compared to things that aren't unique. So that makes me seem kind of salty or rivalrous.

I love making music. There's still plenty to discover. I haven't hybrid all my interests yet. There's Cab Calloway started appearing in some of the music, there's many things that I've enjoyed, the crooning era, that— I'm going to make a record of '40s music to get that out of my system, so that lies ahead of me, the thrill with that big orchestra.

It's the business I don't like, the pigeonholing I don't like, the pitting me against every female that comes along, favourably and unfavourably. That I've had to do because there weren't that many women in the business. I don't like the idea that they make us both put on the gloves, they prod one of them until they say something snotty about me, then hit me over the head with the snotty thing that they said, then get a rise out of me and start these artificial catfights.

Rather than thinking of me as a bitter old fogey, like the young press would like to do, if they thought about it as a mature artist, if it was the old guild system, it would be respected that I knew something, and that maybe my criticisms of these people who outsell me 20 to one, so they really are creating more public interest . . . but there are things, habits that they have gotten into, that aren't great art. False coming in the vocals, whining.

The '40s singers smiled and were elegant, they were drinking and having a high time, they really were more adult, there was a more graceful suffering going on. My generation was a generation of screamers, we were screaming over mountains of amplifiers—not myself per se (*laughs*), I was the only one on with an acoustic guitar, surrounded by The Who's amplifiers, usually (*laughs*). But generally speaking, my generation was screaming over loud electrical impulses, right? And their faces were all contorted, and they were railing, but this next generation has a general tone—they're whiners. I think of Noel Coward: "What's going to happen to the children when there are no more grown-ups/Wot-wot-wot's going to happen to the tots." They're not growing up, this generation, somehow, and they're malformed in a real insipid way, like blaming. And whining. And I just wish they had more character in general. And the over-sexed part of it all, and the guns, you know—it's a degenerate era in the history of music.

But then there are things like the Lilith Fair . . .

I've been invited to play.

Are you going to?

Um, I'm contemplating. It was out of the question because I just didn't want to play, last year. This year I've had a taste of it and I had some enjoyment. I got sick out on this little tour, so I had to do three concerts in the state of delirium, but I managed to stay on my feet, so it was a mixed pleasure. In spite of the illness, I enjoyed myself.

But in light of what you were saying before about false comparisons— because you're all women, say. . .

Yeah, I'm sick of being lumped in with the women. Laura Nyro you can lump me in with, because Laura exerted an influence on me. I looked to her and took some direction from her. On account of her I started play-ing piano again. Some of the things she did was very fresh. Hers was a hybrid of black pop singers—Motown singers—and Broadway musicals, and I like some things also from both those camps.

That record New York Tendaberry . . .

Beautiful record, beautiful. I love Edith Piaf and I love Billie Holiday, but there's no one of that stature among this crop that's come up . . . would you help with this? Because otherwise I'm gonna spend this whole press tour with them pinning me, and me having to deflect—Well, it's *nice*. Because some of it, it's like *culture*.

Like if you look at children's toys. I have a grandson now. Toys are supposed to teach a child the culture. It's frightening to see these killer crushers, the destructive nature of the toys they're exposed to, the vio-lent nature of the toys. This is very bad for culture. Now art can reflect culture or it can deflect culture. I took the stance to sort through my own bullshit and *meshuga,* so to speak, for something that was useful to *me*—my own silver linings. If you could describe the quandary you were in accurately, with some saving grace, so that it was worth it to them to suffer with you, or suffer with the character you're playing—like a good play it had some illumination to it. I don't see much illumination in the work that's coming up.

Could you give me an example of the first case?

Whose work in particular?

Yours or anyone else's.

Well, you'd have to ask different people. For different people it's differ-ent things. [The new lyric] "happiness is the best facelift", for instance. I said that to my boyfriend one day, and he said write that down—or it would've gone up into the air, you know? I think that's a useful phrase.

I got a letter from a guy once who had broken up with his wife. She had had an affair and he hadn't—they were about to get back together, and he couldn't forgive her. And he was putting together a tape of every-thing they were listening to when they were courting—and they were going to the lake of their courtship. And he said, the funny thing was when they were going together I was *her* music, and he was putting all of his music and her music together. But in the final wash, the only thing that was keeping him from blowing this relationship, because he was so mad at her, was "you can't find your goodness because you've lost your heart". And it was that line that was going over and over in his head, so that he didn't just tell her off when she got to the door—"You had an affair and I didn't" (*laughs*)—and blow the whole thing that he was attempting to set up.

People are always telling me that I saved their life or I changed their life. And lately I've taken to saying, How?" Because I have a funny look on my face, they go, "Oh, you hear that so much." And I say, No, the funny look on my face is because I'm wondering, How? Well they always pull a different line. Some of them I wouldn't even think had that kind of power, but it's a little phrase stuck in there somewhere that was just the thing they needed to keep from drowning at a certain moment. I think you'd find it would be different things for different people.

When I see contemporary songs quoted by contemporary music critics, they say, "This is a great lyric," and they'll isolate a line, and I'll think, What's great about that? There's no nourishment in that line. There's not even alliteration or linguistic colour, you know? "Everybody's gay." You know—it's a statement, but there's no art. I mean, OK, am I missing something, is it minimalism here? Is it Barnet Newman? Is it all distilled down to its simplest essence and therefore it's valid? Or do people just not know how to express themselves very well? Are they not thinking? Have they been praised too much in the school system, because the school system changed because they didn't want to give them an inferiority complex? So they gave them an A when they really shouldn't have had one? So they think that's good, and now everybody thinks that's good? I mean, the standards have just dropped so far from Dickens, so far from Kipling. These are masterful thinkers and writers, rich in character . . .

If someone new emerged today and wrote songs with as much depth and meaning as, say, the material you wrote in the '60s, would there

be—in marketplace terms—even an audience for them—one that wasn't tied to some weird nostalgia?

It seems like all we left this generation was shock value. And they're very, very concerned about bodily excretions, in terms of their art and what they say. It seems like that's all we left them or something. I heard, there's a new singer-songwriter—you might know who this is—someone was touting, "Oh, this great new singer-songwriter," and he's got a line, "Strap on the dildo, honey, I want to get fucked in the ass tonight," or something.

I was listening to Noel Coward last night—incredible, incredible craft, incredible wit, incredible social commentary with humour. Stylistically, the language is a bit more formal than certainly this generation would understand. But beautiful and correct, and internal rhyme, and so much skill and so much to say without being *heavy*. I think that's what happened to Bob and I: not to take a poke at drama and the dramatic song, because it's important, and Piaf was one of my first childhood heroes—but I know within the context of my generation I was considered much too dramatic for most people's tastes.

What was the stereotype or misperception about you that bothered you the most?

I guess "that folk singer". Because it's so ignorant. The only thing I've taken from folk music in my art since I began to record is the long lines of the folk songs, to give you the space to put some text to it. A longer line than, "Embrace me, da-dah-dah." [Larry] Klein, from time to time, would provide me with the melody with short lines, and I'd say, Oh, let me parquet words to that just for the exercise, like the Jimmy Swaggart piece, Tax Free. Tax Free had really short, little lines, and I chose to collaborate with him on that just for the challenge— "Front rooms/Back rooms/Slide into tables/Crowd into bathrooms." But generally, "I picked the morning paper off the floor," that's long folk-line singing.

But my chords—nobody in the coffeehouses ever played chords like those. And they're not jazz chords either. Wayne Shorter came in on— what song was it? Ethiopia?—and he said, "What are these chords? These are not piano chords and these are not guitar chords—what are these chords?" And he waded into it like a champ. But harmonically speaking, I'm in my own kind of world.

Did you expect your audience to grow along with you?

I'd hoped. I didn't expect anything. One would hope that it would find an audience.

Do you feel that it has?

It's hard to say, because the last 20 years I've had no record company support, no radio support—the marketplace has been denied me, so I think a lot of those records, there's a bigger audience for it than it received. *Chalk Mark In A Rainstorm* really deserves a big audience, as big as anything the contemporary females have. It's not difficult music. I was disappointed that the company couldn't somehow or other—I was disappointed in the industry at large, that had closed me out from the marketplace, so to speak, that no one would allow me the normal venues that are open to announce that you have product out, with pride. Or that nobody saw. Except Janet Jackson saw it—and she touted it in her interview.

Was that a good thing for you?

Yeah, that was—the best review I got for that record was from Janet Jackson. Yeah. And it really pleased me, it touched me.

Do you think the market access you're talking about is more a function of age or sex?

Both. It's more than that. I'm a long distance runner. Miles was a long distance runner. And I'd have to look up his birthdate, but there was always that restlessness to never rest on your laurels and become a human jukebox. Miles, to the end, was moving forward, still searching and exploring, like Picasso. I belong to that restless camp, you know. Not everybody does. Probably because of the stars, something as simple as that—the moment you popped out (*laughs*). Go figure.

But the industry, to answer your question more tersely, is basically designed to make of you something disposable. That's the way mercantilism in America works. And they get the new improved version of the product. The attention span in this country is shorter, I think, than most. In other countries, if something's good, they're loyal to it. But here, good or not, people get off at a certain point. It's because we're trained—even more so than ever, this batch of babies coming up with the TV—to fear not to be hip. Well hip is a herd mentality, so anything too adventuresome, people are afraid to be the first, or they'll stick out too much. And usually anything that's innovative is not hip, and the copycat gets it all. Once they've heard it the second time, the copier gets the mass approval, because it's kind of familiar by that time. It's been run past them once already.

Another aspect in which you're sort of an uncelebrated pioneer is that in the early '70s it seemed like your private life was the subject of some discussion—but it's nothing compared to what's happening now to people selling 10 million copies of each album. We're so familiar with every aspect of their lives through the media, it's as if they've given over their privacy as part of the deal.

It's become like movie stars. I wrote a poem when I was 16. Having written this poem, why am I in this business? But we had to write a poem, right? It was supposed to be blank verse. So I was getting my hair done for some kind of prom deal, because that's the only time we'd go to the beauty parlour in those days. And I was sitting under the dryer, and they had stacks of movie star magazines. The reigning deities, the teenage idols at that time, were Sandra Dee and Bobby Darin, who were newly married. So the tabloids were full of the misadventures of their marriage. And I just felt so bad for them. And I remember thinking to myself, If somebody wrote this about me in the school paper, I would just *die*. So that's what triggered this poem that had to be turned in for assignment. It was called The Fishbowl.

> The Fishbowl is a world reversed
> Where fishermen with hooks
> That dangle from the bottom up
> Reel down their catch without a fight

Pike, pickerel bass, the common fish
Ogle through distorting glass
See only glitter, glamour, gaiety
Fog up the bowl with lusty breath
Lunge towards the bait and miss
And weep for fortunes lost
Envy the goldfish? Why?
His bubbles breaking 'round the rim
While silly fishes faint for him
And say, "Look there!
I think he winked his eye at me."

How could you end up in show business with that insight, you know? Because I knew it was a trade-off. Blessedly, when I entered into it, there was this brief time when it was viewed as collaborative—because our generation was all in it together—and you were even given the luxury of correcting an interview such as this.

I did an interview with Cameron Crowe and he was allowed—it was before it was them and us, the critic and the artist. I forget what's it's called—a *blow job*, isn't it?—when you write a nice thing about an artist or something. It didn't used to be like that. And people were allowed to write about an artist that they liked, and say nice things. Anyway, Cameron came back with the piece, and I read it over and I said, Oh gee, I didn't really explain this very well—I missed a part, and put in this and this and this. And he said, "Well, Joni, you said that, but I took it out." I said, OK, don't edit me internally—you have to pick your favourite paragraph, because if you take it out in the middle, it's not going to make any sense, because it's such a convoluted thing.

So anyway, he was still living at home at the time. And he'd written a piece about Neil Young, who he adored, and he read it to his mother, whose opinion he valued. And his mother said, "*Cameron*—why would you write a thing like this? You *love* Neil Young." And he realised then that peer-group pressure among writers had caused him to put in some, I don't know, cynical or snotty things about this artist who he simply adored. That's when it began to shift.

Do you think the new artists who sell 10 million records have their own sense of community in the us-versus-them sense, or is it a different scenario altogether?

No—this generation seems to be the most celebrity-loving, celebrity-hating generation that ever lived. And nobody wants to do the mundane job. In my parents' generation, you got a job and you kept it. My father wanted to be a lawyer, but he was a grocery clerk and then the store manager. You got a job no matter what your dream job was. That was your dream job. Then my generation, which was a more affluent generation—no war to deal with, no Great Depression to deal with—saw through and became very critical of the powers that be.

I don't know whether that's good or bad—like certainly the dope wars of Vietnam, the transparency of that, did not deserve the thwarting of the boys coming home. I used to play in Fort Bragg to soldiers, like Bob Hope. I figured I don't care whether it's an unjust war or not, soldiers need singers. So I disagreed with my own generation. I wasn't really of my own generation either. I wasn't an anarchist, I wasn't a nihilist—I never really could find my politics.

The only thing from the hippy thing that I believed in, that I saw evidence of, the only positive thing that I carry on to this day, is the Rainbow Coalition. There we were, white middle-class kids, but we were treated like a grungy minority, and we got a taste of prejudice, which I thought was very healthy and should give us the empathy for all peoples, an insight that no other generation had. The other generations were very apartheid; my parents tried to teach me their ways, which were too narrow for me. Anything different was feared. To me, anything different was compelling and something to explore.

On that level, how was it for you upon being reacquainted with you daughter Kilauren—has she turned out the way you thought a young woman of her generation might?

Her adoptive parents are very like my parents, so her rebellion—I think, and I'm just getting to know her, it's only been a year—is quite similar to my own. I was difficult to raise in my teens, and she was too. Both of us wanted to stretch out and see the world. She took off at 14 with her brother as a chaperone, and modelled quite extensively, 'til 27, all around the world. And she's going through a second rebellion as we speak, you know against me, trying to shock me. Well it's harder to shock me than it was the kids, because they're more like my parents, you know? I loved the experience, everything, with the difficulty and all. We'll be fine, But it's an odd situation and there's much that has to be worked through. So I'm going on Saturday to see her. We had a bit of an awkward encounter, and then we had a beautiful encounter, so we're going through everything intensely in a short space of time. But yeah, there are a lot of things.

Surprisingly, there's less of a gap than there was between my mother and I. My mother thinks I'm *immoral*. I've searched diligently for a morality that applied to the times that I lived in. I keep saying to my mother, Think of me as a Catholic priest that drinks a little with the dock workers (*laughs*). I just don't want to get that *clean*.

Did she hear Facelift?

Yeah.

What did she think?

I think she's getting used to it. I keep saying, It's not our song, Mum, any more, this is so many people's story. This is a story of mothers and daughters; I can say now that I have my own back. There are bad Christmases from time to time. There's a big moral breach. Before I was separated from my husband, my mother introduced us to the man who later became my boyfriend. But the divorce had not come through; as far as she was concerned I was living in sin, flaunting my Hollywood ways in their faces, in their town. Humiliating them. I said, Who am I humiliating you in front of? Your generation is all *dead*. There are no witnesses as far as I can see (*laughs*). My generation is not as intolerant of this. So that's a generation gap song. The funny part of it is, that she's 86 and I'm 55, or 50, when the song occurred.

One of the things that's marvelous to watch was Larry playing onstage with you even now.

He begged me, "Joan, Joan, I'm jealous. You've got to take me on this tour. Who's playing bass?" I said, The seat is open, I'm not cheating on you. I played the bass myself on this last record, but he came in and played the parts that I'd written because sonically the keyboard that I was using wasn't quite right for a couple of songs. He played the bass part that I'd already transcribed. I was really tight on this record that it be my composition all the way down the line. Klein and I always had a broad ability to relate. Great discussions—that never went away. Playing music—that never went away. I said to Donald—Donald's my boyfriend—It's not like Klein and I are out of each other's life, we're just out of each other's hair (*laughs warmly*). He said, "Write that down, that's another song."

Is it an odd thing for you—the boyfriend, the husband, and then even Graham giving you that award the other night?

They're all wonderful men, though. Graham is a sweetheart—and we didn't part with any animosity. A lot of pain—there's always pain in pulling apart. Graham needed a more traditional female. He loved me dearly, and you can see there's still a fondness and everything, but he wanted a stay-at-home wife to raise his children. And I said that I could— a rash promise I made in my youth—and then realised I couldn't. So it all worked out.

The conversation winds down, and a surprisingly cool summer breeze blows, whisking lingering cigarette smoke up into the pure and oxygen-rich air of luxurious Brentwood. By any standard, this is good. And this encounter with the woman who penned *Ladies Of The Canyon* is also good, a significant step up from our first—which took place in a Los Angeles theatre in 1991 and remains a conspicuous exhibit in my own Hall of Shame. Picture this: six-foot-four writer, watching Sting's *Soul Cages* tour, crammed into a seat with his knees pressed hard up against the seat in front of him. Writer shifts in discomfort, unavoidably tugging hard at the hair of the woman sitting directly in front of him. Said woman turns around and fixes the innocent but inescapably tall hair-puller behind her with a glare as cold as a Saskatoon winter.

"I gave you a look that would curl you?" Mitchell grins. She didn't think it was so funny seven years ago.

We descend the staircase leading down from the restaurant and enter a courtyard filled with luxury stores, designer fashion shops, and Brentwood car jockeys who bring very expensive cars in like matadors. And in this paved paradise, can you guess where they keep them?

RADIO INTERVIEW

Jody Denberg | September 8, 1998 | KGSR-FM, Austin (US)

Austin, Texas, air personality Jody Denberg interviewed Joni at the Hotel Bel-Air in Los Angeles in September 1998. She was still talking about *Tame the Tiger* but—as always—did not confine herself to pushing her current album.

Joni offered the colorful, hometown inspiration for the song "Harlem in Havana"—a circus that visited her Saskatchewan town every summer. In a funny aside, she also corrected a phrase attributed to her in the August 1998 *Mojo* interview with Dave DiMartino (included here on page 213), proving that she flyspecked every word of that interview, as she no doubt did with most interviews.

She also talked about her 1996 twofer best-of, *Hits* and *Misses*—the closest thing to a box set she thought she'd get—and about the Roland VG-8 guitar processor that changed her musical life. She also gave an update on her increasingly shaky health, and we hear about her "rich people's" problems of the '80s as well as her belief that the black press "got" her more than the white, mainstream press.

Also lamented by Joni was the "bigotry" of genderization and the resistance she faced trying to make music and maintain some dignity as a mature woman. Her reunion with her biological daughter, Kilauren Gibb, was still in its honeymoon phase, and Joni remarked upon the qualities and quirks they shared.

Note: Portions of this interview aired on KGSR-FM, Austin, and were published in the *Austin Chronicle*. This is an edited transcript of the complete interview. —Ed.

[Jody plays the track "Harlem in Havana."]

Jody Denberg: That was "Harlem in Havana," the opening song of Joni Mitchell's first album of new material in four years, which is

Taming the Tiger. Joni, "Harlem in Havana" sounds like an invitation to a big party.

Joni Mitchell: It does, yeah, in a certain way. It is an attempt to re-create the sound at the end of the mile-long midway. There was a midway [circus] that came up from Florida and played in my hometown every summer, and at the very end of it was the double ferris wheel. Club Lido was along the side—dancing waters, the caterpillar, the motorcycle, cyclotron or whatever it was—all of these things with their own generators, so there was a tremendous cacophony. And the one place that we were all forbidden—any kid that I knew anyway—we were forbidden to stop in front of "Harlem in Havana." My parents said, "Don't let me catch you there." All it was, was black burlesque, and every hour on the hour the band would come out onto the bandstand; and it had a good horn section, and it was my first exposure to black music live. And it was way back on the beat and swampy and a source of total fascination for me. Whenever I heard the "Harlem in Havana Revue" coming out, down I would run. At the age of thirteen, a girl who lived about a block away from me who ripened rather early ran off with the trumpet player from "Harlem in Havana" for the summer and came back a bleached blonde, and I was forbidden to hang out with her. The following year when "Harlem in Havana" returned, she and I went and we stood out in front. And the chorus girls came out with their blue satin capes, these big silver spangles on them and their darned stockings and looking very tired and bored, and chewing gum, some of them. . . . The tallest girl was in the middle, so they made a kind of a pyramid, shorter girls were on the outer edges, and they stood there with their capes and the barker was barking and every once in a while they would open their capes, flap them open, and all they had underneath was a teddy. It wasn't that risqué, but somehow or other this was viewed at that time as very shocking, and my girlfriend said to me, "You see the tall guy in the middle?" And I said, "Yeah." "That's a man." No, I couldn't believe this. The fifties were such an isolated and naive and innocent time. Anyway she got us in—we were both under sixteen—and we watched this show, which was really kind of Redd Foxx comedy and a lot of plumage and high kicking and great music, to my ears anyway. The thickness of the arrangement, the density of it, is an attempt to—in an orderly fashion—create the cacophony and the compressed density of the sound as you listen to that band through the whirring of the generators, of the caterpillar which was adjacent and the screams of people on the double ferris wheel, which was to the other side of it.

Denberg: You mention the horn section. I'm assuming it's Wayne Shorter.

Mitchell: Well, Wayne, and I'm playing horns on the VG-8 [*A Roland-made guitar compressor that made her open tunings much easier to employ —Ed.*] on the guitar, which has in its palette also some horn samples.

Denberg: I knew it sounded like a party, and the thing is, is sometimes people have an image of Joni Mitchell being real serious, but there's always been songs like, "Shiny Toy," "Ray's Dad's Cadillac," "In France They Kiss on Main Street." Those are all kick-up-your-heels dancing swing songs.

Mitchell: Oh, I was a dancer in my teens and kind of a party animal. I think it was a shock to my friends when, suddenly, I bought a guitar and introverted and began to think somewhat deeply. After all, I was a blonde!

Denberg: So do people miss that part of your personality, does it go by them that you like to have a good time?

Mitchell: Not my friends. There's usually quite a mixture of material on an album, especially the later albums. *Blue* was a sad album, for the most part. *For the Roses* was juggling to understand or to find something in lieu of religion, which seemed pretty corrupt, to hang on to. I discovered Nietzsche, who's the bible for the godless, really. . . you have to really kind of sink into the pits to understand Nietzsche, because he looks at more truth than most people could. Even Carl Jung opened up his writings, slammed it shut, and said, "Whew! He'll have no friends."

Denberg: There was scuttlebutt about a year ago that you were going to retire from the music business. What changed your mind?

Mitchell: The VG-8, the guitar, basically. The problems that I had seemed to be many. I seemed to have been blacklisted for about twenty-five years.

Everybody, no matter what I did, nothing seemed to come up to *Court and Spark* for people, including *Hejira*, which was kind of trashed at the time and later was listed as a classic. It just seemed that I was in the game, and not of it. You know, suited up but not allowed to run, or a Man o'War in the pasture [*The champion racehorse of the early twentieth century —Ed.*] . . . in *Mojo* magazine, they translated it into "manure in the pasture"—let's get that typo straight.

And along came this guitar. The other problem that I had was technical, that I had invented all of these tunings and required a rack of instruments around me in order to play—and still never seemed to really get in tune. And I have good pitch and I was frustrated that I spent most of the time in concert in the act of tuning. And along came this instrument which gave me normal guitar player's tuning problems, to have the capacity—not that it was designed for this, but you could use it in this way—you could take over some of the color channels and lie to it basically, because it's all zeros and ones, right? You could file all of my fifty different tunings into this instrument so that I could go from one to the other with a turn of the dial, like a radio station, and I would be in the next tuning. It even has a button on it that if you're in the middle of performance and you're out of tune and you don't want to stop and tune manually, you just hit it and hold it down, and it tunes it back up numerically. So, I'm using it in a way that most people aren't. For most people coming to the instrument, it's just a little box that contains a lot of different amps and a lot of different guitar sounds and some horn sounds and some odd sounds, like a computer guitar. But for me, it's the brain that holds all of these tunings and allows me to perform with facility without this handicap. Yeah, that was the main thing.

Denberg: And also, is it your health? Because I had read that when you were younger, that did keep you off the road.

Mitchell: Yeah. The eighties were very kind of hard on me. I was butchered by dentists, that's a story we don't really want to get into, but I spent about five years in dental hell, and simultaneously in litigation, several court cases. Everybody that could robbed me in the greedy eighties: the government of California, my bank, my business manager, everyone around me. So the eighties were a rough decade for me. And on top of it, I was diagnosed as having post-polio syndrome, which they said was inevitable, for I'm a polio survivor . . . Forty years after you had the disease, which is a disease of the nervous system, the wires that animate certain muscles are taken out by the disease, and the body, in its ingenious way, the filaments of the adjacent muscles send out branches and try to animate that muscle. It's kind of like the Eveready [*Energizer —Ed.*] Bunny, the muscles all around the muscles that are gone begin to go also because they've been trying to drive this muscle for so long. That's the nature of what was happening. So I had it mostly in my back, so you don't see it as much as you would in a withered leg or an arm. But the weight of the guitar became unbearable. Also, acoustic guitar requires that you extend your shoulder out in an abnormal way, and coincidentally some of the damage to my back in combination with that position was very painful.

So, there was a merchant in Los Angeles who knew of my difficulties and knew that this machine was coming along that would solve my tuning problems and he made, on spec, a Stratocaster for me out of yellow cedar that was very light and thin as a wafer . . . an electric guitar is a more comfortable design for my handicap. Then, a genius luthier built me this two and a half pound guitar, which is not only beautiful to look at but it kind of contours to my body. It fits my hip and even kind of cups up like a bra! It's just beautifully designed, and then also, I abandoned regular medicine and fell into the hands first of a kahuna [*A Hawaiian healer, or shaman —Ed.*] and then a Chinese mystic acupuncturist who put down his pins and just points at you. I know this sounds real quacky, but they did some mysterious good to the problem, and I feel fine.

Denberg: So the nineties so far have been a better decade then?

Mitchell: Oh yeah. The eighties were just awful for me.

Denberg: The last album that you did of new studio material, *Turbulent Indigo,* was in '94. It won a couple of Grammys, there were honors coming from every direction. Did you anticipate the higher profile and recognition that followed *Turbulent Indigo*?

Mitchell: No, no. One would never anticipate this.

Denberg: It was a great piece of work though. When you put it out did you think, "I'm just going to cast this stone into the water and see what ripples come back," and then waves sort of came back?

Mitchell: Well, I was fed up, and I put a black joke on the cover, a Van Gogh with his ear cut off, because I was that frustrated. So I kind of cut my ear off in effigy. And I don't know whether people got it, or whether it was catalyst to change, but things did begin to change. I felt that I had been doing good work for twenty-some years, and that it was not being recognized at all. Of course, it was by my fans. I have a loyal body of people that look forward to the next album in the same way, I suppose, that I look forward to [Carlos] Castaneda's next book. I would keep going, keep going.

Denberg: Did you feel a sense of vindication when *The Hissing of Summer Lawns* and *Hejira* first came out, they got slammed by some people and now of course they're heralded. Did you feel vindicated?

Mitchell: Yes and no. I mean, the reviews for instance, of this last concert tour, were very schizophrenic. The laments for the lack of early material in this last performance were also accompanied by some strange statements. For twenty-five years, the public voice, in particular the white press, lamented the lack of four-on-the-floor and major/minor harmony as my work got more progressive and absorbed more black culture, which is inevitable because I love black music—Duke Ellington, Miles Davis. Not that I set out to be a jazzer, or that I am a jazzer. Most of my friends are in the jazz camp. I know more people in that community, and I know the lyrics to forties and fifties standards, whereas I don't really know sixties and seventies pop music. So I'm drawing from a resource of American music that's very black-influenced, with this little pocket of Irish and English ballads, which I learned as I was learning to play the guitar. Basically, it was like trainer wheels for me, that music. But people want to keep me in my trainer wheels, whereas my passion lies in Duke Ellington, more so than Gershwin—the originators, Charlie Parker. I like Patsy Cline. The originals in every camp were always given a hard time.

Denberg: You felt as your music absorbed more of these black influences and it was based less on simple harmony and melody, there was a real resistance, years later.

Mitchell: Believe me, I get my strokes on the street, but I don't generally in the press. The press has a tendency to listen to it, not like it, and then it appears at the end of the year in their top ten list. But they kill the first sales somehow or other with their expectation for it to be something else. And [there's] this tendency, especially from white reviewers, to say that there's no melody there, because white rockers are scared of anything more complex than a seventh chord, and I like wide harmony. I like Debussy, it's modern. I like modern classical music. To me those things are somewhat quaint and charming, but they're no longer an influence and so I can't go back there.

So I feel like for twenty-five years, the criticism levied against me has been unjust. It's asking me to go in a direction that I outgrew. That was easy to assimilate and it didn't really depict my emotionality—blacks and women have a lot in common. We've been repressed and we're entering into a world and trying to find our place. So if a chord depicts an emotionality, our emotionality is going to be more complex. So, wider voicings, I don't suffer in a pure minor. I just don't. I'm not happy in a pure major, there's always some—ever since the bomb dropped, there's always been a second note running through everybody's lives, whether they're sensitive to it or not. But where that second lies, or that eleventh or whatever it is, there's a lot of prejudice levied against that particular kind of harmony in the rock press.

Denberg: What about the latest batch of songs on *Taming the Tiger*? You spent a couple of years making it. Did these songs come from a specific period or were they written ever since the last record came out?

Mitchell: Well, I've been struggling to write since the last record came out. And it's four years, like you say, but you have to understand that the record company, that I turned this in quite awhile ago. And I did *Hits* and *Misses*, which took a lot of research; I had to listen to everything I ever did in the middle. There was a project in the middle, it wasn't just a complete throw out there, there was a lot of thought that went into that, also. The thing that I found was that my experience in the eighties—I got a radical hit of the eighties—the worst part of the eighties fell on me. I had unguarded marbles. So he who has unguarded marbles in a period which is permissive, and it's fashionable to be greedy, suffers, and I did.

And so I had rich people's problems, basically. It wasn't that I was taken down to starvation, but this tiny percentage that I am able to glean from this business, because everybody strips off your profits, then you have 30 percent comes off of that, you manage to get this tiny distillate, you generate a lot of money, but you manage to get this tiny distillate, and then the government of California levied an unjust tax against me. Twelve people in the country received this tax and it was retroactive, it was 15 percent of that tiny little bit that we managed to glean from the record company, who took beyond the lion's share, then the manager, the agent, and then what's left of that, the government. And then they levied a 15 percent tax against the gross. I had financial difficulties. You can't really write about that, it's unattractive. "Oh yeah, the business been good to you." Nobody wants to know. So, as a writer I suddenly found that my problems were those that lacked a universality, they just sounded like kind of a whining. And at the same time my work was being tremendously undervalued, and nobody was being sent to adjudicate it with the intelligence to comprehend it. And so the public statements against it to me were just flat out ignorant. And I had health problems then, on top of all of this, so what am I going to write about? I just got madder and madder and madder at the business. And then all these honors came. Well, the honors kind of fell short. It seemed like it was kind of a copycat crime, that once one was given to me, the others felt the necessity to do it, but they didn't really know why.

And once the honors had kind of passed, we went back into this thing, "Your later work isn't as good as your older work," which isn't true. There's been a tremendous amount of growth. Besides, an actress is not expected to continue to play her ingenue roles. I've written roles for myself to grow into gracefully, but there is no growing into gracefully in the pop world, unfortunately, because the airwaves—everybody is in the same bind. You know this. We're all in this same bind. Since the record business went public, and the men at the top want the graph to go up and nothing else, everybody's getting the squash, including the record company executives. From the top of the business down, we're all now in the same boat, so I'm not just a whiny artist.

It used to be that you could pin it. The business is sick. And music and the genuinely gifted, such as myself, and there aren't a lot in any generation, being shunned from the airwaves in favor of tits-and-ass bubblegum kind of junk food is a tragedy. And there is no other arena for me to make music in. So I feel constantly in a position of injustice. There's a civil liberties thing here. Is it my chronological age? That should never be held against an artist. We're all going to grow middle-aged. We need middle-aged songs. I'm an unusual thing. I'm a viable voice. For some reason, even though I want to quit all the time, you know, I still have a driving wheel to do this thing.

Denberg: One of the songs on the new album actually has the lyrics written by someone else, "The Crazy Cries of Love." I'm not familiar with the gentleman whose lyrics you used for this song.

Mitchell: He's a songwriter from my hometown [*Donald Freed, a poet/ songwriter and Joni's sometime boyfriend, from Saskatoon —Ed.*], and he had these words set to an entirely different kind of music. And I just loved it because I've written a lot about the bridges of Saskatoon, it's called the "city of bridges." "Cherokee Louise" is a story that takes place with an Indian girlfriend of mine in the Broadway Bridge. This takes place on another bridge in Saskatoon, one stormy night. One by one, I'm setting stories on the bridges of Saskatoon, I guess, and it appealed to me on that level. Also I liked the flirty quality of it, and in the mood that I was in, I really wanted to be singing flirty songs but was incapable of writing them. So, I wrote the choruses, he wrote the verses, and I set it to music and I set it to a kind of a Hank Williams, kind of country swing feel.

Denberg: I was wondering how you feel about this unwitting collaboration with Janet Jackson when she sampled one of your songs [*Snippets of "Big Yellow Taxi" are sampled throughout Jackson's song featuring Q-Tip, "Got 'Til It's Gone" —Ed.*]. And then, of course, people are covering your songs, how do you feel about that?

Mitchell: Specifically, the Janet Jackson piece, I love that. As a matter of fact, at that time, I was trying to break down my prejudice to contemporary radio and I was listening to a station. I'd leave it set there, and I'd listen to it for a couple of days to give it a fair shake. And at that particular time, that song sailed out of everything else, I thought. I loved the contouring between her voice and my voice, and "Why you wanna go and do that, uh huh huh." And I loved the video, the video to me was one of my favorite videos ever—the dignity and the liveliness. Picasso would have loved that video. There were a hundred paintings in that video—the spirit of it. I guess it was all taken from a book of photographs taken in South Africa at a certain point, and they reshot it in L.A., although I don't know where they found those squat toilets. I didn't think they existed on this continent. It had a humanity and a quiet dignity. I was very honored to be a part of that.

Denberg: And then of course other people cover your work. Sarah McLachlan did a version of "Blue." Sometimes, in interviews, you seem a little put out by those female singer-songwriters who claim you as an influence. They really can't touch you artistically, but they sell a lot of records. Do you feel like you compete with them in the pop arena?

Mitchell: No, I'm forced to compete by the interview system. I have no problem. I'm honored to be an influence. I think art should beget art, and spark it. And I'm always looking for something to spark me. But I'm less likely to be influenced by a tributary of myself. I mean, you can learn from students from time to time, but what I resent, in a nutshell—and this has been done to me—is to be pitted against them intentionally and be told I'm not as good. Like, there was a radio show, for instance, that was done a while ago that somebody gave me, thinking I'd be honored. It was a lot of the new women coming up. And the interviewer began by saying, "There are a lot of women coming onto the scene these days, all of them claiming Joni Mitchell as an influence. You can even tell what albums they've been listening to. Take this one." And he would play it. "She's been listening to *Court and Spark*." And he'd play the record. I started playing in tunings because I couldn't get at the chords that were in my head on the guitar, they didn't exist on the guitar really. Harmonically, by the time I got to *Court and Spark*, it was very, very deviant. The harmony the girl was using was very primary colors . . . I thought, "How can you say she's been listening to *Court and Spark*? It's an insult to *Court and Spark*, because this is so rudimentary."

"This one's been listening to this and this one's been listening to that." Then the final insult at the end of it was that he said—and this is what gets levied against me a lot—all of these girls are beating her at her own game. She has no sense of melody. And he played a choral piece, "The Reoccuring Dream," as an example of my loss of perspective. That's a beautiful piece of music, but melody is not the point of it. It's textural, and there are snippets of melody. This is one of the hardest things for me to bear is to be told again and again that I have no melodic sense or that there's no melody here. My argument is that—does Marvin Gaye have melody? I try to sing the words, and give them their proper inflection. Every time I sing it, I sing it different.

Denberg: Why would you feel like you have to measure the success of one of your pieces by what someone says in the press about the sales of it?

Mitchell: I don't. But the press has pitted me against the women coming up. It's not a battle of my choosing.

Denberg: I don't feel like you have to compete in that arena.

Mitchell: I don't, either. But one thing that I do get tired of all the way along is the "Women of Rock" articles. There used to be smaller groups, always the "Women of Rock." My favorite compliments have come from the black community. A blind black piano player said to me, "Joan, you make genderless, raceless music." Now that's my optimism and I think that limiting me . . . Let me put it this way, the painters, the women who painted, the women impressionists, you don't really hear about them and they all attended the same academy. There was an extra letter added to their name—associates of the academy. They were never allowed really to be academy members, always *associates* of the academy. By continuously lumping me in with the women, which the white press does and the black press doesn't . . . The black press, recently, in *Vibe* magazine, had an article where they singled out Miles Davis, Santana, and myself, and said, "All you kids with your tight little abs and your two hits, take a look at these guys." I feel that that is a more accurate museum grouping for me. And that genderization is a form of bigotry and not really hearing what I'm doing.

Denberg: The music business, as we've already discussed, is geared to the lowest common denominator and younger demographics. If it wasn't that way, your work would probably be heard by more people. It has always seemed that you're more interested in innovating anyway than being influenced by others. It does seem that your work is apart, it's not influenced by the contemporary artists.

Mitchell: My process of learning has been peculiar. I don't have the right kind of brain for an academic. I learn most intensely by admiration. If I admire something or am interested in something, I become very alert and I take in a lot all at once and it stores and then it mulches and it sifts down. I went and sang in this revue, I sang "Stormy Weather." When I heard the tape back, there's a Ray Charles lick in there, I swear to God. I wasn't even aware I was influenced by Ray Charles. But for the better part of a bar, his presence is on me. There's a lot of Cab Calloway in "Harlem in Havana," certainly a lot of Duke Ellington. Cab Calloway I absorbed as a preteener, pre–rock 'n' roll, because there were a few clips of his that used to run as shorts on our home television station, because they hadn't filled up with commercials yet, so the TV coming up from the States, which had this gap for commercials, we didn't have that many commercials up there yet so they'd fill it in with shorts, and Cab Calloway was one of them. It surprises me every once in a while, like I'll hear, "Oh, listen to that. I know where I got that from." 'Cause all the time I'm trying to be un-influenced by anything, including myself, not to steal from myself. That's one reason I invented the tunings. Because every time I twist and twiddle the strings into a new tuning, pain in the butt as it got to be in terms of performance, I am back to square one, the neck is completely foreign again and I have to discover. I have to find the chords in the tuning. Astrologically, I just found out there's a book of birthdays. I'm born the week of depth and the day of the discoverer, so I have a need to discover because of astrological influence.

Denberg: There's a line in the song "Taming the Tiger," you sing: "Every disc a poker chip, every song just a one-night stand." You describe popular music as "genuine junk food for juveniles." But pop music like that has always existed, hasn't it?

Mitchell: Yeah, it has. But the difference has been radio, for instance, let's take your field. In Toronto, or rather when I lived in New York, I was on the road most of the time playing little clubs. And when I had time off and came back to New York, I would run into the house and I would turn on the radio, and disc jockeys back then were creative. If it was raining, and the disc jockey was an audiophile and he was hired for his talent and his scope, he could play a rain piece by Charlie Parker. If his scope embraced some bubblegum, he could follow it up with that so that you could have an afternoon of rain montage all over the place. I just don't like the segregation that has occurred for the sake of commerce in music. I don't like being told that this album doesn't fit any format, that music of this caliber doesn't fit into a format. I will not pander to a format. Does that mean I never get on the airwaves? If music of this caliber is being made, don't you think it's kind of a crime that it has no outlet that will accept it? I think it is.

Denberg: What can the music industry do to foster its true visionaries? That's not unfortunately the business of the music industry or the radio industry.

Mitchell: No, they're motivated to sell jeans and junk.

Denberg: Joni, there's a beautiful self-portrait on the cover of *Taming the Tiger*, you're holding a kitty cat. I know it's a pretty easy observation to make, but it seems especially on the new album, there's a couple of songs—"Harlem in Havana" and "Love Puts on a New Face"—that share qualities with your artwork. Sometimes they're austere, other times they're bright and bursting with color and imagery. Does painting offer you similar rewards as making music?

Mitchell: Well, I'm a painter first, and a musician second, as it turns out. I had impulses to create classical music when I was seven and eight, but I had my love of it taken away by raps on the knuckles from my piano teacher saying, "Why would you want to play by ear when you could have the masters under your fingertips?" So the impulse to compose in the community that I grew up in was thwarted and it didn't come out for quite a while later. I switched to the guitar with no ambition to be in show business. As a matter of fact, as a teenager, I felt sorry for stars for their loss of privacy, and I wrote a poem about it in high school. So I'm an odd candidate for celebrity in that I didn't practice in front of the mirror and I never really wanted the grand hurrah and I'm not addicted to applause. I have a painter's ego and I get a thrill of juxtaposing one color against another. I get like a private rush.

I'm an only child. It's a form of solitary play. If I put that color next to that color and add another color, you know, I get a buzz. It's the same with music. I don't have any of the musician's languages. I read as a child, but I let the reading ability go. I don't use it in the recording process, because I fiddle around with the guitar so much that I'm not playing it normally anyway. The numerical language that some musicians have doesn't mean anything within my system, nor does the alphabetical system. I don't know what key I'm playing in. So I'm a sophisticated ignorant, is basically what I am. But there are people who can come in, listen to what I play, write it out, and follow it. My harmony is selected by my own interest in the same way that I would select to put that color next to that color. I've produced most of my albums, except during my marriage to [*bassist Larry*] Klein. We did more collaboration so that we could see each other, because albums are kind of consuming. I think of myself as a painter who writes music.

Denberg: And you do both on an instinctual basis. Does the art world view you as a dilettante because of your notoriety as a musician?

Mitchell: Always, because of Socrates, we are a society of specialists, with the exception of the Italians. I think the Italians perhaps could recognize a Renaissance person, but in Socrates's utopia, you couldn't be a poet and a painter and a musician. You had to be one or the other and it was actually against the law in his utopian, just society. And I think that spills over, so that you're not really taken seriously as a painter. Which is fine by me, because I've managed to keep the music pure anyway, even in the pop arena. And the art world, they have the same problem. I'm trying to assimilate too many periods.

I'm glad I didn't make a career of painting, but I'm driven to paint. And they work as a farmer's trick, they summer fallow one another. So when the soil gets sick, I keep the creative juices going by switching from one to the other. So when the music or the writing dries up, I paint. Sometimes you bang into boogie men, so psychologically I think the switching from poetry to painting and back to music, there are three different psychologies really. When you paint, you set down the inner dialogue completely, you come down to synapses, and occasionally a voice like Robbie the Robot goes, "Red in the upper right-hand corner." Poetry is almost insane, you have to stir up overlapping thoughts, chaos in the mind, and then pluck from it. Without the painting to clear the head, I don't think I could do it. And the music is a true gift and has always been kind of soothing to me and not a problem. The poetry is psychologically dangerous, and the painting kind of balances it out.

Denberg: Is there a physical place where you like to paint or write, special places like where you live and certain rooms where you do most of your work?

Mitchell: I'm influenced by environment but not to that degree where I have some kind of *la la* setting, you know?

Denberg: I was thinking about your guitar tunings since we were talking about that earlier, and it just seems to draw this analogy between the colors and the paints and the different tunings that you use. And how did these tunings develop? You were just looking for different ways to do things, rather than just playing the standard major chords?

Mitchell: Well, I wrote my first song, "Urge for Going," in standard tuning, and I guess it's because of the stars. The guitar, in the folk houses, the chords that everybody played sounded the same, while the chords that I heard in my head you couldn't get off the neck, even with tremendous facility. They just don't exist. The chords that I play, if you don't twiddle the strings, you don't get them. I've made the guitar kind of orchestral. It's much wider, it's down into the territory of the bass in some cases. And the chords are very, very wide relative to what guitar chords usually are. You couldn't get that without the tunings. There are traditions of tunings. The Hawaiians, for instance, played in slack key, and they were usually major chords. The old blues guys tuned in banjo tuning, which is open G tuning, which is what Keith Richards plays in. He doesn't even play the sixth string on the guitar. He plays the guitar like a five-string banjo. So, most of the old blues men, coming from banjo to guitar, not knowing anything about Spanish tuning, tuned the guitar into open G or D modal, which is just a dropped D. These tunings were kicking around the coffeehouses. There were about three of them. It was Eric Andersen that turned me onto them one night in Detroit. Because we used to board musicians passing through that town, when I was married to Chuck Mitchell. We had extra bedrooms and everyone was poor, so they usually stayed at our house, and we played music, and if there were songwriters, we shared the songs that had been written since we saw each other last and so on. So in that way I got into the tunings. Well, soon they seemed to be explored, and I didn't seem to be able to get any fresh colors out of them. So then I started tuning the guitar to chords that I heard in my head. And that's the way it went.

Denberg: You've said, I think this might have been in the *Mojo* piece, "My chords reflect my complex life, which is why my simple, old songs don't suit me." And I also read that you saw John Kelly [*A Joni Mitchell impressionist —Ed.*] doing some of your older songs. When you happen to hear one, do you ever feel like rediscovering them? I know you get this from your fans who've been with you from the beginning but why couldn't you ever sing, say, "Little Green"?

Mitchell: First of all, my voice has changed. Secondly, the way I played guitar back then is completely foreign to me. I have no idea how I did it. It's how I did it then. It's like, as a painter, if you ask Picasso to go back and paint in an early period of his, I doubt that he could. You're moving forward and it's always evolving. Basically, the reason I'm so unruly in this business is because I think like a painter, not like a musician. And I never wanted to be a human jukebox. I think more like a film or a dramatic actress and a playwright. These plays are more suitable to me. I feel miscast in my early songs. They're ingenue roles.

Denberg: Maybe Bob Dylan, Van Morrison, and Neil Young don't think like painters, because they seem to have no problem playing those earlier songs or putting those old clothes on that maybe fit.

Mitchell: But their styles didn't change as radically as mine over time, either. It's not that difficult for them to go back. Overall, they haven't changed as much.

Denberg: You had a chance recently to reassess your work when you issued the *Hits* album and then the *Misses* compilations. Did you feel like *Misses* was a way for folks to catch up with you if they hadn't been around for the whole ride or to expose people to your more difficult pieces?

Mitchell: It's hard to say what my reasoning was in the selection there, because most of my work was technically misses. I mean, the *Hits* is padded. I didn't really have enough hits to make a real "hits" album, really, by the hit parade measure. But like "Circle Game," which was never on the hit parade, was distributed through summer camps all across the North American continent and was a hit. It was like "Old MacDonald." The same with "Big Yellow Taxi." I turned on the TV one day, I was like dialing around, and I saw a woman holding an alligator so I stopped. And there were a lot of New York inner-city kids around her. Turned out it was coming from the Bronx Zoo. And she said, "This is Harvey, do you want to pet him?" And all these little grade-three kids got up and looked at him. And then she held up a skin, you know. And she said, "And this is Harvey's brother, look what they did to him." And they went, "Oh." And then she said, "Let's sing a song." She picked up a guitar and she sang "Big Yellow Taxi." And all these little rainbow of kids, little yellow kids and white kids and black kids and brown kids started singing my song, in grade three. And they knew all of the words. And I wept. So that was never a hit either, on the hit parade, because back in the early days, hits were on AM and I was an FM artist or an album-oriented artist.

You have to understand that to go on AM you had to have a band. I couldn't find a band that could play my music till my sixth album, and when I did it was a jazz band, the L.A. Express. And so I entered into that world. Some of the reviews from this last tour said my music was not rhythmic and that there was no melody. The problem is that there's more rhythm there than they can cope with, and a lot of times we're not dealing with the four major beats because we know where they are. All right, we know where they are, so where they're saying there is none, in fact, there's too much. There's too much melody.

Denberg: With Brian Blade on drums how could they say there's no rhythm? You did play some of your older songs on the recent tour, "Big Yellow Taxi" and "Woodstock." Did you feel you could put those clothes on comfortably, still?

Mitchell: "Woodstock," oddly enough, because it should be kind of a curio about an event, still has a life for me. And "Big Yellow Taxi" is just kind of cute. [*Laughs*] It's a ditty.

Denberg: People say, "Joni doesn't have the same melody that she used to and she doesn't write about herself any more, she's always writing about other people." On *Taming the Tiger* there's a great deal of music that's on a first person basis. One of the songs, "Face Lift," tells of your relationship with your mother. Was it easy to write such a seemingly naked song at this stage of the game?

Mitchell: I had no choice because the fight that I had with my mother was so disturbing that I dwelt on it obsessively. I mean, it was a major family squabble. We rocked, you know. It seemed odd that a woman in her fifties—I was fifty at the time—would be having this fight with her mother. Even though it's written as a middle-aged story, I had a girlfriend who went home for Christmas and came back and said, "That's exactly what happened to me." She was thirty, so wherever unmarried sex takes place in this country with parental disapproval it doesn't matter how old you are. The irony is that my mother is still worried about these things in these times when everything like that is so broken down in terms of television. They're not sleeping in twin beds anymore on TV. (*Laughs*)

Denberg: Has your mom heard "Face Lift"?

Mitchell: Yes, she dislikes it, you know, finds it humiliating. You should never get too close to a writer, I guess.

Denberg: Joni, as you say, "happiness is the best face lift"; it seems like you've been having a lot of fun lately. I wanted to ask you about some of the recent projects that you've been doing. The tour that you did with Bob Dylan and Van Morrison, was it a good experience for you?

Mitchell: I think it was a great triple bill, and I took it on that account. I hadn't performed in a long time and I thought, "Oh, that's a good show." But I had a little bad luck. Right out of the chute, I got a virus. We bussed out of Vancouver to the Gorge, and the bus had new carpet with glue, and the glue was really stinky. We burned patchouli like old hippies, to kind of mask it. Also, I'm allergic to air conditioning. To make a long story short, by the time we got to the Gorge, I was really sick and the roof of my mouth was red, and my throat was like hamburger. And they sent me a doctor who gave me really extraordinarily violent medicine. And I played the two Gorge dates very ill—like, delirious, but happy. I was enjoying it, but I was delirious, literally.

And when we got to the eve of the San Jose gig, I couldn't get out of bed, my motor functions—I had to tell myself to walk and tell myself to chew. So, the medicine really worked some violence on me. They sent for another doctor, a Chinese doctor, who recognized it. "Doctor's pills give you brand new ills." [*Laughs*] So I did the whole tour really from behind the wheel in terms of stamina. The San Jose show, in particular, I was afraid to hit a high note. It takes a lot more air to hit a high note. And every time I went to hit a high note, I'd go all pins and needles and start to black out. So I had to kind of jockey things around. And I apologized, I believe, although I don't even remember that show. I said something, but I don't know what it was. The press picked up on it and assumed it was that I was rusty from not having been out of the chute for a long time. But I was just really ill.

Denberg: What was it like playing with your ex-husband in the band, Larry Klein?

Mitchell: Oh, we're really good friends. He called me up. I wasn't going to take a bass player because the guitar has so much bottom on it. And he said, "Joan, you've got to let me come." We're the best of friends.

Denberg: I was surprised that there was no collaboration between the three artists on the bill.

Mitchell: Well, Bobby keeps so much to himself. Van came to me at one point and said, "Have you spoken to Bobby yet?" And I said, "Yeah, I saw him after the Vancouver show."

"Well, he hasn't spoken to me," he said. And I said, "Well, come on, let's crash his set." So there was a song in Japan that closed the show Bob and I were in, in Tokyo, of his, and he kind of short-sheeted me on stage. He pulled a number on me. So I said, "Well, we'll go out on this song of his and we'll get him." So we went out and kind of crashed the set the one night. And Bob got a big kick out of it. It was really rough and I blew the words on it and blew the rhyme and had to make one up. And Bobby was looking at me grinning, "What is she going to rhyme with it?" because I got the first rhyming line wrong.

Denberg: What song was it?

Mitchell: "I Shall Be Released."

Denberg: Also recently you did the Walden Woods benefit in April. You sang "Stormy Weather" backed by an orchestra. Would you ever do an album of cover songs?

Mitchell: That's what I want to do. Rather than tour this album, because I'm so far behind, because they're taking so long to release it, I want to go straight into the studio and record in that genre. That's really where, as a singer, if you separate all these things, just forget Joni the writer, because I write these kind of soliloquies which take more dramatic skills than vocal skills. There's no room to put a trill in. You've got so many syllables to deal with. And you have to enact them, like an actress, as opposed to just singing a mood piece. So I need a break from my own music. And to disappear into standards would be a treat. I did two standards with Herbie [Hancock] and Wayne [Shorter] and Stevie Wonder on Herbie Hancock's album, which is coming out [Gershwin's World, *released in*

1998 —*Ed.*]: "The Man I Love" and "Summertime." And my band and I now, since Woodstock, have an arrangement of "Summertime" that I think is really fresh. And I saw four chins quivering in the audience at Woodstock to that old chestnut. So I know it has a power.

Denberg: You didn't play the original festival. Was this summer's A Day in the Garden concert in Woodstock a good experience for you?

Mitchell: Oh, it was beautiful. It was beautiful. It was a beautiful audience. They loved my band. After some of the prejudice against my music for being too jazzy—all that the West Coast press tends to levy against me—the East Coast doesn't, so much. And there was a banner in the audience about eight-foot long that said, "Joni's Jazz," and all these smiling heads above it. When I hit the stage, I thought, "Oh, good." And they applauded my band genuinely and enthusiastically every time a color entered and left, because, I mean—we took a big leap in growth, I think. It felt like the band was that much more solid. Well, I was, for one thing. And we added [Mark] Isham and the addition of muted trumpet, which is a color that I love. It seemed to flesh everything out. And the audience was wonderful.

Denberg: And there's a TV show that you have in the can that I think was done before the Woodstock show and I guess that's going to come out this fall.

Mitchell: I've got to go up in a couple of weeks and finish editing it. The editing isn't completed yet.

Denberg: And recently there was a beautiful book of your lyrics. And I had read at that time that you might do a short story book or an autobiography.

Mitchell: I'm contracted for an autobiography. But you can't get my life to go into one book. So I want to start, actually, kind of in the middle—the *Don Juan's Reckless Daughter* period, which is a very mystical period of my life, and colorful. Not mystical on bended knee. If I was a novelist, I would like that to be my first novel. And it begins with the line, "I was the only black man at the party." [*Laughs*] So I've got my opening line.

Denberg: Do you have a lot of songs that have been left off of your various projects? I'm sure you're asked the question if you are going to compile a boxed set and bring out some things that have not been released along the way.

Mitchell: In terms of a boxed set, you know, my stock was so low that *Hits* and *Misses* is basically my box set. I don't know what will happen now, but they wouldn't even put out a complete box set. So I got rid of that part of the contract with *Hits* and *Misses*. I never wanted to put out a "Hits" because, like I say, I felt that legitimately I didn't really have that many hits and that the most popular things in my repertoire were not my best work, really. *Hits* and *Misses* kind of fulfils what contractually at that point in my career they would spring for.

Denberg: But is there stuff that didn't make it out that you are holding on to?

Mitchell: Oh yeah, there are *Mingus* outtakes. I cut that with four or five different bands, all-star bands, like the cream of the jazz world. But the *Mingus* album itself was so poorly received that it's archival. I think it would be interesting to people who like music, but the record business, which currently doesn't really care about music, doesn't care about a box set.

Denberg: Finally Joni, there's a poignant song on your new album called "Stay in Touch." Last year, you reunited with your daughter [Kilauren Gibb] who you gave up for adoption after she was born. I don't want to assume that this was written about your daughter, but can I ask you if it was?

Mitchell: When the kids came, Kilauren's boyfriend heard the song and said, "Kilauren, this is about you." And it is. It's about the beginnings of love, conducting yourself through it wisely. I don't think there's another song like it in existence. It's always how foolish we all are when we're smitten. It applies. It wasn't the catalyst for it. Kilauren came in the middle of the project, and one of the reasons why there was a delay in finishing it was because we just had to spend a lot of time with each other. So we'd spend three weeks and then I'd go back in the studio and then I'd go up there and we'd spend some more time and then I'd go back in the studio. And it definitely applies. But it applies to any new, terrific attraction. It's basically how to steer yourself through that smitten period.

Denberg: You had said before that you would send her messages in some of your earlier songs. When I heard you say that, I thought maybe "Chinese Cafe." [*With the line "Now your kids are coming up straight, and my child's a stranger / I bore her, but I could not raise her." —Ed.*]

Mitchell: She [Kilauren] said, "Joan, it's so vague I would never have picked up on that." But the irony is that I sat in flight with my hand on an Evian spritzer bottle, misting my face—because we were traveling a lot, to prevent dehydration—with my fingers over my daughter's face, because she was on the Evian spritzer bottle [*Kilauren was a model —Ed.*] for a long time. So she probably heard the songs but didn't recognize herself, and I covered up her face with my fingers. We were passing each other all over the place.

Denberg: When you met your daughter after so many years, did you see any of your qualities in her?

Mitchell: Oh, well, when we first met, we walked into the kitchen. They arrived, and I was upstairs and I was glazing the cover painting [for *Taming the Tiger*]. I was varnishing it. So I walked out on the balcony of the house with brushes in my hand, and I saw her kind of in the dark. And I ran downstairs. We went into the kitchen and we looked at each other and we said [*giggles*], "Hmm, hmm," exactly at the same time and in the same tone. And our speaking voices are almost identical. And in the first few weeks—well, even now—we say exactly the same thing with the same inflection, like at the same time, which people do sometimes when they're in the beginning of relationships. There's a lot of kind of psychic things. It's terrific. And we've had a couple of little skirmishes. And we're getting to know each other, and it's just terrific [*laughs*]. And I love my grandson [*She sighs*]. Yeah . . .

JONI SAID
On Her Cats

"Nietzsche, in particular, is very vocal. As soon as the guitar stops, he starts talking. But the moment the guitar starts up again, he stops. I wrote a song inspired by Nietzsche called 'Man from Mars.' The night I started, Nietzsche disappeared . . . on the eighteenth day he came back. When I played the song for him, he stood on his hind legs and danced, so he recognized it somehow."

—to Ingrid Sischy, *Interview*, May 2000

JAZZ ROMANCE

Jason Koransky | May 2000 | *Down Beat* (US)

In 2000, Joni, very much a swing baby of the 1940s, was able to fulfill her long-held wish to record an album singing with a full orchestra. The seed had been planted in 1998 when she sang with an orchestra at Don Henley's concert in Los Angeles benefiting the Walden Woods Project. That experience whetted her appetite for surfing the wave of sound created by a big band in full roar.

She spoke to *Down Beat* editor Jason Koransky for a May 2000 cover story that explained how she came to put together the album *Both Sides, Now* with ex-husband Larry Klein. The theme was the drama of love, with Joni interpreting standards such as "You're My Thrill," "You've Changed," and "I Wish I Were in Love Again," and revisiting two of her own classics, "Both Sides, Now" and "A Case of You." Her voice had changed considerably from the 1960s. It was still an instrument of great beauty and nuance, but with deeper colors now.

You can tell that she was expecting Koransky to compare the album with those of pop singers such as Linda Ronstadt or Carly Simon, but that didn't happen, which met with her approval. She saw her world-weary alto as leaning closer to Billie Holiday, and indeed, there was a *Lady in Satin*-like, wounded suppleness to her voice in this period. —Ed.

Joni Mitchell keeps trying to grasp the nuances and subtleties of love. From thrills to rage; passion to ennui; infatuation to indifference; bliss to desperation. This cycle, definite both in its inevitability and unpredictability, has served as a prevalent theme in Mitchell's music for more than 30 years.

In 1967, Mitchell seemingly understood the wheel of love when she penned her omniscient "Both Sides Now." She strummed her solo acoustic guitar as she sang the chorus in her instantly recognizable soaring soprano:

> "I've looked at love from both sides now
> From give and take, and still somehow,
> It's love's illusions that I recall,
> I really don't know love,
> Really don't know love at all."

With its soul-searching, Zen-like lyricism and gentle melody, "Both Sides Now" became a folk music classic, an American standard, recorded over and over by artists looking to share a piece of Mitchell's songwriting genius.

Skip forward to July 1999, to Sir George Martin's London AIR Studios. Mitchell, a mature 55, lays down the tracks for her recently released *Both Sides Now*. The title song is the finale of the 12-track album, and this revisitation comes as quite a departure from the '60s original. For starters, there's an orchestra (your company tends to grow as you get older). Then there's her voice—a husky, confident alto—keyed more than an octave below the '60s recording. It's lower due to the natural aging process, not to mention her several-pack-a-day smoking habit. Mitchell appears as an artist transformed, with the phrasing, intonation and timbre of a classic jazz singer in the mold of Billie Holiday, but with a swagger and intelligence clearly her own.

This is exactly what she set out to do when she started recording *Both Sides Now*, a theme album that comes across as an ode to the drama of love. From "You're My Thrill" to "Comes Love," "You've Changed" to "Don't Go To Strangers," "Stormy Weather" to "I Wish I Were in Love Again," Mitchell sings with aplomb over 10 subtle, lightly swinging standards and two more of her own—"Both Sides Now" and "A Case Of You."

And this album is much more than a tale of love. In a way, it's a tale of Mitchell's musical life coming full circle. After all, she's always been a jazz musician at heart, exploring various avenues of the music in well-documented collaborations with the likes of Charles Mingus, Tom Scott's L.A. Express, Wayne Shorter, Herbie Hancock, Jaco Pastorius and Don Alias. But except for singing "Summertime" and "The

Man I Love" on Hancock's '98 album *Gershwin's World* (winner of the '99 Down Beat Readers and Critics Poll Album of the Year), she had never recorded music in this genre. "Sure, this is new music for me on record, but I grew up with this," Mitchell explained. "I was born in the '40s. Even when rock 'n' roll came along, it was only on the radio from 4–6 p.m. Standards and country and western music were on the radio. So these are really my roots."

Joni's roots, however, do not include performing with an orchestra. In fact, Mitchell never sang with a full orchestra before April of 1998. She took part in Don Henley's "Stormy Weather" benefit concert in her hometown Los Angeles for the Walden Woods Project. Mitchell was one of 10 female singers, including Natalie Cole, Paula Cole, Sheryl Crow, Stevie Nicks and Björk, who fronted the orchestra at this show, and the experience made a dramatic impact.

"I sang 'Stormy Weather' and the Marvin Gaye song 'Trouble Man,'" Mitchell said. "It was such a thrill singing with an orchestra, and all of us decided that we wanted to do more of it. It's a very expensive habit. Charlie Parker got a taste for it and could hardly stand going back to the small bands. I understand that he used to sit in with Lawrence Welk just to feel the big beast around him."

But Mitchell was at first hesitant to sing with the orchestra. Her ex-husband and long-time musical collaborator Larry Klein produced the Walden Woods benefit, and he admits that it took some prodding on his part to get Mitchell to participate in the show. "I had to do some convincing, and I told her that once she sang with a large orchestra, she would want to do it some more," Klein said. "So she went ahead and did it, and predictably loved it. After the event she came to me and said, 'God, I'd love to a record like this.' A couple of other singers who were involved in that show came to me and wanted to work with me on the same thing. So I told Joni that if she was going to do it, she should do it now, and together we began the long, arduous task of producing it."

Mitchell devised the "cycle of love" concept early in the process, and she and Klein then pored through dozens of albums trying to hone down the songs that would fit best into this album. Having once exchanged nuptials (they separated in '92 after 10 years together), the album became personal for Mitchell and Klein. "At one point in the process, I thought, 'Klein and I have been through just about all of this,'" said Mitchell, whose current boyfriend of six years lives in her old home town of Saskatoon, Canada. "If you've been in a relationship long enough, you experience all of these facets."

Once a song for the album was chosen, Mitchell and Klein would come up with a concept as to how to treat it with an orchestra, such as an Ellington-esque swing on "Comes Love," and then send this blueprint to Vince Mendoza for orchestral arrangements. Mendoza had arranged the music and conducted the orchestra in the "Stormy Weather" concert, and for him working with Mitchell proved quite a thrill.

"All of these songs were arranged with Joni's voice in mind," said Mendoza, whose own recent orchestral album, *Epiphany* (Zebra), was nominated for a Grammy. "Her voice has changed a lot over the years ever since the first recording; it has gotten so much more interesting and colorful. Her delivery is so much more interesting. We see her breadth of experience now and the words mean more now than they ever did. I had her contemporary sound in my head. *Turbulent Indigo* is probably one of my most-valued albums—I know it backwards and forwards.

"I approached arranging every piece like a tone poem, like Strauss would write around a vocalist. Understanding the words and knowing when to move and when not to move, when to accentuate the lyrics and when not to. I learned a lot of that from Joni, how she writes and how she delivers the lyrics."

———————

It seems odd that Mitchell, best known for her original lyrics and unique harmonic open guitar voicings, would put down her guitar and pen, and focus solely on her voice on *Both Sides Now*. But following her disappointing commercial and critical release of '98's *Taming The Tiger*, she needed a "personal vacation from the responsibility" of songwriting. And with honesty at a premium in her lyrics, she didn't want to traverse ground that she knew would be uncomfortable.

"I didn't want to think about the millennium when I wrote an album because I am too informed. I wanted a break from writing dark stuff," she related. "We're really in a terrible place as a species. If I went into the studio and did what I usually do—scrape my soul and sing about what I really think of the world—I didn't want to go through that process. I didn't want to think about how screwed up the world is, which is what would have happened if I would have gone in to write. *Taming The Tiger* had a romance to it, but it was against a backdrop of rotten lawyers, the stinking music business."

And she also stopped playing guitar. In fact, the night before we spoke, Mitchell had picked up the guitar and played for the first time in about two years.

"[*Both Sides Now*] is much more derivative than my music is, which is stinkingly original. You know what I mean? My songs are determined to be fresh. Anything that's too original is not very popular," she said. "This album evokes a lot, while in my own music, if I found a lick where I thought I borrowed it, I might take it out. But there are a lot of things here where we borrowed from numerous sources."

In London, Mendoza put together several variations of the orchestra with 22, 42 and 71 pieces. Also invited to the sessions were guest soloists Shorter, Hancock and trumpeter Mark Isham. Peter Erskine sat in on drums and Chuck Berghofer played bass. Bringing Shorter and Hancock into the studio, in particular, brought an element into the music that Mitchell thought necessary.

"Wayne and Herbie's contributions are definitely later 20th Century," explains Mitchell, who used to spend New Year's Eve with Shorter and Hancock at the now-defunct Nuclear Nuance playing in a pick-up band. "I give Wayne total liberty, because he knows how to join into my music so well. You see, what we did with this album was make something both retro and progressive. I was thinking that you would ask me about Linda Ronstadt and Carly Simon. If you see this as another girl making a cover album you are not musically informed. I hope to come in somewhere between Ella [Fitzgerald] and Billie [Holiday], and that I could bring something to the genre that very few did—to bring out the emotional readings on the text. Ella didn't really do that. As beautiful as her pitch and time were, she didn't seem to have the emotional palette of Billie. Billie lived so much, and had this warm transcendental resonation in her voice. It was distinctive. A lot of the women in the genre are hard to nail. They over-embellish. I'm actually not a huge fan of this genre. But what I love about it is the architecture, the melodic curve, the musicality of the chordal movement. But obviously, I abandoned that with the next wave.

"[Billie and Ella are] kind of like Van Gogh and Mauve," continued Mitchell, also an accomplished painter (reproductions of four of her original lithographs, including an elegant self-portrait, appear in a special *Both Sides Now* box released on Valentine's Day). "Mauve was an exquisite classicist. Van Gogh created a new way of painting that looked amateurish to Mauve. But it was rawer, and what it lacked in certain drawing skills, it made up for in emotion. Ella had tremendous classical drawing skills. But she didn't have the emotional coloristic palette. There were things that I thought coming into this project were things that you didn't see evidenced in very many places. That was my optimism. It's a triumph musicality. It's got one foot in the late romantics, one foot in Gil Evans."

Having handed the production reins over to Klein once in the studio ("I'm unproducable, hands-on in the mixes, so I said, 'This time, you be producer. I'm just going to come in and sing.'"), Mitchell concentrated on making vocal magic.

"Vince and I had been preparing the music for months, and it was quite emotional for me to hear them come to life," Klein said. "Her singing was just amazing. When we did 'A Case Of You,' which is entirely her live vocal, the orchestra gave her a standing ovation, and half of them were weeping. It was quite amazing to see an English orchestra get that emotional."

A very visual person, Mitchell established a vivid image as to how she interacted with the orchestra. "The best analogy that I can come up with is surfing," she described. "The difference between this and other beautiful experiences that I've had is the grand scale of it, the enormous power of the orchestra. Contemporary music is very horizontal as far as dynamics. This music, uncompressed, has a lot of thick and thin. It comes down to nothing and then swells up. You can feel these waves building up and getting ready to break. The voice is going from a silent pocket, where it can almost be whispered. Four of the pieces have a 71-piece orchestra, four have 42 and four have 22. With the big beast in particular, such as on 'You're My Thrill' and 'I Wish I Were In Love Again,' when it swells, things tense up in a good way. You have to match the brass, you have to blend.

"Basically I was surfing a wave, so I was very alert. There was a lot internal movement in the chords. Every time I sang it, I sang it differently. My parts weren't written out, so I tried different things. It was really a thrill."

———————

The last time Mitchell headed out on tour, she co-headlined an arena bill in '98 with fellow icons Bob Dylan and Van Morrison. While Dylan cranked the volume up to 11 and reinvented and revitalized many of his greatest hits, Mitchell "wanted to show people that I played guitar in a different way," and played her "unpopular material that was kissed off." In support of *Both Sides Now*, Mitchell has different plans altogether. In May she embarks on a 12-city tour, playing theatres in front of an orchestra assembled from local musicians at each city. Mendoza will conduct the shows on the tour.

This tour, although short, will present jazz at a scale and elegance seen today only at select festivals and events, and through organizations such as Jazz at Lincoln Center and Carnegie Hall. Given the drama that runs through the album, one might expect an accompanying performance to incorporate elements of theatre, perhaps a set, elaborate lighting or choreographed movements. But when this idea is suggested to Mitchell—something simple, perhaps a couch and a fireplace—Mitchell starts laughing.

"An orchestra in the living room? Maybe we could put berry bushes around their music stands and have the orchestra in the bushes, like in black and white cinema! Actually, one night, right after the album was completed, I saw this old movie on TV where everything was playing off the lyrics. It was the story of a trumpet player, with elegant deco settings in black and white. There was a romantic tension. They would sit down and stand up, their eyes would shoot far. And it all played off the music fantastically.

"Maybe we could make [the tour] like a black and white movie, with the curtain going up from the beginning. From the minor note, the way it begins, the Wagnerian entrance of 'You're My Thrill.' It's so dramatic. I can see an old black and white movie, with the curtains rolling up, or bunching up from bottom to top. People don't dress for the theater any more. This show would be a nice occasion to dress up."

But just because this music rings nostalgic to Mitchell, it does not stand irrelevant today. She's trying to make a real musical point, not just rehash old chestnuts. "This was an attempt to make a statement about music at the end of the 20th century, when I feel that all away across the board that music has degenerated so disgustingly."

And Mitchell, Klein and Mendoza aren't stopping now. They're currently working on two follow-up orchestral albums, one focusing primarily on Mitchell's compositions, and one covering various Christmas-themed material. So far, arrangements are in the works for "For The Roses" and "Judgment Of The Moon And Stars."

"From a poetic standpoint and musically, it's such a privilege for me to work on her songs," Klein said. "They exist on so many levels. Honestly, it makes it difficult for me to work on anything else."

For Mitchell, if this music hits a dead end, and she needs to kick the expensive habit, she always has her painting to which she can turn. "I just feel like a derailed painter," she confessed. "At some point I made this detour to the left, and I've been trying to get back to my goal forever. With the evolution of the music, and as the forces against it get more formidable, the desire to evolve [in music] seems so fruitless. But painting has a long way to go in its development."

And thus revolves the cycle of Joni Mitchell's life.

JONI SAID

On Record Companies' View of Women

"They're not looking for talent. They're looking for a look and a willingness to cooperate. And a woman my age, no matter how well preserved, no longer has the look. And I've never had a willingness to cooperate."

—to James Reginato, *W Magazine*, December 2002

JONI SAID

On Her Influence

"I think that Stevie Wonder told me that he had heard me coming in on the radio from Windsor [*CKLW in Windsor, Ontario —Ed.*], that I had influenced some of his pieces. It wasn't like he copped the lick or anything like that, but basically he went in a more adventurous chordal direction than he would have had I not existed. That's the kind of influence that I like. It is not copying."

—to Elvis Costello, *Vanity Fair*, November 2004

JONI SAID

On Selling Your Soul

"I say to young people, well, do you want to be a star, or do you want to be an artist? And they go *dink dink*, they don't know, and I say, you better know right now, because if you make any compromise, if you want to be an artist and they tell you do this, do that—you're screwed, you sold your soul to the devil."

—to *The National*, CBC-TV, January 7, 2005

JONI SAID

On Today's Music

"It's contrived money music. You know, you hear young artists talking and they're talking demographics. And I saw one girl, a fourteen-year-old, you know, with a brand new bosom and she shoved it at the camera and said, 'I want to get my music to the world!' you know? And I thought, There's no muse in this. There's a drive to be looked at, you know? So this is not—these are not creative people; these are created people."

—to *Canada AM* (radio program), April 22, 2005

JONI SAID

On Prince

"Prince attended one of my concerts in Minnesota. I remember seeing him sitting in the front row when he was very young. He must have been about 15. He was in an aisle seat and he had unusually big eyes. He watched the whole show with his collar up, looking side to side. You couldn't miss him—he was a little Princeling. . . Prince used to write me fan mail with all of the U's and hearts that way that he writes."

—Ethan Brown, *New York*, May 9, 2005

PART IV
A Defector from the Petty Wars

Increasingly embittered by the reception to her forays into jazz, Joni retreats more and more to Bel-Air and to her Sunshine Coast retreat in Canada, immersing herself in her painting. She accepts the belated mantle of genius from the pop establishment with grace—sometimes.

HEART OF A PRAIRIE GIRL

Mary S. Aikins | July 2005 | *Reader's Digest* (Canada)

Mary S. Aikins's 2005 interview with Joni for *Reader's Digest*'s Canadian edition revealed Joni, sixty-one, at her most personal. And it's fun to hear that the woman so revered as a pop poet gleefully admitting to having learned vocabulary words from the magazine's "Word Power" feature as a child.

While other interviewers queried Joni about widening harmonies and open tunings, Aikins eschewed such musical detail and encouraged her to talk about her Canadian roots, favorite author, grandchildren, domesticity, and feminism, although—of course—Joni did manage to lob a missile at her old nemesis, Joan Baez. She also expressed a now-familiar disdain for many of her acolytes among the younger generation of women, and a simmering anger, pointing out how many more units Jewel sold than she did.

Note: "Berkley" has been corrected to Berkeley —Ed.

At 61, Joni Mitchell has no plans to write more music. For her legions of admirers—indeed devotees—across Canada and around the world, this is bad news. The good is Joni is alive and well and very busy in her Los Angeles and Sechelt, B.C., homes, painting full-time and enjoying a period of reflection that includes rearranging and re-releasing her music. Her most recent CD, *Songs of a Prairie Girl*, has been released in celebration of the Saskatchewan centennial—Joni's contribution this year to the province and country of her roots.

Born November 7, 1943, in Fort Macleod, Alta., Roberta Joan Anderson and her parents moved to Battleford, Sask., after World War II. The family moved to Saskatoon when Joni was nine. That year, Joni contracted polio, but though briefly paralyzed, she did regain the use of her legs. The experience, however, turned the otherwise healthy young girl towards the arts—painting and music.

Going on to art college in Alberta upon graduation from high school, the young Joni became pregnant and gave birth to a daughter in 1965—a daughter she was unable to care for and gave up for adoption. Later that year she moved to the United States to pursue her music. [Although she married twice, she had no other children.] Joni and her daughter were reunited in 1997, and today she is enjoying being a grandmother to Marlin and Daisy.

Her music is legion and legend. Since 1965 Joni has released 22 albums—*Clouds*, *Blue*, *Dog Eat Dog* and *Turbulent Indigo*, to name but a few. In her more than 40 years as a respected and admired singer-songwriter, she has been awarded three Grammys, two Junos and a Gemini for Best Performance. In 1995 she was given Billboard's highest honour, the Century Award. In 1996 she shared the $150,000 Polar Music Prize awarded by the Royal Swedish Academy of Music [considered by many to be the Nobel Prize for music]. In the same year, she received the Governor General's Performing Arts Award and the National Academy of Songwriters Lifetime Achievement Award. In 1997 she was inducted into the Rock and Roll Hall of Fame. In 2004 she was awarded the Order of Canada.

Joni rarely gives in-depth interviews, but in April she sat down with Reader's Digest at the Hotel Bel-Air in Los Angeles for more than three hours. She wanted to start in the afternoon because that's when she typically begins her day; she likes to paint through the night, "when I'm most creative."

At turns relaxed and intense, her blue eyes flashed with life and there was much laughter. She is clearly comfortable in her skin and with where she is today. She spoke to us about her Prairie childhood, her feelings about yesterday's and today's music, the state of the world, growing old, romance and her painting.

RD: You were familiar with this magazine as a child?

Mitchell: I love Reader's Digest. I grew up on it, played "Word Power." In Grade 7, I wrote a poem and there were two oversized words for an

11-year-old in it. "Saffron" I got from my mother and "equine" I got from "Word Power." I did all my book reviews as a teenager from Reader's Digest condensed books.

RD: We won't go back and tell your Grade 7 teacher.

Mitchell: No, no. [Laughs]

RD: It seems that you have a great fondness for Saskatchewan.

Mitchell: My years there were glorious, really. I loved growing up in Saskatchewan. We always lived on the edge of small towns, so I had the luxury of riding my bicycle into the country, looking for beautiful places, which usually constituted a grove of trees.

You know, I started smoking at age nine. I had a bad year when I was nine [with polio], and I was paralyzed. I prayed to get my legs back and kind of made a deal with something, I don't know what, my Christmas tree, God, Jesus. Then an opportunity arose to join a church choir, and I thought, That's the payback, so I joined it and I became a descant singer because nobody wanted to take that melody—I called it the pretty melody.

Anyway, one of the little choir girls brought a pack of cigarettes to choir practice, and we all went out to the pond behind the United Church in North Battleford and passed them around. There was a lot of coughing and nausea, but I just took to it. For me, it was a grounding herb. I guess I will let it kill me—better it than something else.

RD: You have said certain places there give you a sense of renewal when you go back.

Mitchell: Yes, if I get out into the country—in spring, for instance, when the first crocuses pop up through the snow or when I find a beautiful place in a field, where birds fly in and out.

And driving to my Uncle Lyle's—he had a farm south of Creelman—and seeing a hailstorm coming and knowing how devastating it can be because, up until recently, everything hinged on how the farmers did. So, it is still a province of skywatchers.

RD: Your new CD, *Songs of a Prairie Girl,* coincides with the centennial of Saskatchewan. Where did that idea come from?

Mitchell: Lynda Haverstock, the lieutenant-governor, wanted me to participate as a singer. Well, I've retired. So, then she wanted me to be an emcee, and I thought, well, you need a comic for that. So I talked Rhino Records into doing a limited edition of it [*Songs of a Prairie Girl*] to be given out as party favours at the gala.

RD: How did you choose the songs for this CD to reflect Saskatchewan?

Mitchell: I rounded up everything that had some mention of it. The list was longer than the CD would hold. "Song For Sharon" [was included] for Sharon Bell. Sharon was a childhood friend of mine from Maidstone who studied voice and was going to become a singer. I was always going to marry a farmer. She ended up marrying a farmer and I became a singer. "Urge for Going" is about the long, cold winters, and it's pretty much a soliloquy about Saskatchewan.

RD: Did you find as you started to pull the songs together you did a little bit of crying inside for where you came from? I am, just listening to you.

Mitchell: I don't think I am a greatly sentimental person. I don't look back that much. I try to—you know, I am a Buddhist—live more in the moment. I look back in reflection when I am writing. When I got the collection together I said, "Oh, dear, it's all about the cold weather." So I put on the liner notes, "Get a hot beverage and stand next to the heater before you put this on." [Laughs.]

RD: You had fun doing it?

Mitchell: I am enjoying this repackaging. [I'm] using this retirement as a time to reflect on my work and to organize it categorically.

Rhino Records began with a record they wanted to call *The Best of* and I said, "You know, I am about to get my doctorate from McGill, and there isn't one song on your list that's getting me a doctorate in music. You can call this *Boss's Choices*, [but] *Best of*—in whose opinion?" The songs were the ones that the executives thought were common denominator enough to gamble on in the dog race of it all. But it was nowhere near my best work.

RD: If you were doing this when you were 40 . . . ?

Mitchell: I couldn't have done it when I was 40 because I was intolerant of my early work. The later work had been dismissed, which is the nature of the business. After record six, they try to kill you off, period. They groom for the new. I won a Grammy for *Turbulent Indigo* and the following day there was a newspaper article [about] singer-songwriters then and now, and I was in the "then" column, the day after winning the Grammy. We are just improperly educated about music. [I am] a long distance runner in a sprinter's business. It's a disposable culture.

So this leg of [my career] is not something I knew existed. I thought I was really retired. As it turns out, I am working harder than ever, and there has been a reprise given to a lot of the later work, which was dismissed without any intelligent reason. When I wrote it, it was with intent to educate.

RD: Educate?

Mitchell: [Big sigh] I am very critical of Western society. I think a fundamental error was made and the parts of the Western mind that atrophied were emotionality and sensitivity. So my work would be to give them [emotionality and sensitivity] their just due. The greatest compliment I can receive—a young man came up to me yesterday and said, "Thank you, you changed my life." I said, "Could you in a nutshell explain how?" He said, "Well, I was exposed to you at an early age, and you taught me how to feel." I thought, Okay, that's important, because in a court of law, "I know" counts, "I see" counts, "I feel" does not count and "I sense" does not count. So as a result, no true judgement can take place.

RD: You said earlier, "I am not really sentimental," and now we are talking about the importance of feelings and emotions. How do you reconcile that?

Mitchell: I think Mafia dons are sentimental. People who create great atrocities frequently are sentimental.

RD: But sentimental can be charming.

Mitchell: [Sings] "Going to take a sentimental journey . . ." I try not to look back much, [and] sentiment is kind of looking back. Right now, that is what I am doing.

RD: You're revisiting the music in a very different way. It must have brought up a bit of emotion in you. Who you used to be. We all used to be someone.

Mitchell: I don't know who I used to be.

RD: I just wonder what it meant to you, inside you, as well as the gesture to where you come from, where you see your roots.

Mitchell: Because we moved a lot, as a child, you couldn't let your roots go down too deep, otherwise pulling them up would be extremely painful.

RD: You were born in Fort Macleod.

Mitchell: Then we moved to Calgary, then we moved to Creelman, then we moved to Maidstone, then we moved to North Battleford, all before I was five. So because of all that gypsying—which was good experience for me—it made uprooting easier. As an artist in the pop arena, if you get a formula working, you stick to it. And they kill you off anyway, whether you change or not. But if you do change, you are going to lose an audience and hopefully gain another one. I watched Jimi Hendrix. [He] was at the end of his period and was trying to make it to the second period. He was humiliated by playing the guitar with his teeth and all the flashy things, and he tried to stop doing it, but the audience would say, "Jimi's not himself." And he was really having a hard time with the rejection that goes with going to your next period. He wanted to stand still, get a brass section, but he had banged into Miles [Davis] and Miles had banged into him. Miles plugged in his horn and started wearing patchwork velvet, and Jimi went the other way.

RD: He had trouble pushing himself forward?

Mitchell: He had trouble taking the rejection that goes with changing. For me, travelling around as a child, being uprooted, made it easier to take loss and rejection. Every time I changed, I would receive a lot of rejection.

RD: But you knew . . .

Mitchell: . . . It had to be done. They were going to get you for staying the same, and they were going to get you for changing. So of the two, changing was more interesting. In that way, I am not sentimental. It's easy for me to move.

I had lived in my house here since 1974. But during that time I have also lived part-time in New York. I have a place in British Columbia I get to in the summer. That could be my roots. I tend to be like a drifting air plant.

RD: What are you reading now?

Mitchell: I like Kipling a lot. I think the wisest line in all of literature, including the Bible, is Rudyard Kipling's monkey. "We are the most wonderful people in all the Jungle! We all say so, and so it must be true." There is nothing more pertinent than Rudyard Kipling's monkey at this time in our history.

RD: Can you expand on that?

Mitchell: Really? Okay, ethnocentricity. You hear it everywhere you go: My people are the most wonderful people in the jungle. My people have always said so. That is what war is about.

RD: Do you read modern novels?

Mitchell: No. I read dry books: theology, philosophy.

RD: What I call your poetry, what other people call lyrics—your great language—where do you get . . .

Mitchell: . . . the blarney? [Laughs.]

RD: Does it come from your mom? Does it come from your dad? What about your grandparents?

Mitchell: I think it comes from the Irish side of the family. Definitely I think it is blarney.

RD: When you say blarney, you don't mean it in a derogatory sense?

Mitchell: I mean it in a mischievous sense. I think some nights the blarney is running and some nights it isn't. I was born with a gift of metaphor. I would say all the arts stem from a gift of metaphor.

RD: What's the other blood in you?

Mitchell: My father is Norwegian and Sami, although because of the native tension in the region, he won't cop to that. But, yes, there is Sami.

RD: Did you know your grandparents?

Mitchell: I knew my grandmothers.

RD: Do you feel any connection there?

Mitchell: Not my paternal grandmother. She had so many children and so many grandchildren, she spoke to me only once. We were in the mountains in British Columbia—where she was living—and there was a thunderstorm and I was scared. I was about three, and she said, "Oh don't worry. It's only God dragging his buckboard through the sky."

RD: Are you good friends with your parents?

Mitchell: Yeah, I stay in touch with them. They'll be 94 this year. We have our differences. My mother and I have had a lot of friction. She always said I was too emotional and thought too much and was too sensitive. I was always *too* something, you know. But I think she was a good guide in a lot of ways. We've made our peace.

RD: What about your dad?

Mitchell: My dad was aloof. We were closer in my early childhood than we were in my adulthood. He is three quarters underwater. He's Scandinavian, and he doesn't talk a lot. The things he says when he does speak—you are not sure if you have been insulted or flattered.

RD: When you were at art college [in Alberta], did you have something in mind before you started?

Mitchell: From Grade 2 in school, I forged an image of myself as an artist. I just always knew. That was my identity.

RD: Do you know why?

Mitchell: I'm a boomer. The school was spilling over, so they dragged an old lady out of retirement and annexed the parish hall as an extra school. She was a well-meaning old gal. But she tested us, and when the results came back, she rearranged us in the room. She took the kids who had averaged A and put them in a row and called them the Bluebirds. She took the kids who had averaged B and put them in a row and called them the Robins. And she took the C's and put them in a row and called them the Wrens. The flunkies, she called the Crows. I had just been designated a third-class citizen. I was in the C row, and I liked some of the kids in the D row: They were sensitive and uncooperative in a way, but they were interesting if you could open them up.

So I looked around and I saw the A students, ever so smug about their victory, and I didn't like any kid in that row. I can't remember the exact language that I had in my head, but the gist of it was this, All they did was, she said some things to us and they said it back and then they got to sit in this row. They looked all full of themselves. Well, I didn't want to sit in that row. I took one look and I thought, But I drew the best doghouse. We had to draw a doghouse in perspective, and everyone else's was tall and skinny or inverted perspective, and at that moment—because I had just been called average—I forged this specialty in my mind: I drew the best doghouse.

RD: What an irony—a doghouse.

Mitchell: I'm a pictorial thinker. I would pay attention for maybe the first two weeks of school and my notes would be real orderly and illustrated and nice, and then it would just disintegrate into fashion and poetry.

RD: Early on you knew what you wanted to be?

Mitchell: I had a column in high school called Fads and Fashions and from [age] 12 to 16, I manipulated fashion in a way. Kids used to copy me and I didn't like it. They would wait until I bought my winter coat and then they would get the same one. I have a nose for forecasting. But I worked that out of my system, which was very good preparation for the music business, because it's manipulated. It's in and it's out. And you really don't want that interfering with serious work. You want to create things that are classic.

When I was working with [Charles] Mingus, he told me, "Don't deviate from my melody, no interpretation." So in one song called "Sweet Sucker Dance," I changed one note and he said to me, "You changed my note." I said, "Well, I wanted it to go up here as it goes into the bridge because it goes better with the text to have the inflection go up instead of . . ." "But you sing in the square note," he said to me. I said,

"Well, Charles, that note's been square so long it's hip again." So he said to me, "Okay motherf*****, then you sing your note and my note and you throw in a grace note for God." I don't know if you can put this in your magazine.

RD: We'll work on that.

RD: What made you want to make music?

Mitchell: I was inspired by a piece by Rachmaninoff that I [heard] in the movies. I would go down to the store and take it out of the jacket and listen to it in the listening room. I'd dream that I could drive a car and I could play the piano beautifully. Those were the dreams I had.

One day [my piano teacher] rapped my knuckles with the ruler, saying, "Oh, why would you want to play by ear," whack, "when you could have the masters under your fingertips?" So I quit piano lessons. That kind of brutality drove my love of music underground until I was 18, when I picked up a stringed instrument.

RD: Different place and time.

Mitchell: I was outside the box, completely, from the culture I was being raised in.

RD: Did your parents understand you?

Mitchell: They understood parts. In recent years my mother said to me, "We spent all that money on your piano lessons and you quit." And I said "Look, Mom, I think you got your money's worth, you know what I mean?" [Laughs.]

RD: Do you admire any Canadian female singers today? Do any of them remind you of yourself?

Mitchell: No. I wasn't that crazy about the music of my generation and less so of the generations that have come since. It began to degenerate with my generation. Our generation seemed to be so amateur. Frank Sinatra used to call us the bums. I was on his label and they were making money off us, but it was a big step down in a lot of ways from the musicality and the wit of the writers that came before. I am really a swing-era person.

RD: You enjoyed the female singers of the 1940s and '50s?

Mitchell: Not all of them. I am a poet who doesn't like much poetry. I'm a musician who doesn't like much music, and I am a painter who loves painting. I love so many paintings, and I know so much more about it than I do about music or poetry. But I'm not original. I love too much, so it's harder to synthesize.

RD: You don't feel that need with your art?

Mitchell: Oh, I do. It's hard to find a path untaken, whereas I have an original voice as a poet and I make original music. If I analyze it [pop music], it's a dime a dozen. From singers, I demand something—and even from myself—a nearly impossible emotional sincerity; or, on the other hand, a wry facetiousness.

RD: You've used the phrase "woman as doormat" songs.

Mitchell: A lot of the texts were written by men for women to sing, and they were perpetrating the white picket fence hoax just as feminists perpetrated the woman in the workplace hoax.

RD: You are not a feminist?

Mitchell: No. I am very domestic by nature—cook and decorate.

RD: How do you like to be treated by men?

Mitchell: I don't like to be put on a pedestal. I like a meeting of minds. I love men's company, and I have enjoyed, since early childhood, a kind of honorary maleship, although there were places where they would turn on me: "You can't do that because you are a girl".

I played cowboys all the time [growing up]. And they would never let me be Roy Rogers. Eventually I got a Roy Rogers shirt and a Roy Rogers hat and came out and said, "Can I be Roy Rogers?" "No you can't." "Look, it says Roy Rogers here!" They said, "Well, that means you're Dale Evans 'cause you're wearing Roy's clothes." "Well, what does Dale do?" "Well, she stays home and cooks." In spite of this, I am still not a feminist.

RD: Who were your early female singing influences?

Mitchell: When I first started out, I imitated a girl named Shelby Flint, as a novice singer. She had no vibrato, it was a very girly, breathy voice, easy to mimic. And then a little Joan Baez influence, but I don't care for Joan Baez. She's got a cold tone. She's chilly. She's not a soulful singer. I tend to like black singers. As a singer, I learned more from Miles Davis than I learned from anybody.

RD: I read somewhere that you consider your [early] song "Both Sides Now" a failure and "California" and "A Case of You" as just ditties.

Mitchell: I was so dismissive [because] those are what I [call] boss's choices. There was a certain amount of pressure on me to create hits, because that is where the money was. So, facetiously I created the song "You Turn Me On, I'm a Radio." The tongue was firmly planted in the cheek. It was my idea of a hit. I loved the hit parade when I was a teenager, but by the time I was in my 20s, I had kind of outgrown it. We're in this prolonged adolescence. There are no more adults. We just don't come to maturity, and I blame rock and roll for feeding this prolonged adolescence.

RD: Do you think there is anything right with today's music?

Mitchell: I am sure there is, but I don't know.

RD: You can't find it.

Mitchell: I can't find it, but I'm in a rarefied position.

RD: Have you ever watched *American Idol* or *Canadian Idol*?

Mitchell: I watched a couple of [episodes] because my friends watch them. I find it unbearable.

RD: Do you think it makes kids any more discerning when it comes to music?

Mitchell: No. To be an artist, you have to know when you fail, and you have to know why. None of these kids competing are artists. They are deluded. They don't have the ability to be self-critical, which an artist needs. You have to be able to adjudicate yourself.

RD: You've been called the most influential female artist of the 20th century. How do you feel about that?

Mitchell: That's somebody's opinion. It is not for me to say, is it?

RD: But how do you react to it?

Mitchell: I get a trickle of feedback of my influence on the street. How extensive it is, I don't know. I can tell you this: I sell [fewer] records than any singer-songwriter—any female singer you can name—so either people are taping or they are passing on their record collection to their children. Jewel sells 15 million records. I sell 500,000. From my perspective, my influence is negligible.

RD: Is there someone in this world, alive, that you wholeheartedly admire?

Mitchell: [Nelson] Mandela, Bishop Tutu, the Dalai Lama . . .

RD: Anyone from history you would like to have met?

Mitchell: I would like to have met Nietzsche. I would have liked to have met Picasso. I think I would have been a good friend to van Gogh, who needed a friend desperately. No one in the later generations. I don't think mine was a very interesting generation, in general. Jimi Hendrix I loved, you know. I got to know him a little bit. No, we weren't a great generation, and our children are a less great generation. I don't see any greatness in my generation.

RD: Are you willing to talk about your current boyfriend?

Mitchell: I don't have one.

RD: So at the moment you're single?

Mitchell: Yes, but I have a really good group of male friends. I call them my three husbands. They have been my best friends for many years.

RD: Who is your best girlfriend?

Mitchell: I have several girlfriends; I don't have a best. One of my girlfriends said to me, "Joan, you know, either you are a fan of you or you hate you." You know, my cousins say, "Well, why did you get all the talent and we didn't get any?" I mean, I'm compulsively creative, so it's difficult, I think. It's come down to two cats and a dog. My cats are getting old, one died a few weeks ago and one died a couple of years ago. And

I am an only child and happy with that. I tend to think a lot and need a lot of solitude. All I need are a couple of social outings a week at my age, and the rest of the time I'm quite happy either painting or writing.

Debbie Green and I have become really good friends over the years. She was from Detroit, a friend of Chuck Mitchell [where I get my Mitchell moniker]. Debbie Green was a folk singer. In Berkeley she taught Joan Baez how to sing and play the guitar. So Joan Baez, when she sings, she plays Debbie Green. She's not herself onstage. She has taken Debbie's persona. Debbie in her passive way gave up and let Joan have it. Joan kind of stole her soul and impersonated it.

I am lucky; I have old friends. I did not fare so well with my old friends back home. There's that tall poppy thing there—it was kind of a funny thing, generally speaking, back home. It's a weird resentment. It happens, unfortunately, again and again, and it's not a credit to the Prairie character. There is a pettiness out there.

RD: Do you ever still get the urge to "wreck your stockings in some jukebox dive"?

Mitchell: Oh, yeah. It's been a while since we went to a dance hall, my friends and I. I guess the last one was Celia Cruz, and she died this last year. We went to Palm Desert, and Celia was in her 70s and she stood up and danced all night.

And to the Apollo Theatre. I went to the Apollo Theatre once to see James Brown. And there were people there of all ages, and they were bursting from their seats . . . grannies, get the motion and stand up and dance. These days I am retired but working so hard that my excursions are more local.

RD: Would you love again?

Mitchell: Ah, no, romantic love has become transparent to me. It's like a ruse—it's a trick of nature. In the smitten period the estrogen levels go up in the male, so he becomes tender, and the testosterone levels go up in the female, so she becomes sexually aggressive. Romantic love is totally unstable and it depends on insecurity to keep it fuelled. Do I want to go through those exhausting games? Do I have the energy? No.

RD: Does that mean you are immune to it?

Mitchell: Who knows? You can't rule it out, but I am 61 years old and I heard it in an old movie: Women under 18 are protected by law, women over 60 are protected by nature. [Laughs.] It would take quite a man, I guess, to find me attractive. It's difficult for any man to live with me because they are subject to the Mr. Mitchell thing. He'd have to be tremendously secure and accomplished. And I have a tendency to learn by osmosis, so I will equal him in no time.

RD: Does old age frighten you?

Mitchell: No.

RD: Because . . . ?

Mitchell: It's natural. You know, I like this leg of my journey. When I retired, I thought, Well, I will just paint. But instead, it developed into this reflective period, a reviewing of the work.

RD: We talked a bit about feminism. Do you have a gift or advice to give your granddaughter?

Mitchell: My granddaughter is beyond advice. This is the most independent creature. She was born that way. She's got a lot of rhythm and dancing. I said to her, "How would you like some dance lessons?" She said, "I don't need dance lessons. I am already a good dancer." Daisy is kind of on her own—and wants it that way. She has her tender moments [although she] she is independent.

RD: And your grandson?

Mitchell: Marlin and I—he's the best playmate I've ever had. As a child, I didn't have people I could play with very well—where there was a good rally. I would end up playing by myself with them looking at me.

My father thinks Marlin has the makings of a great man. My daughter once said [of Marlin's father], "It's a wonder he doesn't give me bad dreams." Marlin tugged on her shoulder and said, "But, Mama, bad dreams are good in the great plan."

So I said to him, "How do you know that at three years old? It took me till 40-something to figure that one out."

RD: What did he mean?

Mitchell: It's one of the wisest things I ever heard said. It makes you believe in reincarnation. I mean, he came into this world with a wisdom that belies his years. Whether he will maintain it . . . ? It is not a wise culture.

RD: Why have you continued to live in the West?

Mitchell: I don't know. I have good friends here. I think that is the main reason. Old friends are gold.

RD: If there were one thing you could do differently in your life, what would it be?

Mitchell: In other words, do I have any regrets? Well, bad dreams are good in the great plan. Anything that you might regret, sooner or later there is an opportunity that arises out of it for growth. It may not be instant karma. It may take 20 years. Like polio. I would have been an athlete. I probably wouldn't have been an artist. The Joni Mitchell thing wouldn't have happened.

And it wouldn't be an interesting life without the travail. So, you have to get into trouble. You have to make mistakes.

RD: Did you ever have problems with drugs or addiction?

Mitchell: I did, briefly. I didn't get involved for years, and then I went on [Bob Dylan's] *Rolling Thunder* [tour] and they asked me how I wanted to be paid, and [it was like] I ran away to join the circus: Clowns used to get paid in wine—pay me in cocaine because everybody was strung out on cocaine. It was [Tibetan Buddhist spiritual master] Chögyam Trungpa who snapped me out of it just before Easter in 1976. He asked me, "Do you believe in God?" I said, "Yes, here's my god and here is my prayer," and I took out the cocaine and took a hit in front of him. So I was very, very rude in the presence of a spiritual master.

RD: And he was able to . . . ?

Mitchell: His nostrils began to flare like bellows, and he [began] a rhythmic breathing. I remember thinking, What's with his nose? It was almost hypnotic. They have a technique called emanating grace ways. I assume he went into a breathing technique and a meditation. I left his office, and for three days I was in [an] awakened state. The technique completely silenced that thing, the loud, little noisy radio station that stands between you and the great mind.

RD: And when you came out of that awakened state . . . ?

Mitchell: The thing that brought me out of the state was my first "I" thought. For three days I had no sense of self, no self-consciousness; my mind was back in Eden, the mind before the Fall. It was simple-minded, blessedly simple-minded. And then the "I" came back, and the first thought I had was, Oh, my god. He enlightened me. Boom. Back to normal—or what we call normal but they call insanity.

RD: It was his breathing technique and he managed to pass it on to you. And when you came out of your three days, you were no longer [using] cocaine?

Mitchell: Yes. Ten years later when I learned he was dying, I went back to thank him.

RD: You said once that you had pulled the weeds out of your soul when they were young, when they were sprouting, otherwise they would choke you. Did you get all your weeds out?

Mitchell: No, no. [Laughs.] Do you want to know what I am struggling with?

RD: Yeah.

Mitchell: Well, emotionality. I've got an Irish temper. I have an artistic temperament. So, I am still a work in progress.

RD: Where do you hope to be at the end of your 60s?

Mitchell: I'm a good painter. I am trying to be a great painter. My subject matter is fairly simple: people I know, landscapes I love and, you know, things around me, very personal. I think you have to be a Catholic to be a surrealist. You need early training in that kind of imagination. All the great surrealists were Catholics. I have tried a hand at it, like painting my dreams and things. I am building a vocabulary to attempt that kind of personal work. It's my painting right now that I want to bring to fruition.

RD: Is there a sense of surprise or self-revelation when you paint self-portraits?

Mitchell: No. It's no different to do a self-portrait than any other portrait. I like to paint landscapes, they are freer. But from time to time, as a discipline, I will go into portraits. It's like pool. It's a lot of little abstract angles, and if you get them right . . . It's easier actually to do it from me. It is easier for me to sacrifice myself. Whether it is an attractive portrait or not doesn't really matter. I do self-portraits because the record company insists that your picture on the cover sells more records. You have got this space to decorate and I'm the one to do it.

RD: Did you have a painting teacher?

Mitchell: No.

RD: You don't sell your paintings?

Mitchell: I have. I sold them in Japan to make money to do some videos. I sold a lot. And I regret I did because when I have an exhibition now, they are missing links.

RD: Do you paint mostly in the evenings?

Mitchell: I paint all night, under the wrong light. But the night is quiet and everything shuts down, so night is a creative time for me.

I am nocturnal by nature. So is my mother. We are all cats, maybe, of some kind. [But also] I had a lot of stalkers in my youth. I had dangerous lunatics in my yard, sometimes with machetes in violin cases. A lot of crazed [people] who wanted to marry me or murder me, so sometimes I lived under armed guard, being the night watchman. I've lived a dangerous life. Many of us have been killed, you know, John Lennon . . . It's a dangerous job in many ways because it is so intimate, and you don't know how the words will fall into a disturbed mind.

RD: When you paint, do you listen to music?

Mitchell: No. I've come to hate music. I don't listen to my own music either. I'm doing these [CDs] with a purpose. I only listen to it because I am working with it, and when I am done, when it's complete, I don't listen to it again.

RD: Your early music is very well-known and then you went through a period of releasing albums that weren't as well received. Did that upset you?

Mitchell: It upset me all the way. I just watched as the industry standards got lower and lower. The sediment rose to the top, and crap was being elevated—more formulated, less sincere. It's all very typical of a culture in decline.

RD: So that period was hurtful?

Mitchell: Yeah, but no more hurtful than what van Gogh and Gauguin went through. There is room for improvement in the music, and in some ways, I regret I lost my ability to write it. If I had continued with my education and become fluent in writing music, I think I would probably be scoring. I would be doing more orchestral composition. Not so much symphonies—because they are all in one key and I can't stay in one key in one song—it would be more like ballets or nocturnes, more of the modern forms that are less defined, more pictorial.

RD: What did receiving the Order of Canada mean to you?

Mitchell: It's a beautiful award. But my two highest honours came from black people. In the green room at the Grammys, the door flew open and in came this black girl. She threw her arms out and said, "Girl, you make me see pictures in my head. Give me a hug." Now that's an honour. The other one was a blind black piano player named Henry Butler who said to me, "You make raceless, genderless music."

RD: What difference do you see between Canadians and Americans?

Mitchell: Canadians are caught between the Queen and Yankee Doodle Dandy. That is the Canadian chip—a national inferiority complex which is unnecessary. An inferiority complex can turn into delusions of grandeur.

RD: Are the differences between Canadians and Americans becoming greater?

Mitchell: Up until this [U.S.] government, I didn't see that much difference. I would argue with Canadians who attacked Americans. I would say, "They are not as different as you think they are." But in view of the last two elections, I see a great difference. Never was America so internationally hated, and rightfully so. With this government, my opinion of Americans has dropped considerably. The irony that they could vote this government in on a moral vote—the stupidity, the horror of that. How void of morality can you be to think this is a moral president?

RD: Talking about different places, if you had to choose one place to live out your life, where would that be?

Mitchell: Well, I always thought I'd like to live in Santa Fe. New Mexico during my 20s and 30s was a wonderful place. It's changed a lot. The same thing is happening where I am in British Columbia. When I moved up there [to Sechelt in 1971], it was a lot of poor weekend fishermen, poor people, and now it's being taken over. The millionaires came and then the billionaires came.

RD: Do you have another choice?

Mitchell: I guess I'll stick with what I know. Sechelt is my place, a spiritual sanctuary.

RD: I was driving from Tofino to Port Alberni [B.C.], after doing my research for this interview. I was driving back through Cathedral Grove. There is a park with huge Douglas firs. It has been conserved as a provincial park. There we were, driving on a very rainy day, and up in one of the trees was a handmade sign saying, PAVE PARADISE, PUT UP A PAID PARKING LOT. And I had your music running through my mind, because you were on my mind, and there was this phrase from your writing. And I just wonder, how can you stop creating that?

Mitchell: Because I am so disturbed because the world is so disturbed now. I am like a canary in the coal mine.

RD: Yet you seem happy right now.

Mitchell: I'm happy one day and I'm unhappy the next. The world gets to be too much with me. I take the world on my shoulders, the whole goddamn thing, sometimes, which is not a natural thing to do. But with me it is kind of reflexive because it has been my job for so long to reflect on the world.

I've just come through a kind of a black night of the soul where I have been thinking about a lot of heavy things. Old friends of mine said,

"Joan, you always get like this when you are going to write." But I don't write anymore, so . . .

RD: Is there any hope?

Mitchell: Of writing? Or any hope for the world?

RD: You don't do any songwriting at all?

Mitchell: I haven't since '97.

RD: I don't know your painting well. For me, it's your music and your songs, and I wonder how you can retire from that huge part of yourself?

Mitchell: Easy. It's just like a wind that blew through me, that stopped blowing. It's gone.

RD: You have said you probably wouldn't write music again unless there was a "shift in you." What kind of shift would that take?

Mitchell: It would have to be to reach another spiritual level. All that is in me right now is outrage and social criticism, and I have done that. So to raise my heart in song, I would have to have a kind of spiritual breakthrough.

RD: Do you see that happening?

Mitchell: It is not something you can push or foresee.

JONI SAID

On Her Song "Woodstock"

"The irony is that the line 'I dreamed I saw the bombers riding shotgun in the sky / and they were turning into butterflies above our nation' has been taken as girly and silly and too idealistic. But the point of it is, we've got to do that—if we don't, we're done. There's a genuine urgency. Huge numbers of species have become extinct, and when that many species go, everything is out of whack. Now everybody's got these damn bombs, and they're testing them underground and under the ocean."

—to Camille Paglia, *Interview*, August 2005

JONI MITCHELL'S FIGHTING WORDS

Doug Fischer | **October 7, 2006** | *Ottawa Citizen* (Canada)

Ottawa Citizen reporter Doug Fischer was listening to Joni's 1976 album *Hejira* one night in 2006 when he realized that it was coming up on thirty years since Joni had recorded it.

On a whim, he phoned her agent in Vancouver, BC, to request an interview. Informed that it was a long shot, Fischer promptly forgot about it. A month later, Fischer got a call: Joni would talk to him the following week, but only for twenty minutes, and only about *Hejira*. As it turned out, there was no need to fear she would adhere to that stricture.

"The interview lasted more than ninety minutes, and she talked about everything, including the news she was making her first album of original music in a decade," Fischer recalled. "It turned out that was a scoop, and I wrote a 'newser' about that which the *New York Times* took credit for a week or two later, after [their] sitdown interview." —Ed.

Joni Mitchell's fighting words: When the world becomes 'a massive mess with nobody at the helm,' says the Canadian singer-songwriter, it's time for artists to make their mark.

Joni Mitchell has stepped out of retirement to work on her first album of new songs in nearly a decade, driven by a desire to add a fresh voice to the warnings of pending disaster from war and environmental damage and offer "courage through tough times."

"I was pretty sure that was it, but the music just started coming and so I'm going with it," the Canadian singer-songwriter revealed in a lengthy interview with the *Citizen*. "It feels good."

Ms. Mitchell has already laid down the basic tracks for five songs in her home studio in Los Angeles. The album is still untitled, and she doesn't know when it will be released, or even how—by choice, she is no longer under contract to any recording company.

One of the new songs draws its lyrics from If, Rudyard Kipling's 1908 poetic blueprint for personal integrity, although Ms. Mitchell has changed some of the words to make its message more direct and to "better fit" her own thinking.

Another song, Holy War, is a condemnation of war waged in the name of religion, and while it doesn't name names, it is clearly an open-ended attack on both terrorist groups and U.S. President George W. Bush.

"Since religions have failed and politics have failed and the world is in a massive mess with nobody is at the helm, the job of the artist becomes all the more important," Ms. Mitchell said. "You have to make some kind of an attempt, not to offend leaders and society, but to include and inspire them to be far-sighted."

Besides, she said, "you have to be careful how you put things these days or somebody'll kill you."

Media-shy in recent years, Ms. Mitchell agreed to talk to the *Citizen* on the 30th anniversary of the release of *Hejira*, a deeply personal road album about doomed love, considered her finest work by many critics and fans.

But in an interview that lasted well over an hour, the 62-year-old singer also talked about her views on living in the United States, her worries about Canada, the role of artists in public debate, her difficult relationship with the daughter she gave up for adoption in 1965, her dislike of the music industry and computers, and her first album of new songs since 1998.

Never a star who easily accepted disapproval, nor an artist overburdened with modesty, Ms. Mitchell stopped writing songs after the social and political commentary on 1998's *Taming the Tiger* was knocked by many critics for being excessively negative.

"I blocked myself after that," she said. "People just weren't ready for a lot of my later work—had their heads in the sand, or up their ass, or something. I was just dismissed as Chicken Little and now, of course, everything I wrote is with us in a way that no one can deny."

In characteristic outspoken style, Ms. Mitchell didn't depart the music business quietly.

To fulfill her contract obligations, she put out a couple of albums of standards and her older songs and then went on a verbal rampage. She was ashamed, she said, to have been part of an industry that was a "corrupt cesspool" producing "appallingly sick" and "vulgar" music.

Her opinion hasn't mellowed much since. She's not sure how she'll market her new album—directly to listeners over the Internet seems a good bet—but she's determined the industry won't get a penny.

"The record labels are criminally insane . . . ugly, screwed up, crooked, uncreative, selfish," she told the *Citizen*. "After the last work that I did, the vice-president of the company (Reprise) came up to me and said, 'Joan, this is a work of genius, but we're just selling cars now. We've got cute cars, we've got fast cars, we've got ugly cars—and we just don't know what to do with your car.'"

Like many of her records since 1972's *For The Roses*, Ms. Mitchell's new recording will feature jazz musicians, notably her long-time drummer Brian Blade, saxophonist Wayne Shorter and possibly pianist Herbie Hancock. Ms. Mitchell will also play piano, along with electric and acoustic guitars and synthesizers.

She is still working on the lyrics for several songs, refining and polishing as she goes along, sometimes altering the words enough that she's forced to change the musical accompaniment to suit them.

"There's a lot of back and forth, back and forth," she said. "But it's coming."

Her use of the Kipling poem—not to be confused with crooner Roger Whitaker's soppy 1970s adaptation—marks the second time she's set classic verse to music. On her 1991 album *Night Ride Home*, Ms. Mitchell rewrote several sections of The Second Coming, William Butler Yeats' 1921 lament about society's descent into mediocrity.

The changes are less radical on If, essentially a set of motivational rules for grown-up living that Ms. Mitchell believes remains as relevant today as a century ago.

In one case, Ms. Mitchell changed the lines, "If you can bear to hear the truth you've spoken/Twisted by knaves to make a trap for fools" to

"If you can bear to hear the truth you've spoken/Twisted and misconstrued by some smug fool."

"I thought 'knaves' was too archaic," she said. "And I wanted the message to be more direct. You don't have the same time to savour the words in a song as you do in a poem."

To get rid of Kipling's "macho" ending, she also altered the poem's final line—"And, which is more, you'll be a Man, my son!"—to "And, what is more, you'll be alright," which rhymes with a change made two lines before.

Does she think Kipling would mind?

"Oh no! I've made it better," she said with a big smoky laugh.

While Ms. Mitchell might not lack self-assurance—"she's about as humble as Mussolini," one of her old boyfriends, rocker David Crosby, said once—she can back it up.

Driven by a sort of restless inventiveness, Ms. Mitchell took folk stylings of near innocence in the '60s and transformed them into intensely personal, intelligent pop, jazz, avant-garde and world music in the '70s, presaging the explosion in multicultural music by a decade.

Her refusal to conform to the demands of the recording industry paved the way for female musicians like Ani DiFranco, Tracy Chapman, Alanis Morissette, Shawn Colvin, Chrissie Hynde and Gillian Welch. Her singing and songwriting have been described as an inspiration by artists as diverse as Van Morrison, Pat Metheny, Ute Lemper, Iggy Pop, Cassandra Wilson, Tony Bennett, Renée Fleming, Elton John and Roseanne Cash.

She's in the Rock 'n' Roll Hall of Fame, won or been nominated for a half dozen Grammys and a dozen Junos, and been made a Companion of the Order of Canada. Several of her songs, including Both Sides Now, A Case of You, River, Urge for Goin' and The Circle Game, have become modern standards recorded by everyone from Frank Sinatra to metal headbangers Nazareth.

"Lilith Fair was a playground for Joni wannabes," punk rocker Carole Pope told the Citizen a few years ago. "All those angst-ridden confessional singer-songwriters try so hard to emulate her style, but it's just a pale imitation of her genius."

Ms. Mitchell seems unfazed by all the flattery, and distressed that so little of her influence is apparent in the pop and rock she hears today.

"So much of it is trivial and coarse, and really not sincere. They are preaching to the choir and trying to make the other side angry," she said. "But protest isn't really that effective."

She's become convinced that to have any resonance, the message must contain the seeds of optimism, to provide ways to build rather than just tear down.

Of course, none of that stops her from ripping apart the Bush administration, which she described as gang of thugs trying to sell their war in Iraq as some sort of holy crusade.

"It disgraces the word holy," Ms. Mitchell said. "To carry on that kind of activity under the banner of spirituality is truly blasphemous."

Her bitterness is not reserved for George W. Bush, however. She is equally angry at terror groups who kill and destroy in the name of their gods.

"To do this shows they really can't understand the prophet they purport to represent," she said. "Why can't the holy men get a little holier? The world has gone mad."

Ms. Mitchell said she still finds solace on the 80-acre property she's owned since the early 1970s on British Columbia's rugged Sunshine Coast, where she tries to go for a few months every spring and fall. "L.A. is my workplace, B.C. is my heartbeat," she said.

But even that is in danger from a British company that wants to pave a bit of her paradise by building a $100-million industrial rock mine not far from her home north of Sechelt. The B.C. government has approved the plan pending an environmental impact study, due next year.

Ms. Mitchell said the 4,000 people who signed a petition to keep the mine out have been painted by the government and business press as "just a bunch of farmers and rich retirees who don't know what we're talking about. It's sickening, really."

And while she still sees herself as a Canadian first—she is both a Canadian and U.S. citizen—Ms. Mitchell believes the country is sliding dangerously close to assimilation with the U.S., politically, economically and culturally.

"Canada has got a bad case of Americanitis," she said. "Our governments have become too impressed with America. It's safer sometimes to stand back a bit from the big guys."

If all this makes her seem like a bit of a curmudgeon, Ms. Mitchell doesn't seem to care. She cheerfully concedes she doesn't own a cellphone, a computer or use e-mail.

"I don't believe in them. I just don't want 'em. Computers are eating the earth. They are frying people's brains. They are mental illness personified, and if you really want to know, I think they are part of the manifestation of human insanity."

Reminded she might need the Internet to sell her new album, Ms. Mitchell allowed that computers have "their good side," but insisted they are "just not healthy" overall.

Ms. Mitchell said she's found satisfaction as a matriarch after reuniting with Kilauren Gibb, the daughter she gave up for adoption when she was starting out as a folksinger at 21.

Not surprisingly, perhaps, there have been difficulties between mother and daughter since they came together amid a media frenzy in 1997. But Ms. Mitchell said there are as many good days as bad.

"We're in a difficult phase. She has a lot of issues. Family life does not go smoothly in the best of circumstances, and these weren't the best of circumstances," she said. "I'd say it's a work in progress and will say no more."

In an interview a few years ago, Ms. Mitchell described her daughter as "a difficult girl" and said she was "going to have to forgive me . . . before we can really get along. It's something she's going to have to work through. I can't really help her with it."

But the reunion has also brought Ms. Mitchell two "gifts that mean everything"—grandchildren, Marlin, 13, and Daisy, 7. "I just love 'em like crazy."

THE TROUBLE SHE'S SEEN

Doug Fischer | October 8, 2006 | *Ottawa Citizen* (Canada)

While *Hejira* drew fairly good reviews when it was released in 1976, especially compared to the flogging *The Hissing of Summer Lawns* got, in later years *Hejira*'s reputation continued to grow, and it now ranks as one of Joni's best-loved albums alongside *Blue* and *Court and Spark*. It's thus a treat to have her talk about how the album came about.

Ottawa Citizen reporter Doug Fischer, who'd requested an interview on the thirtieth anniversary of *Hejira*, was delighted to get it. Joni didn't just flout her own request that the interview only touch on *Hejira*, she gave Fischer enough material to present the story over two articles. In the second one, he had her talk about each song on the album—which she did, with a few conversational detours. "I kept having to refocus her on the songs to carry out my initial idea to 'profile' each song," Fischer said. "It was actually exhausting, though exhilarating as well."

Note: "Allan Ginsburg" was corrected to Allen Ginsberg. —Ed.

Doug Fischer talks to Joni Mitchell about her seminal album, Hejira

Whenever Joni Mitchell had trouble sorting out her life, she took to the road. But in early 1976, with a turbulent love affair on the rocks and too many drugs in her body, she hit the highway almost with a vengeance.

"I was getting away from a romance, I was getting away from the craziness and I was searching for something to make sense of everything," she says. "The road became a metaphor for my life."

And it inspired the album many of her fans and music critics consider her masterpiece.

Released 30 years ago this week, the nine songs on *Hejira* form the remarkable personal journal of a nomadic, romantic dreamer whose aural notebook is filled with the stories of doomed love, late night roadhouse dance floors, wedding gown fantasies, lost chances and a deep yearning to escape and start over.

Mitchell is not convinced *Hejira* is the best of the 22 albums that made her among the most influential singer-songwriters, male or female, of the past 40 years. She won't attach that label to any of her albums.

But she concedes *Hejira* is probably her one album that could not have been made by anyone else.

"I suppose a lot of people could have written a lot of my other songs, but I feel the songs on *Hejira* could only have come from me," she said an interview with the *Citizen*.

The stories they tell are so vivid, their observations so naked and the landscapes so haunting that Kris Kristofferson famously urged her in a letter to be "more self-protective . . . to save something of yourself from public view."

But Mitchell says self-confession, no matter how risky and revealing, was essential to her writing during that era.

"My songs have always been more autobiographical than most people's," she says. "It pushes you toward honesty. I was just returning to normal from the extremities of a very abnormal mindset when I wrote most of the songs (on *Hejira*).

"When life gets interesting I get very alert, and life was very interesting. I think that took the writing to another level."

Mitchell talked about the album by phone from her home in Los Angeles, where she revealed she's recording her first collection of new songs in nearly a decade. More wary of public scrutiny these days, the Canadian singer agreed to a *Citizen* request to discuss *Hejira* because, she said, the album recalls an "interesting transitional" time in her life and her career.

Musically, *Hejira* certainly marked a departure from the two jazz-tinged but radio-friendly albums that preceded it. Gone were the hummable melodies, conventional formats and jaunty horn sections she used as Top 40 flirtations on 1974's *Court and Spark* and 1975's *The Hissing of Summer Lawns*.

In their place, Mitchell offered seductively sparse rhythms, lush swirling guitars and the brilliant spark of Jaco Pastorius's fretless bass to create an unceasing musical motion that is as mesmerizing as the highways she travels in her songs.

The album is also a departure lyrically. Using the music's structural looseness to her advantage, Mitchell gives her words a simple directness and poetic polish seldom seen in her music before and rarely found again.

"To me, the whole *Hejira* album is really inspired," Mitchell says. "There is a rootlessness to it, for sure, but also discovery along the road."

Despite good reviews, *Hejira* did not sell as briskly as the more accessible albums Mitchell released during the first half of the 1970s. Although exact numbers are hard to get, there are indications sales of *Hejira* are stronger today than ever.

Voting on jonimitchell.com, an excellent fan-driven website, ranks *Hejira* as Mitchell's most popular album. A critics' poll done in the late 1990s placed the album in a first-place tie with *Blue*, a moody collection of love songs she recorded in 1971.

Mitchell says *Hejira*'s songs were written during or after three journeys she took in late 1975 and the first half of 1976.

The first was a concert tour cancelled amid turmoil after six weeks in February 1976 when Mitchell and her drummer boyfriend John Guerin ended their on-again, off-again relationship, this time seemingly for good.

Soon after, Mitchell signed on with Bob Dylan's Rolling Thunder Review, a ragged, drug-soaked circus that also variously included Joan Baez, Mick Ronson, Roger McGuinn, Ronee Blakely, Allen Ginsberg and members of the Band. She soon became a frequent cocaine user.

"I realized you couldn't stay on that thing straight—you'd be the only one," she explains. "It was just insane." Looking back, she says, the drugs had both "great and disastrous" effects: "I had terrible insomnia but I wrote a lot of epic poems," including Song for Sharon, for many the masterpiece around which *Hejira* orbits.

In danger of losing her equilibrium, Mitchell fled for home in Los Angeles. She was only back a few days when two friends, one of them a former lover from Australia, showed up at her door proposing they drive across the country to New England.

Mitchell eventually dropped them in Maine before heading alone down the coast to Florida, around the Gulf of Mexico and across the southwest back to California.

"I was driving without a driver's license," she remembers. "I had to stay behind truckers because they signal you when cops are ahead. I had to drive in daylight hours only to stay out of harm's way."

In the South, where hard rock and country music dominated the airwaves, Mitchell was a virtual unknown. "It was a relief. I was able, like The Prince and the Pauper, to escape my fame under a false name and fall in with people and enjoy ordinary civilian status."

The cross-country sojourn resulted in six of the songs on *Hejira*, which Mitchell says was originally called *Traveling*—"that wouldn't have been very memorable," she jokes.

While looking through a dictionary, Mitchell came across the word "hejira," an Islamic term for exodus or breaking with the past. It became a song title—and against the will of her record company, which wanted something less cryptic—the name of the album.

"I'd been struggling with a title for the song," she says. "The idea of departure with honour captured the feeling I was after very well."

Joni Mitchell talks to Doug Fischer about the nine songs on Hejira.

Coyote

An upbeat, playful account of an unrepentant ladies' man {"He's got another woman down the hall, but he seems to want me anyway!"} encountered on a roadhouse dance floor. Eventually the cad shows enough humanity to earn the songwriter's pity—and a one-night stand. "People considered it aggressive for a woman to be talking and acting this way at the time," Mitchell says. "They wouldn't have said it if it had been written by a man."

The song is propelled by the explosive fretless bass of Mitchell newcomer Jaco Pastorius, a flamboyant jazz-rock legend whose life ended tragically with a drug overdose in 1987.

"He was the bass player of my dreams." Mitchell says. "I can't imagine *Hejira* without him."

Amelia

Penned as she drove through the burning solitude of the Arizona desert, the song is generally considered one of Mitchell's small masterpieces.

One of several pieces on *Hejira* inspired by her difficult relationship with drummer John Guerin. It takes the form of a conversation with Amelia Earhart—"one solo pilot speaking to another," she says—during which Mitchell questions her ability to love and keep a man.

"Maybe I've never really loved/I guess that is the truth/I've spent my whole life at icy altitudes/And looking down on everything/I crashed into his arms/Amelia, it was just a false alarm."

Mitchell says the song is almost an exact account of her experience in the desert.

"I was driving, I did look up and see six jet trails and they did remind me of the strings of my guitar—and they got me to thinking about Amelia Earhart."

Furry Sings the Blues

The mostly true story of Mitchell's late 1975 meeting with Furry Lewis, a cantankerous old bluesman living in a shantytown off Beale Street in Memphis. In exchange for some Jack Daniels and a carton of Pall Malls, Lewis agreed to sing a few songs for Mitchell as he lay, artificial leg in the corner, on the bed in his shabby room.

In the song, Mitchell owns up to the unfairness of her fame and his poverty—"I don't like you," she imitates the old man growling at her—but the piece's true power lies in her chilling imagery of Beale Street's better days:

"Ghosts of the darktown society/Come right out of the bricks at me/Like it's a Saturday night/They're in their finery/Dancing it up and making deals/Furry sings the blues/Why should I expect the old guy/ To give it to me true?"

After the album came out, Lewis complained Mitchell had exploited his situation for her own gain. But if anything, her song brought his earlier work to the attention of a new audience before he died in 1981. In addition, that's Neil Young on harmonica.

A Strange Boy

Mitchell's sometimes cruel, sometimes self-critical account of the affair she had with one of two men with whom she drove from L.A. to New England in the spring of 1976.

One of the men was a former boyfriend from Australia, the other—the "strange boy" of the title—was an airline steward in his 30's still living with his parents.

"He was psychologically astute and severely adolescent at the same time," she remembers. "There was something seductive and charming about his childlike qualities, but I never harbored any illusions about him being my man. He was just a big kid in the end."

The relationship lasted only a short time, but its flaming early days in an uptight bed and breakfast are recounted in one of the album's memorable verses: "While the boarders were snoring/Under crisp white sheets of curfew/We were newly lovers then/We were fire in the stiff-blue-haired-house rules."

Hejira

The album's most melancholy track opens with a brooding electric bass smear from Jaco Pastorius that quotes Stravinsky and winds down with clarinet swirls from Abe Most that amount to a cry of despair.

Mitchell says the song explores her reasons for running away from Guerin—a "defector from the petty wars," she calls herself—and was probably the toughest tune on the album to write.

Given the blood she let to complete it, it's no surprise Hejira exposes some of the rawest emotions on any of her records.

"I'm porous with travel fever/But you know I'm so glad to be on my own/Still somehow the slight touch of a stranger/Can set up trembling in my bones."

Song For Sharon

For many fans, especially women, this is the album's tour de force.

It was mostly written, Mitchell says, while she was high on cocaine at the end of a long day in New York during which she ferried to Staten

Island to buy a mandolin and visited a fortune-teller on Bleeker Street to see if there was any hope for her love life.

Both incidents turn up in the song, a wistful eight-and-a-half-minute open letter to childhood friend Sharon Bell that meanders over the Saskatchewan flatlands and through small towns, big cities, lost dreams, and life's choices.

As kids, Mitchell longed for married life on a farm and Bell for success as a singer. When things turned out precisely in reverse, Mitchell says, Bell resented her fame while she envied her old friend's close family life.

The two women haven't been in touch since they were teens, but after the song came out, Mitchell says, Bell went to Saskatoon and made a recording of her own songs.

"She was always a beautiful singer. She made the recording not so much for commercial reasons but just to have a record of her own to distribute among family and friends."

Black Crow

A slightly atonal rocker highlighted by Larry Carlton's squalling guitar and punctuated by Mitchell's swooping voice. Black Crow is the only song on *Hejira* inspired by the singer's second home on British Columbia's Sunshine Coast.

"The song is another lament about travel, but this time about the difficulty of leaving there to get on the road," she says. "It is a quite literal description."

"I took a ferry to the highway/Then I drove to a pontoon plane/I took a plane to a taxi/And a taxi to a train/I've been travelling so long/How'm I ever gonna know my home when I see it again?"

Diana Krall, who lives across the Georgia Strait from Mitchell, on Vancouver Island—"She's among the twinkling lights over there," she says—recorded Black Crow in 2004 because she could "relate entirely to the travel difficulties and the rugged terrain it describes."

Although some have speculated the black crow of the title reflects Mitchell's interest in aboriginal culture, she says the idea for the song actually came as she watched a crow diving for shiny objects—"a weakness I can understand."

Blue Motel Room

A dreamy torch song written over a couple of nights at the DeSoto Beach Motel in Savannah, Georgia, it offers the hopeful, humourous view that Mitchell's relationship with Guerin can be rekindled.

Mitchell is no longer sure how long she stayed at the DeSoto, which she recalls as "an old, funky light housekeeping place on the beach."

But she remembers stocking her room with health food and vitamins and running on the beach in the mornings to clean the drugs from her body and "recover from the physical and mental abuse of Rolling Thunder."

Refuge of the Roads

The album's closing song was inspired by Mitchell's encounter with Chogyam Trungpa, a Buddhist teacher she stayed with for three days as she passed through Colorado on her way back to L.A.

"He's the friendly spirit in the song," she says, "I was dragged there against my will and came in looking down on him. But within minutes I realized I was in the presence of a brilliant person."

Trungpa took her to a place of enlightenment where you have no ego and no drive," she says. "It is bliss and it is nothing."

But she concedes with a laugh that Trungpa's advice to stop the self-analysis and work on reducing her ego "wouldn't be much good for an artist like me."

JONI SAID

"To enjoy my music, you need depth and emotionality. Those two traits are bred out of the white, straight males who control the press."

—to Alexandra Gill, *Toronto Globe and Mail*, February 17, 2007

JONI SAID

On Women's Wages

"I was a girl so I was underpaid compared to men's wages. I had two points on my first record, two pennies on *Blue*. That's, excuse me, 'N-word' wages—actually it's less than that. My N-friends [chuckles] were appalled. Basically they robbed me. That awoke me as a political animal and I wrote *Dog Eat Dog*. A lot of the songs I wrote at the time were a warning, which people may be ready for now but they weren't then. It was dismissed as negative and sophomoric."

—Robin Eggar, *Rolling Stone* (Germany), May 2007

TV INTERVIEW

Tavis Smiley | November 9, 2007 | *Tavis Smiley on PBS* (US)

In Joni's first appearance with Tavis Smiley, late in 2007, she chatted with the PBS host about the inspiration that led her to start writing songs again, which had resulted in the album *Shine*.

Joni had often taken abrupt breaks from the music business, beginning in 1970. After her reunion with her daughter, Kilauren, in 1997 and fueled by her increasing anger at the misogyny and ageism inherent in pop music, her threats to stop recording became more frequent. She was weary of the need to prove herself au courant with what she saw as a vulgarized, male-dominated music business that seemed to value female artists for their dancing ability and camera-ready aspect more than their talent. The business, and society in general, had turned away from what she saw as "the feminine principle," so she was happy at home with her cats, her smokes, and her painting. But then an overwhelming feeling of gratitude for her Canadian "peasant's cottage" drove her back to the piano to express her feelings in song.

Typically, Joni defends her smoking habit to Smiley, again citing that helpful Hawaiian kahuna who said it was OK that she smoked and who also helped tamp her aura down so she could be less obtrusive out in public. —Ed.

One of the most influential songwriters of the twentieth century, Joni Mitchell has made music, ranging from folk to pop-rock to jazz, for more than three decades. The Canadian-born icon has five Grammys [*Eight, as of 2018 —Ed.*] and is in the Rock and Roll and Canadian Songwriters Halls of Fame. Mitchell stopped recording in '02 to focus on her painting and poetry. Realizing that she wasn't ready to retire, she's back, with

Shine, inspired by the Iraq war. She also has a mixed-media art exhibit in New York and is working on a ballet based on her music.

Tavis Smiley: Trying to find the right word here. What a delight, what an honor, what a privilege it is to welcome Joni Mitchell to this program. The legendary singer-songwriter is responsible for some of the most enduring songs in the history of popular music. Her first collection of new material in ten years is now available through the Starbucks music label, Hear Music. The disc is called *Shine* and includes an updated version of her classic song, "Big Yellow Taxi." She also has an art exhibit and a ballet based on her music, both of which premiered in New York back in September. So what a pleasure to welcome Joni Mitchell to the program.

Joni Mitchell: Thank you so much, Tavis.

Smiley: I'm so honored to meet you.

Mitchell: Yeah, I listen to your radio show late at night, you know, all the time, so I'm honored to be here.

Smiley: I'm sitting here and I don't want to waste good quality television time, but I want to just sit and look at you. Just stare at you.

Mitchell: [*Laughter*] Well, here I stand on the brink of elderliness.

Smiley: I just want to stare at you. You were supposed to be here on an earlier date and I told my producer, Chris, "If you don't get Joni Mitchell back, you're going to get fired." Just teasing, actually. I love Chris, but I was so afraid that, when your schedule changed, I was never going to get a chance to talk to you.

Mitchell: Oh, no, no. It would happen, you know. No, I looked forward to this myself.

Smiley: Ten years. Long time.

Mitchell: Yeah, it is. I had a dry spell.

Smiley: Why so long?

Mitchell: Well, a few things. Let's see. How do I do this tersely? I handed in my last record—well, I stopped writing, so I did a cover album, a travelogue, with the London Philharmonic. I did actually two albums with them, one of standards.

When I turned it in, they didn't seem to know what to do with it. It was the end of a fulfillment of a contract and the vice president said to me, "Joni, you know, we're just car salesmen now. We got cute cars and we got fast cars. This is a work of genius. We don't know what to do with it." So they dumped me [*laughter*].

You know, prior to that, the last twenty years of my career, I was a little outside the box and they didn't know what to do with me. But I'd always say, "Well, I'll do better. Next time I'll do better." When it comes to that, you say, "What? Now I'm too good?" So that was one of the elements.

I didn't like what had happened to the music industry. I couldn't really relate to it. It was non-melodic. You know, it had kind of lost the feminine principle and become kind of vulgarized. I didn't know how to fit and I just didn't see myself, so I paint. I thought, "Fine. That's my first love anyway. I'll go back and I'll just quit. My contract is up." I wrote one haiku in about ten years, and then one day I started playing—

Smiley: That's a long haiku! [*Laughter*] Oxymoronic, I know.

Mitchell: It's sort of lonely in the decade, you know. Anyway, one day I was sitting staring out to sea at my house in Canada and just feeling so grateful to have such a beautiful place. You know, to live like a peasant costs a lot of money. I've got a tiny stone cottage by the sea. It's kind of like a shepherd's shack. You know, I was so happy there.

I ran in and I played this piece on the piano which is the first cut on the album. I called it "Gratitude" for a long time. Then I wrote a few more melodies and there was something my grandson said, "Bad dreams are good in the great plan," which I thought was profound. So I had that one line rattling around in my head and, from those little bits, I went into the studio.

Oh, and then Valentino discovered the Kipling poem which I studied in school, and I said, "You know, I'm going to set that to music."

Smiley: That's a powerful poem even today. I love that.

Mitchell: Yeah, even more so today because there's more people losing their heads all around you. [*laughter*]

Smiley: Yeah, it's a big "If."

Mitchell: Yeah, if you can hold on and keep your grounding, you know. So I went in with five pieces, you know, one finished song and the rudiments of one and basically three melodies. I told my engineer, "Just get me a good compositional tool." So he got me a synthesizer that had good orchestral sounds, and I just went in and started playing and it was so fun. Then I end up with all these tracks and the words came in the studio.

I'm not used to writing in the studio. As they came, I went, "Oh, not another one." I didn't intend to do so much social commentary, you know. That was part of my blockage. No, no, I'm not going to write love songs. No, no, I'm not going to write social commentary [*laughter*]. So I didn't have much left. But anyway, they all eked out and so here we are.

Smiley: And here we are and I'm glad we are here. I didn't want to interrupt, but you said so much. I was about to jump in because you've given me five different directions I want to move in.

Mitchell: Oh, OK.

Smiley: I don't believe in doing interviews. I believe in conversations and I believe in following the guest. You give me a lot of places to go. I don't know where I want to start. I think what I want to start with is why you toyed around with the title "Gratitude" for that song. I ask that after you give me the state of Joni Mitchell and her view of the world, her view of the music industry. You basically quit and then you go home and the first song you write is called "Gratitude." Gratitude about what?

Mitchell: Well, in 1970 I escaped the music business, which I've done several times, and—

Smiley: We'll talk about that, but go ahead.

Mitchell: I rode up Highway 101 looking for a beautiful place. When I was a kid, the kids were rough. You know, I grew up in a kind of rough neighborhood. Girls were conspiratorial. The boys were OK. Actually, I played a lot with the boys. They weren't as rough as the girls [*laughter*]. When things got too tough, I would grab—I've smoked since I was nine—so I would grab my tobacco which was hidden under the house. I'd get on my bike and I'd ride out into the country, which is only about four blocks to the outskirts in this small city. I'd look for a pretty place and I'd sit in the bushes and watch the birds fly in and out, and smoke. That was the best part of my childhood and it's still a pleasure.

So this place in Canada, I sit on my little deck at this little stone cottage. At night, the Big Dipper like hangs out in front of my door. I stand on the stoop and in the cradle of the mountains is the Big Dipper; and I sing "Follow the drinking gourd" and I feel like a runaway slave.

I've come up here and I've got this place and it's cozy. Sitting on the deck and staring out to sea, I've got seals on a rock and a big blue heron that lives in the outlet next to my house. The house is on a rock. You can't call it an island. The ocean comes around it like a millhouse. You couldn't build like that now.

Smiley: Nobody's ever going to drive by and say, "I was in the neighborhood."

Mitchell: [*Laughter*] No, it's pretty remote.

Smiley: You got to get to it, yeah.

Mitchell: Yeah.

Smiley: Again, you keep giving me so much to talk about. So you've been smoking since you were nine [*laughter*] and I assume you've never heard that smoking can be hazardous to your health?

Mitchell: Well, for me, it's a grounding herb. I mean, some people can drink and some people can't. You know, it's been a good companion for me. You know, I've got a delicate nervous system and I'm sensitive. It's a good focusing herb for me. I went to a kahuna [*a Hawaiian healer, or shaman —Ed.*] one time because, twenty years ago, I was told I had precancer of the throat by a doctor, which wasn't true. He said I had five years to live, like Sammy Davis Jr. So I went to this kahuna that a limo driver recommended to me—she was a smoker.

As a matter of fact, when they found out she had powers, her aunt gave her a pack of black Sobranies [*cigarettes*] and said, "Look, this is the purest tobacco you can get. Don't smoke on the street. It's unladylike. You need this because you got a fine nervous system." So she said to me, "No, the tobacco isn't bothering your throat," I won't go into it, but it's other problems.

So anyway, she said that I was channeling, whatever that means I don't know. But I do know that, in smoking cures, they've tried to hypnotize me and I can't be hypnotized because the gap to my subconscious is wide open. I kind of trance. I go in and out at will. She also told me that my aura sticks out further than normal. They gave me an exercise like an auric tuck so, when I enter a room, I can pull in my antenna from pulling in too much information. That makes you want to smoke [*laughter*]!

Smiley: But it also makes you a genius, though. That antenna picks up a whole lot which is why—and I've been trying to figure out why you are so bright. I get it now, your antenna sticks up better than the rest of ours.

Mitchell: Well, apparently one in a hundred people have this kind of an aura. It's almost like autism, which is more than a hundred fifty now. So it's not that rare, but, yeah, I've had like a thief brush by me and go "thief" as they brush by me, and then Pollyanna myself out of it. So I've kind of learned, you know, that the antenna does work and to trust it more.

Smiley: Now you're really complicating this conversation. I was going to ask you even before I knew the challenge that you have with your antenna being up higher than the rest of ours, which makes sense.

Mitchell: Well, you might have one too. It's one in a hundred.

Smiley: Trust me. I don't. My antenna is way down.

Mitchell: Mingus had it, I'm sure.

Smiley: He had to. That wouldn't surprise me. Charlie Mingus had it.

Mitchell: Charlie, I'm sure, did, yeah.

Smiley: I was going to ask you, and I will now, how it is that you have navigated living a life where your genius expressed through your art, whether it's your painting or through your music, your genius is just—I wouldn't say you're just channeling. You're on a different wavelength. Your gift is so profound and, when you talked about the music business and how you turned in this project and it was just so good that they didn't know what to do with it, how do you live a life where what you're hearing and what you're expressing really is beyond what some of us have the capacity even to grasp or appreciate?

Mitchell: Well, I feel like Jackie Robinson. You know what I mean? In a certain way. In retrospect, everything worked out fine, anything I might have griped about along the way and the frustrations of it, which many an artist has experienced. You know, this is not a renaissance culture. It's a culture of specialists. It's Socratic-based. Lawyer hierarchy, you know, and specialists. Maybe because it's easy for me, taking three subjects is nothing. They do interrelate, being a poet, a painter, and a musician. They do interrelate. I painted this music on. You know, I layered it on stroke by stroke.

Sometimes my music is a little too complicated for people like that, but painters have a tendency to be able to follow it. They'll be painting to it and they'll follow one of the lines one day and another one another day. They go through the layers and then they can assemble it. But for many people, it's like, "Well, there are too many notes. Take some out." [*Laughter*]

Smiley: I'm just wondering whether or not listening to this CD means I will become a good painter. I've always wanted to do it, but I have no talent in that regard.

Mitchell: Are you sure?

Smiley: Positive. You ought to see my stuff [*laughter*]. Maybe this will help me. When you say this is not a renaissance culture, you about backed me out of this chair because that hit me. I hear you, and I feel you on that, more importantly. What's the danger in that? What's the danger of our becoming the kind of society that does not value persons who are in that renaissance tradition?

Mitchell: You know, this is a money-driven culture. You can make more money off of—you know, anything too original doesn't sell, for one thing, so you don't get the mass sales. The better you are, the smaller your audience. Not to say that there aren't good middlebrow things, you know, that have a general across the board appeal. I mean, I can appreciate things on different levels, but as an artist, you know, I want to strive for excellence, which there isn't much encouraging that in this culture. The black culture has always done that because they come from behind—well, women have that in common too. We have to be a hundred times better to be considered half as good. At least, it used to be. Not so much now.

Smiley: How do you adjust, though? How do you navigate your own way juxtaposed against that kind of mediocrity when you know what you're bringing to the table, and not being egotistical about it?

Mitchell: Well, sometimes you do get arrogant because there's no one defending you but yourself. I mean, that's where my arrogance lives in, you know, defending my work. When the record company says of *Dog Eat Dog,* for instance, that album, "You didn't give us anything," to take that project and dismiss it as nothing, it had no popular appeal, but America was a land of ostriches at that time. Rah, rah, rah, Ronnie Reagan. I mean, they've canonized this guy. I'm a Reagan revenue victim, you know. He's no hero to me, you know [*laughter*], but he's a saint in this country and how it's just ridiculous. You'll know, they'll probably saint Bush, and then we'll know how insane this country is [*laughter*].

Smiley: I'm so fascinated. I could do this for hours. I wish they gave me that kind of time today. How have you, again, navigated, dealt with being inside the box that so many people want to put you in, that box of being a 1960s, 1970s artist, and they kind of just want to leave you there?

Mitchell: Well, I keep fighting it. You know, I entered the scene as a folk singer because I picked up the guitar in my teens and I started singing in art school for fifteen dollars a night. That gave me money to go to movies, have a pizza and smoke and bowl.

Smiley: And bowl [*laughter*]?

Mitchell: Yeah, at twenty-five cents a line, you know, so that was basically it. So, yeah, as a seven-year-old, I wanted to compose like Rachmaninoff. I got my wrist slapped, which they did anyway. That's the way they taught piano back then. I remember her saying, "Why would you want to play by ear—*whack*—when you can have the masters under your fingertips?" So the idea of a seven-year-old wanting to compose was not understood and was actually punished.

Smiley: I see why you started smoking at nine, now.

Mitchell: So I quit playing the piano. My mother thought of me as a quitter, and, when I wanted to buy a guitar in my teens, she wouldn't put up the money. So I managed to save up thirty-six bucks and bought myself a ukulele. I bought it on the day that they pulled my wisdom teeth. I went in with bloody sutures in my mouth and plunked down thirty-six dollars. That's pretty symbolic too [*laughter*].

So I entered into this guitar world, but I entered into it with my friends who were kind of wonderful, high-spirited, rowdy, beer-drinking Canadians to accompany bawdy drinking songs at wiener roasts which were basically beer fests [*laughter*]. I learned a few folk songs, but I did enter the arena as a folksinger.

The moment I began to write my own music, I would say my roots began to come out, which was more in classical music from what my mother had in the house, Debussy and so on. You know, I listened to a lot of Miles as a teenager because they used to pay me to do murals and they'd pay me in jazz records, Lambert, Hendricks & Ross—

Smiley: Not a bad way to be paid. Jazz records, wow.

Mitchell: Yeah. But that music was so incredible. I never thought when I was nineteen listening to Miles that I'd be playing with Wayne [Shorter] and Herbie [Hancock]. It never entered my mind. I didn't know that—I was going to art school. I was going to be a painter. So my roots really—

Smiley: Is it Herbie that just did a project of all your stuff?

Mitchell: Yes.

Smiley: I heard some of that. A whole record of Herbie covering Joni Mitchell. [*Hancock's Grammy-winning* River: The Joni Letters —*Ed.*]

Mitchell: Yeah.

Smiley: That's amazing, which leads me to this. How do you process that? When you said you can't imagine you'd ever play with Herbie, here

Herbie is now covering your stuff, but he's just one of so many people that have covered your stuff over the years.

Mitchell: Well, Herbie and Wayne and I are old friends. I mean, we've spent New Year's—there was a restaurant or a bar called the Nucleus Nuance—our families, we had New Year's together with Herbie's sister and my parents, so we go back. There's a comfortability there and a friendliness. Wayne, of course, I adore and he's been on every record except this one since I don't know what year, somewhere in the 1970s.

Smiley: But for everybody else, your stuff has been covered, as I said at the top of the show, so many times and that makes you feel how? Anything?

Mitchell: I do like the idea. It's been said of my music that it's too personal for other people to do. Like I read recently—oh, I know what it was. It was in a review of Herbie's album, *River*, the "overexposed *River*." I went, "Overexposed?" See, that's the new mentality. That used to be a *standard*. The more it was played, it earned its standard stripes, but now it's considered overexposed. Songs are supposed to be disposable and most of them deserve that, you know, because they're made by a committee now. Eight people stand up to take a bow. Eight people can't make a decent song. I'm sorry [*laughter*].

Smiley: [*Laughter*] You got to love Joni Mitchell. You got to love her. Golly, you're putting out too much for thirty minutes. I can't fit all this in in thirty minutes [*laughter*]. So tell me about the new CD. I mentioned earlier that you're the second artist signed on the Hear Music label, Starbucks label. Tell me about *Shine*.

Mitchell: What do you want to know about it?

Smiley: Everything. Whatever you want to tell me about it.

Mitchell: The whole album or the song in particular?

Smiley: The project, yeah.

Mitchell: OK.

Smiley: You had fun doing it?

Mitchell: I had fun doing it. Dano, my engineer, and I enjoyed each other's company. Even after that long layoff, I felt like—I had this wonderful synthesizer. Most producers will tell you, don't play off one instrument. You know, mix it up. Then there's this whole hierarchy of what's the hippest new one and all that. This had great sounds in it, so I just did it on one machine, which means the vibratos match, which is a little tight. But then Duke Ellington's guys played together so long that their vibratos matched. That was my defense of making it all off one machine.

Smiley: It worked for Duke [*laughter*].

Mitchell: It worked for Duke. You know, I'm like, OK, my band's been together for forty years. That's why they play so tight [*laughter*].

Smiley: What made you go back to "Big Yellow Taxi"?

Mitchell: For the ballet?

Smiley: Yeah.

Mitchell: You know, you don't have encores in the ballet, but he said we need to do an encore, so I thought OK. The ballet was composed of my least popular material. It's a war ballet basically. I said to Jean—they had a ballet called "Dancing Joni," which was about my life and he said, "What do you think?" I said, "I think it's kind of fluffy for the times."

I was doing this art show and he saw the mockup on my pool table. I had it all laid out in miniature. He went, "Oh, we must put this in the ballet." I said, "Well, you can't put that with that ballet. It's too fluffy. I'll give you a war ballet, but I warn you that these are my least popular songs . . . your sponsors are Texas oil men. They'll pull out and so on and so on and so on. Nobody likes these songs. I think they're my best songs I ever did, but people don't want social commentary from me for some reason. You know, they want me to suffer personally for them [*laughter*]. I don't know what it is, but your sponsors will probably pull out. Are you willing to take this risk?" He said, "Yes." I said, "OK, let's do it." So they did pull out. He had to hustle to find a sponsor for the ballet and everything, but once we performed it, it was a tremendous success.

The pre-press had me like this monster, "Joni's coming to insult the business community in Calgary," which is oil men, and they had me looking like I'm on the warpath with all of these cracking oil factories behind me. It was on the business page of *Macleans* magazine. Then afterwards, the post-press was remarkable and I got letters saying, "Well, I'm a business person, but I must admit I really enjoyed your ballet." [*Laughter*]

Smiley: That makes you a true renaissance woman, when you're doing records and ballets, to say nothing of the art. Before my time runs out, this catalog. Your painting is wonderful.

Mitchell: It's ink on canvas and they're as large as a door. It's kind of like "Duck Soup," you know, it's kind of like one war turns into another war, just looking at war and torture and just taking a look at it, you know. I wouldn't call it protest, although I certainly have that in me.

Smiley: You couldn't get away from the social commentary if you wanted to. It's just part of who you are.

Mitchell: Yep.

Smiley: So now that you're back ten years later, are you going to stick around for a while or are you going to disappear on us again?

Mitchell: Well, no. I think I'm going to keep going. I'd like to do another one. I mean, this label has been very good. I should have been on a jazz label a long time ago, I guess, because I'm a moderate seller. You know, I have a small, relatively to a pop, audience like Miles. You know, I sell well as a jazzer, but I'm the wrong generation. You know, every generation has a larger constituency built in because there's more people and there's more players in the home and they've been programmed to stick to their demographic. That folksinger from the 1960s, they try to kill you off.

You're not supposed to be able to ride several decades, whereas actors can. It's just the way the music business is structured for money. You're supposed to die so you don't get to a second contract and they don't have to pay you a decent wage [*laughter*].

Smiley: The word icon is way overused in our society. Speaking of what's wrong with our society, the word "icon" used way too easily. It just flows off our lips with ease. But Joni Mitchell is an iconic figure. I revel in your humanity.

Mitchell: Oh, thank you.

Smiley: I'm just delighted and honored that you came by to see us. The new CD from Joni Mitchell on Hear Music. Go to Starbucks and get it anywhere. Joni Mitchell, the new CD is *Shine*. She's back and she promises to stick around for a while. What a delight to have you here.

Mitchell: Oh, my pleasure.

Smiley: Thank you so much. I appreciate it. I'll die and go to heaven now.

MUSIC AND LYRICS

Geoffrey Himes | December 2007 | *JazzTimes* (US)

In this *JazzTimes* dual interview with Joni and Herbie Hancock, Geoffrey Himes explored the pushback both musicians suffered after challenging the firewall between pop music and jazz. Both took heat for their experimentation: Joni from those who wanted her to keep turning out more iterations of *Blue* and *Court and Spark*, and Hancock from jazz purists who were horrified at his funk explorations.

Himes also wrote about an underappreciated aspect of Joni's craft—that she wasn't just pushing for more elastic rhythms and wider harmonies but was playing with the conventions of grammar and style in her lyric writing, as well.

Joni's antiwar sentiments were always bubbling just under the surface, and she speaks about her political anger, which found expression in her 2007 "war ballet" *The Fiddle and the Drum*, created with Jean Grand-Maître of the Alberta Ballet, using her 1969 song. Her thoughts on war and society are a reminder of how missed her feisty commentary is in these years after her 2015 aneurysm.

Himes interviewed Joni and Hancock in a nonsmoking conference room in a Manhattan hotel in 2007. Joni sat down at the round table, pulled out a pack of cigarettes, and asked if anybody minded if she smoked. If they did, nobody was willing to say so. —Ed.

Herbie Hancock has a confession to make: For the longest time, he ignored the lyrics of the songs he played on. Asked if he considered the lyrics when he assembled his poll-topping *Gershwin's World* album, he says, "Not at all," and spreads his hands before his face as if he were pushing the words aside so he could focus on the music.

What's peculiar about this confession is that the veteran pianist makes it in a midtown Manhattan hotel while sitting next to one of the great American lyricists of the late 20th century, Joni Mitchell. Mitchell, wearing a black jacket over a low-cut black dress and balancing an omnipresent cigarette between her long fingers, doesn't seem offended. In fact, she seems amused that her longtime friend and collaborator approaches music so differently. Hancock, wearing a black shirt beneath a black jacket with leather collar, tries to articulate just what that approach is.

"I never paid attention to lyrics," he says, "because I wasn't used to doing it. That's very typical of jazz instrumentalists; we're so dazzled by melody, harmony, textures, all those kinds of nuances, that when we hear a vocal in English it might as well be in Polish. I can't understand the lyrics as they're sung by anybody. I have to shove the music out to understand that it's English, and I have a hard time doing that because the music pulls me in like a magnet."

Mitchell, who still wears her signature blonde bangs and shoulder length hair, has just released *Shine*, her first album of new songs in nearly 10 years. Like all of her recordings, this one is word-drunk, a torrent of metaphor, imagery and run-on verse. She even adapts other literary sources—Rudyard Kipling's poem "If" and Tennessee Williams' play "The Night of the Iguana"—into song. Several songs make angry denunciations of the ecological damage inflicted on our planet.

The title track, though, offers a somber prayer for the planet's healing by asking the sun to shine down on everything from "Frankenstein technologies" to "fertile farmland." Singing over Brian Blade's rumbling drums, James Taylor's patient acoustic guitar and her own atmospheric synth, Mitchell begins with evenly counted lines. But by the second verse she has so much to say that she bursts the bounds of meter to get it all in, relying on Blade's flexibility to make it work. Words are still that important to her. Yet after a long career during which the press and fans have focused obsessively on her lyrics and ignored her music, she seems flattered that Hancock has the exact opposite take on her songs.

For all his willful obliviousness to the words, Hancock has repeatedly worked with this most literary of songwriters. The keyboardist first played with Mitchell on her 1979 project *Mingus*, which combined her lyrics with Charles Mingus' music. Hancock rejoined her for the two orchestral albums, 2000's *Both Sides Now* and 2002's *Travelogue*, and invited her to sing two songs on 1998's *Gershwin's World*. But it wasn't until he devoted his new album, *River: The Joni Letters*, to her music that he sat down and came to terms with her lyrics.

"With *Gershwin's World*," confesses Hancock, sporting purple shades and a trim Afro, "I didn't pay attention to any of the lyrics. In that sense it was business as usual for me. There were other challenges, but that was never an issue. Even with Joni's earlier albums, what attracted me was all the other stuff: the melody, the harmony, the texture. This is the first time lyrics have ever been an issue with me."

Oddly enough, Hancock's breakthrough came not on one of his new album's six vocal numbers, which showcase the singers Norah Jones, Tina Turner, Corinne Bailey Rae, Luciana Souza, Leonard Cohen and Mitchell herself. Instead, it came on one of the four instrumental numbers, his arrangement of "Both Sides Now." It begins with two minutes of spare, impressionistic solo piano before Dave Holland's bass and Vinnie Colaiuta's brushes join in. The familiar melody isn't heard until five minutes into the piece, when Wayne Shorter's tenor sax finally voices it, but the whole piece radiates the feeling of looking at every musical phrase, every feeling, from at least two sides.

"Something happened when I was trying to figure out what to do with that song," he explains. He demonstrates by spreading his fingers and pounding them on the white tablecloth as if looking for a new chord. "I started following what I was feeling, and it was getting more and more interesting. I said, 'It would naturally go here, but I want it to go somewhere it's not expected to go.' I tried something and I said, 'Oh, wow, that's a surprise.'

"But then I thought, 'Wait a minute, these are Joni's words. I haven't really looked at them to see if what I'm doing makes sense in terms of the words.' So I went back and looked at the words. I'd read two lines and I'd have to stop. I'd go, 'She didn't say that, did she? How could she come up with that?' Finally, I said, 'The meaning as I feel it seems to say it's OK for me to do this.'

"Yeah," Mitchell agrees enthusiastically, "because it's a discourse on fantasy and reality."

If Mitchell seems charmed that Hancock thinks of her as a musician first and as a lyricist second, he seems equally charmed that she doesn't care whether he sticks to the jazz tradition or not. They have wound up side by side in the no man's land between jazz and modern pop, even though they arrived from vastly different starting points.

She was born 64 years ago as Roberta Joan Anderson on Canada's western prairie. She got her start singing solo with her acoustic guitar in folk coffeehouses and had her debut album produced by California rock star David Crosby. But in 1975, after six studio albums had established her as the leading female singer-songwriter in the folk-rock scene, she challenged her audience—and subsequently lost many in it—by recording jazz-influenced arrangements with jazz musicians.

Hancock was born 67 years ago in urban Chicago; he was a classical-piano prodigy who was playing with such jazz figures as Donald Byrd and Phil Woods while he was still in college. He was only 23 when he was invited into the Miles Davis Quintet. But after playing a prominent role on some of Davis' most enduring records and releasing his own solo projects such as 1965's *Maiden Voyage*, Hancock left Blue Note Records in 1969 and risked his reputation as the best jazz pianist of his generation by recording such jazz-funk sessions as *Fat Albert Rotunda*, *Mwandishi* and *Head Hunters*. He sold a lot of records but also endured a lot of criticism.

"Herbie and I have the same problem from two different approaches," Mitchell explains. "He was going too far into pop and I was going too far into jazz. They accused him of commercialism, and they accused me of obscurity."

"I learned early on that if I'm feeling what I'm supposed to do," Hancock responds, "that's all I'm supposed to do: no ifs, ands or buts about it. Who's sitting there behind the piano? Me. Not them. Who has to answer to that? Who's it coming out of? It's coming out of me. I have to be honest with myself. She does the same thing."

When James Brown and Bob Dylan and the Beatles revolutionized pop music in the mid '60s, they made a sharp break from Tin Pan Alley pop. In the process, they lost connections to a jazz world that was still tied to show tunes and swing or bop standards or else making its own radical leap into free jazz.

This had unfortunate consequences: Brown never married his revolutionary beats to equally bold harmonies. Dylan never matched his sprawling, dazzling verbiage to similarly elastic music. The Beatles never devoted their studio innovations to the kind of harmonic sophistication or instrumental prowess associated with jazz. Jazz vocalists got stuck in a time warp of the pre-Beatles American Songbook and never got to wrestle with the poetic breakthroughs of Dylan and his disciples. Many jazz instrumentalists who were locked into a template of acoustic swing and bop denied themselves the funk grooves and amplified instruments of the era.

The wall between acoustic postbop and electric funk was breached fairly quickly. Hancock and his employer, Miles Davis, were fascinated by the records that Brown and Sly Stone were making and wanted to make jazz records the same way. That led directly to Davis' *Bitches Brew* and later, Hancock's *Head Hunters*. It took much longer for the wall between Dylanesque singer-songwriters and jazz improvisers to fall. Perhaps it was because jazz vocalists were stuck in a retro phase and all the innovations in jazz were coming from instrumentalists, most of whom, like Hancock, didn't focus on lyrics. Perhaps it was because many of the pop-singer-songwriters were rudimentary musicians.

That was certainly true of Dylan, who never showed much professional interest in modern jazz. But Mitchell, one of Dylan's best heirs, was hiring jazz players for her records by 1974.

"I had jazz records in high school," she recalls, "Lambert, Hendricks & Ross, Oscar Brown Jr., and Billie Holiday. I had race records when nobody in Saskatchewan had race records. This DJ in Edmonton cleared out the radio station library, so I ended up with all these Louis Jordan records, and they were great, 'Saturday Night Fish Fry' and all that. So when rock 'n' roll came along, I went, 'That's nothing new; that's Louis Jordan.'

"I was steeped in swing and I like swing still. I liked Miles, not so much Coltrane. I like the warmth of Johnny Hodges, and I indulged that on *Shine*. No one uses that sax sound with that vibrato anymore because it's corny, but it can be hip again if it has heart."

When Diana Krall released her entry in Hear Music's Artist's Choice series in 2004, a collection of her favorite songs by other artists, Mitchell was flattered because it included her own version of "Amelia." Mitchell contacted Hear and asked if she could assemble her own Artist's Choice CD.

Given the go-ahead, she included only two folk-flavored singer-songwriter selections on the 18-track 2005 release: Dylan's "Sweetheart Like You" and Leonard Cohen's "The Stories of the Street." She put "Saturday Night Fish Fry" right before Chuck Berry's "Johnny B. Goode," so her point about Jordan's link to early rock 'n' roll would be obvious. But she also included Holiday's "Solitude," Duke Ellington's "Jeep Blues," and Davis' "It Never Entered My Mind" to demonstrate how much jazz had meant to her from the very beginning.

"I reviewed everything that has ever given me a major buzz," she explains. "I went all the way, as far back as I could remember to 'Lollipop, Lollipop.' We drafted a list, and some things held up and some things didn't. I asked myself, 'What did I ever care about?' I wanted to include 'In a Silent Way' and 'Nefertiti,' but they were too long so they were left off. But it's a pretty good cross-section."

Mitchell may have loved jazz from her adolescence, but when she was a starving art student in Calgary in 1962, she needed to make some spending money. That was more easily done by accompanying herself on acoustic guitar as she sang folk songs in the local coffeehouses than by putting a jazz combo together. Moreover, a few years later, when she was captivated by Dylan's example of literary expression through song, there was no parallel example in the jazz world.

So she threw herself into the folk-pop singer-songwriter world, traveling from coffeehouse to coffeehouse all over North America and making contacts with the likes of Neil Young, David Crosby, and Tom Rush. Before she even released her debut album, 1968's *Song to a Seagull*, her songs had already been recorded by Rush, country star George Hamilton IV and England's Fairport Convention. Her 1969 album, *Clouds,* included "Both Sides Now," which Judy Collins turned into a Top 10 pop single.

Her fourth album, 1971's *Blue*, unveiled some of her most enduring compositions: "River," "A Case of You" and "All I Want." When Keith Jarrett recorded the latter tune on 1971's *The Mourning of a Star*, a trio project with Charlie Haden and Paul Motian, it was the first indication that the jazz world was noticing Mitchell. She responded by hiring the Crusaders' Wilton Felder and Gerry Mulligan's Tom Scott for her fifth album, 1972's *For the Roses*, which yielded her first Top-40 pop single, "You Turn Me On I'm a Radio."

On 1974's *Court and Spark*, Felder and Scott were joined by Crusader keyboardist Joe Sample and Mulligan drummer John Guerin. The album yielded two Top-40 singles: the No. 22 "Free Man in Paris" and the No. 7 "Help Me." Mitchell was at a crisis point. She had just achieved the greatest commercial success of her career, and yet she was growing bored with the folk-rock formula and was increasingly drawn toward the jazz world.

"I was dating John Guerin," she remembers, "and we were hanging out together. We were in jazz clubs all the time and we went to parties with jazz musicians. That was my world. So naturally when I went into the studio, I leaned in that direction. But they wanted to keep me in that box as a folk singer, even though I hadn't been a folk singer since 1965. Nobody noticed that I was a composer and an arranger; all they talked about were the lyrics. Even on *Court and Spark,* I had sung the parts I wanted and had them transcribed—that cut things loose and they got jazzier."

They got jazzier still on her next album, 1975's *The Hissing of Summer Lawns*. Backed by Guerin, Felder, guitarist Larry Carlton, lyricist Victor Feldman and flutist Bud Shank, Mitchell moved further yet from the singer-songwriter template as she gave her melodies jazz harmonies, elastic rhythms and ever-longer phrases.

She began to rub out line endings so the lyrics ran on until they resembled prose or modern blank verse. While most song lyrics preserve the short lines, even meters and regular rhyme schemes of early 18th-century poetry, Mitchell was looking for a way to give song lyrics the freedom of modern poetry, where lines extended as long as they needed to. It was a breakthrough that she was rarely given credit for, and she could never have done it without the flexibility of jazz.

"When you try to write in long phrases like that," she says, "you suddenly have a bar of 5/4 or 3/4 in there all by itself, but it's only weird if you count it. It was probably Jon Hendricks that started me doing that; the old shoeshine tap dancers also thought in terms of long phrases. As a singer, I'm trying to never sing the same way twice; I'm trying to make the words come out like I've never said them before. So sometimes I'll take an upbeat for a downbeat and turn a phrase inside out and then it'll come back around. But Miles and those guys never had a problem with it."

The Hissing of Summer Lawns is such a crucial transition album for Mitchell that it supplied three of the eight Mitchell compositions on Hancock's *River: The Joni Letters*: "Edith and the Kingpin," "Sweet Bird" and "The Jungle Line." When Nonesuch Records assembled *A Tribute to Joni Mitchell* this year, three more songs from *The Hissing of Summer Lawns* were featured. Elvis Costello sang "Edith and the Kingpin," Björk sang "The Boho Dance," and Brad Mehldau contributed a solo-piano treatment of "Don't Interrupt the Sorrow."

On the same album, Cassandra Wilson sang "For the Roses" backed by her road band. It was the third time Wilson had recorded a Mitchell tune: She also sang "Both Sides Now" on a Pat Martino album and "Black Crow" on her 1993 breakthrough *Blue Light 'til Dawn*. Before she recorded that album, her producer Craig Street challenged her to reconcile the split between her jazz and singer-songwriter enthusiasts.

"Craig did this Freudian thing," Wilson recalled in 2002, "and had me lie on a couch as he asked me questions about how I felt about the music I had grown up with. I told him about playing Joni Mitchell songs on guitar while I was in college in Mississippi, and said, 'But how am I going to be a jazz vocalist and do the folk thing?' He said, 'Why not? It's who you are.' So I decided to come out of the closet.

"I think these songs stand up musically. Joni Mitchell writes great melodies and great chord changes. She writes very freely, maybe because she's unschooled, and the things she does with guitar tunings have always fascinated me. And the language that she and Bob Dylan use is so powerful. Their lyrics are connected to folk, the common folk, whereas Cole Porter and Harold Arlen are more connected to the wealthy, the bon vivant. Dylan, Mitchell and Robbie Robertson are writing for the disaffected, discontented and disenfranchised; they're saying, 'Hey, it's not perfect down here. We have some demons to deal with.'"

Mitchell's move toward jazz faced resistance not only from label executives and folk fans who felt deserted, but also from jazz musicians who felt invaded. "Some people still think I'm trying to be jazz and not quite making it," Mitchell confesses. "My music is a little different from jazz. Jazz has got its own laws."

"What laws?" Hancock interrupted. He seemed genuinely annoyed. "Who says you're not making it? Who cares?"

"Some people are scared of it. Annie Ross once told me," and here Mitchell goes into a nasal impersonation of the jazz singer, "'Joni, don't forget where the one is.' But Herbie showed me that when you get down to the end of the bar, if you can't get in on one, you can get in on two and it's OK. He keeps pushing me until I have to cross the bar."

"I love going across the bar," Hancock agrees. By now the interviewer has been forgotten and the interviewees are talking to each other.

"You and Wayne play together so much that you're used to that," she replies, "but for me it's challenging. I guess you found it challenging to my music, too. It's wide harmonically like jazz, so you have a lot of freedom of choice in notes, but it's not within the laws of jazz. I remember Victor Feldman was gritting his teeth on this one song. I thought, 'Oh, you don't like the words.' And he said, 'I hate the music.' I said, 'Why?' He said, 'It's wrong.'"

"On 'Ethiopia,' Wayne said, 'What are these chords? These aren't guitar chords. These aren't piano chords. What are these chords?' But he jumped in and played like a champ. He called them 'Joni's weird chords.' I tried to get him to explain what was weird about them. One thing that's weird is I'm playing chords that fit complex emotions that I feel. Wayne said, 'Well, they told us at the Berklee [School] of Music to never go from a sus chord to a sus chord. Never stay on a sus chord too long.'"

"Wayne was just saying what he was taught," Hancock responds, "not what he believes. I once wrote a song that's all sus chords except for one: 'Maiden Voyage.' I think that's a pretty good composition."

"I had a peculiar idea about what the bass should do," Mitchell continues, "so I had real trouble with bass players. I started my arrangements in the middle where my voice and guitar are. Then I started overdubbing, up and up. So I said, 'Why can't I do the same thing going down?' 'You can't,' said the bass players. 'Why not?' I said. 'Because the bass has to play the root of the chord.' 'Why do you have to play the root of the chord?' I said. 'Why can't you play this note?' And they said, 'You're trying to tell me how to play my instrument.' This one bass player told me, 'There's this really weird bass player down in Florida who plays with Bob Hope and Phyllis Diller. You'd probably like him.'"

That "really weird bass player" was Jaco Pastorius, and Mitchell did like him. He played on her next two albums, 1996's *Hejira* and 1977's *Don Juan's Reckless Daughter*, joined by Wayne Shorter on the latter. Suddenly, Mitchell wasn't just playing with crossover pop-jazz musicians; she was holding her own with major jazz figures. Charles Mingus, as major as it gets, was so intrigued that he invited Mitchell to recite Bible verses over some new music he had written.

It's a measure of how absent lyrics were (and are) from the thinking of most jazz leaders that Mingus didn't even think to ask one of the era's greatest lyricists to write new words for his music. Mitchell insisted, however, and Mingus was astute enough to agree. Everyone knew the great jazz bassist was dying, so the collaboration was fraught with extra meaning.

"It started off as his record," she recalls, "but then I realized that he wanted a bigger funeral. So I said, 'Let's make it my record, because it will get more attention.' But when it switched over to my record, I took a little more control. I cut the songs at Charles' request with all these bands, and it just seemed tiring; all those solos. But when I got Herbie and Wayne from that Miles band, plus Wayne, Jaco and Peter [Erskine] from Weather Report, it wasn't about solos anymore. Suddenly it was all about dialogues."

"On most of our records Wayne and I have a dialogue," Hancock agrees. "Normally on jazz records you have solos."

Mitchell admired Mingus but wasn't intimidated by him. In fact, she proved as obstinate as the legendarily stubborn composer. He sternly instructed her, for example, not to deviate from the notes he'd written. At the hotel table, she sings his original melody for "Sweet Sucker Dance," going "ba, ba, ba, ba, ba," and descending at the end. She then demonstrates how she altered the tune to fit her words, singing the same line so it ends on a rising note. When she sang the song line for Mingus back in 1978, he was not amused.

"He said, 'You're singing the wrong note.'" Mitchell recounts. "I said, 'The word has to go up there. If it goes down the way you had it, it sounds resigned and it needs some optimism there.' 'But that's a square note,' he said. So I said, 'You know, Charles, that note's been square so long it's hip again.' He said, 'OK, motherfucker, you put in your note and my note and two grace notes too.'"

The finished version of "Sweet Sucker Dance" opens with Hancock stating Mingus' odd chord changes on Fender Rhodes piano. Mitchell enters, contorting lines such as "Tonight the shadows had their say, their sad notions of the way things really are—damn these blues" till they fit Mingus' twisting melody, which does rise optimistically at a crucial juncture. Before long Pastorius and Shorter are taking turns echoing the vocal lines, while Hancock tries to tie all together harmonically. There are no conventional solos, but there is improvised give and take throughout.

Mingus died Jan. 5, 1979, and Mitchell's album, *Mingus*, was released in June. She spent the summer touring with an all-star jazz band that included Pastorius, Pat Metheny, Lyle Mays and Michael Brecker. The Santa Barbara show was released in 1980 as the double-LP album *Shadows and Light*, featuring three of the Mingus songs plus nine tunes from the 1975–77 folk jazz albums. Her next album, 1982's *Wild Things Run Fast*, featured Larry Klein, a 24-year-old bassist who had already played with Shorter, Freddie Hubbard and Joe Henderson. He would marry Mitchell the same year and go on to produce six of her albums as well as Hancock's *River: The Joni Letters.*

Klein was a typical Southern California baby boomer who had grown up on the Beatles and Dylan. As a bassist, however, he quickly realized that he wanted greater technical challenges than rock offered, so he soon turned to jazz. He played both acoustic bop and amplified fusion in Hubbard's band for several years, and backed up singers such as Carmen

McRae and Dianne Reeves. But it never occurred to him that he could combine his newfound love for jazz with his leftover love for the lyrics of Dylan, Leonard Cohen and John Lennon. They seemed like two different worlds.

"I was talking about this with Herbie while we were making the album," Klein says over the phone from L.A. "I know just what he means when he says he never paid attention to the words. When I played a song like 'Just One of Those Things' or 'All the Things You Are,' I never thought about what the words meant. I thought of them as melodic material floating over a series of chords. It was very compartmentalized. Somebody told me that Dexter Gordon was a real stickler for everyone in his bands knowing the words to every song they played, but that seemed like the exception to the rule in jazz."

"I'm 67," Hancock says, "and I started playing piano when I was 7. Through all that time, there was only one song where I paid attention to the lyrics, and that was because for years everyone kept talking about how great the lyric was. I would always say, 'It sure is,' but I had never really bothered to look at the lyrics. Finally, I decided to see what they were talking about. It was 'Lush Life,' and one day I sat down and looked at it."

Hancock mimes spreading a lyric sheet on the hotel table and leaning over to read it carefully. "I looked at every line, and it just tore me apart. I went, 'It's unbelievable someone could write something like this.' I did the same thing with Joni's lyrics this year and had the same reaction."

Klein had a similar epiphany when he got the call for the *Wild Things Run Fast* session. One song on the album described a woman who has shut down emotionally after a bad marriage and life's other disappointments; nothing's left but the "Moon at the Window," as the title put it. The challenge was to find music that worked as metaphorically as the words.

"The most amazing player in this regard is Wayne," Klein exclaims. "The first thing he played against that song was a musical argument between a man and a woman. To me, that's astonishing—to listen to an idea and immediately transform it into music. Wayne's sense of metaphor, the way he plays off words, is incredible. I said to myself, 'Here's how I can pull together all these things I love.'"

Klein and Mitchell were credited as co-producers of her next four albums: 1985's *Dog Eat Dog*, 1988's *Chalk Mark in a Rain Storm*, 1991's *Night Ride Home* and 1994's *Turbulent Indigo*. The last was made while the couple was in the midst of divorcing.

"I started out just being the bass player on *Wild Things Run Fast*," Klein points out, "but when Joni and I became involved romantically, she wanted my opinions as that project was being finished. We ended up working somewhat as a team. Making a record together is not much different from raising a child. You have to do your job really, really well or else it affects a lot of other parts of your life. On the positive side, it's incredibly gratifying to create something together and share the satisfaction of making something of beauty and putting it out in the world.

"In the process of separating, we never lost respect for each other, certainly not artistically. I'd be lying if I said it was an easy thing to collaborate since we've separated. The three records we've made together since then have been difficult records to make, but some pearls have come out of the difficulty."

"We worked through our divorce," Mitchell says. "That was a trip. He'd go, 'What do you mean by that?' and I'd go, 'Oh, come on.' We were so uncooperative it was awful. When we won a Grammy [for *Turbulent Indigo*] we went with his girlfriend and my new boyfriend all together. I hadn't slept in 58 hours, so I was delirious when the thing hit. Klein grabbed me and swung me around and we went onto the stage and I was kind of in a dream state. I let him talk, and he went, 'Uh, uh, uh,' and in my delirium all I could think was 'Gee, this is why we got divorced; I always have to finish his sentences.'"

"He doesn't seem like an overly sensitive guy," Hancock ventures.

"Oh, but he is with me," Mitchell rejoins. "Klein and I are still very good friends. We're still a work in progress. We're working out the bugs in our relationship with humor. We've gotten to the point where some of it is funny, where we can take the teasing without getting touchy. So that's nice."

Mitchell produced her 1998 album *Taming the Tiger* herself, using Shorter, Klein and drummer Brian Blade. After that, though, her writing well seemed to dry up. No new songs were coming to her, so she did what many jazz artists do late in their career: She revisited popular standards as well as her older compositions in new arrangements. Specifically, she wanted to sing with both an all-star jazz band alongside a symphonic orchestra.

The jazz combo included Hancock, Shorter, Erskine and trumpeter Mark Isham, and she called in her ex-husband Klein to pull the pieces together as co-producer and music director. First, they recorded an album of 10 standards and two originals, released as *Both Sides Now* in 2000. Then they recorded a two-CD set of 22 originals, released as *Travelogue* in 2002.

"It was more than just adding the string charts," Klein insists. "What we discovered in doing the two songs of hers in a context of an album of standards was there was real power and a magical thing that happened in hearing her sing these songs as a woman that's gone through a lot of life. In creating a radically different context for them something powerful happened. Herbie and Wayne said they spent one Thanksgiving crying over those two songs. We independently thought, 'Boy, what if we did this to more of her songs? What if we presented more of her songs in this dramatic new landscape?'"

"I couldn't write at that point anyway," Mitchell explains, "so I did what jazz artists do: I went back over my old material. Pop music is supposed to be disposable, but jazz is supposed to endure, so I said, 'OK, I'm going to recut these things.' I turned in *Travelogue*, and the label said, "Joni, you know we're just car salesmen now. We've got cute cars and we've got fast cars. This is a work of genius. We don't know what to do with it.' So they dumped it."

"The industry operates from a fear based on history," Hancock argues. "The history is who bought what yesterday. They don't ask who might be leading the next trend. Or what might people like to hear next. Or what can we do to elevate things. There seems to be no excitement from the business realm."

"The old music guys may have been crooks," Mitchell adds, "but they were music lovers. They said, 'We don't want another Nat "King" Cole.' That's the difference between the old guys and the new guys. The new guys want clones; they don't have any imagination or courage. They don't love music; they love golf and porno. So I said, 'What am I going to do now? I can't get better. What am I going to do, get worse? I'm out of here. That's it, end of the road.'"

Mitchell announced that she was quitting the music business. She re-devoted herself to her first love—visual art—and to the daughter [Kilauren Gibb] she had given up for adoption in 1965 and hadn't found again until 1997. She claims that she would have gladly spent the rest of her life painting canvases and playing with her young grandson if it hadn't been for a broken TV and an unexpected call from Calgary.

"I was retired," Mitchell says, "and then one day my TV broke. I tried to fix it by pushing some buttons and suddenly it was pulsing in green-and-pink negative. At first I was furious, but then I said, 'This is great.' I started taking photographs of the TV with a leftover disposable camera, and before I knew it, I was knee-deep in photos. I went to a photo store, bought out all their scrapbooks and started putting photos in each one. One was called 'War'; others were called 'Cinematic Kisses' or 'Shakespeare on TV.' The 'War' scrapbook had three photos to a page, like a triptych. That looked interesting, so I started fooling around with combinations."

Eventually, those war-photo triptychs were blown up into six-foot-tall panels and organized into an exhibit called Green Flag Song. Typical of the panels is one where an image of a flag-waving female gymnast is atop an image of men in an unemployment line atop an image of crumpled soldiers. Another panel has a silhouette of the U.S. Capitol above the toppling statue of Saddam Hussein above an applauding crowd. All the images are a ghostly, solarized green-and-white. The exhibit has already had gallery runs in Los Angeles and New York.

In the middle of her green-photo frenzy, Mitchell got a phone call from the Alberta Ballet's artistic director, Jean Grand-Maître. He was planning a ballet called "Dancing Joni" that traced the songwriter's life from prairie child to musical legend. She told him it sounded "a little fluffy for the times" and invited him down to California to discuss alternatives. When he walked into her house, he saw the mock-up for her anti-war art exhibit and immediately said, "We must put this in the ballet."

"'If you want a war ballet,'" Mitchell recalls telling him, "'I'll give you a war ballet. But your sponsors are Texas oilmen, right?' Yes, because Calgary is Texas north. I said, 'They'll probably pull out their funding. This is my least popular music. They may walk. Are you ready for that?' He said, 'Yes.' He was so fearless, it was delightful, so I said, 'OK, here we go.'"

Sure enough, the sponsors did pull out, but Grand-Maître raised more money, and the ballet, now called *The Fiddle and the Drum*, took shape. The monochromatic photos from Green Flag Song were projected as slides on the rear backdrop. Older Mitchell songs such as "Sex Kills," "For the Roses," "The Beat of Black Wings" and "Three Great Stimulants" were supplemented by three new recordings: "If I Had a Heart," "Shine," and a new arrangement of "Big Yellow Taxi." Those three tracks would form the heart of her new album.

A documentary film, also called *The Fiddle and the Drum* and directed by Mitchell and Grand-Maître, captures the ballet's performance at the Southern Alberta Jubilee Auditorium in Calgary. When it was screened in New York in September, it revealed that Grand-Maître had not really solved the problem of finding physical gestures that might add to the songs' meaning. At times his gestures were clumsily literal—a "Heil Hitler" salute or a peace sign—and at other times the movement was so abstract it could have accompanied any song. He never found that sweet spot in between where the movement might illuminate the words without simply translating them.

But the ballet project had gotten Mitchell's songwriting juices flowing again. Soon the lyrics were pouring out of her; most of the new songs reflected the same political anger that had fueled Green Flag Song and *The Fiddle and the Drum*.

"It's all work from the same period," she points out, "so it has a natural affinity, because what's on your mind will work its way into how you express yourself. I was mad. I was mad at the government. I was mad at Americans for not doing something about it. They were so quick to impeach Clinton for kinky sex and they're so slow to do something about this. This is what happened in Germany; the Germans went to sleep."

Meanwhile, Hancock was turning his attention to the singer-songwriter branch of modern pop. In 1996, he recorded *The New*

Standard, an album that made the argument that songs by the Beatles, Nirvana, Stevie Wonder and Babyface could be considered standards as much as the songs of Cole Porter or Duke Ellington. There were no Joni Mitchell songs, but the album did include Peter Gabriel's "Mercy Street," which featured Klein on the original recording, and "Scarborough Fair" by the Mitchell-like Paul Simon.

After the critical and commercial success of 1998's *Gershwin's World*, Verve Records was anxious to have Hancock do another songwriter album and suggested he do an album of Mitchell's music with Klein producing. Both men immediately embraced the idea.

"We wanted to avoid all the trappings of a typical tribute record," Klein declares. "One of the ways of doing that was to make it not just an examination of her songs but also an examination of what music and songs that sparked her to go in different directions. I knew she had heard Billie Holiday sing 'Solitude' as a kid, and that it had deeply affected her both as a song and as a vocal performance. I also knew 'Nefertiti' had a big influence on her when she first heard it on the Miles record, as it was to me. And that tune convinced Herbie and I both that we wanted Wayne to be a prominent part of the record.

"We also decided early on we wanted the record to be half instrumental and half vocal. Gradually different songs occurred to me as natural songs to be presented vocally, and others instrumentally. 'Edith and the Kingpin,' for example, is a gritty song about a hustler/pimp kind of guy in a small-town hip spot, and I thought, 'What better voice than Tina Turner's to tell this story?' I don't know if at first she completely understood the lyric, but once she started tying into it, it was just thrilling."

"I based my approach to the project on my limited experience with movie scores," Hancock adds. "Because Joni's music is so deep, I had to ask a lot of questions about the meanings of these songs. Once I had that understanding, I could open myself up to the experience and follow where it led me. As with the ballet, you don't want a graphic representation of the lyrics; you want an interpretation.

"When I finally paid attention to the lyrics, it was like, 'Finally, here's something that points me right to the meaning. Before that, her music had attracted me because it was always fresh. It wasn't like something that someone else figured out. As the same time there was a sense of familiarity, a relationship to jazz there that I could relate to."

On Hancock's new album, Mitchell sings "Tea Leaf Prophecy," a song she had co-written with Klein in 1988. In this new version, one can hear how Mitchell and Hancock have finally closed the musical gap between mainstream jazz and singer-songwriter pop. You can hear how Hancock, finally listening closely to the lyrics, creates a sense of brooding loneliness to support the story of a woman left behind in a small town emptied of men during World War II. You can hear how Mitchell, more comfortable than ever with top-notch jazz players, extends the implications of her melodies into strange, new detours, even trading improvised variations with Shorter's soprano sax.

"Sometimes I'll take an odd interval," Mitchell says, "because I don't question it if it feels emotionally correct with the text. That's why I do it. People keep telling me I'm wrong, so I have to be careful I don't censor myself."

"Right," Hancock agrees enthusiastically. "She comes up with chord resolutions that I myself might not think of just because my orientation has been my traditional training in jazz. In the past I probably would have rejected them because they were, quote-unquote, 'wrong,' but I don't judge things like that anymore, especially when I'm listening to someone like her whose judgment I can trust."

FILM INTERVIEW

Michael Buday | August 20, 2008 | Grammy Museum (Los Angeles, California)

In 2008, Joni agreed to sit for an interview for the Grammy Museum in Los Angeles. The museum staff was making a film, *Life of a Recording*, that focused on artists who had won a Grammy for Album of the Year, and producer Michael Buday wanted to talk to her about Herbie Hancock's 2007 album *The Joni Letters*, based upon her songs, and how her work had inspired him and other jazz artists such as Wayne Shorter.

She also describes the colorful character who stalked her at her remote cabin, inspiring her song "Court and Spark," coins "Coltraning" as a verb, and talks about how her parents' courtship in the early 1940s factored into her song "The Tea Leaf Prophecy."

In this interview, it's only natural that Joni talks extensively about jazz , her friendships with Hancock and Shorter, and her approach to putting together the unique pop-jazz hybrid that she produced over many years. She describes how and why she used sus chords, which she called "chords of inquiry," and allowed them to remain open and unresolved, something that went against traditional music training. Joni saw sus chords as being something a man longed to resolve, while she, as a woman, allowed them to remain open, as a question.

Buday and his crew made the long trek from California to the singer's remote retreat on the Sunshine Coast in British Columbia, Canada—by air, over water, and up a secluded road. They met with her after dusk, when she famously feels most comfortable and alive.

Buday had a few requests before they started filming: would Joni take off her baseball hat, so her face wasn't in shadows, and could she not hold her distractingly cute little dog Coco in her lap? *Done* and *done*.

But when he asked if Joni would refrain from smoking because it caused editing challenges, the answer was a firm no. Cigarettes were a lens through which she saw life, Joni told the director. In the end, he concedes, it worked out. "She was very candid, cooperative, and her 'smoky lens' yielded everything we'd hoped for," Buday said.

Note: The following is an edited transcript from the complete interview that Buday conducted. —Ed.

Michael Buday: When was the first time you met Herbie Hancock?

Joni Mitchell: I can't really remember the first time that I met Herbie. I remember the first time I met Wayne. But Herbie and Wayne and I had a friend in common who had a nightclub. And we spent several Christmases and New Year's—we spent a lot of time in that club, and after hours and jamming.

And sometimes there were the holidays with our families, you know, like with Herbie's sister present and Wayne's family—mother, I think it was, at one point—and my parents and Red's parents, you know, who are a five-star, not Sicilian but Venetian family, you know.

It was this place called the Nucleus Nuance that we frequented and had our social experience. When I worked with Mingus, he provided me with a lot of bands—of his choice. But I wanted to come into jazz, you know, since everybody thought I was flirting with it—in a fresh way, not in a retro way.

And so I, out of courtesy to Charles, ran all his bands, but it always sounded retro to me. And in my mind, the band that I had was this band of Miles's which was my dream band. And that was the band with Tony Williams and Wayne and Herbie, [from] *In a Silent Way* and *Nefertiti*.

That incarnation of Miles's music was while I was playing just instruments, just accompanying myself. That was my idea of cutting-edge music. And I never expected that I would ever be playing with them. It just wasn't even a dream; it was just that's what I admired, but it was another world.

But somehow or another, I guess my music worked its way towards that, enough so that Mingus called for me to write his epitaph, basically. And he didn't really like that band, mainly because it was Miles's band and he was in competition with it. And also, that prejudice that I had encountered in the folk world, where when Dylan plugged in, all of the folkies, you know, shook in their boots because that era was over and folk rock was coming in.

So either they plugged in, or they were a dinosaur. And Mingus was of the old school, that electric instruments didn't take the same virtuosity that acoustic instruments did. Certainly, acoustic instruments are much more strenuous and he said, "Well, it was the touch."

But I was in disagreement. You can still get expression out of electric instruments, absolutely. And Jaco Pastorius, for example, who was the bass player of my dreams, you know, who was doing all of the eccentric things that I was requesting bass players to do, that they refused to do. So he and I were kind of on the same page. Anyway, around that era when I did the Mingus project, we began to fraternize and hang around at this club. From the time that Jaco began to play with me, he also began to play with Weather Report. And it was Jaco that introduced me to Wayne at a Weather Report session.

And once I started playing with Wayne, I had to play with him all up until this last album, *Shine,* when he was unavailable. He just had too much work. He's played on every project, you know, since we met. And he was very busy also when I did the *Travelogue* project.

And his manager and my manager spoke, this was in 2000, and said "Wayne's doing a composition for the Detroit Symphony and will be unavailable." And I thought, no, he can't. He's got to play on this one. This is the culmination of everything. So I called him up.

There was another sax player who wasn't nearly as brilliant as Wayne but was much more popular, so I said to him, "Wayne, you've got to play on this, otherwise I'll get your competitor." And he went, "No, no, no, don't do that. I'm the only one that can crawl across your shit." That's what he said. And it's true. He just crawls across it like a fly, you know. You can just see him studying the architecture, you know, and changing. He's profuse with ideas, like a true genius is, changing concepts midstream, finishing them up six takes down the line.

A talent will come in, get an idea and develop it, and you've got it in four or five takes, and to most ears it will be beautiful and satisfying, whereas a genius, it is not perfect but it's so profuse with ideas that they just coming and coming, and some of them are half baked. So I usually give Wayne twelve takes, just to watch him explore. And now in a situation like Herbie's album where they're playing live, I don't think the vocals went on until later in most cases so the singer had to braid him in. So he's playing off an invisible lyric, and he's a pictorial thinker, so he knows what words are going to be there.

You know, he's very theatrical, which is also a rare, musical gift. Very few people can play more than notes. Wayne is a poet with that instrument and an actor—a method actor.

Buday: What is your process, working with Wayne?

Mitchell: Well, I always work with Wayne as an actor. He's the only musician I ever played with who speaks my musical language. I don't speak the alphabetical language or the numerical language, and I haven't been—I stopped reading [*music*] at eight.

I could read at eight. I took a year of piano lessons so I could read and write in a rudimentary way. But she [*the piano teacher —Ed.*] hit me with a ruler one too many times, I quit and I lost that language. But the language of metaphor, you know, Wayne and I speak.

So I'll say, "OK, you know, you come in here and you get out here, and when you come in, you come in as sad as you can possibly be, and you have to go out really young." And he does it, you know, or something simpler. OK, you're the bird or, you know . . . What are the other instructions that I've given him over time?

The first time that we played together he spoke to me—this was in London—and he said, "I'm going to play it like you're at Hyde Park and there's a nanny and a baby and a boat, and the baby puts the boat on the pond, and the wind is just nudging it. It's just nudging it. That's how I'm going to play." So I went, oh, my God, this guy. That's the way I think, as a painter, about music. And, you know, I think about it in terms of theater. The chords that I add to the text and even the way I marry lyric to melody, I try always to keep the inflection of spoken English and hit the high note at the apex of the idea, that kind of thing.

So there's a point of craft there. Mind you, my songs are more dramatic than your average pop song . . . a song usually has a simple theme. They're not usually this complex.

In terms of cinematic storytelling, you know, sometimes you have to change emotion two or three times within one line, more like a cinematic script.

Buday: When did you move into jazz?

Mitchell: I never was moving into jazz. We should clarify that.

Buday: When were you first aware of jazz musicians gravitating toward your music?

Mitchell: I started writing songs in Detroit and I was a resident of a club called the Chess Mate [*on Livernois at McNichols —Ed.*]. The Chess Mate was folk music—that is to say, acoustic music, 'cause I wasn't a—I haven't been a folk singer since 1965. Once I began to write, that's not folk music, it's more like Schubert, you know. But anyway, once I began to write, I had to have my lead sheets done. So the Chess Mate was folk music from eighty-thirty until midnight, and then it was jazz after hours. So it was the jazz musicians in the club that did my original lead sheets.

And they liked some of it, so they began to play my early songs in their sets. So the black audience, which came to the jazz, started to come earlier and earlier to the sets and so immediately at the beginning my music went and was interpreted by jazz musicians because it's melodic, like standards, it had all of the elements, but it was quirky also from the beginning.

You know, some of my harmonic movement is unprecedented in the history of music, it's really quirky. I guess it's because I'm a woman and it's the way I use sus chords [*unresolved, suspended chords —Ed.*], which I called chords of inquiry, you know, chords of questions. Even Wayne said, "Well, what are these chords? What are these chords? These are not guitar chords and these are not piano chords. What are these chords?" And then he told me that they taught him at Berklee School of Music never to stay on a sus chord too long, and never go from a sus chord to a sus chord.

So my open tunings, a lot of them are in these chords of inquiry. They have dissonance internally, not on the top, so they're kind of running through the middle.

I was born with atomic bombs hanging over me . . . I had been ill all my life, you know, with mystery illnesses that were unsolved. There's just so many mysteries, like unsolved, unsolved, unsolved. So, you know, it's natural that I would gravitate to an unusual use of these chords. And also being a female, it's a masculine nature to need resolution.

So the fact that I would hold onto these unresolved chords longer than you're supposed to, you know, and switch keys, it just makes it difficult to write. You've got two bars of five, four, you know, followed by a sustained sus chord. So there's a lot of quirky stuff going on that, you know, that is now beginning to be examined. It has its validity; it just wasn't done.

But in answer to your question, jazz musicians have always gravitated to my music from the beginning.

Buday: Do you think there is a bias against covering older songs?

Mitchell: Well, here's the thing about the music before our generation. In our generation, there was a thing called standards. And the reason they were standards, 'cause the song was good enough to be repeated a lot of time. Then when you came into my generation, songs became disposable.

You know, they got a short run. They were sprinters and then they died. And most of them deserved to die. You know, they weren't really worthy of a cover or the cover had a—you know, it was a dumb, little song but it had a nice sound to it, you know, like "Tutti Frutti."

I mean, that's not going to be a standard, but it's charming because of the sound of Little Richard's voice and so on. And, you know, the song changed so radically as it went into this market that was being aimed at eleven- to fifteen-year-olds. Right? So the redoing of a song is only abnormal in the last few generations.

Like there was this thing on "River" which keeps being re-recorded at Christmas, because a lot of people are sad at Christmas and it's the sad Christmas song. Right? And the guy gave a couple of columns to it in the newspaper saying, you know, "This song is overexposed."

I thought, well, that used to be the standard, you know? So there's a mental mindset that's a shift, you know. So [*the idea is —Ed.*] that a song that gets re-recorded is overexposed.

Buday: Did you set out to write a Christmas song?

Mitchell: No. I mean, obviously it was coming on Christmas. It must have been near Christmas that I thought of it and, you know, many people get melancholy at Christmas, so I don't really recall what sparked it. Some songs I do, but I don't remember what sparked that one.

Buday: What is the song "Court and Spark" about?

Mitchell: OK. My little house up here in British Columbia is remote and isolated. One day I woke up and there was a tent pitched in my yard and there was this nude lunatic dancing around kind of like in the "seaweed people" Woodstock way, you know, of a "what's he on?" kind of way. You know, like a nature freak.

He jumped around the rocks naked for a whole day and I was kind of trapped in the house. You know, locked my doors at night and the next day he was still bouncing around out there. So finally I just said, "OK, that's it," and I came out and I said to him, "Put some clothes on," which he did.

And some of the song, is in the nature of—some of it is fiction, you know. I made a romance of it, which it wasn't. It was—a lopsided romance. I mean, it was a somewhat loony fan obsessed with me. But some of the images in there were—for instance, "he buried the coins he made in People's Park." There's a People's Park in Vancouver. And he'd been panhandling and he buried them, and he did say to me, "Well, didn't you see me dancing up the river in the dark?" That was his line. It's a crazy line but it's poetic . . .

You know, the possibility seemed offered up when Dylan began to write a more poetic kind of song. So once I heard "Positively Fourth Street," I thought, OK, you can sing poetry now, anything you can think up. But I don't really like poetry, but I do like movies. So I kind of write rhyming little movies, you know, like Tennessee Williams kind of movies.

Faye Dunaway said to me one time, "You're so lucky." "Why," I said. She said, "Well, you can write your own roles." And it's true. So, you know, a lot of the things that I sing in first person are not myself at all. And I am a woman, so the "you" device is a patriarchal device.

Buday: What do you mean by a "patriarchal device"?

Mitchell: If I go "*You*"—you know, "*You've* got a lot of nerve to say"—I couldn't. A woman couldn't get away with that song. It's a patriarchal stance. An angry man is an angry man; an angry woman is a bitch. So you have to find different ways to deliver your theater within the context of your gender, like it or not.

I wrote one album from a "you" stance and people don't want that from me. So if I'm going to pass on human frailty or knowledge, I have to be the sacrificial lamb. I'm the playwright and the actress so I have to sing it in first person, you know, like "I."

That seems to be the device to impart my knowledge that is most palatable to people. Then they have the option of, "that's the way Joni is," or of seeing themselves in it. To see themselves in it is the way to get the value of it, because there is, you know, a human revelation wherever possible in one of these songs, so that it isn't just the clichés that generally make up pop music.

Buday: Do your songs start with music, or lyrics?

Mitchell: I know they always start with melody first, which gives me my structure. And then I see where the apex of the play is, where the dynamic note is. It's the harder way to go but it also keeps you away from iambic pentameter, and is more challenging as a puzzle.

Buday: How did Herbie relate to your lyrics?

Mitchell: Well, Herbie never listened to words in his life. He would admit that. Wayne on the other hand, is listening to the words absolutely. He's playing off the pictures, 'cause he's a story-oriented man. But most jazz musicians, the female singer in the group—even Billie Holliday, who was masterful, really, you know, the best female jazz vocalist ever, on so many levels, still was never one of the boys. And they have a dismissive name for girl jazz singers, the "chirp." And they're kind of tolerated as a party favor and a necessary, decorative element.

But they're not considered really jazz musicians. In Billie's case, I think you have to make an exception. And I think Sarah Vaughan also, because of the force of her personality, never really had a problem with condescension from the bands, 'cause she's sassy.

And Carmen [*McRae*], you know, was so mean that she had her whole band drinking Pepto-Bismol. But it shows in her tone. But, anyway, for whatever reason, Herbie never really listened to lyrics. And Miles was prejudiced against singers too. You know, "They have to do it with the words. I have to do it without it." So he felt, you know, that they had this gimmick that made the communication easier, and his was a harder puzzle, again to use that term. . . .

I can show you the dialogue all through my records that [*Wayne*] has with lyrics. But for Herbie, it was a new experience . . . I mean, he kept his palate as a jazz musician and strayed into what he thought was my territory, although he did some things I wouldn't do in there.

I have a funny prejudice against adjacent vowels and what I call "corny ass doodle oohs," rocking back and forth on the same note. I "coltraned" it a lot. I just don't like it. It reminds me of Bing Crosby, "[*Carolina*] in the Morning." It's like . . . ahhh, corny ass doodle oohs, you know. I don't think I've ever heard Wayne play one of those things. He's more like a descant singer. You know, he takes these wild leaps, like even in the melody to "Nefertiti," even the starting note. Even without a chord under it, it sounds like a blue note.

His melodies, his melodic sense is so unpredictable and interesting to me. So of all of these musicians who are all great on this project, Wayne is my soul. I mean, he's like a kindred spirit. There's nobody on the planet that—he's irreplaceable.

Herbie's a beautiful pianist, a great talent, but because he doesn't know about the words—he does now. This has been an education and he'll tell you so, you know. And they all apprenticed with Miles, of course, and Miles was breaking down the bar, playing across the bar.

I had picked that up too, you know, which was very eccentric for a pop singer, 'cause I'm phrasing crazy, starting in the middle of the first, getting this conversational thing going which is not conducive to pop. You know, it isn't going to be very popular. It's too experimental and people think you're just doing it wrong. But all of that I was familiar with because of my admiration for that experimental pocket in which they all participated. So I brought that authentically to my art, not from so much as a desire to be a jazzer or to belong in any category.

I never wanted to be in a category; I wanted to be an innovator, which I was, you know. I mean, as a painter—and I have a painter's ego more than a musician's ego, you know—you need to, you have the need to discover . . . In the pop arena, that's why I never had a producer, you know.

I mean, [*ex-husband, bassist Larry*] Klein kind of bullied his way into being my producer from time to time, but the main reason that I didn't want a man having authority over my music is that they would wipe the eccentricities out of it in order to popularize it, and there would be no invention taking place. So I had to, I had to. Rather than having to battle an authority figure in the studio, I had to eliminate them. And I had it in my contract early that I would not have a product sicced upon myself.

Buday: What did you think of Herbie's album *River: The Joni Letters* winning the Grammy?

Mitchell: You know, I was so excited for Herbie because he really, really wanted, you know, that. And I was excited, too. It's such a beautifully musical album, it really is. The more you listen to it, the caliber of the playing. [*Drummer*] Vinnie Colaiuta, who I adore, Sting took him away from me. I couldn't afford him anymore. So they're reunited with Vinnie's beautiful playing. 'Cause we were out on the road for nine months and it was a terrific experience. I love that man . . . the solidity of his beat and the versatility, a giant of a drummer.

And since then I've played with Brian Blade—another type of drummer who I also adore, but delicate. He prints in little, little letters and he dots my i's and crosses my t's and plays with me in a delicate way, and grew up loving my music, grew up to play it with me—in a different way than Vinnie, you know.

The guitar player [*Lionel Loueke —Ed.*] is so fresh-sounding on the project. The bass player [*Dave Holland —Ed.*] is wonderful and resonant, and, of course, the way Wayne braids in . . . the more I listen to that album, I was thrilled that such a musical album won the highest award. . . . I wasn't so much personally proud, I was just proud that people were able to recognize that this was worthy of a high award.

It was very exciting. . . . And jazz is coming back. There is a renewed interest among young artists, especially in Canada, you see a lot of young artists going into that field creatively.

Buday: What was your favorite era of jazz?

Mitchell: When jazz to me was at its best—I loved Duke Ellington. You know, you want to go back to the inception. Or Charlie Parker. Wherever the innovation takes place, it's at its freshest. And then it turns into a tradition and within the tradition there emerge some colorful players and so on. But with my appetite for discovery, you know—I don't like copycats. Neither did Mingus. Like he's got this one piece of music called "If Charlie Parker Was a Gunslinger, There'd Be a Lot of Dead Copycats." That cracked me up because I thought I was the only one like that, with just such an appetite for innovation and freshness, that if somebody is second generation, my feeling is, *euhhh*. It's easy once it's been done, you know, to emulate something. And that's fine. I mean, there's room for all in the game. Some people don't have the need to discover and are content to carry on a tradition and that's fine, but for me the innovators are the exciting ones. You know?

So let me just finish telling you about this fellow who was catalyst to "Court and Spark." So he and I are sitting on the front step of my house and talking, and he's telling me all this weird stuff, how he buried this money and he came looking for me, and felt that he and I were predestined. I had a lot of these kind of characters. They came from all over the place, from Sweden—a lot of Jesuses, schizophrenic Jesuses, that I was a magnet to. And they usually all had the same disciples: Bob Dylan, the Beatles, and me.

And I said, "Did it ever occur to you all your disciples are very, very famous?" "Yes, because the Lord hath needed the media," they would say. So I'm sitting with this lunatic who I've just got him to put his clothes on, on my friend's step, and he's an extroverted lunatic, right?

Down the path comes this *introverted* lunatic. And he's twitching, and the extroverted lunatic says to me, "God, look at that guy. That guy's crazy. Aren't you scared being out here all by yourself?" 'Cause I'm in the middle of nowhere, right? And I just laughed. I thought, I guess crazy people don't know they're crazy. But we're all crazy. Anyway, that was "Court and Spark."

Buday: Explain what your song "The Tea Leaf Prophecy" means [from the 1988 album *Chalk Mark in a Rain Storm*].

Mitchell: What can I tell you about this one? "The Tea Leaf Prophecy." OK, a lot of it's in the song, but not all of it. When my mother was thirty years old, the war was on. She was working. She had been a teacher but she was now working in Regina, Saskatchewan, in a bank. And it was hard times, but she and her girlfriend scraped up some money to go to this fancy hotel for high tea. And they put on hats and gloves, and they went and they had these little dainty sandwiches and this tea.

And they had a tea leaf reader there, so the tea leaf reader reads my mother's teacup and says to her, "You'll be married within the month," to which she thinks to herself, there's only farmers and cops here, all the good men are away at the war. I'll be damned if I'm going to marry a farmer or a cop.

"'You'll be married within the month," he says. "You'll have a child within a year. You'll live into your nineties, and you'll die a long and agonizing death," which is a horrible thing. Even if you see it in the cups, I think you probably should have kept that one to yourself.

So two weeks later, she met my dad on leave. She's Gemini, twenty-fourth of May, and my father's Virgo, twenty-fourth of August. And astrologically they're ill-fated. They meet, they feel like they've known each other all their lives. They either move in immediately, or get married immediately, which they did.

They got married two weeks later. Three months later, my mother got pregnant with me, and I was born within the year. And so as she approached her nineties, she was always worried that she was going to die this long and agonizing death. Well, anyway, she beat the gypsy on the last call.

She was a health nut: tai chi, yoga, and nutrition all the way, to fight this curse. And I kept saying to her as the end approached, "Well, look, two out of three ain't bad," or "Them that dies will be the lucky ones." I was trying to think of things to say, because the world is getting so nutsy.

But, anyway, what else can I say about this? When she did die, this mail came from all around the world, a lot of it in other languages, and I had written the poem "Molly McGee" instead of "Myrtle McKee," 'cause she never really liked my portraits of her. We had a very intense relationship and the portraits of our relationship were not necessarily sentimental. They showed a bit of struggle. So this one did as well, 'cause she was always threatening to leave Pop. You know, they shouldn't have been a couple, really. They should have just had an affair and got it over with. But they toughed it out for sixty years. Anyway, that's basically what that song is about. . . .

Now "Edith and the Kingpin" [*from* The Hissing of Summer Lawns —*Ed.*] is kind of interesting. There was a woman up here on the Sunshine Coast [*British Columbia* —*Ed.*] who was Italian. And she claimed she came from a Mafia family, which she said quite proudly, like kind of Mafia chic. And I had a friend who was coming from California to visit me on the weekend, and she said, "Oh, I'm going into town and I'm going to have dinner with some hookers, you know, why don't you come?"

And I thought, you know, I'm a writer, I'm always interested in various stratas of life, and this was before hoes and criminals became mainstream, you know. So the underbelly of things at that time kind of interested me.

So my girlfriend comes in and I said, "Well, come on, we're going to go have dinner, you know, with this woman I know and some hookers." "Oh, God," she says, "*Joni*," you know. So we go to this restaurant. Well, anyway, these women were very unusual. One of them was Swiss Indian, tall and beautiful like a model, and the other one was Jewish and looked like Claudette Colbert.

And you would never think of these girls as even call girls. They weren't cheap-looking. The third one looked kind of Okie, and she had been my next-door neighbor in Laurel Canyon. And I never met her 'cause there was Zappa's house, and then somebody's house—which turned out to be this prostitute—and then mine in Laurel Canyon.

So, anyway, we're having dinner with these women and my girlfriend Betsy was just kind of horrified, and she said she was going to go back to her hotel. But all through dinner they kept talking about this pimp that they had had who was a Native, and they had all stolen from department stores and worked with him. And he was the sweetest guy. They kept touting this guy, touting this guy. So we all went to a discothèque together, and the man came in. He was a big, pockmarked Native man with great posture. But his hands were behind his back and the only thing that betrayed his discomfort was that his hand was clenching like this behind his back.

Well, he came in and invited me to play backgammon with him, which I had never played before, and he was playing with this woman who was my neighbor in Laurel Canyon. And he kind of displaced her for me to sit down and play. So she got bugged and she was kibitzing over my shoulder.

And I said to her, "Look, you know, like get off my back. I've gotta make my own mistakes, 'cause otherwise, if you keep coaching me, I'll never learn this game." . . .

This guy was also a gigolo, kind of being pushed into exploitation. But, still, I thought, well, I'll just keep an eye open, one eye open for what's going on here. Anyway, we were in this disco playing backgammon, and then eventually we moved over to another place.

This is in Vancouver. If you're up after one o'clock in Vancouver, or in Toronto in those days, you bang straight into the life. So, you know— musicians, that's basically the nightlife. In New York it wasn't like that. You could go a lot of different places and meet a lot of different crowds. Same thing with New Orleans.

Well, but Toronto—Canadian cities—everybody was in bed by one o'clock, I guess, except criminals and musicians. Right? So, anyway, we ended up going back to this place and this fellow keeps kind of, you know, patting the seat, you know, "Plant it here, bitch," kind of deal, for me to take up residence next to him.

And I kept saying, "Well, I'm fine where I am." And there were all these Chinese pimps, *ooohhh*, comparing rings, you know: "Eloise gave me this one and this one," and so on. It was kind of sociologically interesting to me. So I finally end up in a conversation with this fellow and it was really a meeting of minds.

It was, you know, where two people have a dialogue, right? And our child met. You know, the man had a beautiful inner side to him, OK? And he had been asking to drive me home all night. So I said, "OK, I'll take that ride now," and he said, "No, now I won't drive you." Right?

So I kind of caught him off guard. The man was a beautiful soul who had come to the city and the nature of the beast is, what is open to you is crime, and within that context, he had won the respect of the women that he worked with and so on, and that was apparent.

So with that as a nucleus again and hybriding it with Edith Piaf—that's where the Edith comes from—it's fiction, you know, like in the same way that Tennessee Williams writes fiction, peppering it with things that you've experienced."

JONI SAID

On Death

"I'm good with death. I'm not morbid about it. I've had a lot of things die in my arms. A robin that had been mauled by a cat. I buried it in my yard. My cats begin to die, one by one. One had two grand mal seizures in my arms. Another one I had named Nietzsche died in the night. He was such an elegant cat and he died twisted like a pretzel, kind of like a Tom and Jerry cartoon. I knew he wouldn't have wanted that, so I shaped his body back to normal before rigor mortis set in."

—to Richard Ouzounian, *Toronto Star*, June 11, 2013

JONI SAID

On the *Los Angeles Times*' Matt Diehl

To whom she said that Bob Dylan was "a plagiarist"
"I hate doing interviews with stupid people, and this guy's a moron."

—to Jian Ghomeshi, CBC, June 10, 2013

JONI SAID

On Dylan

"I like a lot of Bob's songs. Musically, he's not very gifted, he's borrowed his voice from a lot of old hillbillies . . . He's not a great guitar player. He's invented a character to deliver his songs. Sometime I wish I could have that character . . . Because you can do things with that character. It's a mask of sorts."

—to Jian Ghomeshi, CBC, June 10, 2013

JONI SAID

On CBC Reporter Jian Ghomeshi

"You know, I did an interview with a CBC commentator. I exorcised the house after this guy left. I smudged it and opened all the windows. Now it comes out that he has been fired from CBC. People kept saying, 'What a great interviewer.' I didn't think so."

—to Elio Iannacci, *Maclean's*, Nov. 22, 2014

TV INTERVIEW

Tavis Smiley | November 25, 2014 | *Tavis Smiley on PBS* (US)

Joni's first release since 2007's *Shine* would come in 2014: the four-disc *Love Has Many Faces: a Quartet, a Ballet, Waiting to Be Danced*, comprising fifty-three of her songs of love and heartbreak, and much of her art, in a career-spanning box set released by Rhino.

It's to Smiley's credit that Joni requested a return appearance after their first interview. As Joni observers know, even after enjoying an encounter with a journalist she often objected to the way she was depicted in the finished article, no matter how positive. The fact that the PBS host was interviewing her on TV and not for print obviously helped, as her words couldn't be edited or interpreted by anybody. But moreover, the two clearly had bonded.

Compared to her 2007 appearance, Joni did not appear as healthy. In the ensuing years, she had lost both of her parents—first her mother, Myrtle, at age ninety-five in 2007, and then her father, at one hundred in 2012. Her relationship with her daughter had simmered down into a state of functional dysfunction, as Joni often described it. Thus it is poignant to read some of her feistier remarks here, knowing that just four months later, she would be discovered unconscious at her Bel-Air home, having suffered a brain aneurysm. —Ed.

The Rock and Roll Hall of Famer reminisces about her music career, from her coffeehouse days to playing some of the biggest venues in the world.

One of the twentieth century's most influential songwriters, Joni Mitchell has made music, ranging from folk to pop-rock to jazz, for more than four decades. The Canadian-born icon has multiple Grammys and is in the Rock and Roll and Canadian Songwriters Halls of Fame. Mitchell stopped recording in 2002 to focus on her painting and poetry; but, realizing that she wasn't ready to retire, she came back with

Shine—inspired by the Iraq war—and won another Grammy (for the opening track). A talented painter, she also had a mixed-media art exhibit in New York. Her latest musical project, *Love Has Many Faces,* is a curated, four-disc collection of material from forty years of recording that evoke her vision of love.

Tavis Smiley: Joni Mitchell was one of the towering talents of contemporary music. Should anyone be foolish enough to challenge that point, I point them to her new career-spanning four-disc collection of fifty-three of her remarkable songs remastered and reimagined. It's called *Love Has Many Faces: A Quartet, a Ballet, Waiting to be Danced.* Before we start our conversation, first a look at Joni performing "Both Sides, Now" at a tribute to her. She wrote that song when she was just twenty-one. [Clip plays.] Joni—twenty-one? You've been prolific a long time.

Joni Mitchell: Yeah [*laugh*]. There was this trumpet player named Ambrose who's kind of new on the jazz scene and that's what he said to me. He said, "Joni, how'd you do it?" I said, "How'd I do what?" And he said, "How did you do it, twenty-one, whatever it was, albums?" I said, "I don't know. I just, you know, was under contract. I had to deliver." It was some kind of duty, you know.

Smiley: There are a whole lot of folk under contract who ain't put out the kind of stuff you put out for all these years . . . I'm not surprised, knowing you as I do, that you were in charge of this beginning to end, the packaging, everything. We'll talk about that. I mean, it's a piece of art. Aside from the fifty-three songs, the way it's presented is a piece of art, which I want to come to in just a second. But I'm so glad you spent so much time in the liner notes. I love reading liner notes. You learn a lot about artists when you read their liner notes. And speaking of being twenty-one and being so prolific even then, you said that your first husband, Mr. Mitchell, helped make you a philosopher.

Mitchell: If you make a good marriage, God bless you. If you make a bad marriage, become a philosopher [*laughs*]. Anyway, we both married for the wrong reasons. He married—fired his old partner and put me in the duo—so it became Chuck and Joni Mitchell, and he held the purse strings, right? So I had to be a housewife and, you know, bring home the bacon as well as him. It wasn't a good marriage. On our wedding day, even his mother said of him—he was the firstborn—"the first waffle should be used to warm up the pan and then thrown out."

Smiley: Ouch! Hold up [*laughs*].

Mitchell: On our wedding day, he did very badly, very selfishly. He took all the money that was given to us—we were poor—for starting out. He went out and bought himself a Porsche Speedster and was late for the wedding. So his mother—we got off to a bad start. But one thing good that came out of it, he was exploitative, but he set up a publishing company.

When I began to write, it was just inner stuff that I had to work out, though I hadn't really figured out how to do it. It was kind of cryptic in the beginning, you know. "Both Sides, Now," for example, I thought I'd just skimmed the surface of what I was contemplating. I didn't think it was thorough, you know.

I considered it kind of a failure and then other people started to see something in it. In its vagueness, it was very interpretable and I grew into it. Also, it's a funny song for an ingénue. It's not an ingénue song, you know. Singing at twenty-one, what do you know about life? People kind of made fun of it.

Dave Van Ronk sang it very well 'cause he was a young man, but he looked kind of like an old man, like Gabby Hayes who was playing old men when he was—he was one of those kind of old young men. And I thought his version of it was very good.

Mabel Mercer sang it in her seventies and I heard her and paid her a compliment. I said, you know, it takes an older woman to bring that song to life and she went, "Huh?" And I thought, oh, dear, you never tell a woman she's old, you know [*laughs*]. So I found out. I didn't tell her I was the author.

Smiley: Speaking of people laughing, you said laughing and making fun of you. I don't want to overstate that where this passage is concerned, but I do want to share this thing that I found fascinating—

Mitchell: OK.

Smiley: —in this wonderful book and collection of CDs. [*Smiley proceeds to read from the CD booklet —Ed.*] "When the album was finished, I played it for Geffen and Bob Dylan and Bob's buddy, Louie Kemp, who brought a girl with him. Bob had just completed an album, *Planet Waves*, not one of his best. We played it first and everyone was effusive. Then I played *Court and Spark*. I was so proud of it, my first band. Bob Dylan pretended to fall asleep when the last note faded out. Geffen nodded feebly. Louie said nothing. As they continued to comment on Bob's work, Louie's girl came and said, 'Why are they doing this to you?' 'I don't know,' I said. 'I think I'm Jackie Robinson.' [*Laughs*] So with that collection of people around you, the work wasn't given the respect in that moment perhaps that it should have been given.

Mitchell: Well, John Lennon's comment too. Now that's a working-class perspective.

Smiley: Right.

Mitchell: [Lennon]'s just going, "Oh, it's too sophisticated." It's too, you know . . . like that's a class problem, right? That's the way I saw it. But I guess I had a kind of a hard way to go, you know. There weren't that many women in the business. You know, I think it's funny. I mean, I'm not whining, you know. Even trying to lead people, 'cause I had very, very distinctive ideas about how the bottom end should be. I laid my part down and had really good time. So I'd put the bass and drums on afterwards, right? And I just couldn't get anybody until the L.A. Express that could play it.

And [drummer] Russ Kunkel, who was part of the section that played with the "singer-songwriter" camp, they couldn't play it. You know, as John [*Guerin, her drummer and ex-boyfriend —Ed.*] says in here, I found that quote from him because I was thinking figurative like an African instead of one, two, three, four like a schooled white person, you know.

I was throwing in long figures that, if you broke them down and analyzed them bar by bar, John says that you got a bar five-eight or something in there or even "Free Man in Paris" was *don-cha-che, don-cha-che, don, dan, dooka-chica-dooka-chica, dooka-chica.*

You'd have to keep setting up the bar 'cause I'm changing key in the middle of a song. You'd have to keep setting up the bar for two bars where I'd change the time signature. So to do it in notation, it was quite eccentric.

Smiley: You mention bass and drums and your own unique way of writing your music. Who was the drummer you fell in love just 'cause he played?

Mitchell: John Guerin. Oh, he's the one that writes in there like about . . .

Smiley: Yeah, exactly. But you just loved the way he played, yeah.

Mitchell: Oh, everything. I mean, first of all, he could play with me and he rode through those things. Like he says, you have to know what those time signatures are. You know, you're basically playing in a groove and then you go into a shuffle. You go through a transitional thing. I found it very interesting what he said because it's so articulate, you know, from a drummer's point of view.

What was challenging and yet, for him, it was a piece of cake. He rode out and went, huh, that's quirky, and he just sailed through it like a champ. I said to Henry, "Set me up facing the drummer." And he was real cute and flirty too, you know. We just hit it off.

Smiley: And the rest is history [*laughs*].

Mitchell: I fell in love, yeah.

Smiley: So you say that this—I want to get right to the project now. You say, Joni, that this box set is "rising like a phoenix from the ashes of two dead projects, a ballet and a horrendously ill-conceived box set." Tell me how this project ends up being the result of those two failed projects.

Mitchell: OK. So bad management put me into a bad contract with [*inaudible*] and then I got sick. And behind my back, you know, management trying to keep money coming into their pocket, they send, you know—I'll just call him the burglar. I don't want to name names or take him out or anything—they sent a burglar into my stash where I keep my outtakes.

I don't have a lot of outtakes because, as I explained in the liner notes, I didn't have good deals and I had to be really budget-conscious and economical. So I would trick myself. I'd say, "Henry [*Lewy, her engineer —Ed.*], we're going in to make a demo," and then we'd go in and, if it was a good take, I'd start hearing the backgrounds and I'd put them on and we'd take off. So there wasn't a lot of outtakes.

And the things that were stored in my safe place—that's what it was called ironically, a safe place—were there because they were not suitable for release. They needed a lot of work and it wasn't worth it.

I eventually re-recorded it and did it right, you know. But the record company, playing the formula, you know, hired a guy who put together a box set of someone else that they had some success with. So they were, oh, you'll do.

He burglarized my stash. The idea was a two-box set of everything condensed to two, but peppered with these not suitable for release tracks or they need a lot of work. He then brought in an engineer who couldn't comprehend my structures, who had terrible attention deficit. You know, I could have done it over the phone, because I was a shut-in. I was very ill.

I couldn't leave my bedroom really, but I could do it over the phone with the language of Pro Tools. He used Pro Tools, but he couldn't follow or wouldn't follow my instruction, which has been a problem through my career, trying to get men to do my bidding [*laughs*]. You know, I know what I'm doing.

Smiley: That's why I love you, Joni. That's why I love you [*laughs*].

Mitchell: But I know what I'm doing. I just needed a good assistant, and I've had many. Henry was delightful. Jean, my choreographer, delightful. We just worked like champs. We didn't have any of those, you know, dominant—we're just both pulling towards excellence as much as possible. So that's what I needed, a good technician that will enable me.

But these people that, once given the power, were overlording. It's like putting a private in charge of a general. You know, I'm the general. I know what I'm doing, you know. The guy that was gonna do my box set was also gonna do it chronological order, which is a terrible idea because chronologically, there's been so much controversy about how many stylistic changes I went through and they liked young Joni better than old Joni. There's a lot of growth in there, you know. And I lost some fans and picked up some new ones as it went jazzier.

And finally on the *Mingus*, it went straight into jazz, but it was even a little too progressive for Charles, who was like a folkie. He was an acoustic man, you know. I thought, oh, I went through this before in the folk world. He didn't like electric instruments, right? Which I did, and I loved Miles's *In a Silent Way* and that band in particular and, of course, Wayne [Shorter], my beloved Wayne, you know, and Herbie [Hancock]. I loved those guys.

So anyway, I called for that session and it was pretty avant-garde. "Sweet Sucker Dance" on here was conceptually really quite a different approach to working with a singer for jazz, you know.

Smiley: How did you—since we're into this now—you made the point earlier that you didn't want to lay this out chronologically and you didn't.

Mitchell: No.

Smiley: All right. I'm glad you didn't. I mean, I hear your point about growth. But how did you figure these fifty-three tracks? I was amazed by some of the stuff that isn't on here. How did you figure these fifty-three?

Mitchell: Well, something's got to be left out. Like I was thinking—

Smiley: Yeah, of course. You're prolific.

Mitchell: First of all, the first thing that I did was a ballet. Ballet's seventy-five minutes, right? So I tried to get everything I've written about love down to one disc. You know, imagine how much I'd have to leave out there, right? And I even tested it on groups, because usually I don't think about an audience when I write.

But here with the ballet, I had to think about an audience because our war ballet was a triumph. It was a blockbuster. Men were on the edge of their seats. It was exciting, it was war, you know, it was exciting. It was rude and it was like [*laughs*], it was rowdy. It was not like a normal ballet.

So I thought, OK, they're gonna think it's a chick flick. How are we gonna get—this is a topic of more interest usually to women, you know. Take all the things I've written about love and the lack of it, 'cause they're very unorthodox love songs. They're not songs of seduction, you know. They're more the anatomy of the crime [*laughs*].

Smiley: Nicely put [*laughs*].

Mitchell: One old boyfriend said that I was an emotional scientist. That's what he said, you know, and Graham's got a picture of me looking at everything with a magnifying glass. But it's just, Why couldn't we love? was the question. How do you do it?

You know, in the box set in a couple of places, it states how to do it and how hard it is. "Stay in Touch" tells you exactly how to do it and "Corinthians," the love, tells you what love is and what it isn't, you know. But it's really hard and you have to have kind of the same thing—you have to make a religion of blind faith, you know.

You have to bear the imperfections and keep the harmony like the old wives did that were bound by duty and everything. You know, there's a grace to that, to rising above it, if the master, the head of the Victorian household, is a bludgeoning creep, you know, you have to go, "Yes, sir," right?

Smiley: When you are forced—I say forced in a loving way—but when you are forced or compelled to have to sit, to go through all of this stuff—

Mitchell: I didn't listen to it.

Smiley: I know you didn't listen to it, but—

Mitchell: I did in my head.

Smiley: Yeah, but when you're—

Mitchell: And then I listened to it.

Smiley: But when you're forced or compelled to go through the process of putting this together, what's the takeaway for you from you? What's the takeaway for you from what you have done? What do you think?

Mitchell: Oh, the main thing was I was like—it sounded completely fresh to me. I hadn't listened to it for many years and I was delighted by my collaborators, you know. I just really, you know, went, oh, my God, how fortunate I was to play with the London Philharmonic, with Herbie and especially Wayne who suits my music. He's another art student, you know, so he's a pictorial thinker.

I adore Wayne and I put as much there as I could. I always had a legal restriction because of his contract. I could only put him on a few cuts or I would have put him in everything, you know. I just adore his playing and what it adds to my music. You know, when I finally found the people that could enhance my music, could put strokes on my painting, so to speak, and make me go, oh my God, that's fantastic.

Smiley: Speaking of strokes on your painting, tell me about the artwork in this. I mean, as I said earlier at the top of this conversation, this is actually a piece of art. There are four CDs in here with fifty-three of Joni's good stuff, her music, but the art in here . . .

Mitchell: Well, this is all pushing for the ballet. This is Jean and I and a couple of dancers in the dance studios of the Calgary Ballet in Alberta. Everything in this box set, two things I wanted to achieve. One, I wanted to break down by taking it out of chronology into characters so that sixty-five-year-old Joni is up against twenty-four-year-old Joni who can hold a note forever and has a three-octave range. And yet you could see that both of these characters are delivering their text very well, right? The alto and the soprano that can go down into alto, you know. I wanted it to break down a lot of prejudices, but that was the minor part.

The main thing was to find the story line. So act one begins in my youth, although I didn't make music in the fifties. I was a rock and roll dancer then, you know. You know, Lindy Hop in public dance halls and stuff. But the nostalgic pieces, so I started with rock and roll, which is basically Chuck Berry, kids kissing in cars, you know [*laugh*].

That was the theme, right, of the fifties, and it was this emancipation from your parents because of the liberty of the machine. But it was also the car was breaking down the family from the generation before that was the pioneers. They were stuck together on the farm and they all had to pull, right?

Now they're urbanized and Dad's got his car and he goes off to the office. He's got his world. Mom's stuck at home. She's got her world. And when the kids come to be teenagers, I often tell my generation the teenager was kind of trivialized. They weren't an adult yet, but suddenly because of the car, the kids had independence.

So you had people living in a house that didn't know who—that had nothing really in common. The wife with the husband, the children with the parents, and this vague rebellion sprang up that you see in those movies like Marlon Brando, they say, What are you rebelling against? What do you got, right? Like there was just something very wrong, the white picket fence, dream collapse. That gets dealt with in "Harry's House."

So you go from the happy days of fifties, "Birth of Rock and Roll Days," the name of Act One, to the breakdown of the parental dream, you know, into the mercenary litigenous time period that we're in now like beginning in the eighties, you know, the materialistic—where we went from being citizens—

Smiley: Greed is good, yeah.

Mitchell: Yeah. Greed is good and we were being coerced to be consumers as opposed to citizens.

Smiley: My time with you is just about up and I could talk to you for days and hours. There are a couple of things I want to get out, though, in the time I have left. One is we've talked a few times over the years, but I've never asked this question. But this is the right occasion, I think, to ask.

What has been your measure of success? I know it's not about the awards, it's not about the accolades or the Grammys or it may not even be about the sales per se. But what, as a songwriter, as an artist, what's been your measure of success of your work?

Mitchell: Oh. Well, all the songs on here I consider successful, you know, in the distillation. There's nothing here that I want to fix, you know, or I want to read the line different. You know, everybody is playing deliciously. I love this collection. I don't listen to my music, but I would put this on [*laugh*].

As a matter of fact, my friend, we've had three playback parties, well, two of them. We're going to have a third one where we play the whole thing. We take breaks in between. It creates the nicest mood. Everyone gets up and dances. You know, sometimes people bring in someone who don't know my music.

Smiley: You referenced earlier in this conversation the sixty-five-year-old Joni and the twenty-one, twenty-four-year-old Joni. And I ask you what this project means to you now as you look back on your work. Let me ask that question in the reverse. What does the Joni then think of the Joni now?

Mitchell: The Joni then would have no idea where, you know, that I would—I had jazz in high school, you know. Miles's *Kind of Blue* and Lambert, Hendricks and Ross. I knew everything [*inaudible*]. So in my twenties, I would never think that I would be playing with Miles's people, you know, so that's why I guess I'm kind of in awe looking back on it, you know, to see these collaborators who are my friends.

You know, I just hadn't revisited it for a long time. That's what struck me most other than, you know, trying to get the sequence where the story line led and the music led beautifully, you know.

'Cause I had such a range, I could play in any key. So it's not like a symphony where it's all in one key, but it all flowed, you know. It's not, you know, Joni's weird chords—they always said Joni's weird chords. Like I guess I did some things that were innovative in the history of music in the way I used those chords.

Smiley: What they call weird is innovative.

Mitchell: Right.

Smiley: They just ain't caught up with you yet.

Mitchell: You know, I understood the fogies thought they were weird, but when the jazzers thought they were weird or even when they got mad, I thought that was very strange because they were broad, they were polyphonic. They were wide like jazz chords. Wayne [Shorter] would go, "Well, what are these chords? These are not piano chords. These are not guitar chords." Then he'd go in and play like a champ. Wayne said, you know, "What is it? What is it?" But then he just went in and crawled over it like a fly, you know, like amazing.

Smiley: I'm always honored when—it doesn't happen all the time that Joni Mitchell shows up for a rare conversation, and I just pray and hold on for dear life 'cause I know that there's so much going on in this head and in this heart, and I want to stay out of the way. But it's always my great delight to have you on this program, Joni Mitchell.

Mitchell: Mine too. I asked to see you.

Smiley: I know you asked to see me, and that's all I needed to know, that you asked to come back on. Joni Mitchell's new project is called *Love Has Many Faces: A Quartet, a Ballet, Waiting to be Danced*, four-disc set, fifty-three songs and beautiful art all the way through it. I tried to pick some pieces of her notations. There's a wonderful letter handwritten in the back of the project, wonderful liner notes in the front. If you want to learn more about how this mind works, you'll want to get it, listen to it and read it. Joni, congratulations. I'm honored to have you on the program.

Mitchell: Thank you.

Smiley: Thank you, my dear. That's our show for tonight. Thanks for watching and, as always, keep the faith.

JONI SAID

On Unwed Motherhood

"You have no idea how many unwed mothers there were [*In 1965, when she was pregnant —Ed.*]. You know, suddenly the pill wasn't available, but movies had gotten sexier and sexier, and all these girls got caught out. And they all went to the anonymity of the big city so that the homes were full. You know, it was really rough going, and there was so much prejudice. It was like you killed somebody, you know."

—to Renée Montagne, *Morning Edition*, NPR, December 9, 2014

JONI SAID

On "New" Music

"Some music is forever new—Duke Ellington, 'Subtle Lament'? That piece is progressive to this day. Harmonically, just totally original piece of music. 'Kind of Blue,' Miles [Davis]—that's a magnificent piece. There are some things that are magnificent that are always new, it doesn't matter when they were made. I just don't see much that's made that isn't derivative. There's no Charlie Parkers, nobody coming out of the blue."

—to Andrew Hampp, *Billboard*, December 9, 2014

JONI SAID

On Taylor Swift

"I've never heard Taylor's music. I've seen her. Physically, she looks similarly small hipped and high cheekbones. I can see why they cast her [*in a proposed Joni biopic —Ed.*]. I don't know what her music sounds like, but I do know this—that if she's going to sing and play me, good luck."

—to Carl Swanson, *New York*, February 2015

ABOUT THE CONTRIBUTORS

Mary S. Aikins is a senior editor with Reader's Digest International Editions, based in Vancouver, BC.

Jacoba Atlas was a Los Angeles correspondent for *Melody Maker* and also wrote about music for *Circus* before becoming a TV writer and producer. She has worked at NBC News, CNN, and PBS, earning Emmy and Peabody awards.

Michael Buday, a senior producer with Gallagher and Associates, has produced exhibit films and interactive programs for museums including the Grammy Museum (Los Angeles and Mississippi), the Ray Charles Memorial Library, the Woody Guthrie Center, and the National Blues Museum. In the course of his work he's interviewed musical artists such as Joni Mitchell, Graham Nash, Robert Plant, Quincy Jones, Jackson Browne, and B. B. King.

Cameron Crowe is a noted film director who started his career as a music writer, first for the *San Diego Door* in his hometown, then for Detroit's *Creem* Magazine, where he was mentored by Lester Bangs, as seen in his 2000 film *Almost Famous*. It was at *Rolling Stone* that the teenaged Crowe hit his stride journalistically, writing profiles on such icons as Led Zeppelin, the Eagles, Bob Dylan, and Neil Young. His 1979 Joni Mitchell interview, included in this volume, is Crowe's favorite of his *Rolling Stone* stories. His films include *Say Anything*, *Jerry Maguire*, *Singles*, *Vanilla Sky*, *We Bought a Zoo*, and the Showtime series *Roadies*.

Jody Denberg is a veteran of Austin, Texas, radio of more than thirty-five years, having worked for KLBJ-FM, KGSR-FM, and KUTX-FM, the latter an NPR music affiliate where he is currently an on-air host. He has also written for the *Austin Chronicle* and *Texas Monthly*.

Dave DiMartino is the former executive editor of Yahoo! Music in Los Angeles. He is a past editor of *Creem*, where he worked from 1979 to 1986, and later was West Coast Bureau Chief of *Billboard* magazine (1986–1991), senior writer at *Entertainment Weekly* (1991–1993), and executive editor of LAUNCH, a CD-ROM magazine and Internet music site that became Yahoo! Music. After leaving Yahoo! in 2016 he served as editorial director of MusicAficionado.com.

John Ephland has written for *TimeOut Chicago*, *Relix*, and *All About Jazz* and was editor of *Down Beat*. In his eleven years at the Chicago-based jazz periodical he wrote about a variety of artists, including Cassandra Wilson and Joni Mitchell, Miles Davis, Tony Williams, and Dr. John.

Doug Fischer is a newspaper editor and writer living in Ottawa, Canada. He has covered politics, sports, justice issues, arts and social policy, business, and foreign affairs, but writing about music is what gives rhythm to his journalism.

Vic Garbarini was editor of *Musician* magazine, executive editor of *Guitar*, and senior editor at *Guitar World*. He was a music columnist for *Playboy* for seventeen years and wrote for *Rolling Stone*, *Spin*, and other publications. He shares a Grammy nomination with Paul McCartney and won several Billboard Awards. He has done radio and TV music commentary for Marc Maron, CBS News, and Charlie Rose and lectures frequently. He currently is editor of an online music magazine for the Mauli Ola Foundation.

Marty Getz was the producer and **Jeff Plummer** the music correspondent for the 1980s cable television public access show *Quintessential Covina*. For Getz, photography has always been his main "art communication skill," though silk-screen printing and video played their parts too. Plummer now lives on California's central coast.

Geoffrey Himes has written about pop music for the *Washington Post* since 1977 and has served as a senior editor at *No Depression* and *Paste* magazines. He has been honored by the Deems Taylor/ASCAP Awards, the New Orleans Press Awards, the Abell Foundation Awards, and the Music Journalism Awards. His book on Bruce Springsteen, *Born in the U.S.A.*, was published by Continuum Books in 2005.

Jason Koransky was editor of *Down Beat,* the Chicago-based jazz and blues publication for ten years, where he interviewed such notables as Dave Brubeck, Wayne Shorter, Wynton Marsalis, Herbie Hancock, and of course, Joni Mitchell, before giving up journalism for the law. Today he is a practicing attorney in Chicago focusing on trademark, copyright, data privacy, and Internet law.

Larry LeBlanc has been writing about music since 1965 when he wrote a column, *Teenbeat,* for the *Ajax Advertiser* in Ajax, Ontario, for ten cents an inch. He went on to write for *Maclean's, the Toronto Globe & Mail, Record Week, Rolling Stone, Billboard, TV Guide, Hit Parader, Crawdaddy, Record World, Zoo World, Circus, Melody Maker,* and *Zigzag*. He is currently a senior writer at the music trade magazine *Celebrity Access.*

A. L. McClain was a longtime entertainment copy editor for the *Detroit News* who occasionally wrote about entertainment news and movies as well. **Jo Ann Mercer** was one of the few women on the paper's newsroom copy desk in the 1960s, and, like McClain, she also dabbled in entertainment writing. Each had their encounter with Detroit's hot young folk couple, Chuck and Joni Mitchell, in early 1966.

Alanna Nash has written about music and culture for such publications as *Vanity Fair, Rolling Stone, AARP the Magazine, Entertainment Weekly,* and the *New York Times*. She is the author of four books about Elvis Presley, including *The Colonel: The Extraordinary Story of Colonel Tom Parker and Elvis Presley* and *Baby, Let's Play House: Elvis Presley and the Women Who Loved Him.*

Sylvie Simmons is a San Francisco–based author and journalist whose works include biographies of Johnny Cash and Serge Gainsbourg and the acclaimed 2014 biography of Leonard Cohen, *I'm Your Man*. Simmons started her journalism career in her native Britain; over the years her lively stories ran in *Creem*, *Rolling Stone*, and *Sounds*. She interviewed Joni Mitchell in 1988, and part of the interview included here appeared in the German publication *Musik Express*.

Tavis Smiley started his broadcast career as a political commentator on the *Tom Joyner* radio show and has hosted his own telecast on PBS since 2004. He was awarded the NAACP Image Award and has written several books, including *Death of a King: The Real Story of Dr. Martin Luther King Jr.'s Final Year* (with David Ritz). He has interviewed many musicians on his PBS show, including B. B. King, Smokey Robinson, Bonnie Raitt, and of course, Joni Mitchell.

Phil Sutcliffe has been writing about music since 1974, after serving an old-fashioned journalistic apprenticeship on the Newcastle (UK) *Evening Chronicle*. His youth illuminated by Beatles, Beach Boys, and Dylan fandom, he spent his later years interviewing all sorts, including the Police, Kate Bush, Fleetwood Mac, Joni Mitchell, Nirvana, Paul McCartney, Bruce Springsteen, Emmylou Harris, Eric Clapton, Norah Jones, and more for *Sounds*, *Smash Hits*, *The Face*, *The Northern Echo*, *Q*, *Blender*, the *Los Angeles Times*, and *Mojo*. Now "semi-retired," he is self-publishing his foot soldier father's *Memoir of World War 1*.

Michael Watts was US editor for *Melody Maker* for much of the 1970s, when he often wrote about Joni Mitchell. After that, he served as editor at several publications, including the *Financial Times*, the *Independent*, the *Evening Standard*, and *Esquire*.

Dave Wilson has had a varied career in folk music. He founded *Broadside of Boston* in the early 1960s to let people know where and when folk and blues performers were playing in the area, but he'd already been program director of the Boston Folk Song Society, helped found Riverboat Records, and was director of folk music for MIT's WTBS. He also managed and booked performers, and wrote scripts for WGBH-TV's *Folk Music USA*. Today he runs a Broadside of Boston Facebook page, sharing photos and memories with fans.

ABOUT THE EDITOR

Susan Whitall has been a music journalist since 1975, when she became a writer/editor for the iconic *Creem* magazine in Detroit, eventually becoming editor. In 1983 she was hired by the *Detroit News*, where she was a longtime feature and music writer—she continues to contribute stories to the paper. She is the author of several books, including *Fever: Little Willie John's Fast Life, Mysterious Death and the Birth of Soul* (Titan), a biography of R&B singer Little Willie John that was honored as a Michigan Notable Book for 2012. A second edition of her book *Women of Motown* (Devault-Graves), an oral history of the label's girl groups and female artists, was published in 2017. She can be reached at susanwhitall.com.

CREDITS

"Two Single Acts Survive a Marriage" by A. L. McClain, originally published in the *Detroit News*, February 6, 1966, and "Urbanity Revisited: Mode is Mod for City Living" by Jo Ann Mercer, originally published in the *Detroit News*, March 20, 1966. Both stories, and photographs copyright ©1966. Both stories and photographs reprinted by permission of the *Detroit News*.

"An Interview with Joni Mitchell" by Dave Wilson, originally published in *Broadside of Boston*, February 14, 1968. Copyright ©1968. Reprinted by permission of Dave Wilson.

"Joni: Let's Make Life More Romantic," by Jacoba Atlas, originally published in *Melody Maker*, June 20, 1970. Copyright ©1970. Reprinted by permission of Jacoba Atlas.

"Joni Mitchell: Glimpses of Joni" by Michael Watts, originally published in *Melody Maker*, September 19, 1970. Copyright © 1970. Reprinted by permission of Rock's Back Pages and Michael Watts.

"Joni Takes a Break" by Larry LeBlanc, originally published in *Rolling Stone*, March 4, 1971. Copyright ©1971. Reprinted by permission of Larry LeBlanc.

"Joni Mitchell: An Interview, Part One" by Penny Valentine, originally published in *Sounds*, June 3, 1972. Copyright ©1972. Reprinted by permission of Rock's Back Pages and Dan Valentine.

"Joni Mitchell: An Interview, Part Two" by Penny Valentine, originally published in *Sounds*, June 10, 1972. Copyright ©1972. Reprinted by permission of Rock's Back Pages and Dan Valentine.

"The Education of Joni Mitchell," by Steward Brand, originally published in *CoEvolution Quarterly*, Summer 1976. Copyright © 1976. Reprinted by permission of Stewart Brand.

INDEX